WARPLANES OF THE FUTURE

THE MOST EXCITING COMBAT AIRCRAFT BEING DESIGNED TODAY
TO FACE THE THREAT OF WARS TOMORROW
BILL GUNSTON

Published by
CRESCENT BOOKS
New York

A SALAMANDER BOOK

First English edition published by
Salamander Books Ltd.,
27 Old Gloucester Street,
London WC1N 3AF,
United Kingdom.

This edition is published by Crescent Books,
distributed by Crown Publishers, Inc.,
One Park Avenue,
New York,
New York 10016,
United States of America.

h g f e d c b a

**Library of Congress Cataloging in
Publication Data**
Gunston, Bill.
    Warplanes of the future.

    1. Airplanes, Military.   I. Title.
UG1240.G8655   1985   358.4'183   85-9611
ISBN 0-517-46960-X

THE AUTHOR

Bill Gunston is a former RAF pilot and flying
instructor, and he has spent most of his working
life accumulating a wealth of information on
aerospace technology and history. Since leaving
the Service, he has acted as an advisor to several
aviation companies and become one of the most
internationally respected authors and
broadcasters on aviation and scientific subjects.
His numerous books include the Salamander
titles "The Illustrated Encyclopedia of the World's
Modern Military Aircraft", "The Encyclopedia of
the World's Combat Aircraft", "The Illustrated
Encyclopedia of the World's Rockets and
Missiles", "Soviet Air Power" (with Bill
Sweetman), and many of Salamander's
successful illustrated guides to aviation subjects.
He has also contributed to the authoritative
"Advanced Technology Warfare", "The Soviet
War Machine" and "The US War Machine", by the
same company, and carries out regular
assignments for technical aviation periodicals.
Mr. Gunston is also an assistant compiler of
"Jane's All the World's Aircraft" and was formerly
technical editor of "Flight International" and
technology editor of "Science Journal".

CREDITS

Editor: Ray Bonds
Designer: Mark Holt
Color artwork: Stephen Seymour
Line artwork: Maltings Partnership
Color and monochrome reproduction:
    Melbourne Graphics,
    Rodney Howe Ltd.,
    York House Graphics Ltd.
Filmset: SX Composing Ltd.
Printed in Italy by G. Canale e C SpA, Turin.

ACKNOWLEDGEMENTS

The publishers wish to thank all the companies,
various armed services and other institutions who
have supplied illustrations for this book. The
supplier of the illustration is given within each
caption.

CONTENTS

—— PART TWO ——
SYSTEMS OF THE FUTURE 182

—— PART THREE ——
WEAPONS OF THE FUTURE 194

INTRODUCTION

The world's defence community – at least, outside the Warsaw Pact countries – appears at times to be remarkably unprofessional. Time after time weapons and technologies have been ignored for years until someone actually fires something. Then there is a wave of panic, and vast sums are suddenly spent on buying either the weapon, or its countermeasure, or both. Perhaps unfortunately, every new technology that might be useful in warfare becomes the subject of instant funding, far more than new ideas for peace.

In April 1957, on the day that Britain's one and only type of supersonic fighter made its maiden flight, the British government published an official statement explaining that manned combat aircraft were, as a class, obsolete. It noted that the RAF was "unlikely to require" any new fighters or bombers; their place would be taken by missile. As for the supersonic fighter aforementioned (which became the Lightning), this had "unfortunately gone too far to cancel". This lunatic belief caused great schisms in the RAF, crippled the British aircraft industry, handed global markets to France and the USA and set back British airpower an incalculable amount. Yet it was sincerely held, and indeed at the time seemed "obvious" to many intelligent people.

It is thus not easy to discuss warplanes of the future. Since World War II their prospects have been critically dependent upon parallel developments in radars and other sensors, and upon many species of missile – launched both by aircraft and against them. Yet there is nothing new under the Sun. The original development of radar by Sir Robert Watson-Watt stemmed from the Air Ministry's enquiry of him whether or not a claimed "death ray" was feasible. The answer in 1935 was negative, but half a century later the fairest answer is "yes, with reservations". The super-power laser and other directed-energy weapons have now reached the point where the death ray of countless science-fiction writers can now actually be demonstrated, though like the Wright Flyer of 1903 it is hardly a mature technology, and we are miles away from putting a death ray into an agile fighter.

A directed-energy beam able to kill aircraft (or, more easily, spacecraft) at great distances is not a revolutionary capability. We already have anti-aircraft missiles of great speed and power, far transcending anything available in April 1957, and are fast reaching the stage where a totalitarian state such as the Soviet Union could make it very difficult indeed for aircraft or spacecraft to cross its frontier. Of course, in that particular case the frontier is so long that to instal impregnable defences everywhere would be impossibly expensive. But aircraft designers today, unlike in 1957, have to recognise that their offspring will emerge into a perilous world.

In the past there has been no shortage of big and frightening surface-to-air missiles and many other kinds of anti-aircraft weapon, but the guys in the ejection seats seldom had to eject. Most of the missiles were in the wrong places, or for various reasons not combat-ready. If they were actually fired, they often failed to perform as advertised. Crew-members aboard B-52Ds cruising straight and level over North Vietnam could hardly keep tally of the numbers of SA-2s fired at their lumbering monsters. Some struck home, but almost all were confused by chaff and jamming. A few months later, in October 1973, SA-6 missiles took on such more difficult targets as Israeli Phantoms and Skyhawks, and swatted them like flies. Amazingly, nobody had produced ECM to counter a CW (continuous-wave) radar, even though such radars had been guiding Western SAMs since the mid-1950s.

The Soviets, who years before had designed the SA-6 system, were not at all surprised at its lethality because they had studied the failure of Western powers to deploy any CW countermeasures. Perhaps such failures will be rarer in future, though in May 1982 Britain's front-line combat aircraft in the South Atlantic were so totally unequipped for self-defence that chaff bundles were jammed under the airbrake and in the gap between bombs and their ejector racks. Bearing in mind the world leadership in ECM enjoyed by the

RAF 40 years previously, the impartial observer is bound to feel a slight sense of despair, if not disbelief, at such an extraordinary decline.

What it all boils down to is that today the defended sky can no longer be penetrated with impunity. Though we have certainly not reached the stage at which manned combat aircraft really are obsolete, we have to accept the unpalatable facts that airfields can be wiped off the map, agile fighters can be shot down and even air-launched ordance can be destroyed in flight, and with something approaching 100 per cent certainty.

Even such formerly disregarded and seemingly obsolete weapons as the anti-aircraft gun are today to be treated with the utmost respect. Flak in World War II was respected because there was so much of it. In the intervening 40 years it has tended to be almost ignored, because just one or two guns aimed in the general direction of the target are unlikely to score a lucky hit. Today we have a new situation in which each barrel is likely to point in the right direction. As for the SAMs, suffice to say that one company alone, British Aerospace Dynamics, are prepared to demonstrate how to put a Rapier through a tiny Rushton target or use a Seawolf to destroy a shell fired from a warship's main gun. Fighter pilots keep up their morale by tending to discount or disbelieve such things, but a better answer is to go back to the drawing boards at the aircraft factory.

Left: One of the many configurations studied by McDonnell Douglas for the USAF Advanced Tactical Fighter requirement is this straight-wing canard single-seater, which would probably have two 2-D vectoring engine nozzles. The missile is a CW-guided Sparrow.

Above: It is easier to draw a "death ray" than put one into service. This USAF artwork shows a 747SP as carrier vehicle, which gives an indication of the electrical power needed by such weapons. In any case, this is a field where the Soviet Union is judged to be ahead of the USA.

Below: At present the Grumman X-29 carries no death ray, nor any other weapons, but as a new shape in the sky it could be a very large pointer to air-combat aircraft of 20 years hence. Until recently the FSW (forward-swept wing) was structurally impossible to build.

This book is a look at what is on some of those drawing boards. We start with a series of "upgrades" which are hoped to give a new lease of life to familiar aircraft. Many important new warplanes, such as Tornado ADV, are not in this book because they are neither "upgrades" nor designs for the future, and they are fully covered in other Salamander books. The upgrades are self-explanatory, and have their own introduction. Main interest centres on the all-new aircraft, and it must be said at the start that the validity of many can be questioned. Advertisers like to claim they can offer "Tomorrow's airplane today", but a lot of people seem to be bent on producing "Today's airplane for tomorrow".

In designing "warplanes of the future", there is surely no room for sentiment. Decisions must be taken solely on the basis of the available evidence. Thus there is no point whatsoever in creating an aeroplane of traditional form for use in the 1990s if it is going to be destroyed before it can take off, or destroyed after it has taken off. Even quite small modern fighters are expensive by any standard. At something over £60,000 a Rolls-Royce car is beyond the reach of most of us, but the latest fighters cost at least 400 times as much! To buy squadrons of such fighters and then park them on the most heavily targeted spots on this planet does seem questionable logic.

To deal first with vulnerability on the ground, some air forces have clearly failed to address the question at all. Some appear to have taken the view that, as the really destructive or incapacitating anti-airfield systems are difficult to counter, they will instead assume that all their enemies might do is drop a few bombs or anti-runway

Above: As creators of the world's only FSW aircraft Grumman have the credibility to publish artwork of future FSW fighters. This picture dates from 1983 and shows one configuration studied in the ATF programme. Advantages of forward-swept fins are uncertain.

Right: As this is written the nations of Western Europe are trying to work together to build a next-generation air-combat fighter. This water-channel picture by the German firm MBB shows the powerful vortex flows that make canard deltas (MBB call it JF90) so superbly agile.

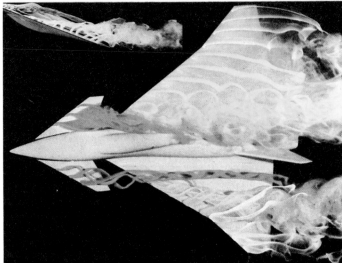

weapons that make craters. These can be largely countered by HASs (hardened aircraft shelters) and a mix of STOL aircraft with a takeoff run of 1,500ft (457m) and fast-reacting engineer teams to fill in the craters. However, wars have never been won by solving the easy problems and ignoring the difficult ones.

It seems self-evident that survival on the ground is possible only by denying the enemy information on where the aircraft are based. This means the widest possible dispersal, the greatest possible amount of camouflage (not just at visible light wavelengths) and frequent moves to the extent that aircraft seldom recover to the place from which they took off. Some air forces will reply that such dispersal and mobility is simply impossible in a world where each fighter squadron needs X electronics test

rigs, Y high-precision workshops and Z gallons of fuel per day. To this the author retorts, "Put it all on wheels". Hitler's Luftwaffe and the Royal Air Force's 2nd TAF were totally mobile, and this was before the era of fighters whose engines had the thrust to lift them straight up into the air (not just the Harrier but almost all new fighters). To put such aircraft on 10,000ft (3,000m) of concrete is the sickest joke in the history of human conflict.

As for survival in the air, this again (obviously) centres on trying to avoid being detected. Today's enemies have eyes, radars, sensitive IR receivers and low-light TV everywhere from ground level to somewhere like 60,000ft (18,300m). Flying at low level helps greatly, and battlefield helicopter pilots can feel better if they can actually hide behind things, but we have to

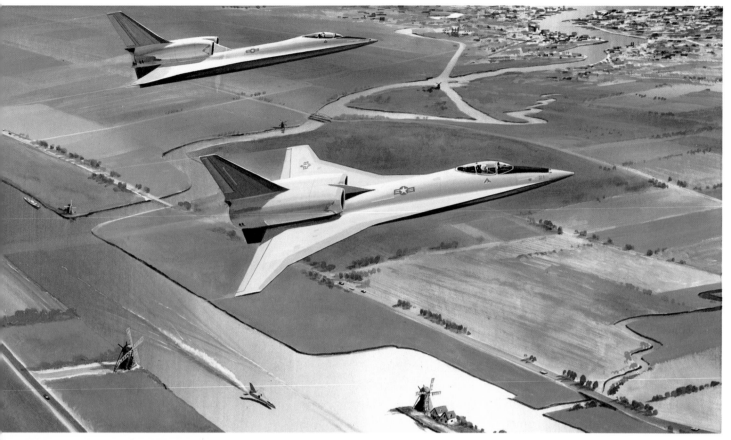

Above: Dutch windmills and placid canals are home to this Lockheed study which combined stealth qualities with a runway of indeterminate length that fills in its own craters! Past attempts to build fighter seaplanes resulted in designs unable to win in the air.

Left: Nobody appreciates better than the British that future warplanes must not depend on identifiable airfields. One problem-ridden answer was the BAe (Warton) P.103, which would have been a fine Jaguar replacement had the engine-out situation not been so fraught.

do much more than this. A few very general rules are: if I can see him, he can see me; if I can foul up his vision with chaff, flares or jamming, his systems were probably designed to stop me doing so; and, the harder it is for me, the harder it is for him. Thus, the pilot of a Tornado making a "ski run" at Mach 1 at near-zero height above the Alps has a harder time than the pilot of an E-3A Sentry orbiting sedately at 29,000ft (8,900m); but he is very much less likely to be shot down. Another ultra-generalized rule is: the most advanced, complicated and expensive systems are likely to be the ones offering the greatest number of ways to counteract them, whereas the man with a manually sighted machine gun is an impossible system to counter except by actually bagging him first.

Of, course, even the simplest system,

such as the unassisted machine-gunner, is going to remain impotent in the presence of undetected targets. One is reminded of the brief Memorandum written by Watson-Watt, Wilkins and Rowe in March 1935 in which the three pioneers of British radar pointed out, "The amount of energy reflected from the target depends not only on its size but also on its aspect and shape", and then went on to note, "In due course it will become natural for the designers of aircraft to seek to minimise reflectivity by all means possible".

There could hardly be any more basic, prophetic and precisely accurate statement than this, and it clearly should have been pinned up in every chief designer's office from the start of World War II onwards. The author discussed the subject with many chief designers in the 1950s and learned

that, at that time, there was not, and never had been, any pressure to reduce RCS (radar cross-section) nor any instruction on how this should be done. Camm, of Hawker, said in effect, "I design fighters; they don't bother about enemy radar". Stafford, of Handley Page, said he was well aware that radars could see big aeroplanes more easily than little ones, and also that shape mattered, but said that the Victor bomber had been designed without any numerical regard to RCS. His words were, approximately, "The problems were great enough on aerodynamic and structural grounds, without having to meet a quantified requirement for low radar reflectivity". So far as the author is aware, the same goes for the B-52, B-58 and B-70.

Having regard to the prophetic statement of 1935 this may seem amazing. For an answer one must look back at the circumstances. In World War II aircraft of traditional types were built in enormous numbers and shot down in enormous numbers. Special units, such as RAF No 100 Group, became very expert at the new science (or art) of EW (electronic warfare), but though a very important part of their work was concerned with jamming or spoofing (confusing or misleading) the enemy, practically no activity was directed to altering or so designing Allied aircraft as to make them harder to detect. In the Korean War the only night interceptions were by the Allies, and EW was almost forgotten. In Vietnam EW emerged again as an important field of activity, but practically nothing was done to assist aircraft to remain undetected in hostile airspace. By this time the RAF and some other air forces had almost forgotten about EW altogether, and though small sums were being spent on RWRs (radar warning receivers) the possibility of buying aircraft specially designed to be hard to see by radar appears to have been repeatedly ignored (though it was given much thought in the design of the cancelled TSR.2).

The urge to "seek to minimise reflectivity by all means possible" stemmed from the covert surveillance aircraft created for the CIA by Kelly Johnson's team at Lockheed's so-called "Skunk Works". This series began in 1951 with what became the U-2, one of which was shot down over the Soviet Union on 1 May 1960. The U-2 was designed unequivocally to fly as high as possible, whilst also having long range, and though radar reflectivity was important it was a secondary consideration, as also was speed. In any case, it was reasoned that a U-2 flying at about 400mph (644km/h) at great height would probably leave a contrail and could hardly expect to remain undetected. It was hoped to survive by being above the effective ceiling of hostile defence systems – which proved not to be the case. By the mid-1950s US designers, the CIA and USAF were studying the prospects for a follow-on spyplane probably burning liquid hydrogen and flying at well over Mach 2, because speed not only cuts down the time available for an enemy's interception but also equates with cruising altitude. With these pioneer supercruise (supersonic cruise) aircraft the altitude promised to go up far above 80,000ft (24,400m).

From the start of work on these remarkable new aircraft great attention was paid, for the first time in history, to minimising RCS. Eventually only one family of aircraft went ahead, and this again stemmed from Johnson's team. Beginning with the A-12, first flown on 26 April 1962, the series led to today's SR-71A, still the only aircraft of its type and with unique capabilities. It is almost certain that future military aircraft will burn liquid hydrogen, but in fact the SR-71A burns JP-7, a liquid hydrocarbon fuel not far removed from conventional kerosenes but tailored to absorb surplus heat from the avionics, cockpit and many other areas without coking or throwing down gummy deposits. Problems of this kind are severe at the SR-71's cruising speed of Mach 3.35, and it is just as well that today we recognise that it is much more important to be hard to detect than to fly at over Mach 3. At present it is difficult to see much advantage in trying to make combat aircraft fly faster and faster as used to be taken for granted. In general, that would merely make them easier to destroy, as explained later.

As one walks around the all-black SR-71 one is struck by its size, its dramatic shapes and its obvious build for fantastic speeds. From the tip of the long nose a sharp chine runs back along each side to join the leading edge of the wing. The underside looks almost as though the fuselage had been held against a giant belt sander until the lower part had been worn completely away until it was flat and level with the wings.

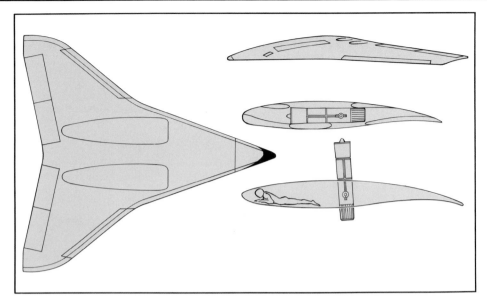

Above: Little more than "thinking aloud", these sketches show one of many possible configurations for a future warplane. Starting with the premise that it must not need an airfield and must be very hard to detect in the air, it is a flying wing V/STOL with two pivoting engines normally housed in the seemingly thick (but mainly hollow) amidships section. Outer wings would be much thinner. In the forward-flight mode the engines would "fire" between upper and lower flap sections which vector the jets, reduce noise, give IR protection from above and below and also tailor the nozzle to the flight regime. (Top right view is from front, three-quarters on.)

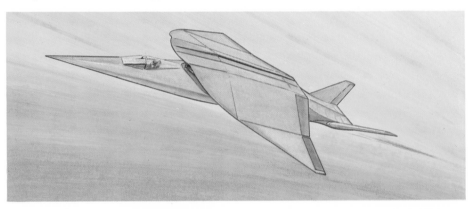

Above: This strange throw-back to the parasol monoplane, one of the configurations of the very first fighters in 1915, was an attempt to get favourable shock-wave interactions at Mach 4.5. But it needs runways, is a non-stealth design and is certainly a non-starter.

Below: USAF Systems Command artwork showing another industry study (from Grumman) along ATF lines. Any rival could point out 15 weak or arguable features, but we can take comfort from the fact the real ATF will do better. Who knows – it might even fly without airfields!

The author first saw this shape on the A-12 (then mistakenly called A-11 by President Johnson) more than 20 years ago. At that time it was explained how the chines reduced drag and improved stability at both low and very high speeds. Looking up at the SR-71 later one was reminded of a hydroplane boat designed for skimming at high speed across the water. Sheepishly the author admits that he never even thought about how the "Blackbird" SR-71 would look on radar, but in fact he was looking at the first stealth aeroplane.

Americans are good at coining words and naming things. The British might have been happy with "aircraft of low radar cross-section", but the evocative word "stealth" encapsulates the most important property of every warplane of the future. There are still people in high places who think of it as an odd and highly specialized

quality possessed by a bomber being built by Northrop for the USAF. Nothing could be more misleading. Stealth is a quality that should have been crystal clear to anyone who read the report written half a century ago by the three British radar pioneers. It is not highly specialized but will have to be a central factor in the design of every future bomber, every fighter, every reconnaissance aircraft, every maritime patrol and ASW aircraft, every military helicopter and every military transport.

Of course, stealth design can never be totally over-riding. It is possibly of highest importance to reconnaissance aircraft, where the payload of sensors is fairly compact; the much greater volume of fuel is conveniently liquid and so can automatically assume the shape of the tankage. With a bomber the position is similar, though heavy loads of bombs and missiles

can be bulky, and in the past were often hung externally. Cruise missiles are henceforth going to be totally stealth-designed, though that still does not mean that it would be better for future bombers to carry them internally. Fighters gain enormously from stealth design, but their compromises have to be slightly greater; in any case, it is in this case that designers will have the greatest difficulty in adjusting themselves to a new scale of priorities. Helicopters pose severe problems, mainly because of the size and characteristic frequency of the main rotor. As for military transports, these have to be capable of swallowing the specified loads, and many of the loads are rigid in size and shape. The designer therefore has to start with a large box-like volume for the payload, and has to introduce stealth qualities in the airframe that goes around this.

Easiest of all aircraft to make virtually invisible to radars are missiles and RPVs because they have no cockpit or canopy. Following the A-12/SR-71 family some of the earliest stealth aircraft to fly were high-altitude RPVs (remotely piloted vehicles), with similarly flat undersides and the engine either integral with the fuselage or above it, to minimize RCS.

It often happens that as a new military technology matures, and the prospects become increasingly exciting, the tightness of the security surrounding it increases. It would be reasonable to assume that stealth technology will dominate the design of all future combat aircraft, though many published configurations are remarkably unstealthy - for example, with giant ventral air inlets giving the enemy radars a seemingly perfect view of the engines. There is only one true stealth design known to be flying in numbers, and that is the "Lockheed F-19". Apart from this, and the Northrop bomber mentioned earlier, the sum total of publishable official information on who is doing what to introduce stealth aircraft amounts to a complete blank. The only additional point made here

Above: The artwork is beautiful, and the subject impressive; but no air force would equip squadrons with billion-dollar Mach 5 fighters with red-hot leading edges. This Lockheed long-range design shows strong SR-71 type stealth influence; but as an IR beacon it's tops!

Below: This Grumman art shows one of the few true stealth (low observables) studies to have been published. In most respects this aircraft, with twin 2-D vectoring nozzles, is very good. All we need eliminate are the fins, canopy and need for airfields.

and in the Lockheed and Northrop entries is that stealth means much more than minimising RCS. The aircraft also has to have minimal or zero emissions or reflectivity at all other EM wavelengths. There is obviously no point in making an aircraft difficult to see on radar if it is pumping out flames from its afterburners, painted Day-Glo red and sending out radio and radar emissions itself! Just how far we can make future aircraft not only invisible but also silent – in the broadest meaning of the word – is anyone's guess.

It so happens that, as this book is written, the US armed forces are burning the midnight oil trying to buy some sensible next-generation aircraft. The biggest potential programme is the ATF (advanced tactical fighter) for the USAF. Not far behind are two VTOL systems, LHX (light helicopter experimental) for the US Army and JVX for the Army, Marines and possibly Navy and Air Force. All are discussed in this book, and all offer good pointers to the future, though with the exception of JVX the information so far published has tended to feature the projects that we can rely upon not being built.

It would be difficult to think of a greater waste of money than an ATF designed for Mach 3, with a length of 80ft (24m), weight of 120,000lb (54 tonnes), blasting out IR and radar emissions at high power, based on a long paved runway and costing about a billion dollars. We can be quite sure that

nothing like this will get off the drawing board, but there is still a faint chance that the USAF might stick to its idea of a 1,500ft (457m) takeoff run, to "take off between the craters". It is fervently to be hoped that this idea is a purely temporary one aimed at increasing the survivability of its existing machines.

A four-page section from page 82 discusses the prospects for future V/STOL, or more correctly STOVL, aircraft in the West. Most countries recognise this as a rather challenging field and, rather surprisingly, are happy to leave the running to others. One recalls the global enthusiasm for VTOL 25 years ago, when one could hardly find a single planemaker who was not drawing pictures of jet VTOL fighters or VTOL airliners or both. The city-centre jetliners were eventually judged to be non-starters, though JVX technology may in due course bring into our city centres tilt-rotor transports cruising at 350mph (563km/h). The jet-lift fighters were variously complex, costly, dangerous and generally impractical as tough front-line weapon systems. Only one made sense: the British conception of a single engine with vectored nozzles. It is a matter for profound regret that the USAF, whose posture in such matters strongly influences not only the NATO alliance but also even the Soviet Union, chose to adopt a scornful attitude to such aircraft, based on the unbelievable misconception that it could rely on always

having its combat squadrons based on intact airfields.

The fact that without STOVL combat aircraft Britain could never have gone to war in the South Atlantic may be irrelevant. Though it is surely unwise for a Defence Minister or Chief of Staff ever to say, "You'll never see us in that situation", perhaps trying to fight a war more than 4,000 miles (6,400km) from the nearest friendly airbase, and without fixed-wing carriers, may indeed be an unusual situation, and the fact that Britain – alone of all the world's countries – could handle it was a matter for sheer chance. It was certainly never planned that way. But the official scorn of the USAF for combat aircraft that need no airfield is a ridiculous posture that should have been discredited many years ago. In the late 1960s the USAF view on jet-STOVL was that it resulted in compromised aircraft that were deficient in almost every important area. In effect the Americans said, "You'll never see our boys having to go to war in inferior things like that!" Whether the Falklands did anything to modify this view is doubtful, because if minds have been closed the last thing they want to do is learn the facts.

But facts are that the Harrier and Sea Harrier are "the Wright Flyers" of jet STOVL, designed when the technique was in its infancy – yet still remarkably effective in the harshest kind of warfare in the worst weather in the world. Whether we need to go beyond Mach 1 is debatable; for fighter missions it helps greatly. What helps even more is that all the most modern fighters have installed engine thrust which at sea level is greater than the clean gross weight. Provided one has a modern aeroplane with a MIL-STD-1553 digital databus linking everything together, there is no reason why we should not have a near-VTOL combat aircraft which in the air is uncompromised and extremely formidable, besides being a stealth design. The drawings shown here illustrate how it would work. Just 30 years ago the US Navy tried turboprop VTOLs and found the control problems, especially on landing, very difficult. In 1957 the USAF found the same trouble with the otherwise prophetic Ryan X-13 Vertijet. Today we can do a million times better. If we don't we won't have an air force.

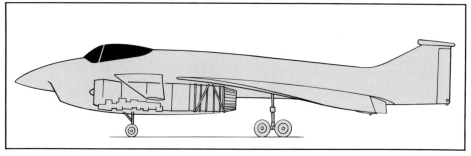

Above: At first glance this somewhat crude-looking jet appears to resemble Soviet radar-equipped interceptors of 35 years ago. On inspection we find the General Electric F110 engine has a double-scarfed rotary section in its jetpipe which can pivot the nozzle down through a right angle. There are left and right nose landing gears, Viggen-type main gears, and RCVs (reaction control valves) on the tail and wingtips. The idea is to show how apparently simple it is to build a "one-poster" STOVL combat aircraft. Of course in the jet-lift mode the powerful jet from the afterburning engine would cause problems with ground erosion and modification of the circulation around the canard and main wing. There are bound to be other problems, but which new aircraft has never had any? To the author it seems only common sense to start making fighter engines lift the aircraft as well as push it along.

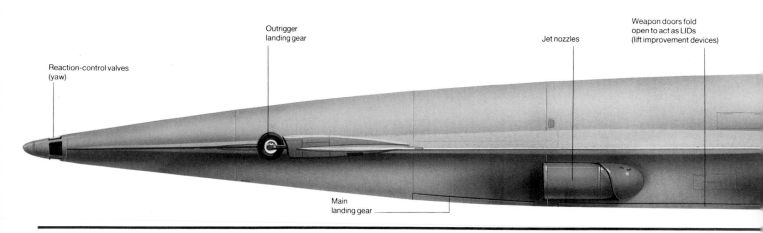

Reaction-control valves (yaw)

Outrigger landing gear

Main landing gear

Jet nozzles

Weapon doors fold open to act as LIDs (lift improvement devices)

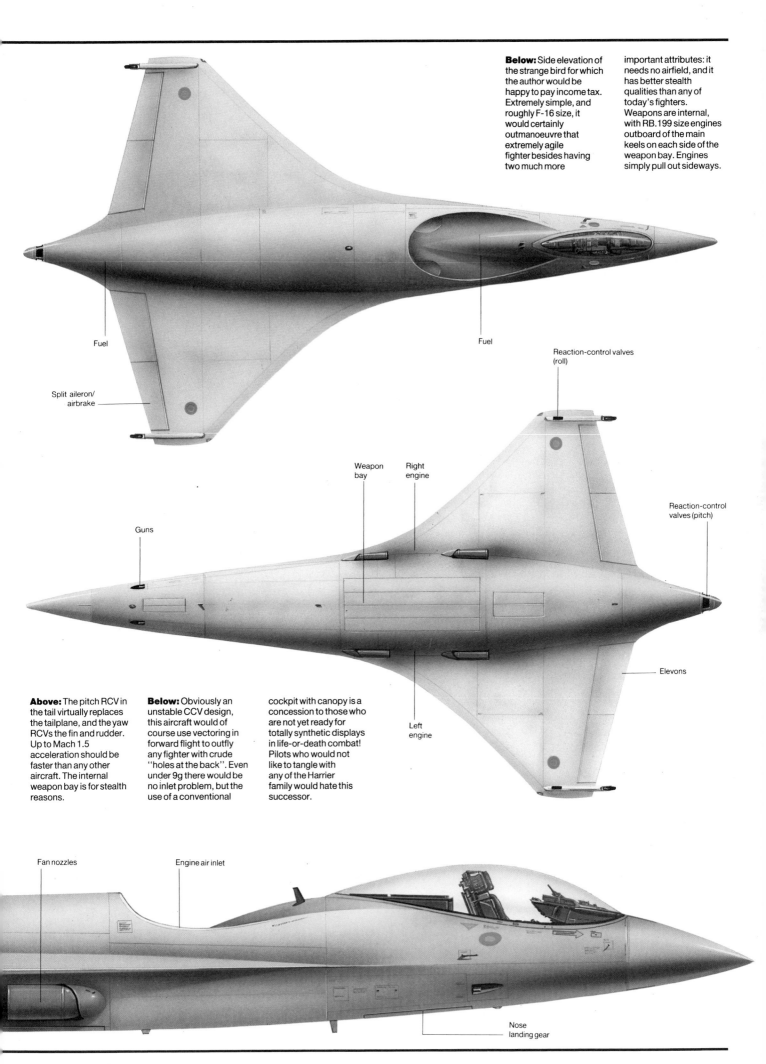

Below: Side elevation of the strange bird for which the author would be happy to pay income tax. Extremely simple, and roughly F-16 size, it would certainly outmanoeuvre that extremely agile fighter besides having two much more important attributes: it needs no airfield, and it has better stealth qualities than any of today's fighters. Weapons are internal, with RB.199 size engines outboard of the main keels on each side of the weapon bay. Engines simply pull out sideways.

Fuel

Fuel

Split aileron/ airbrake

Reaction-control valves (roll)

Weapon bay

Right engine

Reaction-control valves (pitch)

Guns

Left engine

Elevons

Above: The pitch RCV in the tail virtually replaces the tailplane, and the yaw RCVs the fin and rudder. Up to Mach 1.5 acceleration should be faster than any other aircraft. The internal weapon bay is for stealth reasons.

Below: Obviously an unstable CCV design, this aircraft would of course use vectoring in forward flight to outfly any fighter with crude "holes at the back". Even under 9g there would be no inlet problem, but the use of a conventional cockpit with canopy is a concession to those who are not yet ready for totally synthetic displays in life-or-death combat! Pilots who would not like to tangle with any of the Harrier family would hate this successor.

Fan nozzles

Engine air inlet

Nose landing gear

15

PART ONE

WARPLANES OF THE FUTURE

For over half a century the main objectives of the designers of warplanes were to increase flight performance, to be faster, higher-flying or longer-ranged than the enemy. Today, though in some aircraft air-combat agility is important, the objectives are perceptibly different. Overriding all other requirements are two as yet only dimly discerned: the need to operate without airfields of known location and the need to be as invisible and silent as possible.

UPGRADE PROGRAMMES

Since 1919 military customers have been faced with the often agonizing choice of whether to (1) buy a completely new aircraft, to meet a particular mission requirement, or (2) buy new or secondhand examples of an established type, or (3) buy upgrades. Upgrades, also called by such adjectives as "Super", "enhanced" or simply "advanced", can themselves vary widely. Some upgrades are simply existing aircraft given an improvement programme, and this can be done in many ways. Others are new versions so different from the original that conversion is uneconomic, so all the upgrades are newly built aircraft. One of the most outstanding examples in this category is the General Dynamics F-16XL, which has roughly the capability of two of the Brand X model packaged into one airframe!

Some of these new versions are of aircraft which were previously not military at all, examples including the new RAF transport/tanker versions of the VC10 and TriStar. These are impressive and in many ways completely new aircraft, but are not appropriate for inclusion in a book with the title of this one. Likewise, even the Canberra PR.9, now being torn apart and completely refurbished and re-equipped by Shorts at Belfast – which built them originally in 1958-61 – does not appear in this book, but in this case because secrecy prevents disclosure of any details of the modifications being made to this elderly but still useful fleet. If the RAF had adequate budgets it would simply junk the PR.9s and buy a new purpose-designed aircraft to fly the future PR.9 missions, which are classified but clearly involve tactical surveillance, and probably Elint (electronic intelligence) using a new suite of sensors. We do not need to do any journalistic sleuthing to state that the upgrading of the PR.9s will cost much more than the original purchase price of the aircraft. One has only to study prices of the 1958-61 period to be reminded, with a shock, of the effects of inflation. The original price of each PR.9 was never published, but at the time it horrified various watchdog MPs because it exceeded £1 million. Today this sum would just about buy a new set of tyres.

Inflation is one of the chief influences deciding an air force's procurement policy. It is pointless to look back wistfully. Today a Harrier II (AV-8B) will set you back about £38 million (a seemingly astronomic figure arrived at by factoring for inflation the August 1982 price of US$379 million for 12 aircraft, plus spares and support, for the Spanish Navy). When Hawker invited the Press to see the first production Harriers in 1968 it said it was offering to supply them at "from £750,000 to £1 million, depending on quantity and equipment".

The difference between this price and £38 million is staggering, but it is a pointless comparison. It is, however, worth bearing in mind, if only to try to avoid the nonsensical arithmetic that so often afflicts procurement officials and, in particular, fiscal authorities (such as the Treasury in Britain). Once a programme has reached the production stage there is every reason to procure at the highest rate of which the industry is capable. Yet is is common to try to "save money" by reducing the rate, so that less has to be paid each year. This was done in the Tornado programme, which simply means that each aircraft costs considerably more. The only possible advantage is that it stretches out the programme

Below: All the illustrations in this section show aircraft that are the subject of major modifications, one of the most dramatic of which concerns the C-130 AEW jointly marketed by GEC Avionics and Lockheed-Georgia. It contains virtually the complete MSA (Mission system avionics) developed for the Nimrod AEW.3. The forward giant pallet houses the radar itself and signal processors. The enclosed insulated module contains six operator stations. The rear pallet contains communications equipment. The C-130 AEW will have an endurance of up to 12 hours at patrol height of 27,000ft (9000m).

Right: An update as yet little publicised is the Fokker MMVX, an F28 upgrade for US Navy carrier missions. One role is tanker/COD (carrier on-board delivery) with underwing refuelling pods and up to 65 passengers, or other loads. The Sigint/Comint/tanker role demands a belly canoe fairing. Another mission is AEW/targeting/tanker. Increased aileron and spoiler power will give the MMVX adequate lateral control on carrier approach. Tay or General Electric F404 engines will give single-engine climbout on a hot day. Flight evaluation at Pax River was completed in September 1983. The programme is said to be worth $500 million.

so that industry does not have quite such a panic trying to find a replacement to fill the factories in the next decade.

It is largely because of inflation that upgrades of old aircraft which enable them to fly existing missions better, and to fly completely new missions, make financial sense. Over 25 years ago the Pentagon began to talk about "cost/effectiveness", a seemingly useful parameter which attempts to balance a weapon system's combat value against its total costs. It is wise to distrust such slick parameters, though they are useful in some circumstances. The world's chief fighter analysts would certainly say that in air combat in a real war the pilots taking part would throw this parameter out of the window. One is reminded of Lord Hives of Rolls-Royce, who on the day World War II started called his top staff and said "We must win this war; there's no point in coming a good second!" Exactly the same argument applies to air combat, and indeed to much of air warfare. What is the point in saving money by buying a fighter that is anything less than the very best, and then having it shot down? If you end up in "a good

Above: Britain's RAF has taken probe/drogue flight refuelling to a high pitch of development. All its large aircraft will soon be able to transfer and receive fuel. Here the first (camouflaged) VC10 K.2 is about to take fuel from a later K.2, both having once been civil airliners. In July 1984 the first K.3 began flight trials. This aircraft is itself an upgrade of the longer and heavier Super VC 10 with fuel capacity of 22,609gal (102,782 litres). The aircraft will operate with No 10 Sqn.

second" position in a war, cost/effectiveness is clearly zero. This is clearly a good argument against upgrades.

Perhaps unfortunately we live in a real world. Outside the Soviet Union, at least, nobody has the defence funding they would either like or need. The result has to be a compromise, and it is often a severe one. Britain's RAF has since the mid-1960s changed from being a large worldwide force into a small local air force with no responsibilities outside NATO's European theatre apart from the Falklands and a token presence in Belize and Hong Kong. One might have thought this would leave the service exuberantly overstocked with personnel and hardware, and wondering how to spend all its money. Instead it is severely short of aircrew, overspent by a supposed £600 million, and at a loss to balance its books. Yet it was back in 1980 that the decision was taken to modify 95 RAF Hawk T.1 trainers to carry Sidewinder AAMs in the air-defence role, and declare 72 of them to NATO as part of Britain's front-line air defence force. If an air force with such contracted and limited responsibilities suffers such shortages and over-spending problems, despite such cost-saving exercises as turning existing trainers into fighters, the financial and equipment problems of other forces, whose

Above: Test flying the Commander (SMA) Jetprop 1000 began in 1984, with this aircraft equipped with nose radar and a wing-mounted photo pod, both sensors being tailored to surface surveillance. Gulfstream has orders for several SMAs with IR/video, pylons and much more.

responsibilities have remained static or even expanded, must be serious indeed.

It happens that the Hawk features in this section of the book. It does so not only because of the armed RAF interceptor version, the T.1A, but also because the manu-

facturer is offering a completely new single-seat Hawk that is tailored to combat rather than to training. For many years it has been common for obsolescent fighters, with either one or two seats, to be used as trainers. For example, the MiG-15UTI and Lockheed T-33 have far outlasted the original fighter versions in air forces around the world. To take a trainer and turn it into a fighter is much less common, and has previously been done mainly in times of grave national emergency, as in

Left: The colossal jump in capability of the AV-8B Harrier II (nearer camera) is only partially obvious in this formation with a Marine Corps AV-8C.

Below: Red paint highlights the naturally black carbon wing of an AV-8B prototype. The deep pylons and belly LIDs (lift-improvement devices, normally replaced by a twin gun-pod) all help outperform the original AV-8.

Right: Like the Commander (SMA) and other commercially successful existing aircraft the Learjet has also been used as an airframe on which to hang equipment for military missions. Here a Learjet 35A is seen with a tow target (orange) and an Italian ELT/555 ECM jammer pod (blue). The Finnish air force has three 35As equipped for sea patrol, medevac, target towing and other tasks.

Britain in 1940 and Israel in 1948. Today, not only for reasons of inflation, there is hardly a single one of the dozens of piston, turboprop and jet trainer on the market that is not advertised as being suitable at least for the light attack mission if not also for air combat. These are hardly upgrades, as they are armed versions offered from the start, and they are excluded from this book which concentrates on types of basically greater power. The trend is mentioned because, with continuing inflation, what is

Above: An update for a new mission is the ECR Tornado, for the vital electronic combat and reconnaissance missions. This model of

the proposed Luftwaffe and Italian ECR version is carrying HARMs, a jammer, chaff dispenser, two tanks and Sidewinders.

affordable is going to be less and less. The trainer with a couple of AAMs or bombs will increasingly take the place of the newly bought front-line combat aircraft.

Such aircraft are a way for air forces who are mainly in the Third World to acquire

affordable airpower that is effective in their own scenario. Often the ability of such aircraft to operate from tiny hidden airstrips makes them infinitely more valuable than seemingly more impressive machines tied to long paved runways (often the only one in the country). The author has for years preached the doctrine that runways have no place whatsoever in any future major war. He believes that the diverse and expensive efforts of the USAF to try to refute this belief, using quick filling of craters, air-cushion transporters, taking off between the craters and, more difficult, landing between the craters, are utterly futile and stem from blind refusal to accept the plain fact that anything parked in a known location is at risk. As outlined in the main introduction, future major wars clearly demand a total rethink in order that aircraft shall have at least a fair chance of surviving either on the ground or in the air.

Such a major rethink cannot be introduced to existing aircraft by means of a cost/effective update programme, though there have been plenty of attempts in the past. More than 25 years ago, when the USAF had not closed its mind to the belief that airfields might be vulnerable, many fighters were shot into the air by giant rockets in the Zell (zero-length launch) technique. Highly spectacular to eye and

Above: Grumman is refurbishing 40 used A-4L Skyhawks for the Malaysian Air Force, one of which is here seen ready for delivery. Updating the A-4 is good business: IAI in Israel offers a major package, while the New Zealand A-4Ks are to be upgraded by Lear Siegler. In each case the customer has equipment options.

Below: The MiG-23 has had many upgrades. In all versions it has one of the most powerful engines ever fitted to a combat aircraft. This is an all-weather fighter version, with large multi-mode radar. It was itself a considerable advance over the original Lyulka-engined model but was later developed into attack versions (bottom).

ear, it worked well enough; but littering each squadron with massive rockets and spent cases each bigger than a Cadillac, to say nothing of the launcher itself and a mighty ladder to reach the cockpit, proved both unpopular and expensive. The scheme was unwieldy, and each fighter on its launcher was highly visible and vulnerable. Not least, the scheme did nothing to help the pilot land at the end of his sortie, but it was an earnest attempt to update existing aircraft to increase their survivability.

Today the vulnerability of airfields is at least 1,000 times worse, without even resorting to nuclear weapons. Even in the air the situation has become much more perilous, so that "stealth "techniques absolutely dominate the design of all true combat aircraft that are seriously intended to engage in a real war. These techniques involve much more than the addition of defensive electronic packages and perhaps the coating of parts of the external skin with RAM (radar absorbent material). They begin with consideration of the overall shape and configuration of the aircraft, so no update programme is going to have much more than a cosmetic effect (though the F-16XL is exceptional in that it results in a gross modification of aircraft shape).

Discounting the updates for totally new missions, which account for almost half the entries in this section, the unpalatable truth must therefore be faced that we live in a time of unprecedented change in air warfare, and these changes significantly reduce the value of update programmes. The commonest form of update is to fit an improved or different engine, additional EW suites, new cockpit displays and new weapon options. Nobody can fault new displays and weapons. Improved and augmented EW systems are very much better than nothing and, together with IRCM, can give a basically "visible" (and therefore vulnerable) aircraft a rather better chance of survival. New engines are less

Below: Nos 10, 220 and 221 Sqns of the Indian Air Force fly the MiG-23BN. Developing this advanced ground attack version proceeded almost in parallel with the interceptor. Most major airframe portions are very similar, and some are identical. Many versions of the aircraft exist.

Above: The latest, and possibly last, of the Kfir production versions is the C7, which is an update of the C2, itself an improved version of a fighter derived distantly from the French Mirage III. Israel Aircraft Industries have taken this compact design as far as it is possible to go, using currently available technology.

Below: The cockpit of the IAI Kfir-C2 (the C7 is very similar) forms a cost/effective intermediate step between a Mirage III and the very latest fighters. New features include a wide-angle HUD, radar display, MFD (multifunction display), UFC (up-front control), weapon controls and Hotas (hands on throttle and stick) control.

easy to justify, unless the original fit has proved unreliable. Today engines are extremely expensive, and merely to fly a bit faster, further or higher, or pull slightly more g in a turn, is nothing like as important as it used to be.

Thus, any air force that might find itself in conflict with a major power ought to think carefully before spending too much on updates. Its known airfields would certainly be wiped off the map within minutes of the start of hostilities, and it would make no difference whether the aircraft parked thereon were updated or not. But in a limited-war scenario, where all the most effective weapons are absent, updating makes sound sense. This is especially the case where it confers night and all-weather capability, greater firepower, improved weapon delivery accuracy, reliable pinpoint navigation and enhanced protection against enemy systems using radars, lasers, IR or other methods to detect aircraft and shoot them down.

In conclusion, brief mention should be made of the fact that, at least since the dawn of the jet era, combat aircraft need almost constant attention merely in order to stay flying. Like the family car they have to be ministered to between missions, faults must be rectified and not infrequently major items such as engines, avionics boxes and crucial portions of systems have to be replaced. A remarkably high proportion of warplanes of the past two decades have in addition had to receive structural strengthening, including complete replacement of skin panels and/or spars because of the onset of fatique. The trend since 1960 to stay at the lowest safe altitude has greatly accentuated fatigue problems, which on a rough count have been responsible for about the same number of inflight aircraft losses as enemy action in the numerous wars of the past 20 years. Such major rework takes aircraft out of the front line and consumes funds that might have been used for updating or new procurement. It is too early to tell whether the gradual changeover from bulk metal to various forms of fibre-reinforced composite will make fatigue a thing of the past, but on paper there are grounds for optimism.

AIRBUS A300B and A310

Type: Large-capacity medium-range transports.
Engines: Two large turbofans of (A300B) 50,000-58,000lb (22,680-26,300kg) or (A310) 48,000-50,000lb (21,773-22,680kg) thrust, either General Electric CF6-50 or -80 or Pratt & Whitney JT9D-7R4 or PW4058.
Dimensions: Span (300) 147ft 1in (44.84m), (310) 144ft 0in (43.89m); length (300) 177ft 5in (54.08m), (310) 153ft 1in (46.66m); height (300) 54ft 6.3in (16.6m), (310) 51ft 10in (15.8m); wing area (300) 2,799sq ft (260m²), (310) 2,357sq ft (219m²).
Weights: Empty (300, typical) 176,400lb (80,000kg), (310) 168,000lb (76,200kg); maximum (300) 363,765lb (165,000kg), (310) see text.
Performance: Typical cruising speed (both) 550mph (885km/h); range with maximum payload (300-600) 4,100 miles (6,600km), (310-300, typical) 4,000 miles (6,440km).

Now in service with civil operators all over the world, the A300B and smaller A310 were the pioneer aircraft in applying modern high-technology fan engines and wide-body capacity to the twin-engined size. Originally the A300B was quite a short-ranged machine, with stage-lengths of 1,000-1,500 miles (1,600-2,400km), but progressive development has extended the range until the Dash-600 is a transatlantic aeroplane. Likewise the A310, with an even more advanced design of wing than the already supercritical-winged A300B, has been further developed as the A310-300 for long-range operation, one feature being that the tailplane (horizontal stabilizer) is an integral fuel tank. Maximum weight of the A310-300 is increased from the original 291,010-313,055lb (132,000-142,000kg) to 337,305lb (153,000kg).

Though the prime market of both is civil, Airbus Industrie have always been aware of possible military markets. Indeed, the A300B has for almost a decade been studied by air forces, initially the Luftwaffe, as a multirole tanker/cargo aircraft. There is already a dedicated cargo version, the A300F4 and advanced 600F, with a side cargo door 11ft 9in (3.58m) wide and a special freight floor and mechanised and computer controlled loading system. There is no technical barrier to the development of a tanker, with above-floor transfer fuel and three HDUs (hose-drum units). At the usual gross weight of 165 tonnes the payload of the pure freighter is 100,550lb (4,5609kg), but this might be slightly reduced in the tanker by the dead weight of transfer tanks and HDUs.

While a military cargo and cargo/tanker continue to be the front runners in generating a military market for the A300B and A310, the possibility of developing an AEW (Awacs) type variant has become increasingly likely since the 1982 South Atlantic war, and 1983 air battles over the Lebanon, have shown the crucial importance of such aircraft (in one case by their absence). Airbus Industrie produced company-private brochures as far back as 1973 for an A300B with a pylon-mounted rotodome, but – despite development problems with the Nimrod AEW.3 as described on a later page – the most efficient and effective configuration for surveillance radar in an Airbus is now generally accepted as fore and after aerials (antennas) at nose and tail. These avoid interference from the aircraft structure or propellers, give perfect 180° vision, can be roll-stabilized (so that the aircraft does not have to make sickening "flat turns" while on station) giving a picture

---

BRITISH AEROSPACE
HAWK 200

Type: Tactical combat aircraft.
Engine: One 5,845lb (2,6511kg) Rolls-Royce Turboméca Adour Mk 871 turbofan.
Dimensions: Span 30ft 9.7in (9.39m); length 36ft 3in (11.05m); height 13ft 2in (4.01m); wing area 179.6sq ft (16.69m²).
Weights: Empty 8,750lb (3,969kg); maximum 19,000lb (8,620kg).
Performance: Maximum speed (clean) 644mph (1,037km/h) (limit in dive Mach 1.2); combat radius (intercept) 885 miles (1,425km), (four 1,000lb, 454kg bombs, hi-lo-hi) 620 miles (1,000km), (four 1,000lb plus four 500lb/227kg, lo-lo-lo) 155 miles (250km).

Though designed as a tandem dual trainer the Hawk proved so outstanding, and to have such great combat potential, that British Aerospace has now launched the Series 200 single-seat combat version, as well as the two-seat Series 100 multirole version. The latter is basically an uprated trainer with a combat Hotas-type cockpit with an advanced HUD and tactical displays, inertial navigation, comprehensive EW installations and optional FLIR, laser and ECM pod.

The Series 200 is a more complete re-design for combat missions of remarkable variety including airspace denial and air superiority fighting, close air support, battlefield attack and deep interdiction, long-range anti-ship attack (land-based Hawks could hit virtually anywhere in the North Atlantic, carrying Sea Eagle missiles), long-range multisensor reconnaissance and long range deployment over a ferry range of 2,530 miles (4,075km).

Addition of Blue Fox or (later) Blue Vixen radar would confer all-weather capability and compatibility with Sky Flash AAMs. Two 25mm Aden guns, each with 150 rounds, are installed in the fuselage, and Sidewinder AAMs and Alarm anti-radar missiles will be other standard weapons.

The performance figures given above are with the lower-thrust Adour 861; the Mk 871 engine, available for this aircraft from 1988, will give higher performance. With the Mk 861 engine the maximum external weapon load is 6,800lb (3,084kg), but each of the four wing pylons can carry a load of

Below: Simplified cutaway of a current Hawk with the nose of a Mk 200 grafted on. The specified Mk 871 engine will give performance appreciably higher than those listed at left (which are for the 5,700lb/2,586kg, Mk 861), but it fits the same hole without change to the inlets and ducts. So good is the Hawk that the author believes further variants, such as a two-seat Mk 200 and perhaps a version with a raised cockpit, will appear.

Right: Artist's impression of a Hawk 200 with radar operating in the anti-ship strike role with a Sea Eagle cruise missile on the centreline. It would be possible to carry three of these 62 mile (100km) range missiles and still have an effective radius near 620 miles (1,000km). As shown radius exceeds 920 miles (1,480km), weapons being released beyond ship radar range. The aircraft has an extremely wide range of weapon options.

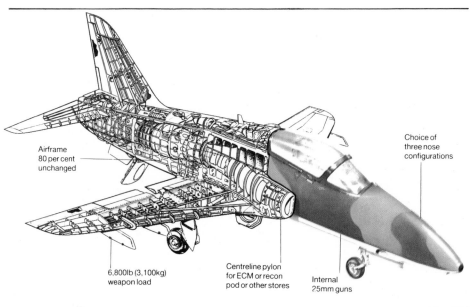

Airframe 80 per cent unchanged

6,800lb (3,100kg) weapon load

Centreline pylon for ECM or recon pod or other stores

Internal 25mm guns

Choice of three nose configurations

aligned with the horizon even in a bank, eliminate cyclic errors and distortions, provide ample emitter depth for precision heightfinding (impossible with the shallow rotodome), make better use of radiated power, reduce aircraft drag and avoid destabilizing effects caused by rotodome lift.

GEC Avionic Systems has done detailed work studying the installation of its modular Skyguardian surveillance system in the A300B, this comprising core radar, IFF, ESM, computers, airborne consoles and secure data links to ground stations. An aircraft as big as the A300B would have no difficulty in accommodating a major operations centre and crew for full inflight processing of all signals and data. Loiter speed and endurance at altitudes over 30,000ft (9,144m) – higher than other AEW aircraft except the Nimrod – are excellent, the main problem with jets being to reduce speed and fuel consumption and extend endurance. The Airbus aircraft all have engines 20 years newer in conception than the JT3D engines of the E-3 Sentry, and correspondingly not only quieter but also much more fuel-efficient. ESM pods would probably go on the wingtips, though they would probably preclude use of winglets.

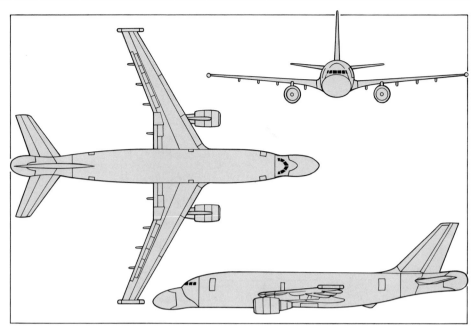

Above: Airbus Industrie has considered advanced tanker/ transport aircraft for a decade, and in 1985 the ultimate inevitability of such aircraft was very slowly being appreciated by various air forces. This sketch based on a BAe proposal shows a typical configuration, using the long-range A310-300. Loral ESM pods are shown on the wingtips. Both the A300B and A310 are cleared to operate at 40,000ft (12,190m), compared with 29,000ft (8,840m) for the E-3 Sentry. The A310-300 would be a particularly good basis for an aircraft in this class.

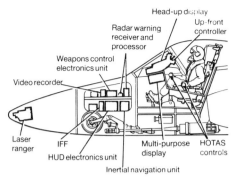

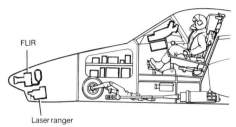

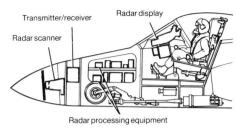

Above: The simplest Hawk 200 nose option is to fit a laser ranger, which could also serve as a marked-target seeker and as a target illuminator to guide "smart" weapons.

Above: Most customers would also require a FLIR, which by presenting a thermal scanning picture converts near-darkness into almost day conditions.

Above: The radar-equipped Hawk 200 ought to prove faster than other models, because of its longer nose. No TFR (terrain following radar) is needed even at treetop height.

2,000lb (907kg), and the centreline pylon is also available (for example, for a Sea Eagle stand-off missile which can be released well beyond the range of a target's radar envelope).

As illustrated above, British Aerospace is offering the Hawk 200 with three different noses, depending on the customer's missions, weather and sensor requirements. All variants will have an AHRS (attitude/heading reference system), Hotas cockpit and basic weapons control electronics. All customers at present (1985) discussing the Hawk 200 would also re-quire a HUD, UFC (up-front control), INS, WAC (weapon-aiming computer) and varying standards of IFF/EW installation.

Normally the INS would act as the central navigation reference, linked to all other avionics via the digital databus. A laser is regarded as essential for all non-radar Hawk 200s to provide target slant range. This is inputted to the WAC for providing real-time solutions to the problems of aiming free-fall or unguided rocket weapons. A FLIR is highly desirable for any air force which wishes to operate at night, and also has important capabilities in target detection at all times, relying on slight thermal differences instead of visual appearance. Either of the radars, with which the Kingston/Dunsfold/Brough engineers are already familiar, would greatly enhance all-weather capabilities, especially in the air-to-air and anti-shop missions. A radar-equipped Hawk 200 would be able to carry up to six medium-range Sparrow, Sky Flash or AIM-120A AMRAAM missiles.

Such a load would give great combat persistence, and this is also achieved by the extraordinarily high efficiency resulting

BRITISH AEROSPACE
NIMROD AEW.3

Type: Airborne early-warning aircraft.
Engines: Four 12,140lb (5,507kg) Rolls-Royce Spey 250 turbofans.
Dimensions: Span (over ESM) 115ft 1in (35.08m); length 137ft 8.6in (41.97m); height 35ft 0in (10.67m); wing area 2,121sq ft (197.0m²).
Weights: Empty not published but about 87,000lb (39,460kg); maximum 192,000lb (87,090kg).
Performance: Maximum transit speed 575mph (926km/h); operating ceiling 40,000ft (12,192m); endurance over 12h; range 5,755 miles (9,265km).

In 1977 Britain decided not to wait for a decision on a NATO-common AEW aircraft for Europe (the E-3 was eventually chosen) but to go ahead unilaterally with its own aircraft using 11 available Nimrod MR airframes. The AEW.3 version is the first aircraft to use the surveillance aerial arrangement in which radomes at nose and tail each cover a 180° sector, working in exact synchronization. As explained in the entry on the Airbus A300B, this offers a considerable number of major advantages over the traditional "saucer" arrangement using a pylon-mounted rotodome, and in theory results in a dramatically superior surveillance platform. Moreover, as it was started roughly ten years later than the Boeing E-3 and its Westinghouse radar, the British aircraft promised to be technically superior and in particular to be better matched to the local requirement in which more than half the area to be covered is water.

Unfortunately severe difficulties were experienced with the basic radar and associated dedicated computer. The striking differences in aircraft shape, first seen on AEW.3 XZ286 flown on 16 July 1980, caused almost no trouble and flight development of the basic aircraft has been exemplary. The serious difficulties all stem from excessive demands made on the main

Right: This photograph is one of the best to show conversion of Nimrods to AEW.3 standard. Today practically all the airframe work has been finished, but problems with the aircraft are still not fully solved. The latest date for initial operational service is some time in 1987, about five years late.

Above: Impression of a Hawk 200 with "iron bombs", and a second with radar and anti-ship missile.

Right: Impression of a T-45A Hawk arriving on a carrier. This model is in full-scale development at Douglas Aircraft.

from the unique combination of wing and engine. No other aircraft can come anywhere near the Hawk's ability to engage in close combat at low and medium levels for long periods. Combat fuel flow (defined at 16°/s and 6g sustained turn rate) is under 30kg/min, compared with (for example) 150 for an F-5E, 220 for an F-20A and 620 for an F-4.

Quite apart from the Hawk 200, BAe/Douglas are soon to fly the first T-54A, the carrier-capable US Navy Undergraduate Jet Flight Trainer. The T-45A has new landing gears, hook and lateral airbrakes.

GEC Avionics radar and computer. The radar demands more power than originally calculated, and this strains the main electrical generators and causes problems in heat dissipation. Because the fuel is used as the heat sink this means that a heavy fuel load is required whenever the radar is operating, so that much more fuel must be brought back from each mission, thus reducing endurance and time on station, which is further reduced by an overload weight problem which makes it impossible within the limits of gross weight to take off with a maximum fuel load. More fundamental is the radar's initial poor reliability and inability to pick out targets from background clutter, which – together with changing and generally increased demands by the customer - has grossly overloaded the processing capacity of the computer.

With increasing maturity there is a chance that improved radar reliability and

Below: XV285, first so-called "production standard" Nimrod AEW.3. The production Mk 3 actually has a probe, and also required several further years of extremely detailed systems development before it was acceptable.

discrimination will bring back signal-processing demands to a level within the capacity of the computer, but this looks a forlorn hope. The alternative is to switch to a different computer, but the only examples available in Britain are apparently commercial types not designed for severe Ministry of Defence and airborne applications which could call for substantial redesign to meet temperature, acceleration, shock-load and similar requirements. The signal-processing demands appear to have been underestimated, and as a result, even if the radar reliability were to become consistently acceptable, the computer and main generators would still be at the limit of capability with nothing in hand.

The bright spot in a generally troubled scene is that the basic aircraft, radar and computer perform outstandingly on the rare occasions when everything works. This colossal project was clearly yet another where the effort, time and cost were underestimated at the start; then, because of the MoD(PE)'s crippling shortage of funds, the difficulties were side-stepped or "worked around" instead of a bold decision having been taken to upgrade major elements in the system.

By spring 1985 BAe Manchester site had converted all 11 Nimrods, but only one had been "delivered" to RAF Waddington, and that remains in MoD hands with test crews from Boscombe Down and the various main contractors. No 8 Sqn RAF was due to be operational in 1982, but it looks like being 1986 before this unit can at last pension off any more of its stalwart but totally obsolete Shackleton AEW.2s and become operational with a single Nimrod AEW.3.

The total development bill of £800 million was expected to rise to perhaps £1,300 million, which by any standard is a high price for the R&D on a fleet of 11 aircraft. Moreover, the delay of some three years in introducing the Nimrod AEW has had major repercussions on RAF planning.

Top: Roll-out of the first AEW.3, 30 April 1980. At that time some observers wondered if the grotesque nose and tail would cause handling problems. In the event aerodynamic and structural difficulties have been few.

Above: The AEW.3 has six operator consoles arranged along the left side of the cabin. Here the Marconi Elliott trials team work keyboards and rolling-ball inputs in the early stages of flight development.

BRITISH AEROSPACE
SEA HARRIER

Type: STOVL ship-based multirole combat aircraft.
Engine: One 21,500lb (9,752kg) Rolls-Royce Pegasus 104 vectored-thrust turbofan.
Dimensions: Span 25ft 3in (7.70m); length 47ft 7in (14.5m); height 12ft 2in (3.71m); wing area 201.1sq ft (18.68m^2).
Weights: Empty 12,990lb (5,892kg); maximum 26,200lb (11,880kg).
Performance: Maximum speed (high) Mach 1.25 or 828mph (1,330km/h), (low) 740mph (1,191km/h); combat radius (hi intercept mission) 460 miles, (low strike mission) 288miles (463km); ferry range 2,300 miles (3,700km).

After years of delay the Sea Harrier FRS.1 was permitted to go ahead in 1975, the designation signifying Fighter, Reconnaissance, Strike. The first flew in 1978, and without the puny force (28 out of a total available of 32) of Sea Harriers the whole idea of a Task Force to recover the Falkland Islands in 1982 would have been a pipedream. This was pure chance, because the delay in getting going on the programme was largely due to the vehement belief that no such aircraft was needed (it was said "the Royal Navy can rely on the RAF for protection").

Eventually total orders for this outstandingly agile, effective, versatile, tough and reliable aircraft reached 57 for Royal Navy squadrons, plus 16 Mk 51s (and four tandem-seat Mk 60 trainers) for the Indian Navy. Few aircraft have ever exceeded expectations as has the Sea Harrier, but it is now recognised that, there being no money for a next-generation aircraft (because of plain shortsightedness in Whitehall), there must be an MLU (mid-life update). This was argued about over a long period, but was at last announced in February 1985.

The chief elements in the Sea Harrier MLU are the replacement of the Blue Fox radar by the new Ferranti Blue Vixen pulse-doppler radar, giving complete "look-down shoot-down" capability, and imported AIM-120A (Amraam) "fire and forget" medium-range AAMs. These will give the updated Sea Harrier FRS.2 a long-range kill capability against multiple targets. A completely new set of software programmes will be provided, and other changes will include secure voice and digital data links via the US-developed JTIDS (joint tactical information and distribution system), the new Marconi Defence Systems Guardian radar warning system, which is microprocessor-controlled instead of hard-wired and shows threat information pictorially or alpha-

Shackleton maintenance was being rapidly run down (to a planned stop in 1984), while large facilities and servicing teams were built up in 1982-3 at Waddington to handle the Nimrods (most of the personnel have been re-posted). Shackleton major overhaul is no longer possible as BAe's Bitteswell site was shut in 1983.

All these unfortunate difficulties divert attention from the fact, not mentioned by the media, that in most respects the Nimrod AEW.3 is potentially the best surveillance aircraft in the world. The basic advantages of the powerful pulsed-doppler radar have already been referred to, the Cossor Jubilee Guardsman IFF is an outstanding new set that uses the same aerials as the main radar, and the ability to interleave high and low PRFs for optimum picture discrimination in different land and sea conditions is unique. Of course, navigation, communications and EW/ECM installations are to the very highest standard, the Loral ESM passive receivers being in wingtip pods feeding analysers of all received signals.

The first production-standard Nimrod AEW.3 is XV263, flown in mid-1984, but the first delivered to Waddington – largely to give the RAF ground staff experience on the aircraft – was XZ285. Probably all 11 aircraft will be away from Manchester by the end of 1985, but it is doubtful that any will be truly operational until 1986. It is to be hoped that the interlinked problems of these aircraft, which stem largely from the cheeseparing procurement system and have nothing at all to do with any of the fundamental principles, will not cripple future efforts of GEC Avionics as a major supplier of AEW systems.

Indeed by mid-1985, the whole AEW.3 system did seem, at last to be coming "out of the wood", though the official RAF view continued to be that operational capability would not be achieved until at least the second quarter of 1987.

Above: XV263 was the first AEW.3 to reach the true production standard. This view shows the overall "hemp" colour, flight-refuelling probe, reversers on the outer engines, ram-air inlet between the main engine inlets to serve the heat exchangers, equipment cooling inlet on the left of the fin and APU exhaust on the right of the fin. Unlike the Nimrod MR.2, the AEW.3 needed no auxiliary fins on the tailplane to counter the destabilizing effect of the probe.

numerically on a cockpit display, a modern data-bus system for rapid and effective handling of information, a cockpit redesigned for Hotas controls to reduce workload in combat, and provision for carrying Sea Eagle anti-ship missiles (which in fact is preceding the MLU). Features previously published, but absent from the official MLU announcement, are addition of LERX (leading-edge root extensions) to enhance manoeuvrability as on the AV-8B Harrier II and RAF Harrier GR.5, and extra weapon pylons including Sidewinder launch rails on redesigned wingtips.

Left: Artist's impression of a Sea Harrier FRS.2, which – in the absence of LERX and wingtip missile rails – will now be identifiable chiefly by the rather larger and less-pointed radome. The planned mid-life update will have a very large effect in increasing capability in the 1990s.

BELL
AH-IT+ SUPERCOBRA

Type: Close-support and attack helicopter.
Engines: Two 1,625hp General Electric T700-401 turboshafts.
Dimensions: Diameter of main rotor (two blades) 52ft 0in (15.85m); length of fuselage 48ft 2in (14.68m); height 14ft 2in (4.32m); main-rotor disc area 2,124sq ft (197.3m²).
Weights: Empty not published but about 8,900lb (4,040kg); maximum, probably to be set at 15,000lb (6,804kg)
Performance: Maximum cruising speed 184mph (296km/h); range (original fuel) about 250 miles (400km), but fuel load can be increased.

Produced as a private venture in 1965 to meet an apparent need for a slim-bodied armed helicopter, the HueyCobra immediately won massive orders from the US Army and was soon in action in Vietnam. Early versions were powered by the 1,400shp T53 engine, in common with most UH-1 "Huey" multirole transport helicopters from which the Cobra was developed, but when in 1968 the US Marine Corps placed an order it picked the AH-1J SeaCobra with a PT6T (T400) engine of 1,800shp with twin power sections giving twin-engine safety.

Over 1,000 Cobras have been rebuilt as AH-1S modernised machines, in several sub-types, most with a T53 uprated to 1,800shp, with IR-suppressed exhaust and numerous other features to enhance survival on the battlefield, and visually distinguished by having the smooth moulded canopy replaced by flat glass panes which reduce glint and make the helicopter less conspicuous in NOE (nap of the Earth) flying. All these advanced versions carry eight TOW anti-armour missiles, the stabilized sight being in the nose; late sub-types have a FLIR-augmented sight giving greatly improved capability in darkness or through fog or smoke.

These in-service versions carry a wide range of armament schemes. The original AH-IG was delivered with a TAT-102A chin turret with a 7.62mm Minigun firing 4,000 shots/min. This was replaced by an M28 turret, a Minigun and an M129 grenade projector with 300 rounds of 40mm grenades, or two of either. Stub wings carry various loads including Minigun pods or up to 76 rockets in 19-tube launchers. Some AH-IGs were re-armed with a 20mm M61 six-barrel cannon, but the AH-1J was from the start equipped with the lighter M197 three-barrel version firing at 750 shots/min. All TOW variants have the Hughes M65 system with two quadruple launch tubes carried on the outer sub-wing attachments, and the sight low in the nose (which forces the entire helicopter into full view of the enemy). A universal chin turret is installed in the Up-gun AH-1S and Modernised AH-1S, able to mount either a 20mm or 30mm gun, and with improved management of the stub-wing stores.

The AH-1T, first flown in 1976, introduced many upgraded airframe features, including a 1,900shp T400 coupled engine unit, a wide-chord main rotor and new transmission able to accept the full power

DASSAULT-BREGUET
MIRAGE 3 NG

Type: Multirole fighter/bomber.
Engine: One 15,873lb (7,200kg) SNECMA Atar 9K50 afterburning turbojet.
Dimensions: Span 27ft 0in (8.22m); length 51ft 4.3in (15.65m); height 13ft 11.5in (4.25m); wing area 381sq ft (35.4m²).
Weights: Empty 16,094lb (7,300kg); loaded (clean) 22,050lb (10,000kg), (maximum) 32,400lb (14,700kg)
Performance: Maximum speed (clean) Mach 2.2 at high altitude (1,460mph, 2,350km/h), or 863mph (1,390km/h) indicated airspeed; combat radius (hi-lo-hi, two bombs of 882lb/400kg size) 391 miles (630km).

By far the best-selling fighter from Western Europe since World War II, the Mirage delta family (Mirage III, 5 and 50) were obviously coming to the end of their competitive marketing life in the late 1970s. To sustain customer interest Dassault-Breguet first offered the Mirage 50, powered by the uprated 9K50 engine, as fitted to the Mirage F1 family, and then carried out a thorough-going upgrade which alters the airframe structure, aerodynamics and systems as well as avionics and weapons. Called 3 NG (Nouvelle Génération), it is immediately identified by its fixed sweptback canard foreplanes mounted on the upper part of the inlet ducts. These canards are geometrically almost identical to those of the IAI Kfir, and indeed one of the objectives of the Mirage 3 NG is to try to secure export sales that might otherwise have gone to the Israeli product.

Whereas the Kfir has a pure delta wing with a dogtooth and extended-chord outer leading edge, the 3 NG has no dogtooth but a sawcut slot at about 50 per cent semi-span and an important improvement in a sharply swept leading-edge root extension. Together with the canard this gives very much better lifting capabilities at high AOA (angle of attack), enabling the 3 NG to operate at increased gross weight and manoeuvre with much improved capability, though this is still not in the same class as the Mirage 2000 or other modern fighters.

The flight-control system has been completely replaced by an FBW (fly by wire) system, similar to that of the Mirage 2000, and this also improves performance and handling. The navigation system is now inertial, and combat effectiveness is improved by adding a HUD and customer options which include updated Cyrano IV radar, a laser ranger or Agave air/surface radar. The prototype 3 NG can be seen to have a comprehensive RWR (radar warning receiver) system with an aft-facing receiver aerial near the top of the fin and two forward-facing receivers on the leading edge near the wingtips. A flight-refuelling probe can be provided, and to take advantage of the considerable increase in allowable gross weight four new lateral stores attachment points have been added across the underside of the fuselage.

Of course, a wide range of advanced weapons can be carried, some of them not compatible with the Mirage III and 5. A dedicated reconnaissance version has also been studied, and another alternative is a multisensor reconnaissance pack carried by an otherwise unchanged 3 NG. At the time of writing, however, no customer had come forward. A 3 NG update of existing Mirages is not very likely.

of both engine power sections together. In 1980 this served as the basis for the first AH-1T+, by far the most powerful of all Cobras. Powered by two of the new T700 engines, each more powerful than the single engine of early Cobras, the T+ (T-plus) also features a new combining gearbox to handle the much greater power (3,250shp) and various new airframe and systems items, all planned to keep this helicopter competitive into the 1990s, by which time the completely new LHX (see later pages) should be coming into service. Among AH-1T+ armament schemes are 76 rockets of 2.75in (69.85mm) calibre or 16 Zuni rockets of 5in (127mm) calibre, or two AIM-9L Sidewinder or Stinger AAMs plus 750 rounds of ammunition for the M197 gun, or eight TOW wire-guided or Hellfire laser-homing anti-armour missiles.

The prototype AH-1T+, named Supercobra, first flew in November 1983, and in early 1984 Congress gave approval for this powerful new version to be procured for the Marine Corps. The current production

is of two blocks each of 22 helicopters funded under Fiscal Years 1984 and 1985, these being due for delivery in 1986-7. They will escort transport helicopters, carry out "reconnaissance by fire" missions, search and target acquisition, multiweapon fire support and anti-armour missions. Further batches may be permitted, depending on progress with LHX.

Above: The prototype SuperCobra has now been painted in USMC drab olive for prolonged battlefield evaluation. Comparison with earlier versions emphasizes the greater size of the new twin-T700 engine installation, though the engines themselves are small, most of the extra volume being essential exhaust IR suppression. The chin turret houses a GE M197, a three-barrel lightweight version of the M61 gun used in US fighters. The Super is seen on a Yuma range with standard TOW missiles.

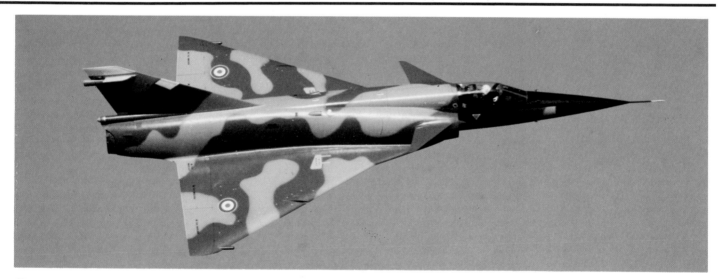

Above: From above all the 3 NG electronic warfare sensors can be seen, the comprehensive suite of receivers and dispenser/jammers being one of the most important advances over the Mirage III and 5. Main contractors would be Thomson-CSF and Electronique Marcel Dassault.

Left: Even from this angle, on takeoff, there are many features which distinguish the NG. Conversion of an existing fleet would probably not be cost/effective.

Right: Looking up at the 3 NG soon after its first flight on 21 December 1982. Though in many ways attractive, the NG had not attracted a customer by mid-1985.

DASSAULT-BREGUET
MIRAGE 2000

Type: (C) Single-seat fighter, (B) two-seat trainer, (N) two-seat low-level attack aircraft and nuclear-missile carrier.
Engine: One 19,840lb (9,000kg) SNECMA M53-5 afterburning bypass turbojet; from 1986 2000N will have 21,830lb (9,900kg) M53-P2.
Dimensions: Span 29ft 6.34in (9.0m); length (except 2000N) 47ft 6.86in (14.5m), (2000N) 47ft 8.8in (14.55m); height 17ft 6in (5.3m); wing area 441sq ft (41m²).
Weights: Empty (2000C) 16,315lb (7,400kg); loaded (air intercept mission) 33,000lb (14,969kg), (maximum) 36,375lb (16,500kg).
Performance: Maximum speed (clean, high altitude) 1,320mph (2,124km/h, Mach 2.2); maximum attack speed at low level 690mph (1,110km/h); combat radius (four bombs, high altitude) over 920 miles (1,480km).

Designed in 1975 to meet the future needs of France's Armée de l'Air, this small tailless delta has also secured major export sales despite a basically very high price. Its design is tailored to the supersonic high-altitude mission, but - in sharp contrast to the company's initial philosophy on the Mirage III – great efforts are being made to carry the maximum number of offensive stores and other external loads to achieve the greatest mission versatility.

One variant not yet built is the dedicated 2000R multisensor reconnaissance model, though the existing 2000C1 as now in service can carry any of four types of external pod for this mission. More serious is the absence from current literature of the planned Thomson-CSF RDI radar. The pulse-doppler RDI was planned to give greatly enhanced capability to this aircraft from 1985, but its development has been de-layed and all current 2000s have the simpler and older-technology RDM. Thus, most current aircraft are either 2000C1 fighters for the original customer, or tandem-seat 2000Bs, or export aircraft differing only in small details, and still powered by the M53-5 engine.

At present the only new model coming into production is the 2000N for the Armée de l'Air. This is a two-seater, the backseater being concerned mainly with navigation, avoiding hostile defences and systems management. Dassault-Breguet state that the 2000N airframe has been "strengthened for flight at 690mph (1,110km/h) at 200ft (60m)" which is the same as the maximum speed at low level of the 2000C1, and in any case does not compare favourably with the 920mph (1,480km/h) of Tornado. The 2000N is fitted with ESD Antilope V terrain-following radar and the new AHV12

DASSAULT-BREGUET/DORNIER
ALPHA JET and LANCIER

Type: Advanced trainer, close support and reconnaissance aircraft.
Engines: Two 2,976lb (1,350kg) SNECMA/Turboméca Larzac 04-C6 turbofans (NGEA, 3,175lb/1,440kg 04-C20).
Dimensions: Span 29ft 10.8in (9.11m); length (close support) 43ft 5in (13.23m); height 13ft 9in (4.19m); wing area 188.4sq ft (17.5m²).
Weights: (Close support) Empty 7,749lb (3,515kg); maximum 17,637lb (8,000kg).
Performance: Maximum speed, clean, sea level (C6 engines) 621mph (1,000km/h), (C20) 645mph (1,038km/h); combat radius, lo-lo, gun pod and wing stores 363 miles (583km).

Left: An Alpha Jet NGEA on weapon-carry trials with 99gal (450litre) drop tanks, centreline gun pod (one 30mm DEFA cannon) and two Matra Magic close-range missiles. The chisel nose is caused by the Thomson-CSF laser ranger; other avionics include SAGEM Uliss inertial system, Thomson-CSF HUD, TRT radar altimeter and SFIM standby compass. By 1985 Dassault-Breguet had sold this model to Egypt and Cameroun.

The Alpha Jet was developed jointly by France and Germany to meet mutual demands for an advanced jet trainer. Features include stepped tandem cockpits with ejection seats, two small turbofan engines and a shoulder-high wing with anhedral. The wing position was adopted partly to give plenty of clearance for underwing stores, and the Luftwaffe purchased a special Alpha Jet A version for use in the close-support and reconnaissance roles, three JaboG (fighter bomber wings) each having 51 aircraft, and a further 18 equipping another unit for weapons training. They are austerely equipped in comparison with more powerful modern attack aircraft.

In April 1982 the partners first flew the Alpha Jet "alternative close support version", developed by Dassault-Breguet and with close kinship with various Mirages. This is recognised by a long anteater-shape nose with an oblique chisel tip housing a laser ranger. Other equipment includes a HUD, inertial platform and radar altimeter. This variant was adopted by Egypt as the MS2, and the Helwan factory tooled up to build it under licence (the production run is now likely to terminate at No 11).

A second-generation development is the

Alpha Jet NGEA (Nouvelle Génération pour l'Ecole et l'Appui), which again has been developed chiefly by Dassault-Breguet. This is a natural next stage beyond the MS2 and related sub-types, and its chief upgrade feature is the slightly more powerful Larzac 04-C20 engine. The nav/attack subsystems are closely similar to those of the MS2, though customers are offered various optional upgrades. Addi-

Above: The NGEA demonstrator photographed with two tanks and two rocket launchers (standard types are F4 firing 18×68mm rockets, LAU-3B/A firing 19×2.75in or CEM 1 firing 36×68mm). A major difference in the Lancier is its ability to carry heavier stores.

tional aerials (antennas) can be installed in a long dorsal spine along the centre of the existing spine fairing the canopy into the fin. A Thomson-CSF gun camera is a radio altimeter, two Sagem inertial platforms, Thomson-CSF colour cockpit display (though, unlike the Hornet, it still has ordinary cockpit instruments), an Omera vertical camera and upgraded ECM. The original 2000 was fitted with the Thomson-CSF Serval RWR system and Matra's integrated chaff/flare dispenser at the rear of the wing roots.

The chief weapon of the 2000N will be the ASMP long-range (62 miles, 100km) nuclear cruise missile. This will usually be carried on the centreline, together with two large tanks and two Magic self-defence AAMs.

Right: A Mirage 2000N on flight test with a typical load comprising a mock-up ASMP on the centreline, two 374gal (1,700litre) tanks and two self-defence Matra Magic AAMs on the outer pylons. The 2000N is a two-seater specially configured for attack missions.

standard fitting, and among new external stores options are Magic 2 close-range AAMs, Maverick ASMs and different auxiliary fuel tanks, including 99gal (450litre) size on all four pylons or 137.5gal (625litre) tanks on the inboard pylons.

Dassault-Breguet is busy with marketing this NGEA version, and with its further upgrading. Dornier, however, has not incorporated several potentially important upgrade features which the German company studied in 1980-82, such as DSFC (direct side-force control) imparted by separately controllable left/right split rudders on each of four enlarged underwing pylons. With these the Alpha Jet could almost have rivalled the F-16/AFTI in manoeuvre capability and air/air and air/ground weapon aiming without the need to make banked turns.

Above: The Dassault-Breguet Lancier had not been built as this book went to press, though its nose was exhibited at the 1985 Paris airshow. This demonstrator is virtually a Lancier without the Agave nose radar, FLIR or improved HUD. It is shown carrying an AM39 Exocet (1,438lb, 652kg), one tank and two self-defence Magic air-to-air missiles. The Lancier will have the same type of digital multiplexed bus system and CP 2084 computer as the Mirage 2000. It has been hurried along to try to compete with the more thoroughly engineered Hawk 200.

AFTI/F-16

Type: Advanced-technology research fighter aircraft.

Engine and other numerical data broadly as for General Dynamics F-16A and C described in many other publications.

First flown on 10 July 1982, the AFTI/F-16 is the most important research aircraft in the history of air fighting. The aircraft itself is merely a carrier vehicle which happens to be based on an F-16. What matters are the flight-control systems, computers, software, programs and complex control laws and dynamics which from the start have explored totally new territory. A great deal of the work could be, and is being, done on the ground, both with basic computer studies and with large research tools.

The objective is to create fighters of the future with previously undreamed-of capabilities. The basis was the CCV (control-configured vehicle) concept, which was briefly explored with a rebuilt YF-16 prototype from March 1976. That aircraft was visibly distinguished by its two down-sloping canard control surfaces, but it had an analog flight-control system, and was thus limited in capability. Today's AFTI (advanced fighter technology integration) F-16 has a very advanced FBW (fly by wire) DFCS (digital flight control system) which with ongoing research and development enables the full potential of the aircraft to be realized. The AFTI aircraft likewise has canard control fins, and most of its additional research and test equipment is housed in a dorsal spine which leads from the cockpit to the fin.

The basic feature of the AFTI is its six flight modes, all of which are decoupled from the others in a way impossible with conventional aircraft. There is no need to describe how ordinary fighters fly, except to comment that they generally go where they are pointing and can change trajectory only in carefully defined and often rather laborious ways. For example, to turn left or right it is necessary first to roll left or right into a bank and then proceed to move the nose along the horizon with (probably) careful combination of pedal pressure and backward pressure on the stick before finally rolling out wings-level as the desired new heading is reached.

With the AFTI, and any similar aircraft, the ability to impart control forces simultaneously at the front and rear opens up new possibilities, to the extent that the limiting factor is almost always the pilot's ability to withstand the imparted accelerations and unusual forces. For example, in the pitching plane it is possible to do two things: point the aircraft's nose up or down through a considerable angle (the limit depending on indicated airspeed and other factors) whilst maintaining height exactly unchanged (or even in terrain-following flight following the contours of the ground), or alternatively to move the aircraft up or down, with very large vertical speed, whilst holding the fuselage in the level attitude. Likewise, it is possible either to move the aircraft instantly to the left or right without changing the direction in which it is pointing or, alternatively to swing the nose left or right, rotating the aircraft about the Z (vertical) axis, without changing the direction of travel. These manoeuvres, together with those of conventional aircraft, are commanded by the pilot's stick, pedals and a throttle twist-grip. The aerodynamic surfaces used are the front canards, used in unison or in opposition, the wing flaperons (which behave as flaps or as ailerons), the tail-planes and the rudder.

For example, an AFTI pilot seeing a target for ground gunnery approaching could depress the nose precisely on to that target, open fire and keep every round on that target over a considerable distance, without the aircraft changing its height above the ground. Lining up for a bombing run he could move left or right instantly with wings level. In air to air combat no conventional fighter could even approach the AFTI's extraordinary ability either to move in "impossible" directions or to continue moving in one direction whilst rotating about any axis to point in another. In current research the pilot wears a helmet mounted sight which among other things shows by small lights when a particular target is centred in the sight's crosshairs; then, with Hotas controls the pilot can slew the radar, FLIR or other sensor (such as the IR homing head of an AAM) exactly on to the same target.

The limitations of the possibilities are obviously the ability of the pilot to withstand side accelerations exceeding 2g whilst still being centred in the cockpit and looking accurately through the HUD. Possibly the longer-term result will be renewed belief in the 1956 philosophy that the pilot ought not to be aboard the aircraft.

Below: The AFTI/F-16 began life as F-16 No. 6 FSD. Conversion was a major task, the dorsal spine and front canards being only the visible items. It is seen here with the engine nozzle fully open for maximum 'burner.

Above: On 24 April 1985 the AFTI first flew with a new laser FLIR tracker, supplied by Westinghouse. Unrelated to the twin Lantirn pods carried by regular F-16Cs, the pod is mounted conformally to give minimum drag. It provides precise information on where the aircraft should be in any kind of weapon-delivery situation. The FCC (fire-control computer) then steers the aircraft as instructed.

Dorsal spine covers
AFTI dedicated avionics

Tacan

AFTI/F-16
USAF NASA USN

AF 75 750

Nozzle open

Canted ventral fins

Main-gear compartment

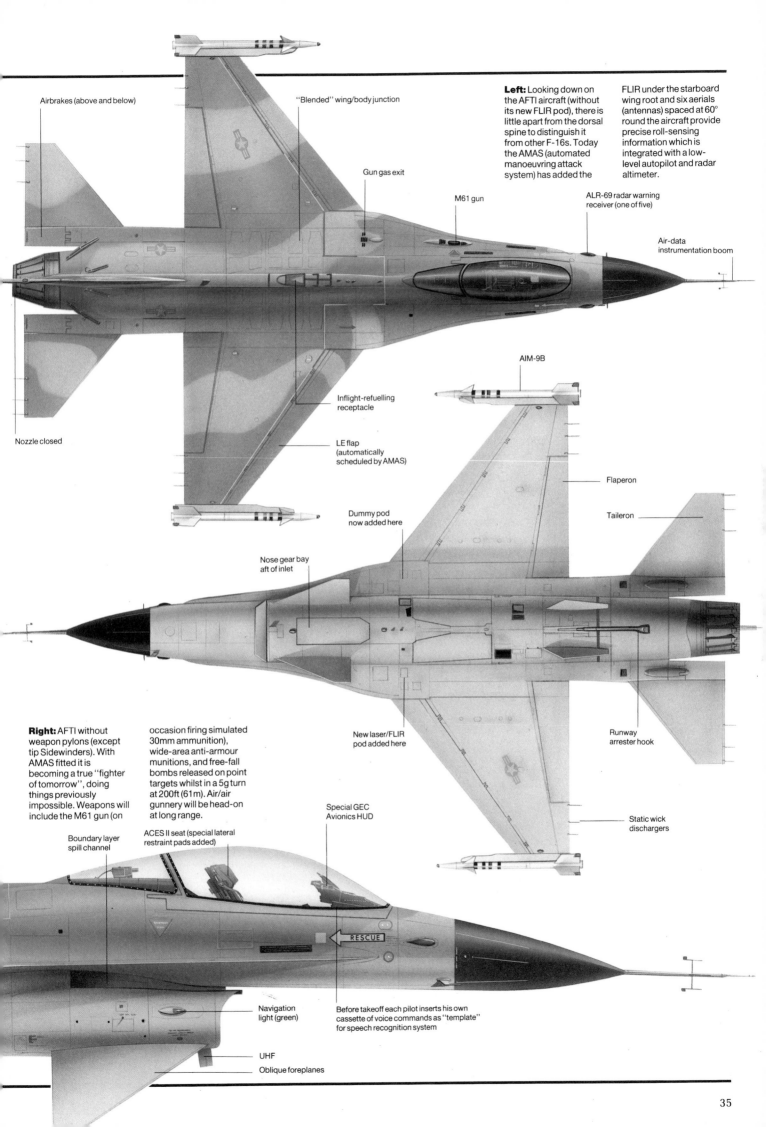

Airbrakes (above and below)

"Blended" wing/body junction

Gun gas exit

M61 gun

ALR-69 radar warning receiver (one of five)

Left: Looking down on the AFTI aircraft (without its new FLIR pod), there is little apart from the dorsal spine to distinguish it from other F-16s. Today the AMAS (automated manoeuvring attack system) has added the FLIR under the starboard wing root and six aerials (antennas) spaced at 60° round the aircraft provide precise roll-sensing information which is integrated with a low-level autopilot and radar altimeter.

Air-data instrumentation boom

Nozzle closed

Inflight-refuelling receptacle

LE flap (automatically scheduled by AMAS)

AIM-9B

Flaperon

Taileron

Dummy pod now added here

Nose gear bay aft of inlet

Special GEC Avionics HUD

Runway arrester hook

Right: AFTI without weapon pylons (except tip Sidewinders). With AMAS fitted it is becoming a true "fighter of tomorrow", doing things previously impossible. Weapons will include the M61 gun (on occasion firing simulated 30mm ammunition), wide-area anti-armour munitions, and free-fall bombs released on point targets whilst in a 5g turn at 200ft (61m). Air/air gunnery will be head-on at long range.

New laser/FLIR pod added here

Static wick dischargers

Boundary layer spill channel

ACES II seat (special lateral restraint pads added)

RESCUE

Navigation light (green)

Before takeoff each pilot inserts his own cassette of voice commands as "template" for speech recognition system

UHF

Oblique foreplanes

F-16XL

Type: New-generation multirole combat aircraft.

Engine: Prototypes flown with 23,840lb (10,814kg) Pratt and Whitney F100-200 and with 29,000lb (13,154kg) General Electric F110-100 augmented turbofans.

Dimensions: Span 34ft 2.8in (10.43m); length 54ft 1.86in (16.51m); height 17ft 7in (5.36m); wing area 663sq ft (61.59m²).

Weights: Empty, not published; design mission 43,000lb (19,504kg); maximum 48,000lb (21,772kg).

Performance: Maximum speed same as F-16C at 1,350mph (2,173km/h), Mach 2.05; maximum range more than 2,875 miles (4,630km).

When the F-16's predecessor, the General Dynamics Model 401, was in the preliminary design stage one of the configurations that appeared most promising was a modification of the tailless delta which GD called the cranked-arrow wing. Though it was not picked for the F-16, the overall configuration offered such possibilities that the design team at Fort Worth continued to study it, and in 1980, when the F-16 was in production, GD funded a complete detail design and programme to build at least one prototype. The USAF became equally excited about the enhanced capability of the changed configuration and leased back to GD two development F-16 airframes, an F100 engine and a new tandem-seat cockpit. What came out was two striking and impressive aircraft called

F-16XL, one a single-seater powered by the F100 and the other a two-seater powered by the General Electric F110. The first flight dates were, respectively, 3 July and 29 October 1982.

Both the XLs are considerably longer than the regular F-16, and the tailless big-wing configuration is completely new. The wing can be regarded either as an ogival (Concorde-type) delta with extra conventional wings added at the tips, or as a conventional swept wing fitted with such gigantic leading-edge strakes that they obliterate the whole wing except the tips. The sweep angle of the leading edge is 70° inboard and 50° outboard, though the inboard leading edge sweep is reduced, partly to improve crew downward view. Overall area is more than doubled, and the skins are graphite/polyamide composite to achieve the necessary strength and rigidity. Movable surfaces comprise inboard flaps, outboard ailerons and powered leading edge flaps over the outer section.

GD originally called the redesigned aircraft the Scamp (Supersonic-cruise aircraft modification program), and one of the areas where the new wing originally showed to advantage was in supersonic flight, where it offered better efficiency and lower drag than the conventional shape. During the redesign GD took every opportunity to enhance the capability of the XL, and this, combined with the fact that it is a basically larger aircraft, means that direct comparisons with the "Brand X" model are not

quite fair. GD claims that the XL carries "double the weapon load 45 per cent further". Internal fuel, already good on the F-16, is increased by no less than 82 per cent! Completely new weapon carriage results in there being 17 stores stations, many in tandem to give a total of 29 main hardpoints. Instead of requiring pylons, where the stores offer maximum drag, conformal stowage is used with the stores recessed into the aircraft to reduce drag by at least 58 per cent. No other "fighter type" aircraft in history has ever had the potential to carry such a varied load of weapons.

Thanks to the enormous wing area and advanced flight controls the XL can outperform even the F-16C in almost every part of the air combat repertoire. Pitch and roll rates are roughly doubled, though this probably enters areas where the limiting factor is the pilot. Low-level penetration speed is increased, and these greater speeds can actually be reached as a result of the conformal weapon carriage and more powerful GE engine. Slow-flying ability is remarkable, full control being maintained at 30° AOA at 90kt (104mph, 167km/h). Takeoff and landing distances are about two-thirds as long as for the F-16C.

The XL narrowly lost to the F-15E in the USAF Enhanced (Dual-Role) Fighter programme, but development is continuing for future use in the 1990s. A production XL with the F110 engine would probably be designated F-16F, and production could begin in the second quarter of 1991.

Below: Side elevation of the first F-16XL, rebuilt from the No. 5 FSD (full-scale development) F-16 prototype. This aircraft is a single-seater and is powered by the F100 engine, whereas a production derivative would more closely resemble the second XL, with two seats and the more powerful GE F110 engine. The extended rear fuselage, below the rudder, houses a braking parachute as on F-16s of Norway and Venezuela.

Right: Another view of the original single-seat F100-engined F-16XL. The more powerful two-seater is FSD aircraft 75-747 (No. 3 FSD) rebuilt. An FSD decision of this far more capable version is expected in 1986.

82 per cent more internal fuel (fuselage and wing) than F-16C

Production aircraft would have GE F110 engine

Drag chute (option Loral Rapport ECM)

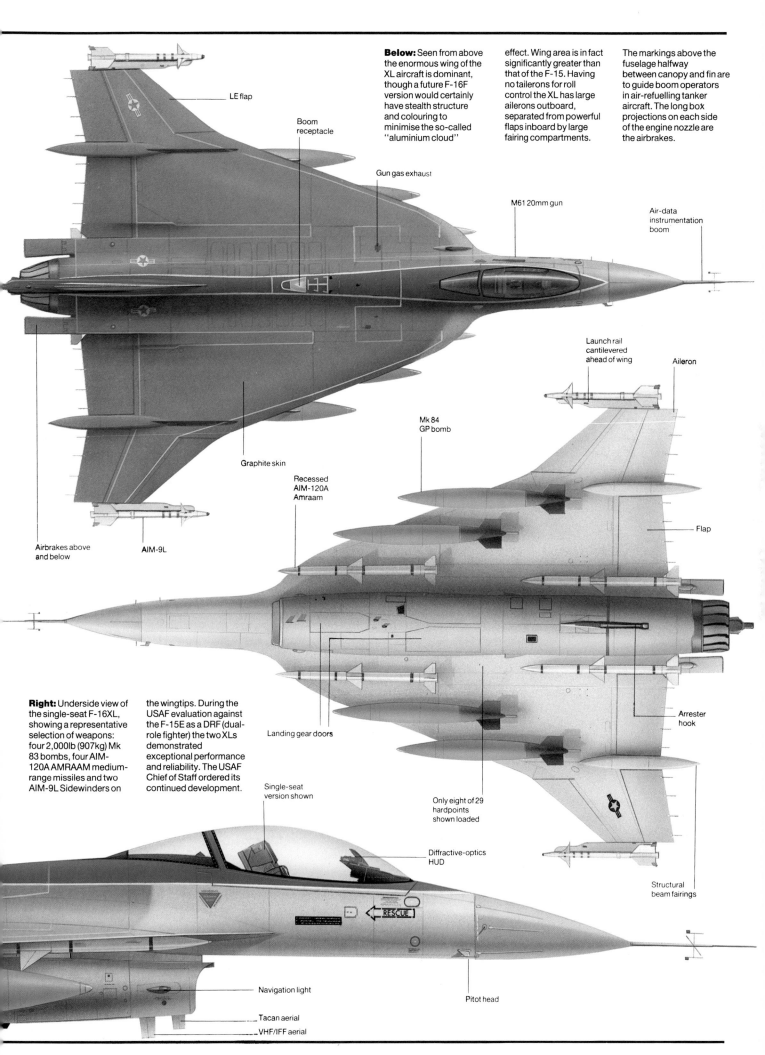

LE flap

Boom receptacle

Gun gas exhaust

M61 20mm gun

Air-data instrumentation boom

Below: Seen from above the enormous wing of the XL aircraft is dominant, though a future F-16F version would certainly have stealth structure and colouring to minimise the so-called "aluminium cloud"

effect. Wing area is in fact significantly greater than that of the F-15. Having no tailerons for roll control the XL has large ailerons outboard, separated from powerful flaps inboard by large fairing compartments.

The markings above the fuselage halfway between canopy and fin are to guide boom operators in air-refuelling tanker aircraft. The long box projections on each side of the engine nozzle are the airbrakes.

Graphite skin

Launch rail cantilevered ahead of wing

Aileron

Mk 84 GP bomb

Flap

Recessed AIM-120A Amraam

Airbrakes above and below

AIM-9L

Landing gear doors

Arrester hook

Only eight of 29 hardpoints shown loaded

Right: Underside view of the single-seat F-16XL, showing a representative selection of weapons: four 2,000lb (907kg) Mk 83 bombs, four AIM-120A AMRAAM medium-range missiles and two AIM-9L Sidewinders on

the wingtips. During the USAF evaluation against the F-15E as a DRF (dual-role fighter) the two XLs demonstrated exceptional performance and reliability. The USAF Chief of Staff ordered its continued development.

Single-seat version shown

Diffractive-optics HUD

Structural beam fairings

RESCUE

Navigation light

Pitot head

Tacan aerial

VHF/IFF aerial

Type: Tactical or strategic attack aircraft (EF, electronic warfare aircraft).

Engines: Two Pratt & Whitney TF30 augmented turbofans (from 18,500lb/ 8,390kg TF30-1 to 25,100lb/11,385kg TF30-100, depending on sub-type).

Dimensions: Span (wings spread) 63ft 0in (19.2m) (FB-111A, 70ft 0in, 21.34m); length 73ft 6in (22.4m); height (most) 17ft 2in (5.22m); wing area (most) 525sq ft (48.77m^2).

Weights: Empty, ranges from F-111A at 46,172lb (20,943kg) to FB at over 49,800lb (22,590kg); maximum (EF) 89,000lb (40,370kg), others ranging up to FB at 114,300lb (51,846kg).

Performance: Maximum speed, clean, high altitude, all about 1,450mph (2,335km/h); cruising speed 571mph (919km/h); range (F-111F, max internal fuel) 2,925 miles (4,707km).

One of the world's best-known warplanes, the swing-wing F-111 is still the only aircraft in the USAF inventory capable of flying high-speed attack missions at night or in adverse weather. Moreover, it is now distinctly long in the tooth; it stacks up extremely badly against the Panavia Tornado, which in every single respect has demonstrated not only higher flight performance and lower operating heights but also better navigational accuracy, more precise weapon delivery, significantly higher reliability and much lower maintenance manpower burden. Yet the F-111, with its colossal internal fuel capacity, is basically an outstanding and valuable aircraft, and the airframes are calculated on present usage to be safe for continued operation until 2010. The avionics, however, were deliberately chosen in the early 1960s to be state-of-the-art, partly to avoid introductory problems and poor reliability with new LRUs (line replaceable units).

In the event the USAF perhaps got the worst of both worlds. It began procuring the F-111A, switched to the F-111E with almost the same primitive avionics, then switched to the F-111D with the so-called "Mk II" avionics (more advanced and totally dissimilar to anything in earlier models), found horrifying problems of cost and unreliability and finally completed the programme with the F-111F which has an avionic suite which attempts to get most of the capability of the F-111D with better costs and reliability. (To confuse matters further Grumman has completely rebuilt 42 F-111As into EF-111A Raven tactical jammer platforms, with no weapons but very large radar warning and jamming systems, and retaining most of the original tactical avionics suite.) Achieved avionic performance of the F-111 series has for many years been a cause for serious concern. For example, achieved MTBF (mean

Right: The basic plan for updating the USAF fleet of active F-111 aircraft, which is the most extensive – and one of the most costly – in history. It is really a compliment to the F-111 (which it must be remembered had a most controversial and troublesome time early in its career) that it is considered of such value to the USAF, and to have such a long airframe life ahead of it, that it is worth spending at least as much as the original cost of building the aircraft in updating them for continued front-line duty until the year 2010.

Right: The aircraft will be redelivered in two main timeframes. Top priority is being given to the FB-111A bombers of Strategic Air Command, which have a particularly poor availability record and will benefit by the total transformation. Detail changes to the D and F are also already taking place for 1987-88.

RELIABILITY IMPROVEMENT MODIFICATIONS

	FB-111A	F-111A/E	EF-111A	F-111F	F-111D
Advanced microelectronic converter	X	X	X	O	O
Weapons navigation computer	(2)	X	X	O	O
Combined altitude radar altimeter	X	X	X	O	O
Inertial navigation system	(2)	X	X	O	O
Attack radar	X	X	X	X	O
Terrain-following radar	X	X	X	X	X
Doppler radar	X				
Controls and displays	X	X	X		

O = Items being updated *external* to the F/FB-111 AMP programme
X = a/c getting programmed changes

AMP DELIVERY SCHEDULE

Fiscal year	1987				1988				1989				1990				1991				1992			
Qtr	1	2	3	4	1	2	3	4	1	2	3	4	1	2	3	4	1	2	3	4	1	2	3	4
FB-111A (57)	2	9	9	9	9	9	9	1																
F-111A/E (120)													12	13	13	13	13	13	13	13	12	5		
EF-111A (38)																	6	6	6	6	6	6	2	
F-111D/F TFR (166) (field installation)	7	11	14	18	27	27	27	35																
F-111F ARS (88) (field installation)				8	20	20	20	20																

Left: The 100th F-111 from USAF Europe to be refurbished by BAe at Filton (Bristol). These aircraft, F-111Es of the 20th TFW (tail code UH) and F-111Fs of the 48th TFW (tail code LN) were, until arrival of Tornados in 1982, NATO's only all-weather interdiction aircraft in Europe.

Above: Though taken at Filton, this scene broadly resembles that at Sacramento Air Materiel Area between 1987 and 1992 as the entire USAF F-111, FB-111 and EF-111 force is electronically updated. The basic airframes are considered good for intensive combat duty until the year 2010.

time between failures) for the bomb/nav system of the FB-111A varies from 2 to 4h, the figures for the F-111A/E, D and F respectively being 6h, 2h and 5h. For comparison, the goal for ATF is 200h, with a much more complicated system.

MODERNIZATION PROGRAMME

The task of upgrading F-111s, known as F-111/AMP (for avionics modernization programme), was preceded by years of planning, culminating in a final review on 24 January 1984. A total of 381 aircraft are to be upgraded, with first delivery due in December 1986 and subsequent deliveries according to a timetable reproduced here. Total cost in then-year dollars is put at $1,141,500,000, but this is bound to be exceeded, if only because of one or two extras that have been admitted. By far the most important of these extras is the decision to develop and install a DFCS (digital flight control system), which will begin in Fiscal Year 1986 and call for a major development effort.

All USAF F-111s are looked after by Sacramento Air Logistics Center, but integration of AMP hardware, and subsequent test and warranty, is the responsibility of the original prime contractor, GD Fort Worth. A table shows which major avionics elements are being replaced in each F-111 sub-type. There is no dramatic change in contractor. General Electric provide the new attack radar, Texas Instruments the TFR, Singer Kearfott the weapons/nav computer, Litton the INS, Rockwell Collins the integrated CNI (com/nav/IFF), Sperry a new MFD (multifunction display), Teledyne Ryan the doppler radar (FB-111A), Novatronics the aux com panel, TEAC the VTR (video tape recorder) and GD Fort Worth the VTR controls, avionics power control and the FB-111A's SRAM inertial buffer unit.

Most of the changes are intended to improve the previously appalling level of reliability and greatly reduce the maintainability man-hours needed. Some will improve system performance; for example, the attack radar is being given a HUD display of nav and weapons data, improved

ECCM capability and a new close (2.5 nautical mile/4.63km) range selection, while the vital TFR is being given wider terrain coverage in banked turns and a higher probability of detecting low-reflectivity terrain (such as sand dunes or snow-covered mountains) and terrain seen through heavy rain. This will be a boon to the 20th and 48th TFW operating in Europe.

Throughout the AMP the emphasis is on testing, demonstration, verification and the overriding insistence that, this time, everything has to work as advertised. The task is made more difficult by the fact that the aircraft are not being gutted and fitted with totally new integrated systems. Instead each major element, such as the attack radar, is being torn apart, the boxes showing poor reliability replaced and a new subsystem created out of a mix of old and new hardware, all most carefully integrated. Much of the new hardware is being supplied in kit form for field modification. At all times secondary objectives are to reduce operator workload (for example by installing modern menu-driven MFDs) and improve damage tolerance, which in the past has been low by modern standards. At the end of the day the USAF F-111 force may not look different, but the difference in operational effectiveness will be several hundred per cent!

GRUMMAN
A-6F INTRUDER

Type: Carrier-based all-weather attack aircraft.

Engines: Previously 9,300lb (4,218kg) Pratt & Whitney J52-8A turbojets, now 10,800lb (4,899kg) General Electric F404-400D turbofans.

Dimensions: Span 53ft 0in (16.15m); length 54ft 9in (16.69m); height 16ft 2in (4.93m); wing area 528.9sq ft (49.1m²).

Weights: Empty (E) 26,746lb (12,132kg), (Upgrade) about 26,000lb (11,794kg); maximum 60,400lb (27,397kg) (cat limit 58,600lb, 26,580kg).

Performance: Maximum speed, clean, SL 644mph (1,037km/h); combat range (hi-lo-hi, max military load), (E) 1,011 miles (1,627km), (Upgrade) over 1,600 miles (2,575km).

Grumman's A-6 Intruder is one of the oldest combat aircraft still in front-line use by US forces, and in many ways its design may superficially appear obsolescent. It is therefore testimony to an outstanding aircraft to note that, when the US Navy sought a next-generation all-weather attack aircraft for the 21st century, it picked an upgraded A-6. Of course, the A-6 has been upgraded previously. Grumman built 488 of the original A-6A version, many of which were updated with defence-suppression systems and a FLIR/LLTV turret for all-weather attack on targets inadequately defined by radar. In the A-6E, first flown in November 1970, the aircraft received a quantum-jump update with stronger structure, multimode radar (replacing two in the A-6A), IBM computer and solid-state electronics. With the TRAM (target-recognition and attack multisensor) adding a FLIR and laser designator, as well as ACLS (automatic carrier landing system), inertial navigation, new CNI (com/nav/IFF) and other updates the A-6E remains in production. In 1981 it was decided to modify the A-6E to fire the AGM-84 Harpoon anti-ship cruise missile; 50 aircraft were modified and the capability is built into aircraft now on the line.

In the early 1980s the US Navy studied how best to acquire a next-generation all-weather attack aircraft for use from its carriers. Obvious needs were introduction of across-the-board new technology to improve availability, reliability, ease of maintenance, navigation accuracy, weapon aiming accuracy, penetrative capability and combat survivability.

Externally not even a boy spotter will find it simple to tell an A-6E Upgrade from the regular A-6E. (It is now known the aircraft will receive the designation A-6F). The nose radome will be new, but the profile will not alter greatly. The inflight-refuelling probe will be offset to the right instead of centred ahead of the windshield. There will be a third weapon station outboard under each wing, normally to be occupied by Sidewinder or Asraam self-defence AAMs. The leading edge of the wing roots will be aerodynamically redesigned with a slat and glove vane similar to that fitted to the derived EA-6B Prowler EW aircraft. On the EA-6B the slat and vane were added to enable gross weight to rise to

GRUMMAN
F-14D TOMCAT

Type: Carrier-based all-weather interceptor and multirole attack/recon aircraft.

Engines: Two 29,000lb (13,154kg) General Electric F110-401 augmented turbofans.

Dimensions: Span (spread) 64ft 1.5in (19.54m), (swept) 38ft 2.5in (11.65m); height 16ft 0in (4.88m); wing area 565sq ft (52.49m²).

Weights: Empty about 41,000lb (18,600kg); loaded (clean) about 59,000lb (26,760kg), (maximum) probably 75,000lb (34,020kg).

When the F-14A Tomcat entered service with the US Navy in October 1972 it brought air-defence capabilities which were not only of a totally new order but which in many respects still have no equal 13 years later. Chief among these capabilities are a stand-off kill ability from distances of about 100 miles (161km) and the pilot's choice of using an M61 gun, or a close-range dogfight missile, or a medium-range radar-guided missile or an ultra-long-range missile with its own active homing guidance. The F-14 also has tremendous versatility and can fly attack missions with ordnance loads of up to 14,500lb (6,577kg), though this has not been utilized. It is, however, at present having to fulfil the Navy's reconnaissance missions, carrying an external multisensor pod.

From the start of Fleet service the F-14 has been improved in various ways. The biggest and most sustained effort has concerned the TF30 engine. At the start, in the 1960s, this engine was expected to power only the first two blocks of F-14As, subsequent Tomcats being F-14Bs with the more powerful P&W F401. This engine flew in Tomcat No 157986 in September 1973, turning it into an F-14B, but the new

Above: Grumman and GE found success in flying the powerful F110 engines in the Super Tomcat demonstrator. Rated at almost 30,000lb each, the new engines give 34 per cent more thrust for 5 per cent less fuel, 77 per cent more cold thrust, cut time to height by 61 per cent, and use 50 per cent less intercept fuel.

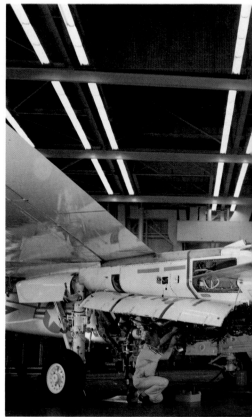

engine was never put into production. The next ten years with the TF30 have been less than happy, and between July and September 1981 No 157986 carried out a most successful test programme with a much newer engine, the General Electric F101DFE (Derivative Fighter Engine). The results convinced the Navy the time had at last come to replace the TF30, and plans went ahead to buy 300 future F-14s powered by the production derivative of the F101DFE, the outstanding F110.

Before that happens, however, Gruman is already well into a major update programme on the original F-14A, turning these aircraft into much more modern F-14Cs. The central feature is a general switch from analog to digital electronics. The Hughes AWG-9 radar fire control remains but with many new features the most important of which is programmable software, mainly managed by a new touch-

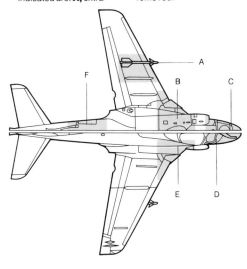

Above: Plan views (left half from below, right from above) of the Upgrade, which is to be designated A-6F. Items indicated are: **A,** extra store station; **B,** F404-400D with AMAD; **C,** new radar; **D,** offset FR probe; **E,** new fillet/slat geometry; and **F,** doppler removed.

65,000lb (29,483kg). On the A-6E Upgrade its purpose is to reduce landing speed by up to 12mph (19km/h) to reduce stress on the landing gear, which in turn will allow aircraft to land at increased weights on carriers. The present field limit of 45,000lb (20,411kg) is reduced to only 36,000lb (16,329kg) for carrier operation. This has frequently demanded that unexpended stores be jettisoned, and while this is acceptable with "iron bombs" it is extremely costly with high-technology missiles. The high-lift wing of the Upgrade will probably mean that no more stores need be wasted on the grounds of MLW limitations.

By far the most important new features of the Upgrade will be internal. The F404 engine is the same as that of the F/A-18A, giving massive commonality advantages. The augmentor is removed and a short adapter and bypass airsplitter added. It is a smaller and lighter engine than the J52, but its biggest advantages lie in reduced fuel burn and across-the-board improvements

in maintenance effort and other related factors. These will be enhanced by fitting an AMAD (airframe-mounted accessory drive), as in other modern aircraft, so that changing an engine will become almost simple. Another big plus will be the addition of an APU (auxiliary power unit), making the Upgrade independent of yellow ground service carts.

The doppler radar will be removed, but the brand-new main radar will be a multi-mode design with an air/air combat capability, and ground mapping will be enhanced by DBS (doppler beam sharpening). The flight deck will be completely upgraded with a new HUD, Kaiser AYK-14 tac computer (common to the F-14 and -18) and a range of advanced panel displays also common to those other Navy/Marines aircraft. Stores management, CNI and EW suites will also be new, one major addition being the ASPJ (airborne self-protection jammer). The E Upgrade should look and fly like today's model but be roughy 100 per cent more effective.

Left: Apart from the dramatic increases in power, economy and reliability, the F110 opened up the Tomcat's flight envelope (Mach plotted against altitude) and manoeuvre envelope (angle of attack versus sideslip). In each case the F110 set record new levels. Allied with this the F-14D has fully updated avionics.

Above: Artist's impression of the proposed General Dynamics Pomona AMS (Advanced Missile System), firing tandem-boosted missiles from a retractable box, and with associated look-down, shoot-down radar in an underwing pod and the missile guidance in a pod on the other wing. AMS could replace Phoenix.

panel display in front of the backseater. Reliability, maintainability and resistance to hostile jamming should be transformed. At the same time the missile suite is being upgraded to comprise the AIM-9M, AIM-7M and AIM-54C. Ongoing updates over the next four years will add digital data highways, new central processors, programmable MFDs (multifunction displays, as in the F/A-18) in both cockpits, new inertial navigation and stores-management

subsystems, and the ALR-67 threat warning and recognition system. As they become available three major additions will be the JTIDS, ASJP and AIM-120A Amraam missile. The new avionics will also facilitate further radar updates.

Coming in parallel with all these improvements will be the welcome new engine, which almost incidentally increases takeoff thrust per engine from 20,900lb (9,480kg) to the 29,000lb

(13,154kg) class. The changeover comes in FY87, the year ending 30 June 1987, in which of the annual buy of 24 Tomcats half will be F-14Ds with the GE engine. Subsequent buys will be F-14Ds exclusively. Deliveries are expected from March 1990, and the plan is to buy 300 at 30 per year. This underscores the importance in the modern world of getting a fighter design right, because the F-14 is now fairly assured of a production life of 30 years.

HUGHES
AH-64 APACHE

Type: Battlefield attack helicopter, studied for Marine and Navy missions.
Engines: Two 1,696shp General Electric T700-701 turboshafts; Navy/Marines would use 1,729shp marinised T700-401.
Dimensions: Diameter of main rotor 48ft 0in (14.63m); length overall, both rotors turning 58ft 3.1in (17.76m); height over top of air-data sensor 16ft 9.5in (5.12m); main rotor disc area 1,809.5sq ft (168.11m²).
Weights: (Standard Army version) empty 11,015lb (4,996kg); maximum 17,650lb (8,006kg).
Performance: Maximum speed 186mph (300km/h); range on internal fuel 428 miles (689km); endurance (anti-armour) 1h 50min.

After a long and extremely expensive development the AH-64A Apache is in full production at the new Mesa, Arizona, plant for the US Army as the latter's dedicated anti-armour and battlefield attack helicopter. In 1984 the total buy was increasd from 515 to 675 through FY88, so all these should have been delivered by about 1991. By 1986 deliveries will be at 12 per month.

From this powerful, very well protected and comprehensively equipped Army helicopter Hughes Helicopters, now a subsidiary of McDonnell Douglas, is promoting two marinised versions, one for the US Marine Corps and the other for the Navy. The Marine AH-64 would fly the following missions: transport helicopter escort, LZ (landing zone) suppressive fire, anti-air fighting, visual armed reconnaissance, airborne FAC (forward air control), surface convoy escort, anti-armour/hard-point destruction, and spotting for naval or Marine gunfire.

Hughes claim the Apache to be the first operational helicopter equipped for precision navigation and weapons delivery 24 hours a day and in adverse weather. It already has FLIR, laser and low-light TV sensors, and carries a 30mm M230 Chain Gun, Hellfire laser-homing missiles and conventional rockets. The Marines' model could add TOW missiles, AIM-9 Sidewinder AAMs, Stinger missiles, Sidearm anti-radar missiles, 5in (127mm) rockets and a different gun if specified. It would also have complete anti-corrosion measures, auto blade folding, doppler/inertial navigation, electromagnetic radiation shielding and floating-base maintenance provisions.

The company is trying to develop this version so that deliveries could begin in calendar year 1988. With 38 rockets, four Hellfires, 1,200 rounds for the Chain Gun and two Sidewinders for self-defence it

ILYUSHIN
Il-76 "CANDID" AND "MAINSTAY"

Type: Airlift transport, tanker and AEW platform.
Engines: Four 26,455lb (12,000kg) Soloviev D-30KP turbofans.
Dimensions: Span 165ft 8in (50.5m); length 152ft 10.25in (46.59m); height 48ft 5in (14.76m); wing area 3,229sq ft (300m²).
Weights: (76T) Empty about 176,400lb (80,000kg); maximum 374,785lb (170,000kg).
Performance: Maximum speed 528mph (850km/h); cruising speed 466/497mph (750/800km/h); range with payload of 88,185lb (40,000kg) 3,110 miles (5,000km).

Seemingly very similar to the USAF Lockheed C-141, the Il-76 is in fact much more powerful, and better equipped for operations from short unpaved airstrips. It has proved most successful and by 1982 was already in service in five identifiable versions. The basic Il-76 had been replaced in production by the Il-76T transport with additional centre-wing tankage and heavier payload (world record was set at 154,590lb, 70,121kg). The Il-76M is a purely military update with a twin-23mm rear gun turret and five ECM fairings at nose and tail. The Il-76TD is an extended-range version, and the Il-76MD is the long-range military counterpart. Some 350 of all transport versions had been delivered by spring 1985, of which almost 300 were serving with the VTA (Soviet military transport aviation). Deliveries to Nos 25 and 44 Sqns of the Indian AF began in 1985.

Since before 1978 the Ilyushin design bureau, led by Genrikh Novozhilov, has been working on upgrades for other missions. The first to be identified was an air-refuelling tanker. The VVS (Soviet air force) has a large ongoing need for tankers, the chief existing aircraft being a converted form of M-4 "Bison". These are old and few in number, and a new and highly capable tanker has been an important project. It is not yet known whether the tanker Il-76 is a dedicated one-role aircraft or a multirole tanker/transport. Few hard facts are available, and it may even be that the new tanker will be based on a different aircraft type, but in 1985 it was expected that the Il-76 tanker would be on the point of entering service. No rigid-boom air refuelling has been seen in the Soviet Union, but it is known that the hose/probe/drogue system has been developed in that country to very high flow rates. It may be expected that the tanker Il-76 will have three hose-drum

LOCKHEED
P-3 (AEW&C) ORION

Type: Airborne early warning and control aircraft.
Engines: Four Allison turboprops, initially 4,910ehp T56-14, later 5,250shp (5,625ehp) T56-427.
Dimensions: Span 99ft 8in (30.37m); length (with MAD boom) 116ft 10in (35.61m); height 33ft 8.5in (10.27m); wing area 1,300sq ft (120.77m²).
Weights: (P-3C) Empty 61,491lb (27,890kg); maximum 142,000lb (64,410kg).
Performance: (P-3C) Maximum speed 473mph (761km/h); operating speed (AEW&C) 200-250mph (322-402km/h); endurance 14h.

Virtually the standard long-range land-based ocean patrol and ASW aircraft of the Western world, the P-3 Orion has already passed through numerous upgradings in its primary mission, current deliveries having the designation of P-3C Update III.

Virtually all the upgrading has been in avionics, mission systems, equipment and weapons. Among other items P-3C Update III has a new IBM Proteus acoustic processor to analyse signals picked up from sonic devices in the ocean, a new sonobuoy receiver, improved APU and an upgraded ECS (environmental control system) to get rid of greater heat from avionic items and improve crew comfort. Update III deliveries began in May 1984.

Mention should also be made of the extremely extensive P-3B Orion Upgrade programme managed by Boeing Aerospace Co for the Royal NZ Air Force, which uses this older P-3 variant. After redelivery by Boeing the P-3B Upgrade is packed with some of the most modern maritime surveillance sensors and avionics available, including new radar and infra-red detection systems, inertial and Omega navigation, and new computers, data highways and displays.

All current P-3 Orion aircraft have the A-14 engine, which has been in production many years. Allison Division of General Motors has continuously upgraded the T56/Model 501 family of engines, and also has a much more powerful new-generation engine in the T701. The immediate next-generation engine for US Navy aircraft is the A-427, with increased airflow and many minor improvements to enhance power and reduce fuel consumption. Initial deliveries are for E-2C Hawkeye AEW aircraft, but in due course it is planned to introduce the Dash-427 to the P-3 series, giving enhanced mission performance at greater weights. This could be particularly useful to the AEW&C version, would have a maximum speed of 175mph (282km/h), mission radius of 142 miles (229km) and endurance of 2.8h.

The Navy version is slightly more fluid, but is envisaged as carrying surface search and target acquisition radar and either Harpoon or Penguin anti-ship missiles, in addition to previous options listed. It could stand off at the edge of a task force (Hughes say "up to 150 miles (241km) away") to search for, identify and destroy hostile ships. It would have the option of substituting fuel for weapons in order to patrol well beyond the horizon. Hughes see this version as being especially useful when a task force carrier is for any reason unable to provide fixed-wing airpower.

Right: Future seagoing Apaches would have all present weapons capability plus Sidewinders, seen here, and a wide range of other Navy/Marine stores for air/surface operations.

units, one in the rear fuselage and the others under the outer wings.

Satellite reconnaissance has kept the Pentagon informed about another Il-76 update, for the AEW or Awacs (airborne warning and control system) mission. At first dubbed "Suawacs" for Soviet Union Awacs, it now has the NATO reporting name "Mainstay", because only transports have names beginning with C. Not much is yet known about "Mainstay" apart from the belief that it has a radar rotodome mounted on a pylon above the trailing edge of the wing and has a slightly stretched forward fuselage with an inflight-refuelling probe.

Right: This artist's impression of the Ilyushin "Mainstay" appeared in the 1985 edition of the US official publication "Soviet Military Power". It predicts the fielding of five per year.

which needs generally higher power in order to carry the greatest possible load of radar and fuel to the highest altitude.

Immediate sales prospects for the AEW&C include Australia, which provided the former P-3B airframe used for initial aerodynamic and control test flying from 14 June 1984. In 1985 the 24ft (7.32m) rotodome was to be linked with the General Electric APS-138 radar, with ARPS (advanced radar processing system) as carried by the E-2C. Partly because of its short wingspan the P-3 ceiling is only about 28,000ft (8,500m), rather less than the E-2C, but the A-427 engine would increase this. The big advantages over the E-2C are greater internal room and endurance.

Right: Owned by Lockheed-California Company, the AEW&C prototype is a rebuilt P-3B ex-RAAF. In 1985 an operative radar was being installed for research purposes.

McDONNELL DOUGLAS/BMAC
F-4 MODERNISED

Type: Multirole fighter.
Engines: Two 20,600lb (9,344kg) Pratt & Whitney PW 1120 augmented turbojets.
Dimensions: Span 38ft 5in (11.7m); length 63ft 0in (19.2m); height 16ft 3in (4.95m); wing area 530sq ft (49.2m²).
Weight: Empty about 28,500lb (12,928kg), depending on original aircraft; maximum, 61,000lb (27,670kg).
Performance: Maximum speed, clean, high altitude 1,500mph (2,414km/h) or Mach 2.2 (1,464km/h) or Mach 1.19; takeoff run at 58,610lb (26,585kg) 2,950ft (900m); range, conformal tank and two wing tanks (58,610lb/26,585kg) at high altitude 788 miles (1,240km).

By far the most numerous front-line fighter in the Western world, with over 2,700 in operator inventories, the McDonnell F-4 Phantom is still a formidable aircraft in many fighting, attack and reconnaissance missions. Some existing Phantoms have been updated in various ways, and McDonnell Douglas itself is offering a carefully designed update which concentrates on structure life, avionics and other details to yield an aircraft that will go on doing a superior job longer, and at a lower cost.

Externally the F-4 as updated by the original manufacturer would not look very different. BMAC (Boeing Military Airplane Co), however, are well advanced with a visibly more extensive upgrade. It involves a change of engine, and so is offered in partnership with Pratt & Whitney, which eagerly wants new military business.

The new engine is the PW1120, virtually an F100 (engine of the F-15 and F-16) with the LP compressor (fan) reduced in size so that the bypass ratio is only 0.19. Thus the PW1120 is to all intents and purposes a straight turbojet, the bypass air serving to cool the carcase of the engine so that it needs no surrounding airflow when installed. Other changes include a single-stage uncooled LP turbine and revised augmentor (afterburner) and nozzle. The engine weighs 2,848lb (1,292kg) and is 162in (4,144mm) long, compared with about 3,847lb (1,745kg) and 208.7in (5,301mm) for the existing J79. Takeoff thrust, however, is up from about 17,000 to over 20,000lb, (7,711 to 9,072kg) and a particularly important factor is that fuel consumption is appreciably reduced, despite the much higher power. Though the PW-1120 is a new engine, the fact that it has the

extremely mature core of the F100, allied with its close relationship throughout to that engine, is expected in the near term to result in parts-life, reliability and maintenance burdens better than those of even the most mature older-technology engine.

The PW1120 was picked by Israel to power the IAI Lavi (see separate entry), and thus Israel has a keen interest in the BMAC Modernised Phantom. As one of the world's biggest Phantom operators, the Israeli AF is the biggest and most immediate customer for the update. As an initial research tool a Phantom is being converted

McDONNELL DOUGLAS
F-15 EAGLE

Type: Multimission fighter.
Engines: Two 23,830lb (10,809kg) Pratt & Whitney F100-100 or F100-220 augmented turbofans (see below).
Dimensions: Span 42ft 9.7in (13.05m); length 63ft 9in (19.43m); height 18ft 5.5in (5.63m); wing area 608sq ft (56.5m²).
Weights: Empty (A) 27,381lb (12,420kg), (C) 28,970lb (13,141kg), (later versions) not disclosed; maximum (A) 56,000lb (25,401kg), (C) 68,000lb (30,845kg), (E) 81,000lb (36,742kg).
Performance: Maximum speed, clean (high altitude) 1,650mph (2,655km/h) or Mach 2.5, (sea level) 912mph (1,468km/h) or Mach 1.2; mission radius, not published; ferry range 2,878 miles (4,631km), (with conformal Fast Pack tanks) 3,570 miles (5,745km).

Generally regarded as the natural successor to the F-4 Phantom as the top fighter of the Western world, the F-15 has been continuously upgraded since it first flew in July 1972. At the time of writing McDonnell (and Mitsubishi in Japan) had delivered about 895 Eagles. Of these 361 were F-15As and 58 two-seat F-15Bs. All the rest were F-15Cs and two-seat F-15Ds with internal fuel increased from 11,600lb (5,260kg) to 13,455lb (6,103kg), programmable instead of hard-wired radar signal processors with memory increased from 24K to 96K, provision for Fast (Fuel And Sensor Tactical) packs in the form of conformal fuel tanks attached on each side of the fuselage, and stronger landing gears. The conformal tanks add a further 9,726lb (4,412kg) of fuel with no extra drag, and themselves provide

accommodation for a wide range of reconnaissance sensors, EW equipment and weapon-aiming devices, as well as low-drag "tangential carriage" of up to 12 bombs of 1,000lb (454kg) or four 2,000lb (907kg) and AIM-7 Sparrow missiles whilst leaving existing pylons unoccupied. An addition introduced during C/D production is an overload warning system which enables the pilot to manoeuvre at up to 9g throughout most of the flight envelope at flight design gross weights.

In general the performance and reliability of the F-15A/B/C/D has been

exemplary. Just over 1,000,000h have been flown, only 39 USAF aircraft have been lost and the FMC (fully mission capable) rate has set new records. The FMC rate is the percentage of all aircraft of one type in an air force that, at a particular chosen time, are ready for immediate action, including all those on major overhaul, being repaired after damage or simply suffering trivial (or even suspected) snags. The FMC rate for the entire USAF force of nearly 800 F-15s was 78.1 per cent in September 1984, 79.5 in October and 80.2 in November, Eglin and Langley hitting 88.7 and 86.7.

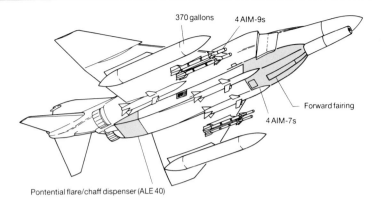

Left: Installation of a mock-up PW1120 in a USAF F-4D. Airflow is greater than in the original J79, but the fit is good.

Right: The Boeing/PW conversion results in a major change in appearance, the belly fairing appearing to contradict the Area Rule which calls for body cross-section to be reduced near the wings! Conversions may be done in users' own countries.

370 gallons   4 AIM-9s

Forward fairing

4 AIM-7s

Pontential flare/chaff dispenser (ALE 40)

as a demonstrator for that air force. It is to resume flying in late 1985 with one J79 replaced by a PW1120 for comparative testing. BMAC is also converting a second F-4E for the USAF Systems Command ASD (Aeronautical Systems Division), with both engines replaced. The conversion of the engines is straightforward and requires no all-through rebuild of the ducts or engine bays. The engine diameters are comparable, and the increased airflow of the PW1120 is within the capacity of the existing installation. The reduced engine length and weight means that in a fully engineered conversion there is additional volume and mass available for fuel.

Taking advantage of this, BMAC goes on to add a giant conformal tank, with a capacity of 916gal (1,100US gal, 4,165 lit) on the underside of the fuselage. The tank extends from ahead of the air inlets to the engine nozzles, and despite the great weight of fuel is stressed to the full aircraft g limits, even when carrying additional stores on its underside. It is, in effect, the same technology as the F-15's Fast packs but turned through 90° to lie on the underside of the aircraft. Stores that can be attached include two AIM-7 Sparrow or AIM-120 Amraam missiles or four bombs. Thanks to careful profiling and compliance with Area Rule aerodynamics the giant tank has no significant effect on top speed or Mach number.

It is BMAC's intention to carry out a complete structural audit of each rebuild Phantom, repair any cracks, introduce small modifications to avoid future fatigue and add about 3,000h to the operational life of the aircraft. It is expected that most aircraft presented for modernisation will be F-4Es, but other variants could be similarly updated, probably for a price to be negotiated separately for each contract. The price would in any case vary with the desired avionic fit. As a baseline suite BMAC propose installing a MIL-STD-1553B digital databus linked to a wide variety of items including a Hughes APG-65 multimode radar (Hornet type), GEC Avionics wide-angle holographic HUD (F-16C type), GEC avionics air-data computer, Honeywell ring-laser gyro INS, and Sperry MFD (multifunction display) system for the cockpits.

BMAC discussed prospects with F-4 users, and announced the scheme in 1984.

Left: The first (November 1983) artwork showing the "STOL F-15" being developed for the USAF. Not much has been published on manoeuvrability of fighters with canards plus tailplanes.

Above: A later artist's impression of the "STOL F-15" in the pipedream situation that appears to be taken seriously by the USAF. The 2D nozzles are to a later standard than those in the other picture.

Great effort has been applied to the F100 engine, which through the 1970s suffered stall-stagnations and turbine failures that affected operating performance and caused severe maintenance burden and high support costs. Today the basic Dash-100 engine has been trimmed to a fleet average of 97 per cent thrust, and at this level, after prolonged detail improvements, these engines can fly 1,800 TAC mission cycles without any refurbishment, even to such crucial parts as the HP turbine. Now coming into production is the new F100-220, with DEEC (digital electronic engine control), a new gear-type fuel pump and an ILC (increased-life core) planned to fly 4,000 TAC missions between refurbishment!

This engine will power the F-15E DRF (dual-role fighter), a two-seat version with greatly enhanced night and adverse-weather attack capability. The airframe and landing gears are restressed for operation at double the clean gross weight, the maximum bombload being a theoretical 24,500lb (11,113kg), with tangential carriage along the Fast Packs. Both cockpits have electronic MFDs (multifunction displays), the pilot having three and the backseater four (two for radar, one for monitoring enemy tracking systems and one for weapon selection and guidance). The pilot has a new CNI control and wide-angle HUD, and new sensors include a LANTIRN pod and FLIR. Air-combat capability will be enhanced rather than degraded, though of course at 81,000lb (36,742kg) the ratio of thrust to weight is unimpressive and this formidable aircraft would normally seek to expend its attack ordnance before engaging enemy fighters. The USAF expects to receive 392 of this version from 1986. Pratt & Whitney had hoped to produce its 27,410lb (12,433kg) PW1128 engine for the F-15E, but this was not chosen.

Meanwhile, advanced features are being studied in almost every part of the F-15. On 24 June 1983 an F-15 arrived at Edwards AFB to begin testing a new Lear Siegler digital flight control system. McDonnell's George Vetch said the coupling of the flight-control system with the engines, fire control and navigation systems "provides significant improvements in aircraft performance without expensive changes to the airframe or engines. Coupling the flight controls and engines, for example, can provide more than a 10 per cent increase in thrust, which results in greater acceleration and higher turn rates for air combat". This digital integration helps the heavy F-15E manage with the existing engines.

Another exciting new development is the self-repairing flight control system which though not peculiar to the F-15, could find its first application on the F-15. As previously noted, the idea was spurred on by a pilot bringing back an F-15 which had lost half a wing.

In September 1983 the USAF asked McDonnell to propose a scheme for a STOL F-15 to operate from supposed cratered runways. Apparently believing that all an enemy would do would be to make a few pock-marks, the idea is that a STOL F-15 should takeoff and land "between the craters". McDonnell's proposal is to add movable canards and 2D vectoring engine nozzles, these working in unison to add lift at front and rear. After landing the nozzles would apply reverse thrust. Fitted with the digital integrated control system. the STOL F-15 should also offer enhanced manoeuvrability in all flight conditions. The first converted F-15 should fly in 1988, and it is expected that this will become the standard version. There seems every chance that retroactive modification will be possible to existing F-15s, though no funds for this have been accepted.

McDONNELL DOUGLAS/BRITISH AEROSPACE
AV-8B/HARRIER II

Type: STOVL multirole tactical combat aircraft.

Engine: One Rolls-Royce Pegasus vectored-thrust turbofan, (AV-8B) 21,500lb (9,752kg) F402-406, (GR.5) 21,750lb (9,866kg) Pegasus 105.

Dimensions: Span 30ft 4in (9.25m); length 46ft 4in (14.12m); height 11ft 7.8in (3.55m); wing area, including LERX root extensions 238.4sq ft (22.15m^2).

Weights: Empty (AV) 12,922lb (5,861kg), (GR) 12,750lb (5,783kg); maximum (VTO) 19,550lb (8,867kg), (STO) 29,750lb (13,494kg).

Performance: Maximum speed, clean, SL 679mph (1,093km/h), (high altitude) 727mph (1,170km/h, Mach 1.1); combat radius (hi-lo-hi, seven Mk 82 Snakeye bombs) 691 miles (1,112km).

So great an update as to be a wholly new aircraft, the Harrier II is a joint programme, both in development and production, between McDonnell at St Louis and British Aerospace Weybridge Division's Kingston and Dunsfold sites. Compared with the first-generation Harrier and Sea Harrier the Harrier II has a completely new wing, carefully revised aerodynamics in the vertical-lift mode, new stability/control system and computer-controlled Sperry autopilot, new cockpit with raised seat and high-visibility canopy, totally new avionics and displays and greatly enhanced weapon-carrying capability. The overall result is an aircraft offering approximately twice the range or weapon payload of the original Harrier, with virtually no change in engine power. At the same time the cockpit takes it into the modern era, and among other things greatly reduces pilot workload, whilst at the same time enhancing versatility and weapon-delivery accuracy.

The new wing has a supercritical section and much greater span and internal volume, internal fuel capacity being in-

ceased by 50 per cent. Structure is almost wholly of graphite fibre composite, the result having limitless fatigue life yet weighing no more than the original; indeed, amazingly, this bigger and much more capable aircraft has an empty weight appreciably less than the original Harrier. The LERX (leading-edge root extension) enhances dogfight manoeuvrability, which with Viffing (vectoring in forward flight, to use engine thrust intelligently in a way denied to all other aircraft) was already of an extremely high order. The only drawback is that, while at high level the Harrier II is supersonic on the level, at sea level it is slower than the orignal.

The initial customers are the US Marine Corps, which is taking an announced 328 production AV-8B aircraft, and the RAF which will receive 60 Harrier GR.5s for use in Germany. Both versions are fitted with the Hughes ARBS (angle rate bombing system) in the nose, which uses TV and laser wavelengths to acquire, track and destroy surface targets. Primary navigation system is the Litton ASN-130 INS, used in conjunction with Tacan, an advanced AHRS (attitude/heading reference system) and Smiths HUD with symbol generator and dual combiner glass. AV-8Bs have the ALR-67 RWR installation, with small receiver aerials (antennas) on each side of the tail projection for the reaction-control jet,

Above: The first Harrier GR.5 (Development Batch 1) flew on 30 April 1985, on a schedule set three years earlier. A typical in-service load would be seven BL.755 cluster dispensers, two Sidewinders and the two 25mm guns. It has two pylons more than AV-8B.

under the forward fuselage (omni-aspect) and looking ahead from each wingtip. Standard chaff/flare dispenser is the widely used ALE-39.

The RAF has wisely decided to protect its GR.5s with a specially designed (but costly) integrated defence aids system, produced by Marconi Defence Systems as Zeus. This comprises interlinked RWR receivers and an internal multimode jammer, with a Northrop transmitter, plus chaff/flare decoy dispensers, a digital processor and cockpit display with manual controls. The RWR is derived from the RHAWR fitted to Tornado F.2 interceptors.

Weapons are all carried externally. The AV-8B has twin belly pods, specially configured to serve as LIDs (lift-improvement devices), containing on the left side a General Electric GAU-25 gun and on the right 300 rounds of 25mm ammunition, fed across through a streamlined bridge duct. The RAF has adhered to using two self-contained gun pods, but the 30 mm Adens used in the Harrier GR.3 are replaced by the new 25mm Aden which has a higher muzzle velocity, improved trajectory and greater rate of fire. Each gun has its own 110-round magazine above and to the rear.

The basic AV-8B carries 9,200lb (4,173kg) of stores on seven hardpoints (not including the gun attachments).

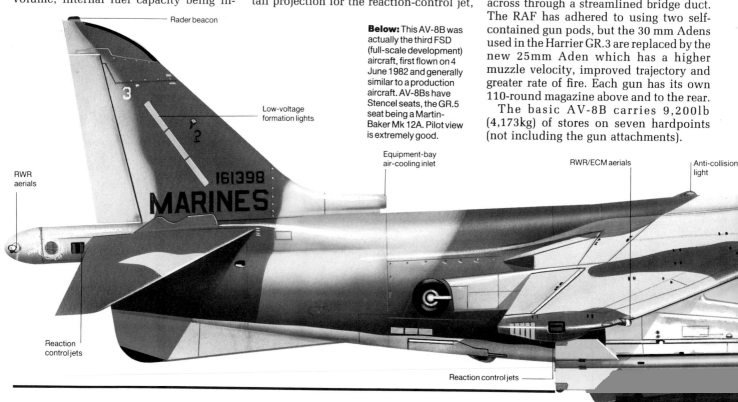

Rader beacon

Low-voltage formation lights

Below: This AV-8B was actually the third FSD (full-scale development) aircraft, first flown on 4 June 1982 and generally similar to a production aircraft. AV-8Bs have Stencel seats, the GR.5 seat being a Martin-Baker Mk 12A. Pilot view is extremely good.

Equipment-bay air-cooling inlet

RWR/ECM aerials

Anti-collision light

RWR aerials

Reaction control jets

161398 MARINES

Reaction control jets

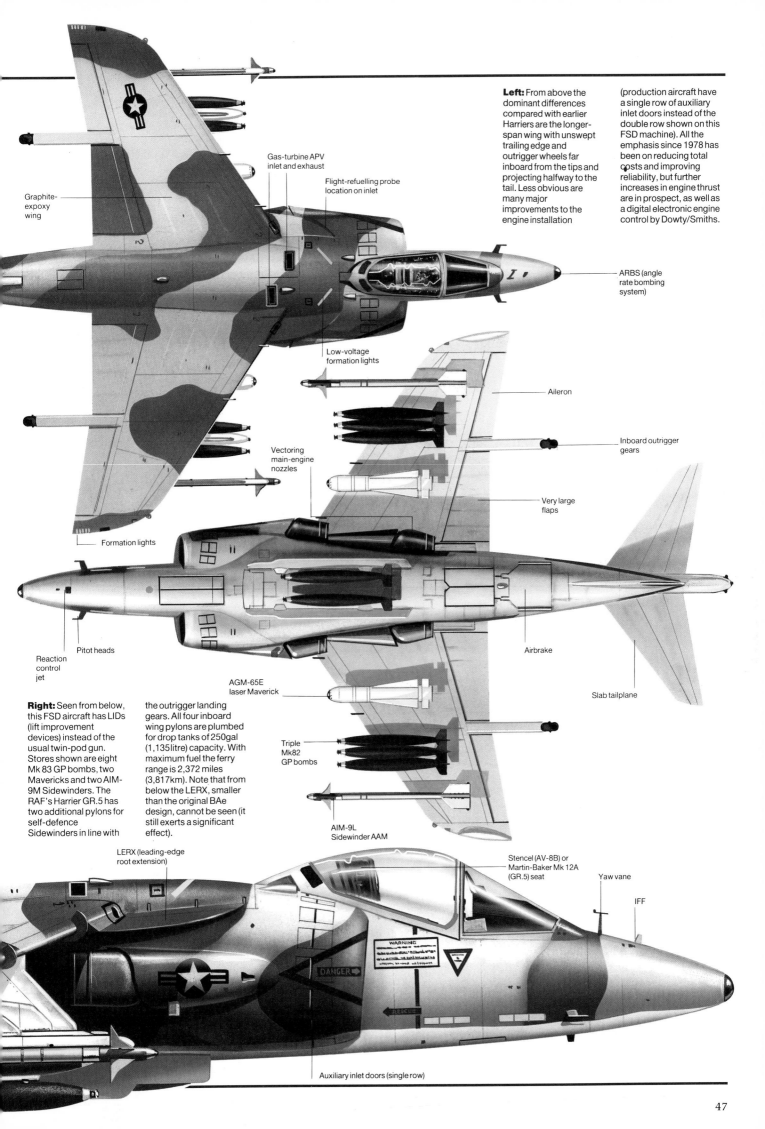

Graphite-expoxy wing

Gas-turbine APV inlet and exhaust

Flight-refuelling probe location on inlet

Left: From above the dominant differences compared with earlier Harriers are the longer-span wing with unswept trailing edge and outrigger wheels far inboard from the tips and projecting halfway to the tail. Less obvious are many major improvements to the engine installation

(production aircraft have a single row of auxiliary inlet doors instead of the double row shown on this FSD machine). All the emphasis since 1978 has been on reducing total costs and improving reliability, but further increases in engine thrust are in prospect, as well as a digital electronic engine control by Dowty/Smiths.

ARBS (angle rate bombing system)

Low-voltage formation lights

Aileron

Inboard outrigger gears

Vectoring main-engine nozzles

Very large flaps

Formation lights

Airbrake

Pitot heads

Reaction control jet

Slab tailplane

AGM-65E laser Maverick

Right: Seen from below, this FSD aircraft has LIDs (lift improvement devices) instead of the usual twin-pod gun. Stores shown are eight Mk 83 GP bombs, two Mavericks and two AIM-9M Sidewinders. The RAF's Harrier GR.5 has two additional pylons for self-defence Sidewinders in line with

the outrigger landing gears. All four inboard wing pylons are plumbed for drop tanks of 250gal (1,135litre) capacity. With maximum fuel the ferry range is 2,372 miles (3,817km). Note that from below the LERX, smaller than the original BAe design, cannot be seen (it still exerts a significant effect).

Triple Mk82 GP bombs

AIM-9L Sidewinder AAM

LERX (leading-edge root extension)

Stencel (AV-8B) or Martin-Baker Mk 12A (GR.5) seat

Yaw vane

IFF

WARNING

DANGER

RESCUE

Auxiliary inlet doors (single row)

PILATUS BRITTEN-NORMAN
ISLANDER/DEFENDER

Type: Multirole, see below
Engines: (Islander/Defender) two 300hp Avco Lycoming 10-540-K1B5 piston engines, (BN-2T/Castor/AEW/ASW) two Allison 250-B17C turboprops each flat-rated at 320shp.
Dimensions: Span 49ft 0in (14.94m), (extended tips) 53ft 0in (16.15m); length (standard) 35ft 7.7in (10.87m), (weather radar/Maritime) 36ft 3.8in (11.07m), (extended nose) 39ft 5.3in (12.02m), (Castor/AEW) about 40ft (12.19m); height 13ft 8.8in (4.18m); wing area (standard) 325sq ft (30.19m²).
Weights: Empty (basic) 3,815lb (1,730kg), (Defender) 4,020lb (1,824kg), (BN-2T) 4,120lb (1,869kg); maximum (Defender and BN-2T) 6,600lb (2,994kg), (BN-2T with extended-tip fuel) 7,000lb (3,175kg), (Castor/AEW/ASW) 8,000lb (3,628kg).
Performance: Maximum speed (Defender, clean) 174mph (280km/h), (Defender, pylons loaded) 166mph (266km/h), (BN-2T, also max cruising speed) 197mph (317km/h), (ASW) 195mph (315km/h); range (Defender) 309-1,723 miles (497-2,722km) depending on payload, (BN-2T) 366-838 miles (589-1,349km), (ASW radius of action, 4h on station) 115 miles (185km).

Well over 1,000 BN-2 Islanders and military Defenders are in use, and production is continuing with both the piston and BN-2T turboprop versions. The basic Defender has four NATO pylons, the inners each rated at 700lb (317kg) and the outers at 450lb (204kg). The Maritime Defender has a Bendix search radar in the nose and much special equipment for offshore patrol duties.

Using the BN-2T turboprop airframe three new military variants are now flying. Least strikingly modified, the ASW Maritime Defender can be equipped to customer specification, but equipment would normally include a surveillance radar with all-round coverage, FLIR, sonobuoys, MAD boom and acoustic processing and displays. Four wing pylons can carry two Sting Ray or similar torpedoes, depth charges, ECM and ESM pods, rocket launchers, gun pods, survival packs or other stores.

More grotesquely altered, the AEW Defender carries the mighty Thorn EMI Searchwater radar, as fitted to the Nimrod MR.2. This occupies much of the fuselage, together with a second operator tactical display which allows data exchange with other air or surface platforms. The main scanner has 360° long-range surveillance, and is particularly effective against targets flying at low level over the sea. The radar features real or synthetic-aperture processing and on-board real-time processing and recording, with optional ground data link. In one mode it offers precise range/azimuth of selected ground targets. The AEW aircraft has very low radar cross-section itself, and can carry ECM amd ESM pods on wing pylons.

The Castor Islander gets its name from Corps airborne stand-off radar. It is under development for the MoD for the British Army, to operate in conjunction with the Phoenix RPV to provide an overall picture of a land battle. Ferranti provide the lightweight multimode I-band radar, which provides all-round cover against fixed and moving targets. The aircraft can be managed by a crew of two, and despite the ungainly nose flies perfectly. Processed radar data are fed to ground stations.

Right: Unlike the Castor Islander the AEW Defender carries its radar – now called Thorn EMI Skymaster – in a nose shaped like an American football. Skymaster is a multi-mode radar based on the Searchwater fitted to the Nimrod MR.2.

SEPECAT
JAGUAR

Type: Tactical attack and reconnaissance aircraft.
Engines: Two Rolls-Royce Turboméca Adour augmented turbofans (for thrust ratings see below).
Dimensions: Span 28ft 6in (8.69m); length, excluding probe (single-seat) 50ft 11in (15.52m), (two-seat) 53ft 10.45in (16.42m); height 16ft 0.5in (4.89m); wing area 260.27sq ft (24.18m²).
Weights: Empty (typical single-seat) 15,432lb (7,000kg); loaded (clean) 24,149lb (10,954kg), (maximum) 34,612lb (15,700kg).
Performance: Maximum speed, clean (high altitude) 1,056mph (1,699km/h) or Mach 1.6; (sea level) 840mph (1,350km/h) or Mach 1.1; combat radius (hi-lo-hi, typical) 875 miles (1,408km).

The production run of 573 Jaguars for six countries includes various degrees of upgrading, both new and since delivery. One basic variation is engine thrust. RAF and Armée de l'Air Jaguars were delivered with Mk 102 engines with maximum rating of 7,305lb (3,313kg). RAF aircraft were subsequently refitted with the Mk 104 engine of 8,040lb (3,647kg), the initial export models having the Mk 804 of the same thrust. Later export Jaguar Internationals have the 9,270lb (4,205kg) Mk 811 engine. The performance figures given above are for the original Mk 102, and can be appreciably uprated for the Mk 811 engine, which has a particularly beneficial effect with heavy external loads of up to 10,500lb (4,763kg).

Export Jaguars have an avionic fit

Above: Strong vortices streaming from the tips show how hard the ACT Jaguar wing works at low speed, with leading edge slats extended. This totally unstable aeroplane has a unique flight control system, with no reversion possible: no unaided human pilot could handle it.

generally based on RAF aircraft, with inertial navigation, HUD, projected map (or COMED, combined map and electronics display), laser in a chisel nose and ARI.18223 RWR with receivers facing to front and rear near the top of the fin. French attack Jaguars have no inertial system but instead a twin-gyro platform and doppler.

The final 30 for the Armée de l'Air are upgraded to the extent of having a Thomson-CSF Atlis II TV/laser pod used in conjunction with LGBs and AS.30L missiles. Jaguars of the Sultan of Oman's Air Force have a Marconi Avionics 920C mission computer and, like most Internationals, carry overwing AAMs, in this case Sidewinders. Indian-assembled Jaguars have an advanced HUD and weapon-aiming system based on that of the Sea Harrier, with Magic overwing AAMs. Anti-ship Jaguars have Thomson-CSF Agave nose radar, with the option of a laser in a chin blister, and can

carry AM.39 Exocet or similar anti-ship missiles.

Major research programmes in Britain have including design and test of a complete Jaguar wing in carbon-fibre composite material, design of a larger wing offering substantially enhanced manoeuvrability and greater fuel capacity with no penalties, and of course the BAe Warton ACT (active control technology) research Jaguar. The ACT aircraft is not intended to be a production aircraft, but is to support the design of the EAP prototype. The benefits of the changes are very great, and

Above: Taking off, the ACT Jaguar shows the upswept inboard rear section of tailplane (also visible, left). This part of the tailplane is set at 2.5° in regular Jaguars, but on the ACT aircraft the angle is 6°. Input to the EAP has been absolutely crucial, EAP also being an unstable aircraft.

the costs of the modification not high, particularly as RAF Jaguars are being subjected to a major upgrade in any case. If the RAF had any money it would probably study the cost/effectiveness of such a modification programme.

The first candidate for upgrading in RAF Jaguars was the INS (inertial navigation system), which is being replaced by the Ferranti FIN.1064. This advanced modular system has appreciably enhanced accuracy and reliability. The readouts and push-button interfaces fit into a very neat panel in the upper left of the cockpit coaming. It is a digital system, though most of the aircraft remains analog. The next update is adding an advanced VOR radio navigation receiver and new ILS (instrument landing system) receiver to enhance bad-weather capability. To provide an interim EW capability in 1983 a small box was added in the tailcone under the parachute bay for ejecting up to six chaff/flare cartridges. Some Jaguars have received the Westinghouse ALQ-101-10 active ECM jammer pods bought secondhand from the USAF and originally carried by Buccaneers.

In 1984 ASR (Air Staff Requirement) 633 was issued calling for an integrated EW installation, such as should have been specified back in 1966 when the RAF Jaguar was originally planned. The MoD expects seven companies or teams to bid, and there are many possible fits, nearly all using existing hardware items. RWR information will be presented on a new Ferranti COMED similar to that used by India. The new suite will replace the ARI.18228 and will almost certainly include a microprocessor and power manager responsive to threats and commanding jammers and dispensed payloads which will probably be external, probably mounted conformally. When all updates are complete the Jaguars will be redesignated GR.1A. No schedule for redelivery of GR.1As has been published.

SIKORSKY
S-76

Type: Multirole helicopter (see below).
Engines: Originally two 650shp Allison 250-C30 turboshaft engines; military variants will probably have the 735shp Allison 250-C34 or 960shp Pratt & Whitney Canada PT6B-36.
Dimensions: Diameter of main rotor 44ft 0in (13.41m); length overall, rotors turning 52ft 6in (16.0m); height overall 14ft 9.75in (4.52m); main-rotor disc area 1,520sq ft (141.21m^2).
Weights: Empty (utility) 5,600lb (2,540kg), (AUH, equipped) 6,680lb (3,030kg); loaded (utility and AUH) 10,300lb (4,672kg), (H-76N/ASV) 10,953lb (4,968kg), (PT6B or C34 engines) 11,000lb (4,989kg).
Performance: Maximum speed limited to 178mph (286km/h) though a regular C30-engined S-76 has set speed records such as a 500km circuit at an average of 214.833mph (345.74km/h); range highly variable from about 207 miles (333km) with maximum payload (PT6B engines) to 691 miles (1,112km) with maximum fuel.

Extremely successful as a civil and military utility and passenger helicopter, the S-76 is now being upgraded both in engine power and weight and also in equipment to fly specialized combat missions. The C34 and PT6B-36 engines dramatically enhance the already sparkling performance, particularly with digital engine control which is a feature of the Allison engine, Designation S-76 Mk II is unchanged with the C34 engine, but becomes S-76B with the more powerful Canadian engines, which also enable the tail rotor pylon to be slightly reduced in size.

The AUH-76 gets its designation from Armed Utility Helicopter. Sikorsky had previously offered as customer options a strong cargo floor, sliding doors and armoured crew seats, and the AUH now adds such extras as weapon pylons, an optical sight above the instrument panel, self-sealing crashproof tanks, provision for door-mounted weapons and, in conjunction with guided missiles, either a roof-mounted or mast-mounted sight (MMS).

Above: The armed H-76 was originally certificated for podded and door-mounted weapons. The trials were flown by this prototype, at company expense. Here the load comprises pods of Mk 66 rockets of 2.75in calibre. Note that at this time no MMS was fitted, and also that landing gear is extended for weapon-trials photography. In 1985 Sikorsky was building a prototype of the proposed naval H-76N, to fly in 1986. The company's initiative looks like paying off.

WESTLAND
LYNX 3 AND WESTLAND 30

Type: Multirole (see below).
Engines: (3) Two Rolls-Royce Gem 60 turboshafts with contingency rating of 1,346shp, (30) two General Electric CT7-2B turboshafts with contingency rating of 1,712shp.
Dimensions: Diameter of main rotor (3) 42ft 0in (12.8m), (30) 43ft 8in (13.31m); length overall, rotors turning (3) 50ft 9in (15.47m), (30) 52ft 2in (15.9m); height overall (3) 10ft 10in (3.3m), (30) 15ft 6in (4.72m); main rotor disc area (3) 1,385.4sq ft (128.7m^2), (30) 1497.7sq ft (139.14m^2).
Weights: Empty (3) not published, (30-200) 7,520lb (3,411kg); maximum (3) 13,000lb (5,896kg), (30-200) 12,800lb (5,806kg), (30-300) 15,500lb (7,030kg).
Performance: Maximum speed (3) 190mph (306km/h); cruising speed (30-300) 166mph (267km/h); range with max fuel and 20min reserves (3) 385 miles (620km); range of 30-300 or 17 armed troops 247 miles (398km).

Both these helicopters are upgraded derivatives of the original Lynx. The Lynx 3 is to be developed in both army and navy versions, but the former is earlier in timing, and a prototype has been flying since June 1984. The more powerful engines drive an enlarged rotor with BERP (British experimental rotor programme) tips giving greater efficiency (40 per cent is claimed). The fuselage is bigger and more stream-

lined, the engines, main gearbox and main rotor are mounted on a raft isolated from the fuselage by vibration-absorbing mountings, the landing gears (by Fairey) are entirely new, and the entire systems design has been completely upgraded. Westland has long been working on MoD contract on fibre-optics looms for transmitting data by light, and such technology is likely to be introduced to these new helicopters.

Above: The prototype "army" Lynx 3, ZE477, on troop exercises. Ordinary Lynxes can carry a squad of 10, but Lynx 3 has much greater weight-lifting capability. When this photograph was taken its multisensor sight was on the cabin roof, but an MMS is an option.

or TOW, Hellfire, Sea Skua or Stinger missiles. Without guns 16 TOW or Hellfire missiles can be carried, the same load as the much more costly Apache.

The naval H-76N was announcd in 1984. It is, like the tactical AUH, designed for practically every role imaginable including ASW, ASV surveillance and attack, over-the-horizon targeting, SAR and utility, operating from frigate-size ships. Surveillance versions would have Ferranti Sea-spray 3 or MEL Super Searcher radar, with the scanner in a chin radome offering perfect view. For ASW sensors would include dipping sonar and processor, weapons including Mk 46 or Sting Ray torpedoes. ASV weapons would include two Sea Skua missiles. Planned upgrades include dual digital flight controls, doppler, autohover, target-information data link, tac-nav system, inflight (hover) refuelling from ships, roof or mast-mounted FLIR, ECM pod, chaff/flare dispensers, strengthened landing gear, folding blades and haul-down/anchoring to the deck.

Self-protection systems include IR suppressed exhaust pipes, an RWR, IR jammer and chaff/flare dispensers. Normal seating will be provided for a load of 10 armed troops, or seven when the MPPS (multi-purpose pylon system) is installed carrying practically every available missile, rocket pod and gun option, including torpedoes,

---

Avionics for the army Lynx 3 were fast reaching a definitive state in 1985, though many features remain customer options (for example, whether the main sensor group should be on the nose, on the roof or in an MMS package). Westland has been working with avionics companies on many advanced features, such as the Racal mission-management system flown since 1983 on a British Army Air Corps Lynx and now enhanced by a cockpit CDU (control display unit). The next-generation DCAS (digital core avionics system) is to start flight development in the winter 1985-86. Lynx 3 will from the start have a MIL-STD-1553B digital databus, so that all future subsystems and devices can be immediately connected. Expected equipment includes Apache-style PNVS (pilot's night vision system) and TADS (target acquisition and designation system), together with a comprehensive EW suite. Weapon options include guns, and Hellfire, TOW, HOT and self-defence Stinger AAMs.

The big-fuselage Westland 30 is being developed in civil, utility (including battlefield transport/casevac) and naval versions. Its big cabin will in the Series 300 version be allied with a five-blade rotor to absorb the increased engine power.

FUTURE FIGHTERS

In the introduction to this book the fundamental questions of stealth design and the need to operate completely away from all known airfields were discussed at some length. These questions are, and will remain, the two central factors determining the design of all future combat aircraft. Oddly, they are taking a long time to be understood, and this is simply because they pose major problems and involve tradeoffs and compromises which inevitably knock one or two percentage points off what can be achieved by future fighters which ignore these issues.

Thus today's chiefs of staff appear happy to commit themselves to future fighters which can do the best possible peacetime job, but which would all cease to exist on or before Day One of any future war with a major power. The only ones which might escape would be the odd aircraft which happened to be away from their bases at the crucial time.

Of course, it may be that the outpourings in Western media on the USAF's proposed ATF and the Europeans' hoped-for EFA (or FEFA) are cunningly contrived to mask the true design objectives, and thus mislead potential enemies. The author does not believe this is so. In a free society it is extremely difficult to manipulate the media, and it seems reasonable to assume that the open discussion – for example, in the trade and technical press – of ATF and EFA really does reflect the current design objectives. So far these objectives have concentrated entirely on the easily solved problems, such as those associated with particular air-combat capabilities, weapon loads and mission radii. In the case of ATF stress has also been laid upon reliability, operational readiness, maintainability,

support costs and similar factors which are all very important to an air force which does a lot of flying and wants to be effective 168 hours a week.

In late summer 1985 the USAF ATF specification had been disclosed only in general terms. We can certainly take it for granted that the gigantic supercruise (supersonic cruise) "fighters" seemingly 100ft (30m) long and costing astronomic sums, which have figured in much American artwork, will never actually be built. Not even the USA has so much spare cash that it can squander billions on such useless and vulnerable hardware. In Europe, however, a fantastic situation arose in 1981-82 in which the main NATO powers

plus France all discovered that they are going to need a new fighter in the early 1990s. At first glance there seemed to be no problem: Panavia desperately needs a new follow-on programme, and the new fighter is the obvious choice. But, despite the existence of this giant body of three-nation expertise and experience, nothing has been done in three years except produce mountains of paper and two rival prototypes which are at daggers drawn.

The reason for the impasse is the existence of the French company Dassault-Breguet. This company demands "technical leadership" of any EFA programme, plus 46 per cent of the work on a cost basis, plus a design tailored "to the requirements

Above: Sweden's Saab 39 Gripen, or JAS, is a refreshing change from study projects because it is actually being built. British Aerospace are building the graphite-fibre wing. The Gripen promises to be the least expensive of all the current crop of future fighters.

Below: Originally called TKF90, and now JF90 (fighter for 1990), this MBB study is virtually the same aircraft as the British EAP. A go-ahead by Panavia (the existing company linking MBB of West Germany, British Aerospace and Aeritalia) is the one thing Dassault-Breguet fears.

of l'Armée de l'Air and l'Aéronavale". It also wishes to delay an EFA in order to sell as many Mirage 2000 fighters as possible. Other countries have better things to do than "knock" their allies, but Dassault-Breguet has issued a deluge of publicity material explaining why its own Rafale is the only "future fighter" worthy of consideration. It has also published the December 1983 OEST (Outline European Staff Target), which shows exactly what kind of animal the EFA is likely to be.

In the air-to-air mission the EFA will have to be capable of intercepting and destroying bombers, fighters, attack aircraft and helicopters expected to be operational in the 1990-2010 timeframe. RPVs, cruise missiles and hovering or slow-moving helicopters must also be taken into account. The EFA must thus carry six AAMs such as four medium-range interception missiles and two close-range air-combat missiles or a different mix. The medium-range missiles must be of the latest active self-homing type in order for EFA to launch them in rapid succession against a numerically superior hostile force. The EFA will also need an internal gun and an internal ECM suite.

In the air-to-ground role the Chiefs of Staff require a minimum 3.5 tonnes (7,716lb) of ordnance to be delivered on a target 300-350 nautical miles (345-403 miles, 555-649km) from takeoff. This armament must include advanced stand-off "launch and leave" missiles to enable the EFA to stand well away from its targets. EO (electro-optical) systems must play an increasing part in weapon delivery systems. Avionics must also include a radar with acquisition range in the 50 nautical mile (57.5 miles, 93km) class. Radar signal processing will have to be very advanced: typical demands include "look down, shoot down" capability, ability simultaneously to track eight hostile aircraft, and automatically carry out threat assessment and assign priorities.

As the airbases are so vulnerable, the EFA must not need long runways. It must be able to take off in 1,640ft (500m) with full internal fuel, two AMRAAMs and full gun ammunition. It must also be capable of being refuelled in flight. Finally, the price must be "reasonable". To this end the equipped empty weight has to be kept down.

Even this single factor of empty weight has become a subject for interminable argument. At the Paris air show Benno Vallières, Président Directeur-Général of Dassault-Breguet, explained that France wants a limit of 9.5 tonnes, while other countries want 9.75 tonnes! This terrible crisis overlooks the undoubted fact that all such limits will be altered or forgotten long before anything gets near production. One is reminded of countless occasions in the past where rigid numerical limitations — such as the weights set for the F-111 — looked ludicrous a few years later. But in 1985 the name of the game at Dassault-Breguet was "Keep out British Aerospace and Turbo-Union", both far more deadly foes, obviously, than any design bureau in the Soviet Union. At a press conference the

Above: This mock-up at British Aerospace Warton shows the P.103. At least this design recognized that future fighters must be able to operate without known airfields, but in other respects it was not an impressive design. But in the author's view EAP is a retrograde step!

Below: Dassault-Breguet want their hastily schemed Rafale, designed for French air force and navy, to be the basis for an EFA in which the French company would be "leader" and have the lion's share of the work. This posture overlooks the importance of EFA.

suggestion was made that the tri-national Turbo-Union RB.199 might be used in Dassault-Breguet's Rafale. The answer in exact translation, was "No, it is a larger engine, and it needs much more airflow to deliver the same thrust; and it is designed for low altitudes and is not suitable for fighter manoeuvres at altitude." Now, today's RB.199 is not ideal for future fighters, and in fact Rolls-Royce is building a next-generation XG40 engine which takes technology even further; but it is a pity to see Dassault-Breguet so concerned not to have any truck with established European programmes that it calls an engine which is actually much smaller, "larger".

This book will still be a useful reference long after the EFA arguments have been resolved. For the moment we merely echo the British Secretary of State for Defence, Michael Heseltine, who observed: "If everybody is tending to make statements based on deep-seated rivalries it will get us nowhere. If we can't find a compromise there will be no winners, only losers." This book appears just at the time when the European NATO nations are, once again, being offered the chance of collaboration on a multinational programme which would also do much to improve NATO's 30-year failure to emulate the Warsaw Pact with totally interoperable standardized equipment.

Re-reading the OEST requirements one inevitably feels that they describe a fighter of today, not of the 1990-2010 era. In most respects the demands come nowhere near what the F-14 has offered since 1972, and as a target for the next generation the whole approach seems amazingly dated. Nothing is said about the two crucial issues mentioned previously, and in any case the idea of the European NATO air forces spending most of their budget on such conventional airfield-based fighters, whose design is tailored largely to taking on the Bad Guys in head-to-head close combat seems extraordinary. Assuming that some NATO fighters survive the start of hostilities, they might score one-for-one (a better result than anyone could expect today against MiG-29s), and that would very soon leave WP forces with about a 2,000-to-nil superiority.

Possibly some of the ATF submissions are highly unconventional. Of future fighters whose design features are known virtually all follow the current fashion of having anhedralled canards used as primary flight controls, a cropped delta wing of large area, a simple fixed ventral inlet (in the Rafale divided into two) and a single fin. One can date the aircraft in this class by their structural materials. Those started in 1979-80, such as the Lavi and Gripen, incorporate extensive carbon-fibre composites in the primary structure. Those started in 1983, such as the EAP and Rafale, have even more carbon and also large amounts of Kevlar, aluminium-lithium alloy and SPFDB (superplastic forming and diffusion bonding) titanium. The latter, for example, is used for the Rafale's wing leading-edge flaps.

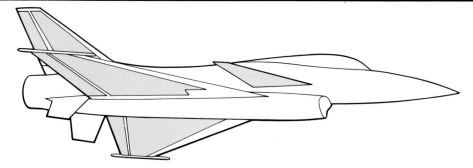

Above: This drawing of the Israeli Lavi shows for the first time some of the major portions being made from graphite/ epoxy composite material. Grumman is a vital contractor responsible for some of these, including the wing.

Below: Black panels betray the graphite (carbon) composite structure of these wings about to be delivered for France's Rafale. Lavi, Gripen, Harrier II and the B-1 are examples of major projects with "imported" carbon.

Advanced structures make these future fighters relatively light, despite their size. EAP and Rafale each have about 560sq ft ($52m^2$) of wing, about the same as a wartime Ju 88 bomber. Moreover, the structure has to be stressed to carry very heavy loads of ordnance (3.5 tonnes hardly looks impressive compared with the 10.7 tonnes carried by today's F-15C) and manoeuvre at load factors up to 9ğ, as does today's F-16 (and certainly the MiG-29 can equal this). These demands inevitably result in a ratio of installed engine thrust to aircraft weight "far superior to one" (Dassault-Breguet's words). Is it not strange, then, that despite engines powerful enough to lift the fighter-mission aircraft straight up into the sky, instead tomorrow's fighters should need 1,640ft (500m) of smooth firm terrain in which to accelerate to flying speed? Worse, they need at least as much space in which to effect a safe landing. Dassault-Breguet proudly boasts its Rafale will land at "under 120 knots" (138mph, 222km/h); anyone with the slightest ability to picture future war would wonder why this was considered good.

It is doubtful that anybody believes in VTOL fighters, unless they have invented something quite new. But fighters which need half a kilometre in which to get into the air (and much greater distances when carrying ordnance for air-to-ground missions) and which then have to slam on to the ground at high speed and hope to slow down safely are obviously not merely imperfect but likely to be unable to operate in any conceivable European war. Even the USAF now accepts that future fighters *must* have something better than the crude

nozzles which have been taken for granted in the past and yet which cannot point the engine's thrust in different directions.

For 45 years the designers of rockets, with jets much hotter and faster than anything in a fighter, have vectored the thrust in all directions, giving complete trajectory control of ballistic vehicles devoid of aerodynamic control surfaces. Vectoring the thrust can play a crucial role in getting future fighters off the ground without a 500m run and can also dramatically improve combat manoeuvrability. Harrier-type nozzles are increasingly unsuitable as the required flight Mach number rises beyond unity, and even the "three-poster" has its limitations. Alternatives, such as the tandem fan (one of several schemes discussed in this section) are

inclined to be relatively complex and heavy. The author has yet to be convinced that a good STOVL fighter cannot be built with a single vectored afterburning nozzle.

Be that as it may, it seems obvious that, with the passage of time, to plan an EFA with two plain holes at the back will be seen to be mistaken. Designers at present are excited at the excellent field length possible with such machines, but time is likely to show that it is not good enough to avoid going near airfields, and thus surviving. In any case, the crunch situation is recovery after the mission, and here there is an overwhelming need not only for the ability to stop before landing but also for stealth characteristics so that the enemy's satellites cannot see where the aircraft landed.

Type: Tactical attack and reconnaissance aircraft.

Engine: One 11,030lb (5003kg) Rolls-Royce Spey 807 turbofan (licence-built by Italian companies).

Dimensions: Span (excluding AAMs) 29ft 1.37in (8.874m); length overall 44ft 6.4in (13.575m); height 15ft 0.16in (4.576m); wing area 226.04sq ft (21.0m²).

Weights: Empty 13,228lb (6,000kg); maximum 25,353lb (11,500kg).

Performance: Maximum speed (sea level, full external mission load) 723mph (1,163km/h) or Mach 0.95; mission radius (lo-lo-lo, 6,000lb/2,722kg bombload)230 miles (370km).

There is no longer over-riding pressure on designers to make combat aircraft fly as fast as possible. One has only to reflect for a moment to understand that, if it is necessary to try to penetrate defended airspace at the lowest possible altitude, very high speeds are possible only over water or over land that is absolutely flat and featureless. Over real landscapes it is preferable to stay really low and fly at about 570mph (920km/h), which in turn means that the aircraft can be relatively simple and cheap in comparison with a Mach-2 aeroplane. This philosophy produced the highly successful A-7, and in 1977 was the basis of the AM-X, which replaces the G91 and F-104G in the AMI (Italian air force) and provides a modern aircraft able to fly close-support, interdiction and reconnaissance missions which would otherwise demand use of the long-range and much more costly Tornado.

Work went ahead with Italian industry, thus the designation stems from Aeritalia/Macchi Xperimental. Aermacchi was already working with Brazil on a proposed A-X to replace the Aermacchi M.B.326GB (built by EMBRAER as the AT-26 Xavante). In 1980 the Brazilian government decided to link in a joint programme, the final work-sharing being 46 per cent Aeritalia (centre fuselage, radome, fin, rudder, elevators, flaps, ailerons and spoilers), Aermacchi 24 per cent (forward fuselage with gun/avionics integration, tailcone and canopy, and EMBRAER 30 per cent (wings, slats, tailplane, inlets, pylons and fuel tanks). The engine was picked in October 1978 because it was well matched to the mission and offered maturity and competitive fuel burn. It is produced under licence by Fiat, Alfa Romeo and Piaggio, and assembly of production aircraft takes place at Turin Caselle (Aeritalia) and Sao José dos Campos (EMBRAER).

Before World War II there would have been nothing unusual in either Italy or Brazil producing a new type of combat aircraft. Today, even in collaboration it represents an enormous burden and sustained commitment, and is a unique example of professionalism in writing operational requirements winning over the emotional appeal of the supersonic fighter. The AMI is fortunate to have the F-104s as a Mach-2 all-weather interceptor armed with radar-guided medium-range AAMs (Sparrows or Aspides) and this has enabled the AM-X to be designed with great care for all the limited-radius offensive missions. In the past such missions have often been flown by obsolescent "fighters", and at first glance the AM-X might be thought to be broadly similar to such long-established machines as the MiG-17, F-84, F-100 and Hunter. Such similiarity is misleading. Aircraft designed in the 1980 era are fundamentally superior in aerodynamics, airframe structure, materials, systems and above all in integrated avionic systems to their predecessors.

In most respects the AM-X is conventional. The unaugmented engine is short

Above: With 30 per cent by value of the programme, Brazil is playing a full role in development and manufacture. Here Model 2C is seen in an EMBRAER tunnel with slats, flaps, landing gear and tip AAMs. EMBRAER is fatigue-testing a wing, and the first tests of auxiliary tanks and the reconnaissance pallet have begun on the Brazilian No. 6 aircraft.

Below: There is not a lot to distinguish the AM-X from fighter/attack aircraft of the 1950s. Only upon detailed examination can the Italo/Brazilian aircraft be seen to be a 1980s product. Many other nations have contributed to it, including British and US accessory and equipment suppliers. Martin-Baker tested the AM-X seat with a sled-mounted forward fuselage. Another mockup forward fuselage was used to qualify the M61 gun during firing trials in the USA, where the design of blast deflector was established. The same rig was then shipped to Brazil where it was used to optimise the installation of the twin DEFA 30mm guns. Aermacchi was meanwhile testing canopies against bullets at 500 knots airspeed.

Elettronica RWR (front and rear)

Powered rudder

Fixed nozzle (no afterburner) of Spey 807 engine

Anti-collision light

IFF

UHF

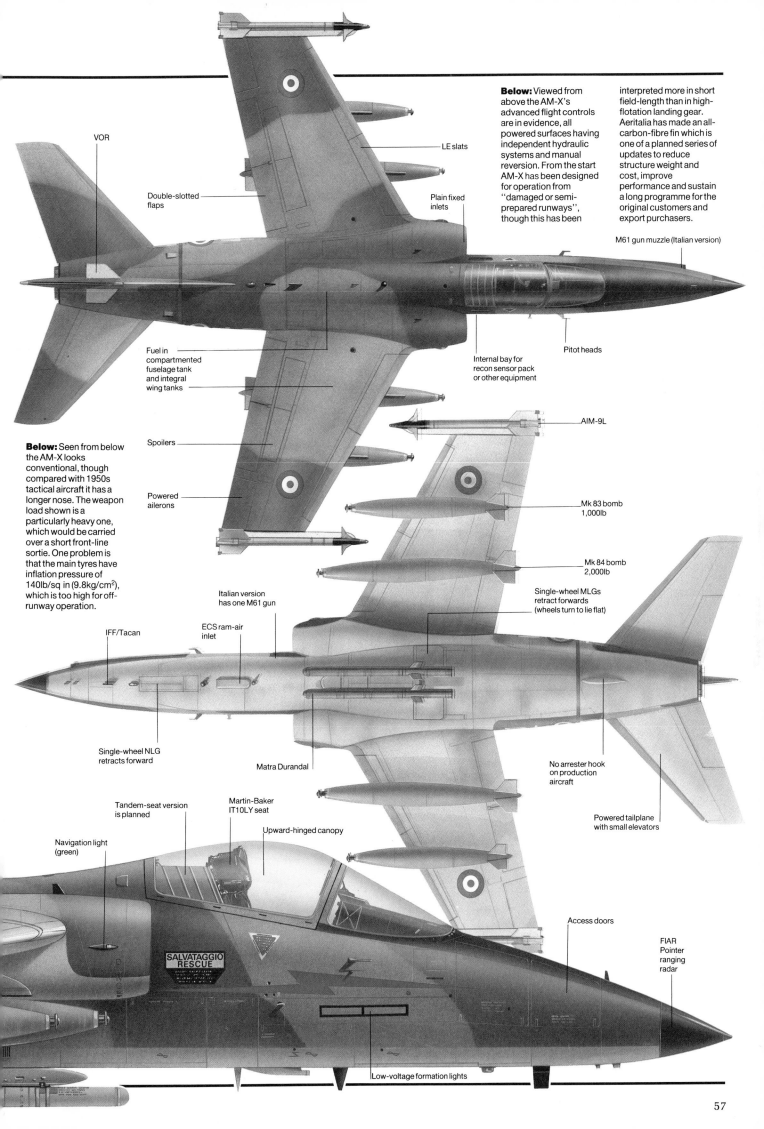

VOR

Double-slotted flaps

LE slats

Plain fixed inlets

Below: Viewed from above the AM-X's advanced flight controls are in evidence, all powered surfaces having independent hydraulic systems and manual reversion. From the start AM-X has been designed for operation from "damaged or semi-prepared runways", though this has been interpreted more in short field-length than in high-flotation landing gear. Aeritalia has made an all-carbon-fibre fin which is one of a planned series of updates to reduce structure weight and cost, improve performance and sustain a long programme for the original customers and export purchasers.

M61 gun muzzle (Italian version)

Fuel in compartmented fuselage tank and integral wing tanks

Internal bay for recon sensor pack or other equipment

Pitot heads

AIM-9L

Below: Seen from below the AM-X looks conventional, though compared with 1950s tactical aircraft it has a longer nose. The weapon load shown is a particularly heavy one, which would be carried over a short front-line sortie. One problem is that the main tyres have inflation pressure of 140lb/sq in (9.8kg/cm^2), which is too high for off-runway operation.

Spoilers

Powered ailerons

Mk 83 bomb 1,000lb

Mk 84 bomb 2,000lb

Single-wheel MLGs retract forwards (wheels turn to lie flat)

IFF/Tacan

ECS ram-air inlet

Italian version has one M61 gun

Single-wheel NLG retracts forward

Matra Durandal

No arrester hook on production aircraft

Powered tailplane with small elevators

Navigation light (green)

Tandem-seat version is planned

Martin-Baker IT10LY seat

Upward-hinged canopy

Access doors

FIAR Pointer ranging radar

SALVATAGGIO RESCUE

Low-voltage formation lights

and can be fed by plain fixed-geometry inlets which curve in across the wing roots giving an area-rule compliant profile, and with enough duct length to avoid F-111 type airflow distortion and mismatch problems. The engine is right in the tail, and is accessed by unbolting the entire rear fuselage with tailplane. Fuel is housed in a compartmented fuselage cell and an integral tank forming each wing box, and all four wing pylons are plumbed for drop tanks. There is provision for an inflight-refuelling probe to be added, but neither of the two original customers has tanker aircraft.

The airframe is mainly conventional light alloy, though the fin, elevators and some other minor parts are of carbon-fibre composite. The wing is slightly swept and has little taper, the broad tips carrying self-defence AAM launch rails. Powerful high-lift devices comprise full-span leading edge slats and large double-slotted flaps extending well outboard. Even at maximum gross weight the takeoff run is no more than 3,120ft (950m), and on most missions it will be little more than half this. Roll control is by small outboard ailerons and two pairs of inboard spoilers which also can be opened in unison as airbrakes or, after landing, as lift dumpers. The ailerons are mechanically signalled and hydraulically driven, but small enough to be controlled manually in emergency. The

Above: AM-X prototypes (this is No. 2) adorned with four arrowheads in the colours of the two countries. Note the four deep NATO-standard pylons, the avionics aerials and the runway arrester hook.

spoilers are FBW (fly by wire). An important role of the slats and flaps is to enhance combat manoeuvrability at typical speeds around Mach 0.6, where their variable-camber effect will greatly improve agility with heavy bombloads.

The vertical tail has been considerably enlarged as a result of tunnel testing under conditions of high AOA (angle of attack). A GEC Avionics/Aeritalia flight-control computer governs all primary flight controls, the broad rudder being FBW. Should both electric wires or both hydraulic systems fail, the rudder is locked central. The tailplanes are really slabs, with dual hydraulic power, but small carbonfibre elevators are hinged to the primary surfaces to provide a get-you-home manual reversionary capability in emergency. Thanks to the flight control computer all trimming is done within the system, no tabs being needed.

Like all new types the AM-X is planned for maximum availability with minimum maintenance effort whilst operating from austere airstrips. Almost all items are modular, immediately accessible through

BRITISH AEROSPACE
EAP

Type: Advanced fighter technology demonstrator.
Engines: Two very slightly modified Turbo-Union RB199 Mk 104 augmented turbofans, each rated in the 17,000lb (7,711kg) class.
Dimensions: Span 36ft 7.75in (11.17m); length 48ft 2.75in (14.7m); wing area 560sq ft (52.0m²).
Weights: Not yet published, but air-combat gross was estimated in 1984 at 35,275lb (16,000kg) and thrust/weight ratio has been described as "always greater than unity".
Performance: Maximum speed in the Mach 2 class, ie 1,320mph (2,128km/h).

The chiefs of staff of the air forces of five major European nations agreed in early 1984 on a common joint requirement for a FEFA (Future European Fighter Aircraft) and have reaffirmed that almost unbelievable agreement since. Unfortunately, the whole grand design is likely to founder because of the existence of two major aircraft manufacturers each with the capability of handling such a programme; BAe and Dassault-Breguet. BAe has long experience of collaborative programmes, with many companies in many countries, but Dassault has never overcome immature feelings of superiority, and its idea of collaboration is to permit lesser nations to built parts of its own aircraft. This inevitably makes it very difficult for the five

nations to move from the agreed requirement to an agreed design.

The naive observer might have thought that the existence of Panavia, as a three-nation industrial consortium already in being and highly experienced in the field of modern combat aircraft, (Tornado) might have provided the obvious foundation upon which to build. Panavia is owned by Aeritalia, British Aerospace and MBB, and its large staff have enormously broad and detailed experience of aircraft design, defence contracting, specifications, requirements, quality control, service support and all other aspects of producing modern fighters; the organization also urgently needs a major new programme to take over as Tornado tapers off. Unfortunately this has proved a pipe-dream, and indeed Britain's continental partners in Panavia have, for purely national reasons, been forced to back-track from the initial position of mutual collaboration.

Perhaps the high point was in April 1982 when the three Panavia partners formed a joint design team. Italy at that time had not firmed up a definite new fighter design, but MBB had drawn a TKF 90, later restyled JF 90, as described later. BAe had progressed through numerous studies and projects at both Kingston and Warton, and by 1981 the Warton P1110 had gradually evolved to meet the purely British AST (Air Staff Target) 414. This could hardly fail to be

very similar to JF 90 in configuration, because fighter design is strongly influenced by fashion. Fortunately it was also virtually identical in size, weight and thrust, whereas the P.106 and other earlier studies had been smaller and single-engined. Features included two RB199 engines fed by long lateral inlet ducts carrying large swept canards mounted high at the rear of the cockpit and above the level of the large wing with a kinked leading edge. MBB had decided in favour of a single chin inlet, of a severe rectangular form, partly because of its superior performance at extreme AOA. For commonality this was adopted by BAe, along with MBB's pair of large anhedral canards set further forward and much lower on the fuselage. Called the ACA (Agile Combat Aircraft), this was exhibited in mock-up form by BAe at the 1982 Farnborough airshow, when it was also seen that MBB's tail, with twin canted fins, had also been adopted.

With no visible difference between ACA and JF 90 the way looked clear for some kind of go-ahead, but at this stage Dassault-Breguet decided it could hardly stand idly by and watch European partners going ahead with a collaborative programme. It quickly schemed the ACX (described later), the configuration being extremely similar to that of BAe's earlier P.106. As Dassault hoped, this was enough to stop the German government and MBB in their the mass of hinged doors that cover most of the fuselage. Despite the substanial under-fuselage stores capability the AM-X sits low to the ground, and it is rare for any ladder or trestle to be necessary. Basic aircraft systems are standard, but predictably the Italian and Brazilian air forces differed in armament and avionics. Great credit is due to the design team for reconciling the differences without compromising the aircraft or significantly adding to its size or cost. Moreover, good planning in the conceptual definition phase is now paying off in facilitating the addition of subsystems and equipments that were not in existence when the AM-X was designed.

Primary navigation system for the AMI is a Litton Italia INS, but the Brazilian FAB preferred traditional VOR/ILS. VOR, which relies upon ground radio stations, has obvious shortcomings in low-level missions deep into hostile territory, and in 1985 the FAB was studying add-ons to upgrade their self-contained navigational accuracy. Both air forces are at present buying AM-X with a simple ranging radar built by FIAR and derived from the Elta EL/M-2001B as used in some Kfirs. This may suffice for day attack in good weather, but again there is likely to be a future update, either by fitting a multimode radar or (or possibly and) a FLIR and TV/laser installation to permit all-weather operations. Common to all versions is the Microtecnica air-data computer and Litton computer-based weapon aiming system, in conjunction with OMI/Selenia HUD and stores management and a panel-mounted MFD (multifunction display). Most cockpit instruments are conventional, and include an attitude/heading reference system and an alphanumeric data display.

Both customers were insistent on having a gun, but in 1980 the gun selected, the 20mm M61A1, had not been cleared for export to Brazil. Thus the AMI has a single M61 on the left of the nose, with a 350-round drum mounted transversely immediately in front of the cockpit, while the FAB has two 30mm DEFA 553 (554) cannon, each with 125 rounds. Under the centre fuselage is a single twin-pylon attachment whose stores fit neatly between the main landing gears. The three units of the landing gear all have levered suspension, and though made in Italy by ERAM (main) and Magnaghi (nose) were designed in France by Messier-Hispano-Bugatti. There is an airfield arrester hook but no braking parachute or reverser. The centreline and inboard wing pylons are rated at 2,000lb (907kg), the outers being limited to 1,000lb (454kg). Total stores load is at present limited to 7,716lb (3,500kg), the design load factor being 7.33.

One of the farsighted decisions was to reserve a bay in the right side of the fuselage, ahead of the main gear and under the inlet, which can accommodate various specially tailored pallet payloads. Initially the pallets will offer a choice of reconnaissance systems, such as panoramic, TV or photogrammetric cameras. Later other sensors might be added. For AMI use the Elettronica ELT/156 RWR has been selected, with forward and aft receiver aerials on the fin. Elettronica and Selenia have both worked on the EW suite, which is to be internal. This does not preclude adding further external ECM in a pod, but with just five pylons it would on occasions degrade mission capability. Even as it is the centreline pylons may be needed for an IR/optronics pod, and great efforts are being made to keep EW systems internal.

Altogether the AM-X will certainly be a very useful aircraft, and probably to customers additional to Italy and Brazil. Loss of the first prototype on 1 June 1984 has not significantly affected the programme, and the last of six prototypes should have flown well before the end of 1985, nos 4 and 6 being assembled in Brazil. If the AM-X were being designed today Stealth technology would have played a part in the basic configuration and shape, but this should make little difference to the success of today's aircraft. The AMI expects to deploy 187 aircraft (which may receive a different designation or name) from 1986, and the FAB 79. Export aircraft will be available from 1988.

tracks. MBB pulled out of the ACA, except for a very small ongoing design effort (and BAe continued to place contracts with German Tornado suppliers for certain items of avionics).

Italy, however, never wavered in its belief in a collaborative programme, and has made a major contribution to the main wing of ACA. Great assistance has also come from the British accessory industry, including GEC/Marconi Avionics, Ferranti, Smiths Industries, Lucas and Dowty. As early as the 1983 Paris airshow these companies had spent an estimated £25 million of their own money on research and testing for the ACA programme. Rolls-Royce, on behalf of Turbo-Union, had also

Above: Predecessor of the EAP, BAe Warton's ACA (Agile Combat Aircraft) mock-up in summer 1982. In the background are Tornado vertical tails, one of which actually went on the EAP in place of the twin verticals seen here.

made a significant contribution, and MBB and Aeritalia had contributed to the joint design and project team at Warton.

At the 1982 Farnborough show the British MoD had stated its intention to "make a financial contribution" to the ACA programme, and this took a very tangible form when on the eve of the 1983 Paris show, on 26 May 1983, the MoD placed a contract with BAe Warton for a single technology demonstrator aircraft, the EAP (Experimental Aircraft Programme).

The ultimate objective of the European nations is a Future European Fighter Aircraft (FEFA). Nobody yet knows what form this will take, nor who will build it, but it will probably look like the pictures already published. The ACA is the hoped-for joint design by the Panavia partners, which if it ever goes ahead will probably be managed by Panavia's present organisation though possibly with shareholding modified to admit additional partners. The EAP is a purely national British effort, the tangible result of which is the single demonstrator now being built. Of course, the EAP is almost the same as the ACA, except that it is being produced to a minimal budget and lacks internal features that would be required by a definitive fighter. What one cannot even suggest is that there is any link between the EAP and the FEFA, because the latter aircraft may be based on Dassault's rival demonstrator, or on some as-yet unknown design, or it may never happen.

Construction of the EAP began in summer 1984, and in mid-1985 was fast taking shape at Warton, pretty much on schedule and on budget. The wing is almost a delta, but with a kinked leading edge and a major LERX (leading-edge root extension) which continues around above the inlet to form a sharp-lipped splitter plate. The wing is very large for the size of aircraft, and BAe is trying to keep wing loading lower than for any recent fighter.

This has a profound effect on takeoff/ landing performance and on inflight agility at all speeds, and it is again powerfully assisted by the wing's supercritical profile and variable camber features with powered flaps along both edges.

The flight-control system is based squarely on the world-pioneering quad digital FBW system flying in the ACT (active controls technology) Jaguar. Of course the EAP will have all its avionics and on-board systems linked to a MIL-STD-1553B databus, and the "fail oprational" flight controls will be the most important single element. When the EAP design was almost frozen the decision was taken to go back to a single vertical tail, and a spare Tornado fin/rudder is being fitted, which saves time and cost and exerts very little penalty, besides increasing commonality with Dassault.

The main wing, like most of the other aerodynamic surfaces, is to a considerable degree a carbon-fibre composite structure of very advanced form. Aeritalia has made a second wing and will test this as a major contribution to the programme. According to Frank O'Gara, ACA deputy project manager, use of leading and trailing flaps results in a 40 per cent increase in maximum lift/drag ratio, as indicated by tunnel testing. This would again make a massive contribution to field length and combat manoevrability. The canards are now aerodynamically almost perfect. Driven by the FBW quad system, they are not only primary flight controls but also instantly responsive surfaces for gust alleviation, as also seen on the B-1B. According to BAe this improves area ruling and lift/drag ratio, apart from making life much more comfortable for the pilot and greatly reducing the stresses imposed on the air-

frame. The trailing edge flaperons can be separated into outboard ailerons and inboard flaps, though there are regimes in which all four sections act together.

Much of the EAP armament is fairly obvious. Though not shown in drawings, a gun will be fitted (presumably a 25mm Aden or 27mm Mauser), and AAMs will be carried in minimum-drag configurations. MBB showed traditional conformal carriage of Sparrows similar to an F-15, but BAe has three times produced artwork showing Sky Flash or Sparrow AAMs recessed side-by-side under the flat inlet duct and tucked away into the angle under the root of the wing, the missile fins being recessed. This is a novel location, and may offer not only low drag but also slight benefit in stealth quality. To accommodate these two missiles the wing root is extended aft of the trailing edge and fixed, the flaps terminating further outboard. Side-

winders are shown in one drawing on tip launchers; in another they are on underwing pylons located at the kink in the leading edge (where a small dogtooth has appeared), the tips being occupied by small streamlined bodies which might be large enough to accommodate ECM jammers. The Tornado fin already has the ARI.1824l/1 RHAWS (radar homing and warning system), and a good place for chaff/flare dispensing would be the fixed wing trailing-edge roots.

According to O'Gara no attempt has been made to fit 2D vectoring nozzles. Takeoff distance would in any case be "dramatic", and presumably there is little point in taking off where a fighter cannot land, and EAP has no reversers! At least Mr. O'Gara believes that "almost any aircraft these days should be able to operate away from airfields" – from highways and good fields – so EAP should have much going for it.

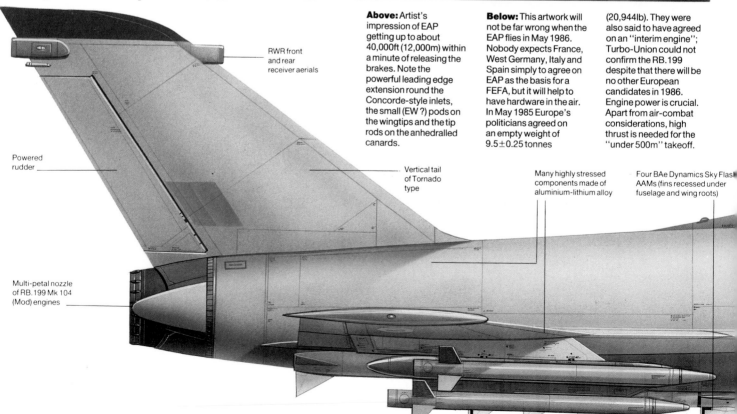

Above: Artist's impression of EAP getting up to about 40,000ft (12,000m) within a minute of releasing the brakes. Note the powerful leading edge extension round the Concorde-style inlets, the small (EW ?) pods on the wingtips and the tip rods on the anhedralled canards.

Below: This artwork will not be far wrong when the EAP flies in May 1986. Nobody expects France, West Germany, Italy and Spain simply to agree on EAP as the basis for a FEFA, but it will help to have hardware in the air. In May 1985 Europe's politicians agreed on an empty weight of 9.5±0.25 tonnes

(20,944lb). They were also said to have agreed on an "interim engine"; Turbo-Union could not confirm the RB.199 despite that there will be no other European candidates in 1986. Engine power is crucial. Apart from air-combat considerations, high thrust is needed for the "under 500m" takeoff.

RWR front and rear receiver aerials

Powered rudder

Multi-petal nozzle of RB.199 Mk 104 (Mod) engines

Vertical tail of Tornado type

Many highly stressed components made of aluminium-lithium alloy

Four BAe Dynamics Sky Flash AAMs (fins recessed under fuselage and wing roots)

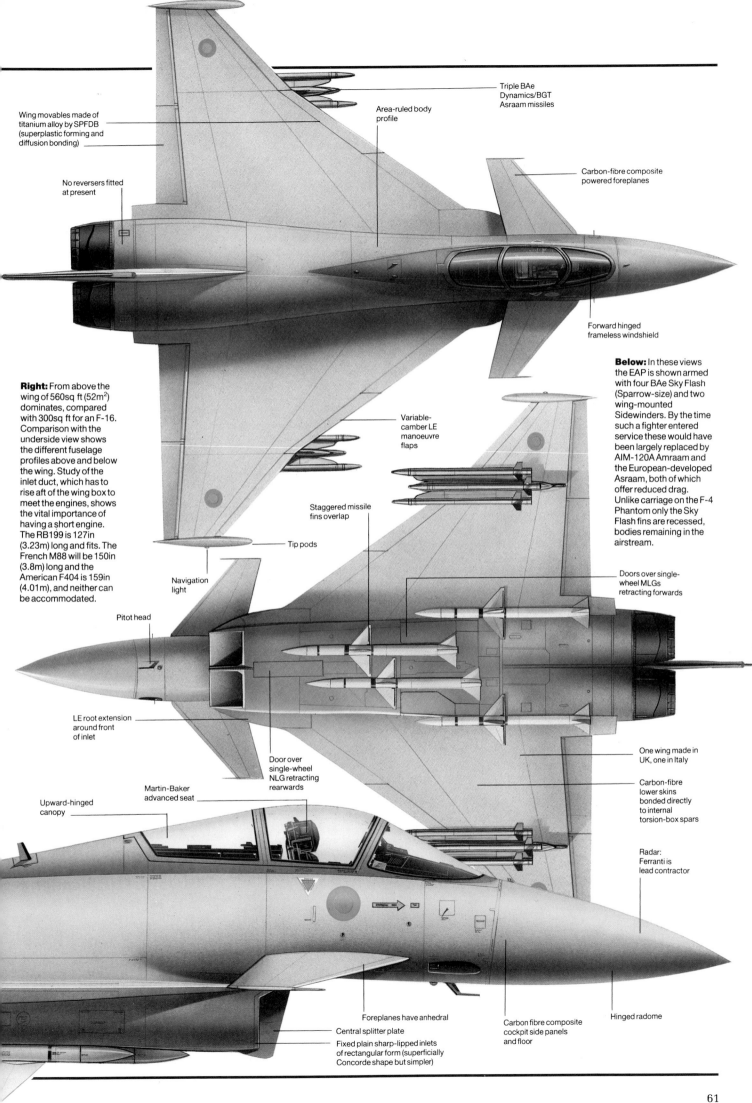

Wing movables made of titanium alloy by SPFDB (superplastic forming and diffusion bonding)

No reversers fitted at present

Triple BAe Dynamics/BGT Asraam missiles

Area-ruled body profile

Carbon-fibre composite powered foreplanes

Forward hinged frameless windshield

Right: From above the wing of 560sq ft (52m²) dominates, compared with 300sq ft for an F-16. Comparison with the underside view shows the different fuselage profiles above and below the wing. Study of the inlet duct, which has to rise aft of the wing box to meet the engines, shows the vital importance of having a short engine. The RB199 is 127in (3.23m) long and fits. The French M88 will be 150in (3.8m) long and the American F404 is 159in (4.01m), and neither can be accommodated.

Below: In these views the EAP is shown armed with four BAe Sky Flash (Sparrow-size) and two wing-mounted Sidewinders. By the time such a fighter entered service these would have been largely replaced by AIM-120A Amraam and the European-developed Asraam, both of which offer reduced drag. Unlike carriage on the F-4 Phantom only the Sky Flash fins are recessed, bodies remaining in the airstream.

Variable-camber LE manoeuvre flaps

Staggered missile fins overlap

Tip pods

Navigation light

Doors over single-wheel MLGs retracting forwards

Pitot head

LE root extension around front of inlet

Door over single-wheel NLG retracting rearwards

One wing made in UK, one in Italy

Carbon-fibre lower skins bonded directly to internal torsion-box spars

Radar: Ferranti is lead contractor

Upward-hinged canopy

Martin-Baker advanced seat

Foreplanes have anhedral

Central splitter plate

Fixed plain sharp-lipped inlets of rectangular form (superficially Concorde shape but simpler)

Carbon fibre composite cockpit side panels and floor

Hinged radome

61

DASSAULT-BREGUET
ACX (RAFALE)

Type: Advanced combat experimental aircraft.

Engines: Two 16,000lb (7,258kg) General Electric F404-400 (possibly F404-400D to be fitted later).

Dimensions: Span 36ft 8.9in (11.2m); length 51ft 10.0in (15.8m)

Weights: Combat weight 30,865lb (14,000kg).

Performance: Maximum speed over Mach 2 (1,320mph, 2,128km/h).

Design of a new combat aircraft began at Dassault-Breguet in 1982 to produce a production ACT (Avion de Combat Tactique) in the 1990s to replace the Jaguar A, and a closely related ACM (Avion de Combat Marine) for deployment aboard the two new nuclear-powered carriers of the French Navy Aéronavale. At first Dassault-Breguet did not wish to proceed too quickly with a next-generation fighter that threatened to compete with the company's Mirage 2000, whose international marketing might thereby have been adversely affected. The emergence of a major international market for a future European Fighter Aircraft (FEFA) triggered a sudden decision to compete with British Aerospace and build a technology demonstrator, in the hope that this might even enable the Paris-based company to gain a commanding position in a future collaborative programme.

At first Dassault-Breguet claimed that, as it had "unquestioned leadership in delta-wing fighters", and an "unequalled record in international sales", therefore it should be awarded clear project leadership, 46 per cent by value of the entire multinational programme and the ability to dictate the design according to the requirements of the Armée de l'Air and Aéronavale. It also insisted that a collaborative programme should not "add to the time or cost". After much unpublished discussion, part of which hinged on the obvious fact that the other four nations – Britain, Germany, Italy and Spain – might just go ahead on their own, Dassault-Breguet has predictably eased its demands, reportedly to a programme share of 25 per cent but it still wants "programme leadership". This is a childish notion, because Panavia has demonstrated that the concept of one partner being able to overrule the others is unworkable. On the entire Tornado programme every decision was talked through until all partners were in agreement that they had arrived at the correct or best choice, and it must be the same in the FEFA programme.

ACX was announced at the 1983 Paris show, and a model was displayed showing a configuration very similar to the BAe P.110 of 1981, with a broad kinked-delta wing with square tips, large single fin, twin engines fed by curved inlets on the flanks of the fuselage, and large swept canard foreplanes mounted above the inlets just to the rear of the cockpit and above the level of the wing. The landing gears retract into the fuselage, the main units having narrow track and the nose gear twin wheels. Inlets have conical centrebodies larger than those of Mirages, translating in and out with variation in Mach number (the BAe EAP has a chin inlet with a hinged lower lip).

Though France does not yet have experience with advanced digital systems, the Mirage 2000 does have CCV aerodynamics controlled by a quad FBW system without manual reversion, and this has provided valuable experience. The ACX will go as far as current technology permits, and is to have fibre-optic data transmission (FBL, fly by light) over selected circuits, as well as (it is hoped) voice-activated controls as now being pioneered by USAF Aeronautical Systems Division. The cockpit will have three head-down MFDs and an advanced Thomson-CSF HUD.

The wing, which in an eventual ACM would fold at the kink, will have full-span slats and three-section flaperons on each trailing edge. The canards will be primary flight controls, and the company has suggested the embodiment of anti-turbulence ride control (though this may not fly at the start of ACX flight testing). Structure naturally includes advanced Kevlar and graphite composites, and in 1985 the Armée de l'Air Chief of Staff, Gen Capillon, was shown the "side of the pilot's seat, internal structure of the central tank and titanium elements in the wing slats" as advanced structural parts. He was also shown the "areas especially dense in equipment: main landing gear bays, accessory gearbox zone, engine compartment, air conditioning, radio bays and the fairing from canopy to tail". Defence Minister Charles Hernu also visited St Cloud to see the mockup and progress with the actual aircraft, a new model showing Magic AAMs carried on wingtip rails far ahead of the lading edge. Gen Capillon "was impressed by the determination of the manufacturer to develop the smallest possible aircraft, to comply with the wishes of the French air force"; in fact the announced span is greater than that for the British EAP and length about 3ft (1m) greater.

Right: The ACX mockup. Dassault-Breguet has a second string to its bow in the proposed ACM (Avion de Combat Marin) for equipping France's two big nuclear-powered aircraft carriers now entering construction. No other European country has a conventional (non-STOVL) carrier, so France is likely to try to reject any FEFA not based on its own Rafale/ACM.

RWR (front and rear)

Low-voltage formation light

Very large fin

Anti-collision beacon

Powered rudder

Brake chute

ACX

AMD-BA

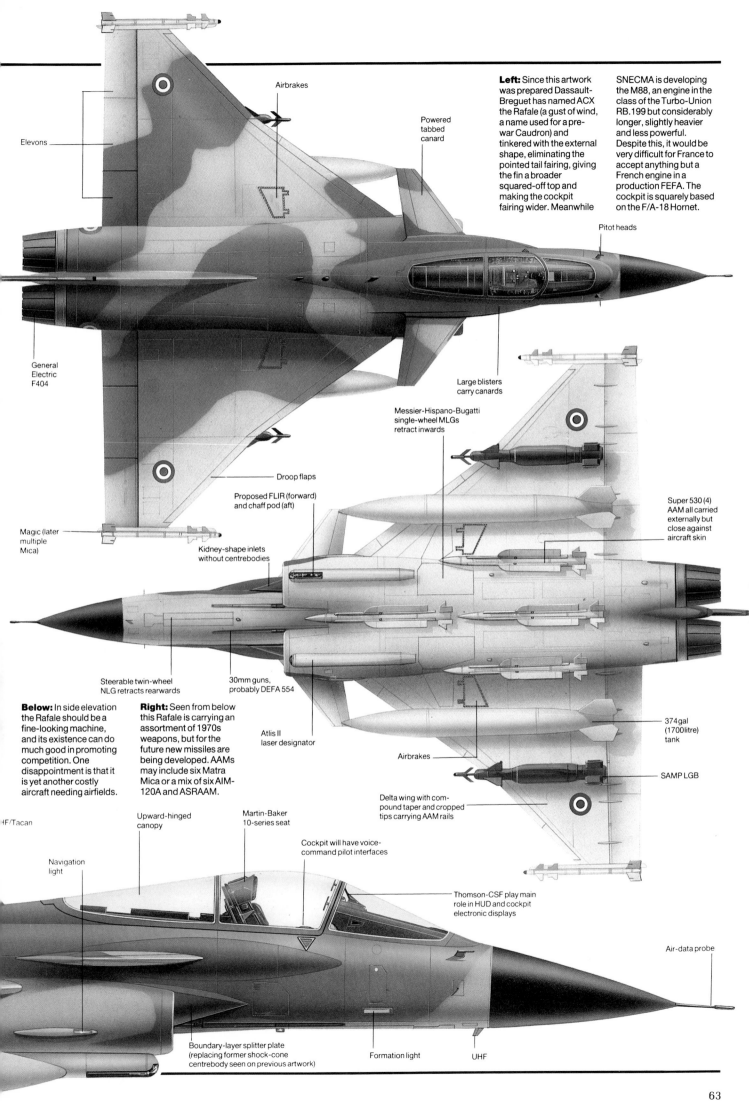

Elevons

Airbrakes

Powered tabbed canard

Left: Since this artwork was prepared Dassault-Breguet has named ACX the Rafale (a gust of wind, a name used for a pre-war Caudron) and tinkered with the external shape, eliminating the pointed tail fairing, giving the fin a broader squared-off top and making the cockpit fairing wider. Meanwhile

SNECMA is developing the M88, an engine in the class of the Turbo-Union RB.199 but considerably longer, slightly heavier and less powerful. Despite this, it would be very difficult for France to accept anything but a French engine in a production FEFA. The cockpit is squarely based on the F/A-18 Hornet.

Pitot heads

General Electric F404

Large blisters carry canards

Messier-Hispano-Bugatti single-wheel MLGs retract inwards

Droop flaps

Super 530 (4) AAM all carried externally but close against aircraft skin

Magic (later multiple Mica)

Proposed FLIR (forward) and chaff pod (aft)

Kidney-shape inlets without centrebodies

Steerable twin-wheel NLG retracts rearwards

30mm guns, probably DEFA 554

Atlis II laser designator

374gal (1700litre) tank

Airbrakes

SAMP LGB

Below: In side elevation the Rafale should be a fine-looking machine, and its existence can do much good in promoting competition. One disappointment is that it is yet another costly aircraft needing airfields.

Right: Seen from below this Rafale is carrying an assortment of 1970s weapons, but for the future new missiles are being developed. AAMs may include six Matra Mica or a mix of six AIM-120A and ASRAAM.

Delta wing with compound taper and cropped tips carrying AAM rails

UHF/Tacan

Upward-hinged canopy

Martin-Baker 10-series seat

Cockpit will have voice-command pilot interfaces

Navigation light

Thomson-CSF play main role in HUD and cockpit electronic displays

Air-data probe

Boundary-layer splitter plate (replacing former shock-cone centrebody seen on previous artwork)

Formation light

UHF

N/D 102

Type: Study for advanced fighter aircraft.
Engines: Two 13,550lb (6,146kg) Pratt &
Whitney PW1120 turbojets.
Dimensions: No precise details published,
but span about 27ft (8.2m) and length about
50ft (15.2m).
Weights: Not published except "in the
25,000lb (11,340kg) class".
Performance: Maximum speed about
Mach 2 (1,320mph, 2,128km/h).

Though not as big as MBB, nor a member of
a consortium such as Panavia, Dornier
GmbH is one of the most high-technology
companies in West Germany. It has been
prepared to spend substanial sums of its
own money in a seven-year study of future
fighters to replace the F-4F Phantoms of the
Luftwaffe in about 1995. It has a large staff
of research engineers, and has deeply
explored CCV technology, active control
technology, direct side force controls
(using an Alpha Jet research vehicle, which
of course is in part a Dornier aircraft) and
many technical aspects of the ideal flight

control system. Partly as a research tool,
but also very seriously as a proposed future
fighter, Dornier teamed with Northrop
Corporation Aircraft Group to design a
fighter smaller and lighter than most rival
proposals, and thus affordable in greater
quantity. Submitted as a JF 90 (previously
TKF 90) contender for Luftwaffe consideration, it was revealed at the 1983 Paris airshow as the N/D 102.

Though it has a few obvious Dornier
features, the N/D 102 also immediately
betrays the identity of the US partner,
notably in the wing, inlets and overlying
Cobra-style LEX (leading-edge extensions).
Its most striking feature is that it has
neither a horizontal tail nor a canard, and
while tailless deltas are not uncommon it is
most unusual to find a tailless fighter with
an almost conventional wing planform.
The wing profile is in part supercritical,
Dornier being a leading exponent of such
technology. Details of wing movable surfaces were not visible on the displayed
model, but comprise full-span flaps along

both leading and trailing edes, the trailing
surfaces being also used for roll control.
Unstable in CCV manner, the N/D 102
would be controlled by a quad FBW system
and in the pitching plane would use
vectored engine thrust as well as wing
camber.

Dornier drew attention to the fact that
here was a fighter light and small enough to
need no afterburners. Not only does this
itself reduce cost and weight, and make a

JF90

Type: Project for advanced multimission
fighter.
Engines: Two advanced Turbo-Union
RB199 augmented turbofans.
Dimensions: Span about 36ft (11m); length
about 49ft (15m); wing area about 560sq ft
(52m^2).
Weights: Empty about 17,600lb (8,000kg);
maximum about 35,000lb (16,000kg).
Performance: Maximum speed, clean, over
Mach 1 at low level, over Mach 2
(1,320mph, 2,128km/h) at high altitude.

Though the Helicopter and Military Aircraft Group of Federal Germany's biggest
aircraft company has never seriously enter-
tained the idea of going ahead on its own, it
has for many years studied new fighter
configurations which might replace the
Luftwaffe's F-4Fs in the 1990s. At first
these were true multirole machines
generally known as the TKF 90 (tactical
combat aircraft for 1990), but since 1980
the emphasis – following the temporary
fashion, rather than an objective assessment of requirements - has swung in favour
of dogfight type air-combat aircraft, known
as JF 90 (fighter for 1990).

From early in the studies the favoured
configuration has been the currently
popular canard delta with a kinked leading
edge and wing geometry varied in profile
instead of in plan. All published artwork
and models have twin canted tails above
twin engines, and for reasons of inlet
efficiency, particularly at high AOA, MBB
has looked to a rectangular chin inlet.
Whether this choice would be modified in
the light of stealth technology has not been
made public.

At the start of TKF 90 the company was
working closely with its Panavia partners,
BAe and Aeritalia, but though a few

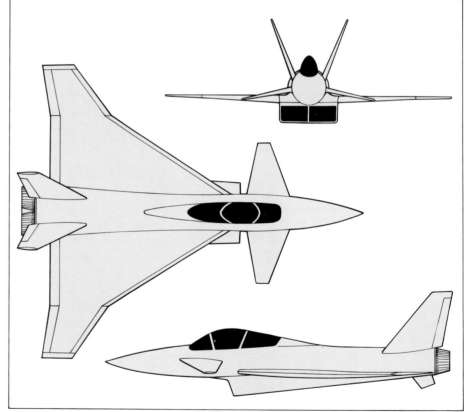

Above: In some
respects, the German
MBB scheme for a JF 90
has strong resemblance
to the MiG-29, the main
difference being that
hundreds of the Soviet
fighter already exist. The
dominance of the engine
inlet is almost certainly
exaggerated, and whilst
this geometry is excellent
for the engine at all flight
angles of attack, it is also

extremely bad from the
stealth viewpoint. Aircraft
designers from now on
will be forced to accept
often very severe
penalties in flight
performance, weight and
even cost to achieve the
highest possible
"invisibility" at all
electromagnetic
wavelengths, including
optical (visual) and IR
(heat emission).

Right: A JF 90 carrying
four Sparrows or AIM-
120A Amraam missiles
along the body chines
and Sidewinders on the
wingtips. This shows the
almost total coincidence
of thought with BAe
Warton, whose EAP
originally was almost
identical (but is being
built with an existing
single vertical tail). It may
be that, by the time the

1990s come, AAMs will
seldom be carried
externally. The author
feels the currently
fashionable fighter,
which has to have two
engines fed by a chin
inlet, a canard and broad
kinked delta wings, is
merely a passing phase
which will gradually
disappear because of its
inability to meet basic
survival requirements.

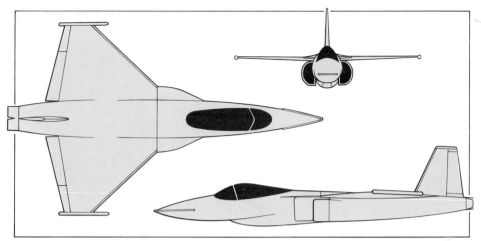

Left: Though the N/D 102 has practically no chance of being built, its design gives several useful pointers to fighters cheaper to build and operate than those more generally considered fashionable. This model showed that even such a small fighter could carry four AIM-120A missiles side-by-side recessed under the fuselage. The bulge just ahead of the missiles could cover reconnaissance systems or forward-firing guns.

Above: Three-view of the N/D 102 as it was originally planned. Since 1983 the design has been further refined, and without disclosing classified technology Northrop has introduced stealth features (it was already good in this respect). Computer studies suggest that this tailless and canardless configuration could outperform most existing fighters. Northrop really needs a new fighter programme.

major difference to fuel burn, but it makes it easier to fit vectoring nozzles. In discussion with Dornier designers it was learned – as must eventually be appreciated everywhere – Dornier believe in using directed engine thrust in whatever ways are possible to achieve pitch pointing, direct lift control and all the other new degrees of freedom practised (without vectored thrust) by the AFTI/F-16. It is certainly remarkable that a company so competent in fighter design for maximum agility should have done away with any auxiliary horizontal surface.

The model showed four AIM-120A Amraam missiles recessed under the belly – indicative of cunning "out and down" extension of the main gears – and a prominent bulge which deepens the fuselage below the cockpit. This is needed for aerodynamic, electronic and systems reasons, and also fits in with nose landing gear geometry. Air inlets are related to those of the F-18L, though LEXC/bleed geometry is quite different.

engineers are still based at Warton MBB has distanced itself from a joint project in order to preserve an impartial approach regarding Dassault-Breguet. Unfortunately there is still much disparity of opinion within the Federal German government and Lutfwaffe on precisely what is needed, one powerful faction having favoured a lower-cost fighter in the 25,000 (11,340kg) class.

Whatever is actually agreed, if anything, MBB continues to provide itself with knowledge of CCV unstable flight vehicles with a much-modified F-104G, originally built by the company over 20 years previously and recently fitted with a destabilizing fin and canard foreplane above the forward fuselage, together with totally new flight-control systems, autopilot and associated computer and software. Phase III testing was complete in 1983 and explored aircraft handling throughout the flight envelope including flight with manually switched emergency software programmes and, in extreme cases, mechanical emergency control systems. Since early 1984 Phase IV testing has been exploring completely new possibilities using an integrated digital autopilot with very advanced software, as well as two laser inertial systems, one by Honeywell and the other by Litton/Litef.

All this work is directly relevant to JF 90, which it is hoped will be built as the German designation of a multinational programme. As this is written the British EAP demonstrator aircraft is virtually indistinguishable from current MBB thinking on what is needed, apart from the fact that to save money it omits numerous items which would be required in a production aircraft.

LAVI

Type: Close-support fighter.
Engine: One 20,680lb (9,380kg) Pratt &
Whitney PW1120 afterburning turbojet.
Dimensions: Span 28ft 6.9in (8.71m);
length 47ft 2.53in (14.39m); height 17ft
3.88in (5.28m); wing area 349.8sq ft
(32.5m^2).
Weights: Empty about 15,500lb (7,031kg);
takeoff clean 21,305lb (9,664kg); maximum
37,500lb (17,010kg).
Performance: Maximum speed, clean
(high altitude) 1,221mph (1,964km/h) or
Mach 1.85; low attack speed with eight
750lb (340kg) bombs and two AAMs
619mph (997km/h).

If the world was impressed by IAI's capability of creating (admittedly out of the
Mirage) the excellent Kfir, it must have
been amazed when Israel announced the
Lavi ("young lion"). A totally indigenous
design, though with tremendous engineering assistance in many parts of the aircraft
by US industry, the Lavi appeared an impossibly large task for a still small and very
young aircraft industry.

The USA's Grumman Aerospace designed the complete main wing and is
delivering the first 50 shipsets. Like most
other aerodynamic surfaces this surface is
almost entirely graphite (carbon) epoxy
composite material. The list of US suppliers to the Lavi programme almost reads
like a who's who of the US industry, and
this has (at least for the time being) given
the USA political control of the project.
This control was suddenly made visible
when the US State Department prohibited
"technology transfer" to Israel, but sanc-
tioned only the export of finished parts.

Far more than most of the new fighters,
the Lavi is planned primarily as a close-
support attack and interdiction aircraft, to
replace the Skyhawk from 1990. Air combat capability is expected to be chiefly
self-defence during penetration of hostile
airspace, and the thrust/weight ratio at
maximum weight of 0.55 shows that the
designers have not fallen for the fashionable "agile dogfighter" class of aircraft. At
the same time 0.55 compares with only 0.4
for a typical Skyhawk, and combined with
an extremely close-coupled canard configuration with large surface areas the Lavi
will have manoeuvrability in a different
class from its predecessor. Indeed it is expected to out-turn a Phantom, and except at
very high weights to have better acceleration, partly because of the fast-spooling
engines, which were originally developed
by Pratt & Whitney for the Israeli aircraft.

In some respects the Lavi configuration
resembles that of the EAP/ACA/JF 90 in
Europe, though it is a smaller aircraft,
similar in weight but with half the engine
power. This alone underscores the different emphasis put on fighting and attack
by the two design teams.

Construction of five prototypes (reportedly including three tandem two-seat
versions) was authorised in early 1982. A
detailed mock-up was revealed in early
1985, and first flight is hoped to take place
in February 1986, with production deliveries due in 1989. The Heyl Ha'Avir is
reported to have a requirement for 300
Lavis – if inflation permits their purchase –
including some 60 two-seat trainers with
combat capability. Deliveries will build up
to 30 to 36 per year, to replace first the

Skyhawks and then the Kfirs. Despite the
US sanctions on technology Israel Aircraft
Industries is determined to acquire self-
sufficiency in advanced composites and
has established a new subsidiary company,
MMCA Ltd., specifically to manufacture
such parts in the Lavi programme.

The inlet is based on that of the F-16 and
has no variable features. Internal fuel in
fuselage and integral wings adds up to
732gal (3,330 litres), with the option of
adding a remarkable 1,121gal (5,095 litres)
externally for ferrying. There is no announced inflight refuelling facility, though
this appears certain to be included (probably with a probe).The radar is the very
latest design from Elta, derived from the
M-2021B and now on test in a Phantom. It
has a coherent transmitter and stable
multichannel receiver for such modes as
the TWS (track while scan) and look down/
shoot down (though this is a secondary
function). High-resolution mapping can be
enhanced by DBS (doppler beam sharpening), and the programmable signal processor, backed by a network of smaller
embedded computers, is expected to give
great flexibility for power management,
updating of algorithms (computing procedures) and future growth.

Main navigation system will be inertial,
a field in which Israeli industry already has
appreciable experience (originally relying
on a Singer Kearfott licence in the Kfir
programme). Lear-Siegler is the chief back-
stop for the quad-redundant digital FBW
flight control system, the reversionary system being not manual but electronic analog.

Altogether there is no reason to doubt
that the Lavi will perform as advertised.

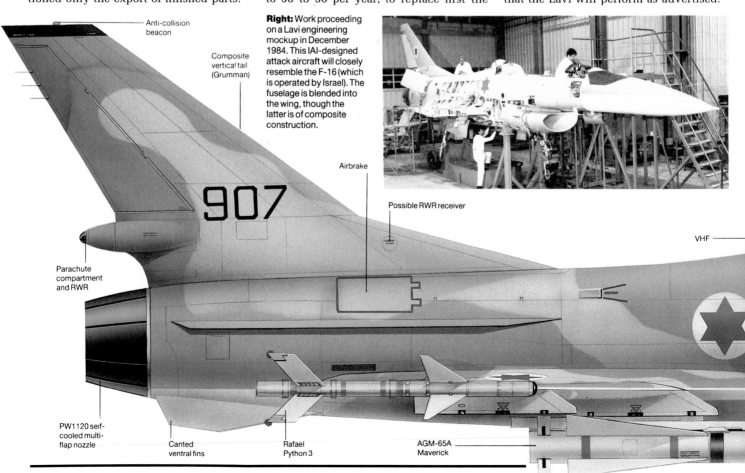

Anti-collision
beacon

Composite
vertical tail
(Grumman)

Right: Work proceeding
on a Lavi engineering
mockup in December
1984. This IAI-designed
attack aircraft will closely
resemble the F-16 (which
is operated by Israel). The
fuselage is blended into
the wing, though the
latter is of composite
construction.

907

Airbrake

Possible RWR receiver

VHF

Parachute
compartment
and RWR

PW1120 self-
cooled multi-
flap nozzle

Canted
ventral fins

Rafael
Python 3

AGM-65A
Maverick

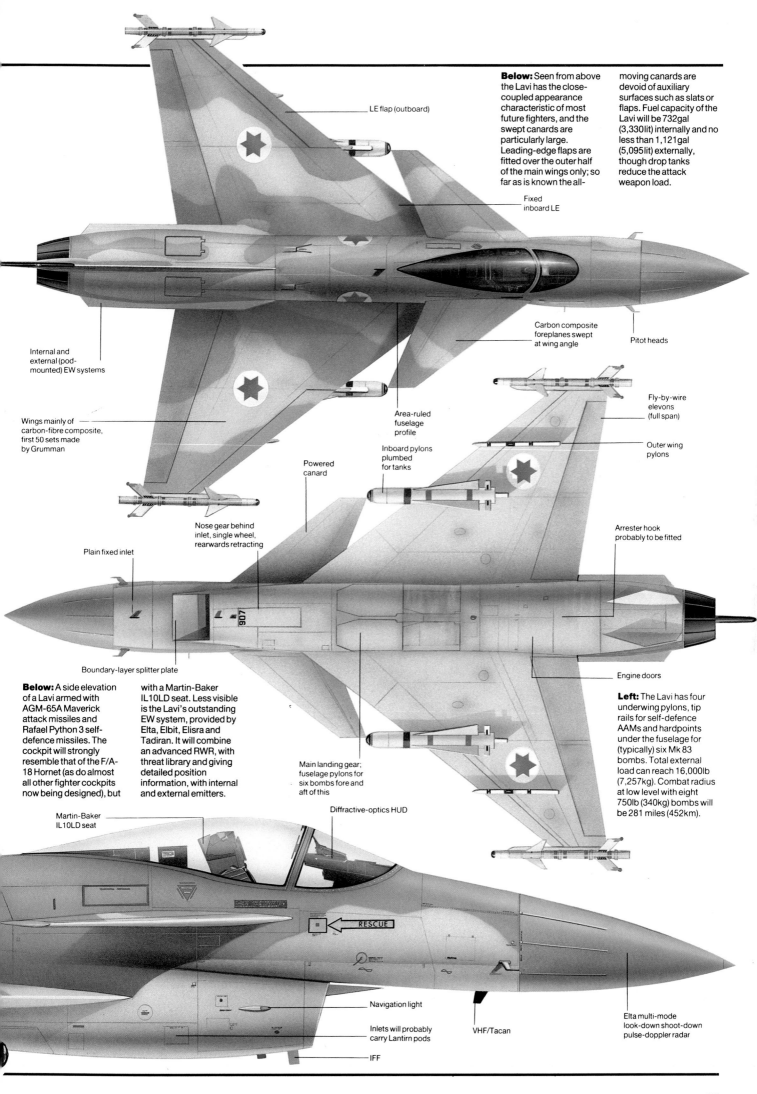

LE flap (outboard)

Below: Seen from above the Lavi has the close-coupled appearance characteristic of most future fighters, and the swept canards are particularly large. Leading-edge flaps are fitted over the outer half of the main wings only; so far as is known the all-moving canards are devoid of auxiliary surfaces such as slats or flaps. Fuel capacity of the Lavi will be 732gal (3,330lit) internally and no less than 1,121gal (5,095lit) externally, though drop tanks reduce the attack weapon load.

Fixed inboard LE

Internal and external (pod-mounted) EW systems

Carbon composite foreplanes swept at wing angle

Pitot heads

Wings mainly of carbon-fibre composite, first 50 sets made by Grumman

Area-ruled fuselage profile

Fly-by-wire elevons (full span)

Powered canard

Inboard pylons plumbed for tanks

Outer wing pylons

Nose gear behind inlet, single wheel, rearwards retracting

Arrester hook probably to be fitted

Plain fixed inlet

Boundary-layer splitter plate

Engine doors

Below: A side elevation of a Lavi armed with AGM-65A Maverick attack missiles and Rafael Python 3 self-defence missiles. The cockpit will strongly resemble that of the F/A-18 Hornet (as do almost all other fighter cockpits now being designed), but with a Martin-Baker IL10LD seat. Less visible is the Lavi's outstanding EW system, provided by Elta, Elbit, Elisra and Tadiran. It will combine an advanced RWR, with threat library and giving detailed position information, with internal and external emitters.

Main landing gear; fuselage pylons for six bombs fore and aft of this

Left: The Lavi has four underwing pylons, tip rails for self-defence AAMs and hardpoints under the fuselage for (typically) six Mk 83 bombs. Total external load can reach 16,000lb (7,257kg). Combat radius at low level with eight 750lb (340kg) bombs will be 281 miles (452km).

Diffractive-optics HUD

Martin-Baker IL10LD seat

RESCUE

Navigation light

VHF/Tacan

Inlets will probably carry Lantirn pods

Elta multi-mode look-down shoot-down pulse-doppler radar

IFF

F-19 STEALTH AIRCRAFT

Type: Reconnaissance/strike aircraft.
Engines: Two jet engines in 12,000lb (5,443kg) class, reportedly GE 404 unaugmented turbofans.
Dimensions: Span probably about 33ft (10m); length about 56ft (17m); height about 12ft (3.6m); wing area about 550sq ft (51m²).
Weights: Empty possibly 15,000lb (6,800kg); maximum possibly 30,000lb (13,600kg).
Performance: Maximum speed probably supersonic except at low level; radius (high altitude) probably over 500 miles (800km).

Technically one of the world's most interesting aircraft, the so-called Lockheed F-19 also goes under the acronym COSIRS, from COvert Survivable In-weather Reconnaissance Strike. This explains its mission, but not its place in history as the first low-observables, or stealth, manned aircraft to go into service anywhere. It is yet another of the amazing products of Lockheed Aircraft Corporation's highly secure Skunk Works at Burbank, founded and directed for many years by Clarence L. "Kelly" Johnson. Today this is officially Lockheed Advanced Aeronautics Co., and its president is Johnson's able aide (chief of propulsion systems on the U-2 and A-12/SR-71), Ben Rich.

Practically nothing has appeared on the record about COSIRS, and unlike the Northrop ATB – another classified low-observables programme – it has never appeared in the annual list of ASD (USAF Aeronautical Systems Division) projects published by the *Air Force Magazine* in Washington. Writing in the same magazine in early 1985, John W. R. Taylor reported: "People living around Burbank Airport tell of C-5 Galaxy transports that land at night, pick up well-wrapped shapes from the Lockheed plant, and whisk them off to a heavily guarded top-secret airfield in the Nevada desert." The *Baltimore Sun* newspaper has reported that "between 300 and 400 of the Lockheed Stealth fighters will be delivered, beginning in 1986-87, in a program worth $1.4 billion annually by 1988". But the aircraft did not appear in the 1984 *Statements* by top USAF personnel before any of the subcommittees of the US House of Representatives Armed Services Committee, and they covered everything else that the USAF was doing or even thinking about.

By far the most informative story was written by Bill Sweetman for a 1984 special edition of *International Defense Review*. He stated that, soon after the shock of Israelis being unable to jam SA-6 mssiles over the Sinai in 1973, the US DARPA (Defense Advanced Research Projects Agency) launched the Have Blue programme for a small stealth prototype that might be suitable for recon and strike roles. Like the entire Blackbird family (A-12/YF-12/SR-71) before it, the XST (experimental stealth tactical) flew from Groom Lake, otherwise known as The Ranch, in southeast Nevada, in 1977. Several additional XSTs, possibly including some by contrac-

tors other than Lockheed, joined the programme and were flown against US and Soviet defence systems on the Tonopah range. According to Sweetman, Lockheed received the first production contract in 1981, the initial 20 XST-derived aircraft being designated F-19. If the Baltimore newspaper is correct, many more F-19s must have been ordered since.

There is no reason why this, the pioneer low-observables aircraft, should not be a useful and uncompromised design capable of flying effective reconnaissance and strike missions. Among the profusion of other unofficial statements printed concerning it are: it is a double delta; it has a planform resembling the Space Shuttle; it is about the size of the F-18 Hornet; it is extremely quiet in flight; it is powered by two 12,000lb (5,443kg) jet engines; its contract was funded by DARPA but actually placed by the ASD Flight Dynamics Laboratory; and C-5 Galaxies will carry F-19s to bases outside the USA for operational deployment.

All these statements are plausible and probably true. For the record the only public listing of FDL major programmes in 1985 is: AFTI/F-16; X-29; STOL/manoeuvre technology; the GD/Martin Marietta

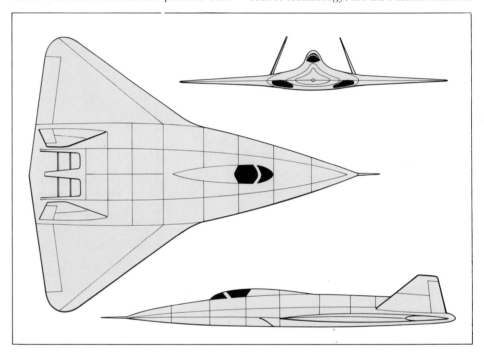

Above: This three-view is loosely based on drawings which appeared in *International Defense Review* in 1984. The layout is very plausible, and shows obvious kinship with the A-12 family previously produced by "The Skunk Works" and which were designed for Mach numbers exceeding 3 – most unlikely to have been the case with the F-19. Configurations of this shape gain enormously from body lift at high supersonic speeds and also at high AOA.

Below: A contrasting alternative configuration for an F-19-type aircraft showing less-reflective dorsal inlets. Stealth design is already requiring a massive upsurge in fundamental aerodynamic research, some of it contracted to universities and NASA. The author is convinced that vertical tails should be replaced by vectored engine nozzles, which can still be shielded from ground observers. It also helps if cockpit canopies can be replaced by synthetic vision.

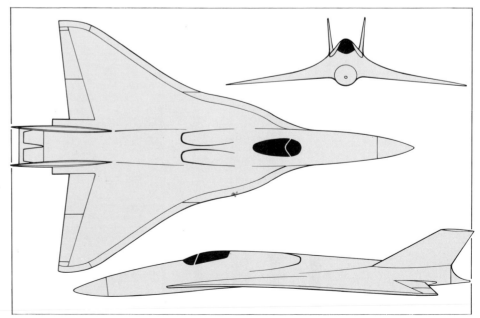

strategic boost/glide vehicle; and the F-111 MAW (mission-adaptive wing).

The accompanying illustrations are unofficial, of course, and the source of each is named. The ones that accompanied Sweetman's article had "flush ventral air inlets". The drawing by the author suggests dorsal inlets simply on the score of low observability. There are, of course, further ways of reducing the observability of such an aircraft at all wavelengths. One is to eliminate the canopy and give the pilot exterior vision inside the cockpit. This is perfectly feasible, and as the pilot could select the sensor wavelength his view in bad weather or at night would be much better than through a canopy. Another obvious possibility is to replace the vertical tails by reaction control jets using engine bleed air, as on the hovering Harrier. It will be noted that the engines, which have no afterburners or other boost system, discharge their quite cool jets through nozzles shielded from observation from below. There is no reason why a similar shroud should not shield the nozzles from an IR sensor carried in an interceptor high above.

In the strike role some or all of the F-19's weapons could be expected to be carried internally. This happens to reduce drag but it also reduces internal fuel capacity, so heavy weapon loads are not to be expected. The author's drawing suggests a nose radar, but this is the last thing a covert stealth aircraft wishes to use, and there is little point in carrying it if it is never switched on. Inertial navigation, astro tracking, passive IR reception, RWR installations, TV and human eyes are all fine, but anything that emits detectable radiation is taboo, or the whole objective of stealth is negated.

Of course, the one thing that appears quite beyond the capability of contemporary technology is to propel a fast aeroplane by engines that emit no easily detectable heat. The F-19 has been verbally described to the author as "a thousand times less detectable by IR than, say, an F-15". This sounds great, but when one considers the IR emission plot for an F-15, dividing it by even 1,000 still seems to leave enough for today's most sensitive devices to lock-on to – after all we can "detect a cigarette at 50 miles".

In due course all will be revealed. Lockheed have certainly not bungled the F-19, because the company – probably Lockheed Missiles & Space Co., a different outfit located at Sunnyvale – is now working on the first stealth cruise missile for the USAF.

Left: Some years ago Lockheed-California published this fine study of a future "supercruise" fighter with methane-fuelled vectoring engines. Apart from the inlets, this flat blended design appears to have good stealth qualities.

Below: This Lockheed monster has traditional nozzles but odd inverted inlets for stealth rather than pressure recovery. Four giant turboramjets could hardly remain undetected, even at cruise thrust!

MiG-29 "FULCRUM"

Type: All-weather multirole righter.

Engines: Two augmented turbofans (or possibly turjobjects), assumed to be related to the Tumanskii R-13 or R-29, each rated at about 20,000lb (9,000kg).

Dimensions: (Estimated) Span 33ft 8in (10.25m); length 50ft 10in (15.5m); height 17ft 2in (5.25m); wing area 360sq ft (33.4m²).

Weights: (estimated) empty about 18,000lb (8,200kg); loaded (clean) 28,000lb (12,700kg), (maximum) 36,800lb (16,700kg).

Performance: Maximum speed (clean, high altitude) 1,520mph (2,450m/h) or Mach 2.3, (sea level) 912mph (1,468km/h) or Mach 1.2; combat radius (DoD figure, conditions not stated) 500 miles (800km).

The facility with which the Soviet Union can maintain security is shown by the fact that in spring 1985 virtually nothing was known about the MiG-29, apart from a general idea of what it looks like when seen from above (in US satellite imagery). Indeed, despite the latter pictures, which must now run into thousands, the "official" published shape has kept changing, and in 1984 the estimated span was changed from 39ft 4in to 33ft 7.5in (a foolishly "pseudo-accurate" figure which here has been rounded up to the nearest inch above!). All this complete absence of hard fact applies to an aircraft that has been flying so long and in such large numbers that it is being supplied to the Indian Air Force and may soon be built under licence in that country. (If it comes to that, Hindustan Aeronautics is already in licence-production with the MiG-27M, and there is plenty the Western world still does not know about that previous-generation aircraft.)

Comparison with the MiG-27M shows the dictates of fashion in fighter design. The variable-geometry swing wing is temporarily out of favour, and the Russians have gone for aerodynamic configurations that closely follow the F-15, F-16 and F-18.

From the first hints of its existence, when it was merely a blurred image on a picture of Ramenskoye test airfield and known as Ram-L in US Department of Defense lists, this aircraft has been regarded with considerable respect. It has always been described as having outstanding manoeuvrability, and a few years ago there was a story that Britain had a ciné film of it showing manoeuvres that no F-16 could emulate. It was also said to have full lookdown shoot-down capability, which at present the F-16 lacks. For the past 50 years the Soviet Union has been second to none in aircraft cannon.

Further uncertainty surrounds the tail. Several Western drawings, including the most recent ones published by DoD in Washington, show twin outward-canted fins mounted on the fuselage above the engines. The latest artwork, however, shows an arrangement much more like the F-15, with the fins mounted on cantilever booms alongside the engines, and carrying swept tailplanes extended well aft of the engine nozzles. Recent drawings show the engines well separated, even at the nozzles, indicating considerable internal capacity for fuel, APU, systems, avionics and possibly weapons.

The Soviet Union has an unparalleled range of AAMs, though most are much larger and heavier than Western missiles of equivalent range and capability (that is if Western assessments are not self-deluding). Standard kit of the MiG-29 is said to be six missiles, though it is uncertain whether this means six medium/long range AA-10 weapons or (as interpreted by most observers) four of these and two dogfight missiles such as "AA-8 Aphid" (whose true designation is reported as R-60). Some artists have shown the latter on wingtip launchers, but these are absent from the latest interpretations. Just how the larger AAMs are carried is anybody's guess; the DoD has shown underwing pylons, but it would be sensible for low-drag conformal carriage along the flanks of the fuselage to

have been adopted, if not internal stowage along the bottom of the inter-engine space.

No designation for this fighter has been known other than the VVS (air force) one of MiG-29. The NATO reporting name is "Fulcrum". The standard machine is a single-seater, though doubtless tandem dual versions exist which in due course could also double as "electronic combat" and multisensor reconnaissance platforms.

Wing movable surfaces are thought to comprise large-chord inboard flaps and full-span leading-edge slats or droops. If there are no other movables the primary roll control must be taileron use of the tailplanes. Thrust/weight ratio is calculated to be better than unity in all flight regimes, though fairly obviously the engines must be of a previously unknown type, smaller than the other fighter engines in recent MiGs. It is evident that, in conformity with long-established Soviet practice, the MiG-29 shares common aerodynamics with the larger Su-27, just as in the case of the MiG Ye-2A and Su-7, MiG-2l and Su-9 and MiG-23 and Su-24. In each case the Sukhoi aircraft has been on a larger scale of size, though this is probably coincidental.

From the first Washington assessments the MiG-29 has been described as an uncompromised air-superiority fighter, freed from the close ground control that was previously exerted on Soviet fighter pilots and able to operate autonomously. It has been taken for granted that the Soviet Union has from 1971 known all about the Hughes APG-63 radar fitted to the F-15, and the MiG-29 radar has been designed to outperform this. What is taken for granted is that the Russian design engineers have not been able to keep pace with their Western counterparts who have, for example, virtually duplicated the capabilities of the APG-63 in the much smaller and lighter APG-65 fitted to the F-18. Likewise the fact that Soviet AAMs may be larger or heavier than, say AIM-120A Amraam, is always taken to mean uncompetitive technology, not greater range and warhead size.

Grouped RWR/ECM/IFF aerials

Canted vertical tails resemble MiG-23/27

Right: Satellite photograph published in early 1985 in *Air Force Magazine* showing one of the first MiG-29 prototypes, probably at Ramenskoye. Overall similarity of shape to the F-15 is obvious, though the Soviet fighter is slightly smaller.

Brake chute container

Probable VHF

Widely spaced canted ventral fins

Broad tips usually have no AAM rails

Vertical tails are mounted on structural beams outboard of engines

LE manoeuvring variable-camber flaps

Below: Looking down the artist can get most of the details right, because this is the aspect seen by satellites. No gun is shown, though it was suggested unofficially in the West in early 1985 that the MiG-29 has two guns in the tops of the long wing root

extensions. The twin vertical tails are very far apart, and like the tailerons (tailplanes) are almost certainly attached to structural beams on the outer sides of the engines as was done in designing the F-15. Certainly the F-15 greatly influenced the Soviet

designers, but whereas both the F-15 and MiG-29 were originally designed as uncompromised air-combat fighters, both are now multirole aircraft, with what the Defense Department calls "swing force" capability (air/air or air/ground).

Large fixed LE root extensions

Two guns believed to be installed above inner wings

Possible airbrakes above and below

Dorsal spine above tankage between engines

Possible AS-7 Kerry ASM (AS-10 and other types also carried)

Possible ailerons

Broad-chord flaps, probably with spoilers upstream

AA-2-2 Advanced Atoll shown on pylons under inlet ducts: normal load said to be six AA-10

Possible doppler radar

Air-data instrumentation boom

Twin-wheel NLG bay with ground access to maintenance panels

Single-wheel MLG bay doors

Below: Bearing in mind that satellite surveillance is from above, it is easy to understand the years of uncertainty concerning the MiG-29's engine inlets, weapon carriage and all other factors on the underside. The

artwork on these pages is believed to be more accurate than any published previously. Certainly the more we in the West learn about the MiG-29, the better it is seen to be. It could be the best there is.

Above: Standard air/air armament is said to be six of the new AA-10. This missile's configuration is classified and the inner wing pylons here are mere guesses. Body air-to-air missiles are Atolls.

Outboard wing pylons (usually AA-10, as yet unknown in West)

Graphite-epoxy slab tailerons project well aft of jetpipes

Root extension alongside cockpit

Main multimode "look-down shoot-down" radar with all-round access

Oblique sharp-lipped inlets far below bottom line of fuselage

MIKOYAN-GUREVICH
MiG-31 "FOXHOUND"

Type: All-weather interceptor.
Engines: Two large augmented turbojets (very unlikely to be turbofans), probably 30,865lb (14,000kg) Tumanskii R-13F.
Dimensions: (Estimated) Span 45ft 11.2in (14m); length 82ft 0in (25m); height 20ft (6.1m); wing area 624sq ft (58m²).
Weights: (Estimated) Empty 48,115lb (21,825kg); maximum 90,725lb (41,150kg).
Performance: (Estimated) Maximum speed, clean (high altitude) 1,586mph (2,553km/h) or Mach 2.4; combat radius (conditions not stated) 930 miles (1,500km).

When the MiG-25 appeared in the late 1960s it was considered such a specialised type that it was expected to remain a rare "oddball" in PVO (air defence forces) regiments. It was originally designed to intercept the Mach-3 XB-70 Valkyrie, and when this bomber was cancelled there did not seem (to Western observers) much point in building the MiG-25, a fantastically fast fighter which burns enormous quantities of fuel and has to travel in straight lines. Any attempt to turn results in the greatest-radius turn in history, unless speed is allowed to bleed right off.

It was therefore surprising when the defecting Lt Viktor Belyenko said in 1976 that the familiar MiG-25 "Foxbat" was the subject of major update programmes, which eventually resulted in emergence of so-called "Foxbat-E", or MiG-25M, with uprated engines and various improved avionics, notably including a new radar with "limited look-down shoot-down capability".

Belyenko also said that the MiG-25M had been strengthened to permit supersonic flight at low altitudes. The design load factor of the original MiG-25 had been quite low; it was for this reason, as well as for the extremely high speed and exceptionally high wing-loading, that it had such poor power of manoeuvre, and at low levels it was restricted to speeds in the order of

575mph (925km/h), slower than a fully loaded Tornado. The MiG-25 was thus a perfect candidate for conversion as a reconnaissance aircraft, and might have some merit in the high-altitude Elint and EW roles, but did not seem a very good basis for a next-generation fighter for use against all aerial targets including those flying at minimum altitude. Nevertheless, the MiG design bureau has worked on the MiG-26, or Ye-26 family, and by about 1978 must have been well into test flying what is now believed to have the VVS (air force) designation of MiG-31. Remarkably, not a word appears to have leaked out, and when the Washington DoD announced its reporting name as "Foxhound" in 1983 it added that this fighter was already in full production and being deployed with fighter regiments.

The DoD also said the MiG-31 was "The first Soviet fighter to have true look-down shoot-down capability". Such a capability seems to have been a fixation with Western analysts, who have ascribed its possession to four Soviet aircraft previously, though sometimes with the prefix "limited" or "partial". Why the Soviet radar designers should have found the development of pulse-doppler radars so difficult has not been explained; certainly an examination of the MiG-25 radar may have given Washington a falsely jaundiced view of Soviet capabilities, because this 1959 set is contemporary with the APQ-72 fire control fitted to the first Phantoms. Be that as it may, there is no longer any doubt in the Pentagon's collective mind, and the full "shoot down" capability is said to be possessed by the MiG-31. It is also credited with having remarkable combat persistence, for its normal weapon load is said to be "eight AAMs". These are said to include a new radar-guided weapon dubbed AA-9. Bearing in mind the giant size of "AA-6 Acrid" carried by the previous-generation MiG-25, the AA-9 may be expected to have considerable range capability. This would

go well with a 1970s-technology radar fitting into the vast nose of the MiG-31.

The aircraft itself is clearly a stretched MiG-25, restressed for high speeds at low level and with very much greater power of manoeuvre at all heights than its predecessor. It is partly on the score of manoeuvrability that the Mach limit has been downgraded from the MiG-25's 3.2 to a mere 2.8, though it should be remembered that in practical missions with AAMs on board this (or, to be precise, 2.83) was the authorized limit for the MiG-25. Certainly 2.8 ought to be adequate to catch anything in the sky until 1990 at least, though faster cruise missiles are clearly possible. Early MiG-31 reports also spoke of an internal gun, but this is not mentioned in post-1983 assessments.

The airframe has a wing closely resembling that of the MiG-25 but with leading-edge root extensions and apparently with rather greater sweepback. It is clearly strong enough for heavier underwing loads, and drawings show the outer pair of four large pylons carrying tanks which must each weigh at least 5,000lb (2,268kg). No real information is available on weapon carriage, and on this very fast aircraft it would be amazing if there were to be no lower-drag attachments than pylons hung under the wing.

All reports insist that the standard "Foxhound" is a tandem two-seater, the backseater probably handling the navigation, systems and electronic-warfare devices. Adding a seat is an interesting comment on an age in which new technology is making it easier for a single-seat aircraft to fly all-weather missions.

The more powerful engines are almost certainly different from those fitted to the MiG-25M (Foxbat-E). The latter has jetpipes of the original length, whereas in the MiG-31 the big variable nozzles project much further aft, almost to the point where they are beyond the line joining the trailing edges of the tailplanes. Another major change concerns the air inlets and ducts, which seem matched not only to greater airflow but also, oddly, to increased flight Mach numbers; at least, the ducts are extended forward and the sharp lips are most acutely inclined.

Production at a plant in Gorkii began not later than 1982, and the estimate was that more than 50 MiG-31s were operational by April 1984. Total numbers are unlikely to be very large.

Multiple communication and RWR/IFF aerials

Small powered rudders

Below: Like all Soviet combat aircraft "Foxhound" looks extremely fit for its purpose; but just how it looks is still partly conjectural. The fuselage is said to be "longer ahead of the wings" and to have "an extended rear section", yet most official estimates say it is shorter than the MiG-25!

Dorsal spine

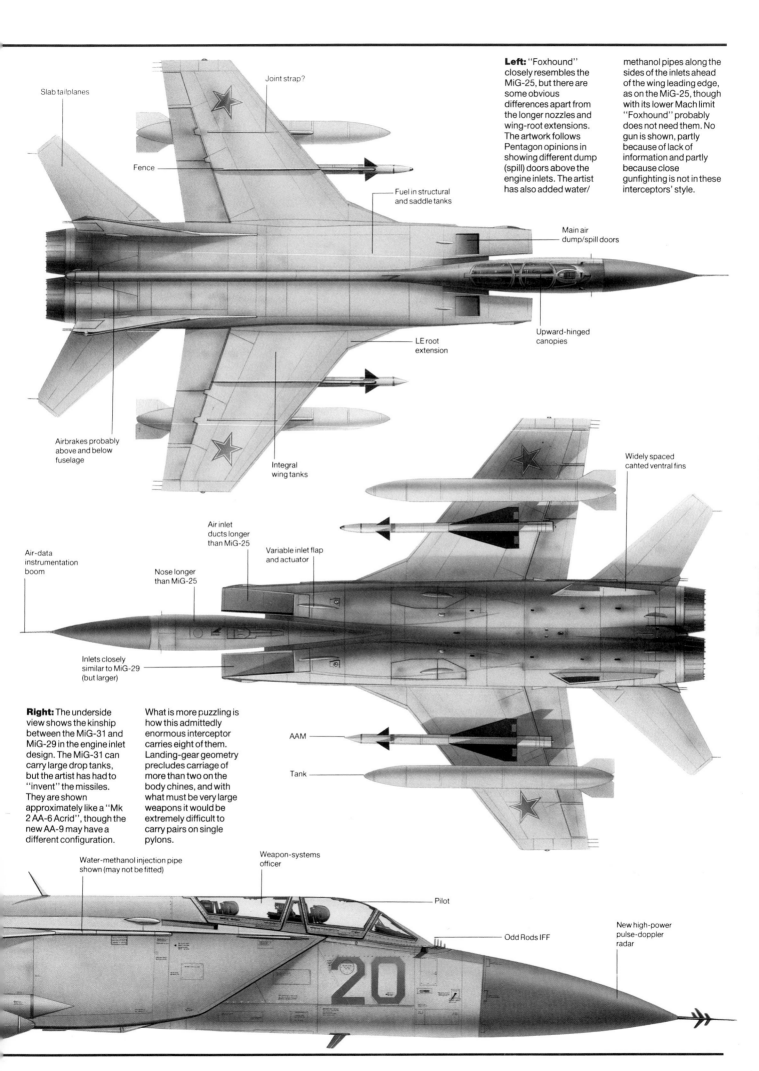

Slab tailplanes

Joint strap?

Fence

Fuel in structural and saddle tanks

Left: "Foxhound" closely resembles the MiG-25, but there are some obvious differences apart from the longer nozzles and wing-root extensions. The artwork follows Pentagon opinions in showing different dump (spill) doors above the engine inlets. The artist has also added water/ methanol pipes along the sides of the inlets ahead of the wing leading edge, as on the MiG-25, though with its lower Mach limit "Foxhound" probably does not need them. No gun is shown, partly because of lack of information and partly because close gunfighting is not in these interceptors' style.

Main air dump/spill doors

Upward-hinged canopies

LE root extension

Airbrakes probably above and below fuselage

Integral wing tanks

Widely spaced canted ventral fins

Air-data instrumentation boom

Nose longer than MiG-25

Air inlet ducts longer than MiG-25

Variable inlet flap and actuator

Inlets closely similar to MiG-29 (but larger)

Right: The underside view shows the kinship between the MiG-31 and MiG-29 in the engine inlet design. The MiG-31 can carry large drop tanks, but the artist has had to "invent" the missiles. They are shown approximately like a "Mk 2 AA-6 Acrid", though the new AA-9 may have a different configuration.

What is more puzzling is how this admittedly enormous interceptor carries eight of them. Landing-gear geometry precludes carriage of more than two on the body chines, and with what must be very large weapons it would be extremely difficult to carry pairs on single pylons.

AAM

Tank

Water-methanol injection pipe shown (may not be fitted)

Weapon-systems officer

Pilot

Odd Rods IFF

New high-power pulse-doppler radar

F-20A TIGERSHARK

Type: Multirole tactical fighter.

Engine: One 17,000lb (7,711kg) General Electric F404-100A augmented turbofan.

Dimensions: Span over empty missile rails 26ft 8in (8.13m); length 46ft 6.7in (14.9m); height 13ft 10.15in (4.22m); wing area 200sq ft (18.6m²).

Weights: Empty 11,810lb (5,357kg); loaded (clean) 18,200lb (8,255kg); maximum 27,500lb (12,474kg).

Performance: Maximum speed, clean (high altitude) over 1,323mph (2,128km/h) or Mach 2; combat radius (hi-lo-hi, five Mk 82 bombs, AAMs and two tanks, allowances for combat and reserves) 633 miles (1,019km).

The Tigershark is so good that a customer will probably eventually emerge, but as this is written in 1985 it could fairly be described as "the best fighter never bought". Originally designated F-5G, it was given the new DoD number to emphasize its dissimilarity to previous F-5s. The number does not, however, imply adoption by any of the US forces, though for a time the F-20A was shortlisted as a candidate for the US Navy Top Gun "aggressor" fleet. Northrop developed the aircraft for sale to foreign customers, like the F-5 family before it.

By far the dominant new feature of the F-20A is its engine, which is an uprated and otherwise modified derivative of the engine used in the F/A-18 Hornet. This powerplant's swift maturity, sparkling performance and oustanding reliability and maintainability spurred Northrop into going ahead in January 1980 and building three development aircraft. These flew on 30 August 1982 (with analog avionics, F-5E

canopy and Dash-400 engine), 26 August 1983 (with digital avionics and larger canopy giving improved all-round view) and 12 May 1984. The loss of one prototype in 1984 was not due to any fault in the aircraft and did not affect the development programme.

Externally the main differences compared with an F-5E are the single engine (giving 70 per cent more thrust than the twin engines used previously), redesigned inlets and LEX (leading-edge extensions), enlarged "shark nose" of flattened oval section, enlarged and raised canopy, new spine at the base of the fin with a ram-air cooling inlet at the front, revised fin cap and generally enlarged rear fuselage. Less obvious is the greater internal volume

resulting from elimination of the area ruling of the fuselage and inlet ducts across the top of the wings. Other airframe changes that might not be obvious are a general strengthening of the structure (such as thicker wing skins, especially over the inboard sections) to permit the combat load factor to be raised to 9g, a complete revision of structural methods (for example, the fin is a slab of cast aluminium with skins welded on and completed with honeycomb sandwich leading and trailing sections, while the horizontal tails are full-depth aluminium honeycomb cores with graphite/epoxy spar, ribs and skins), and, most important of all, complete revision of the systems and avionics.

Northrop had to tread a careful middle

Above: First picture of a Tigershark with Sparrow AAMs (AIM-7M on left wing and 7F on right). This aircraft actually fired the 7F, scoring a direct hit on an airborne target. Capability with these large missiles had not previously been claimed, and in fact gives the F-20A a temporary edge over the F-16 (temporary because of the development of AIM-120 AMRAAM).

UHF aerial

Tacan

IFF

Fuel jettison

Navigation lights

Anti-collision strobe light

ECM aerials on parachute doors

Ram-air cooling inlet

VHF aerial

Multi-petal nozzle of F 404-?

RWR aerials

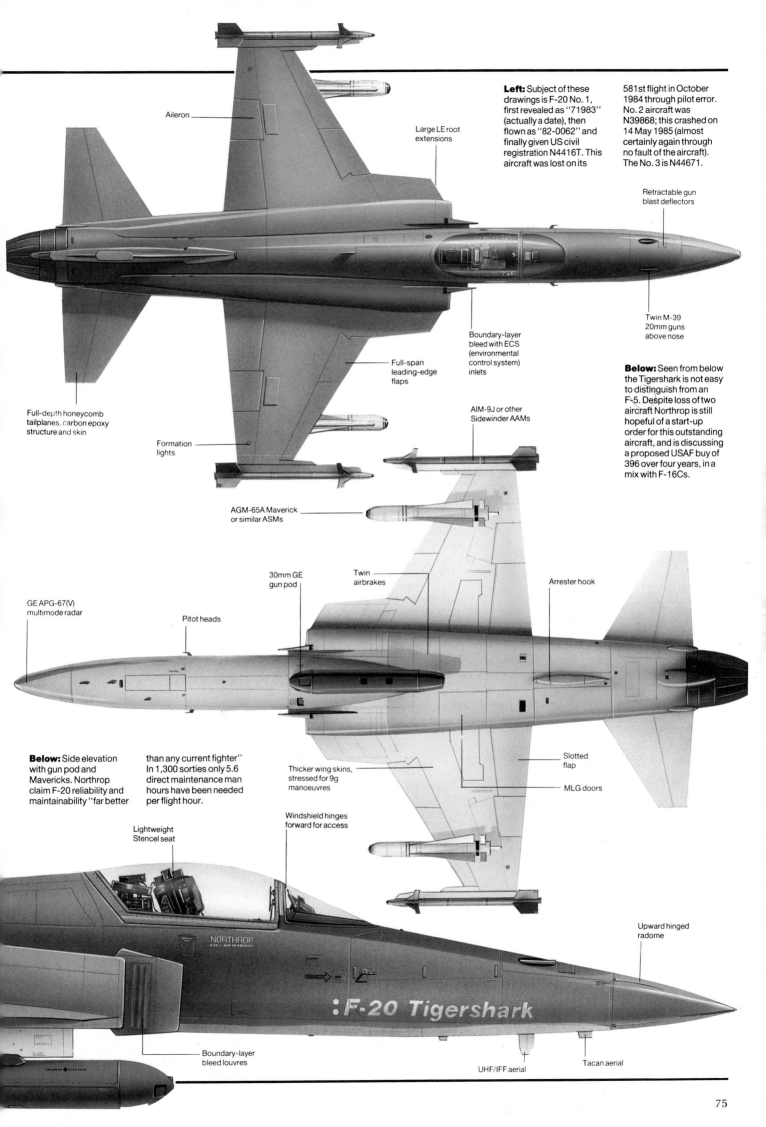

Aileron

Large LE root extensions

Left: Subject of these drawings is F-20 No. 1, first revealed as "71983" (actually a date), then flown as "82-0062" and finally given US civil registration N4416T. This aircraft was lost on its 581st flight in October 1984 through pilot error. No. 2 aircraft was N39868; this crashed on 14 May 1985 (almost certainly again through no fault of the aircraft). The No. 3 is N44671.

Retractable gun blast deflectors

Boundary-layer bleed with ECS (environmental control system) inlets

Twin M-39 20mm guns above nose

Full-span leading-edge flaps

AIM-9J or other Sidewinder AAMs

Below: Seen from below the Tigershark is not easy to distinguish from an F-5. Despite loss of two aircraft Northrop is still hopeful of a start-up order for this outstanding aircraft, and is discussing a proposed USAF buy of 396 over four years, in a mix with F-16Cs.

Full-depth honeycomb tailplanes, carbon epoxy structure and skin

Formation lights

AGM-65A Maverick or similar ASMs

GE APG-67(V) multimode radar

30mm GE gun pod

Twin airbrakes

Arrester hook

Pitot heads

Below: Side elevation with gun pod and Mavericks. Northrop claim F-20 reliability and maintainability "far better than any current fighter" In 1,300 sorties only 5.6 direct maintenance man hours have been needed per flight hour.

Thicker wing skins, stressed for 9g manoeuvres

Slotted flap

MLG doors

Windshield hinges forward for access

Lightweight Stencel seat

Upward hinged radome

NORTHROP

:F-20 Tigershark

Boundary-layer bleed louvres

UHF/IFF aerial

Tacan aerial

path in developing the Tigershark. The company recognised that it would in general have to find the development and flight-test money itself, even though since 1983 the USAF Aeronautical Systems Division of Systems Command has been involved with the programme. For this reason it wished to preserve maximum commonality with the F-5E, and this also has obvious advantages to any customer, especially one already using the F-5E. On the other hand, the whole purpose of the development was to offer a superior fighter, and there was a very strong incentive to make it as dramatically modern as possible. One team even studied the costs of major changes, such as going full-tilt into unstable CCV (control-configured vehicle) and stealth technology. The company was especially interested in stealth because it is a world leader in this field, but eventually decided to adhere fairly closely to the established F-5E Tiger shape, partly because a lot of stealth technology is classified and not usable in a product intended for export and partly on reasons of overall technical risk, cost and timing.

Any objective observer is bound to conclude that the company have got it exactly right. The F-20A is a tremendous performer, possibly the fastest-climbing fighter in the world and probably in some respects also the most agile, in both the horizontal and vertical planes. The systems and avionics are dramatically later in concept and higher in performance than those of the F-5E, and the difference in specific and overall capabilities between the F-5E and the F-20A is much greater than that between the F-5A and F-5E.

Perhaps the only surprising choice is the retention of twin M-39 20mm cannon mounted above the nose as in previous F-5s. For one thing this is now an old gun, which since retirement of the F-100 is not used by any other US fighter. Moreover the Tigershark is designed to fly at night, and the muzzle flash when the guns are fired is severe. Northrop must have studied the prospects for installing an M61 or GAU-12, the latter a new and powerful gun, in the lower part of the nose and reshuffling the nose avionics racking to accommodate the gun, the ammunition staying in the same

SAAB
JAS 39 GRIPEN

Type: All-weather multimode fighter.
Engine: One 18,000lb (8,165kg) Svenska Flygmotor RM12 augmented turbofan.
Dimensions: Span 26ft 3in (8.0m); length 45ft 11in (14.0m); height and wing area not finalised.
Weights: Empty, not disclosed; "normal maximum" 17,635lb (8,000kg); maximum, probably about 25,000lb (11,340kg).
Performance: Maximum speed, clean (high altitude) about 1,323mph (2,128km/h) or Mach 2, (sea level) supersonic (ie, over 760mph, 1,223km/h); combat radius not disclosed.

Despite the enormous cost and technical risk Sweden has designed its own fighters since World War II, and has achieved total success with each generation. The Saab 37 Viggen is the fifth in line, and when the project was launched in 1964 many observers thought it would be the last. Throughout the 1970s, however, the Flygvapen (air force), Swedish air board and Saab-Scania AB studied the alternatives for the sixth generation, to replace first the AJ37 version of the Viggen in the all-weather attack role, then the SF37 and SH37 reconnaissance aircraft and finally, towards the end of the century, the JA37 all-weather interceptor. The studies gradually hardened into a canard tandem delta aircraft of minimum proportions, which could fly all the missions, be affordable by Sweden and be likely to win over future opposition. Project definition and initial engineering were funded in June 1980.

Sweden is the only country already to have a tandem canard combat aircraft in service, the Viggen having adopted this configuration largely to meet the vital

demand that it should be capable of operating well away from any known airfields. Far more than NATO air forces, Sweden has realised for many years that in a war an airfield is likely to be the very first place to be wiped off the map, and the Viggen, like the J35 Draken before it, was designed to combine Mach-2 performance with such good low-speed handling and short field length that it could both depart from and recover to short stretches of country road and even farm tracks. This also demands "high flotation" landing gear, which in the case of the Draken was met by very large main wheel tyres and in the Viggen by two main wheels in tandem on each leg. The Viggen's very large wing and efficient flapped canards combine to give outstanding STOL capability.

None of these requirements was in any way relaxed for the next-generation aircraft, which was first identified as the JAS, from the Swedish words for fighter/attack/reconnaissance. Later it was designated the Saab 39 and in 1982 the aircraft was named Gripen (Griffin). Its development is being managed on behalf of the Air Board by Industri Gruppen JAS, comprising Saab-Scania, Volvo Flygmotor, LM Ericsson, SRA Communications and FFV. This powerful group has been required to match the financial commitment of the government. The initial design was designated Saab 2105, and submitted for approval in June 1981. This was slightly modified and the resulting aircraft carefully evaluated against rival fighters which might be imported. In April 1982 procurement of the Swedish aircraft was recommended, and approved a month later. Work is now going ahead on five prototypes, the first due to fly

in 1987, and the final go-ahead on tooling for a planned run of 140 aircraft (including about 25 tandem two-seaters) was decided in April 1983. Early in the project the possibility of collaborating with another country was examined. The obvious closely similar project is Israel's Lavi, but the idea of a joint aircraft foundered partly on

gets), but the F-20A has the General Electric APG-67(V), one of the neatest and most modern sets available from a company which, though not one of the two main US producers of fighter radars, lacks nothing in expertise in the technology. The APG-67 occupies only 3cu ft (less than $0.1m^3$), weighs 270lb (122kg) and was designed for 200h between failures at a time when the F-15 radar was specified at 60h. For air/air operations it offers search, track and air-combat modes, whilst in air/ground operations (in which up to 8,300lb, 7,365kg of weapons can be carried) it can be switched to any other following modes: ground map, DBS (doppler beam sharpened) map, ranging, sea states 1 and 2 and freeze.

Pilots who have flown the F-20A have been excited at its handling, radar and capability all round. The cockpit is a judicious blend of F-5 and 21st century, with Hotas controls, an advanced HUD and MFD (multifunction display). Sadly, the legal dispute with McDonnell Douglas over the F/A-18 had in 1985 expanded to include an action by the latter that Northrop have copied the cockpit of the Hornet.

Left: McDonnell Douglas accused Northrop of copying the cockpit of the F/A-18, but it is difficult to see how else the Tigershark "office" could have been designed. Two MFDs flank the UFC (up-front control) under the head-up display, with Hotas stick.

Above: The No. 1 F-20 lets go five Mk 83 (1,000lb, 454kg) bombs. One Tigershark made eight fully planned bombing missions between dawn and dusk. Overall mission reliability rate has been a remarkable 97 per cent, and overall cost levels have been low.

place. Something like this may yet be done eventually.

By far the most important updates offered by the F-20A, transcending even the enhanced flight performance, are in the field of avionics. The F-5A had only a small ranging radar, the F-5E had a small I/J-band pulse radar giving a useful but limited search/track capability, primarily in the air/air mode) not against low-flying tar-

political reasons and also because the Lavi is tailored more heavily to attack, whereas the JAS is true multirole with no compromise in air-combat capability.

However, other nations were turned to for specialist high-technology expertise and experience. British Aerospace Warton is collaborating on the design of the super-

critical delta wing, with slats and four-section elevons, the structure being almost wholly of carbon-fibre composite; BAe is making the wing for the first prototype. General Electric's F404 was picked as the engine, further developed and licensed to Flygmotor in Sweden. BAe Dynamics provide the ECS (environmental control sys-

Above: This Gripen model appears to be painted silver, but in fact the Swedish air force is as interested as other forces in finding the best "stealth" external finish. A pale grey is already being used with Viggens, together with plain matt white on JA37 fighter Viggens. National insignia are still conspicuous, but reduced in size compared with the size on this model. Of course, small overall size helps greatly in remaining undetected.

tem) for the cockpit and comprehensive yet compact avionics. The seat is a Martin-Baker Mk 10. Ferranti are collaborating with Ericsson on the lightweight radar, being responsible for the aerial pedestal and signal processor and part of the system architecture. The aerial is a carbon-fibre planar array and the as-yet unnamed radar uses "a flexible waveform" with FM, pulse compression and synthetic-aperture techniques. Sundstrand provide the main electrical system, Lear Siegler the triply-redundant FBW flight-control system, Dowty the hydraulics with Abex pumps, Moog the elevon and rudder power units, Lucas Aerospace the "geared hinge" drives for the leading flaps (and also the complete canopy), Hughes the advanced HUD, SRA the three cockpit MFDs (making the cockpit very similar to the obvious model, that of the Hornet), AP Precision Hydraulics the neat landing gears (this time with single wheels), Microturbo the gas-turbine APU/starter and Mauser the 27mm gun mounted in the left side of the belly.

Had Northrop made the F-20A an "all new" aircraft the result might have resembled the Gripen, which puts a later version of the same engine into the newest airframe that could be created outside the USA and Soviet Union in the early 1980s. The geographical qualification is needed because stealth technology outside those two countries is inevitably limited. Obviously since 1980 Sweden has been carrying out the most intensive research into this technology it can afford, and it is possible that certain details of the Saab 39, such as the inlets, are being left fluid so that the results of this research can be incorporated.

Maximum weapon load has not been

Above: Illustration of two Gripens configured for the air-to-air mission (further) and surface-attack missions (nearer). They are shown in the present standard Swedish camouflage, which is likely to be replaced by overall grey.

disclosed but is probably some 14,000lb (6,350kg). Sidewinders go on the wingtips, and four wing pylons carry the RB71 Sky Flash AAM or RBS15F anti-ship missile. A FLIR pod can be attached under the right inlet. TFR is not fitted, but the main radar

has an obstacle-clearance function for low-level attack.

Service entry is due in 1992. It is a telling reflection on cost of modern weapon systems that in 1985 this Swedish programme was the only one for a new fighter going ahead anywhere in Western Europe. Traditionally Sweden has put strict neutrality in front of weapon exports, but if the policy were to change this aircraft could probably achieve massive global sales.

RM12 multi-petal nozzle

VHF 1

Airbrake   UHF/IFF

Below: Subject of these drawings is a JAS 39 Gripen operating in the anti-ship attack mission with two RBS15F cruise missiles, each weighing 1,320lb (600kg). As an alternative the Gripen can carry four BAe Dynamics (RB71) Sky Flash radar-guided AAMs. In June 1985 BAe Dynamics and Sweden were reported close to launching Sky Flash 90, with active radar homing superior to that of the troubled AMRAAM, to arm Gripen and European Fighter Aircraft EFA.

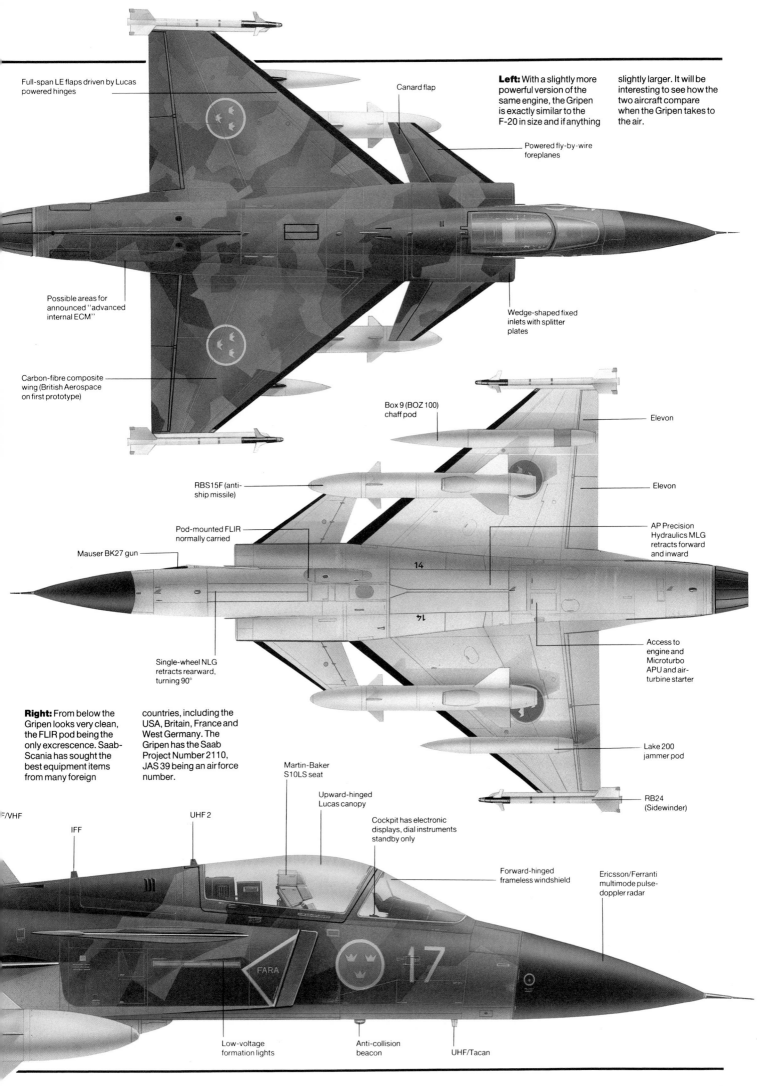

Full-span LE flaps driven by Lucas powered hinges

Canard flap

Left: With a slightly more powerful version of the same engine, the Gripen is exactly similar to the F-20 in size and if anything slightly larger. It will be interesting to see how the two aircraft compare when the Gripen takes to the air.

Powered fly-by-wire foreplanes

Possible areas for announced ''advanced internal ECM''

Wedge-shaped fixed inlets with splitter plates

Carbon-fibre composite wing (British Aerospace on first prototype)

Box 9 (BOZ 100) chaff pod

Elevon

RBS15F (anti-ship missile)

Elevon

Pod-mounted FLIR normally carried

AP Precision Hydraulics MLG retracts forward and inward

Mauser BK27 gun

14

Access to engine and Microturbo APU and air-turbine starter

Single-wheel NLG retracts rearward, turning 90°

Right: From below the Gripen looks very clean, the FLIR pod being the only excrescence. Saab-Scania has sought the best equipment items from many foreign countries, including the USA, Britain, France and West Germany. The Gripen has the Saab Project Number 2110, JAS 39 being an air force number.

Lake 200 jammer pod

Martin-Baker S10LS seat

RB24 (Sidewinder)

Upward-hinged Lucas canopy

Cockpit has electronic displays, dial instruments standby only

F/VHF

IFF

UHF 2

Forward-hinged frameless windshield

Ericsson/Ferranti multimode pulse-doppler radar

FARA

17

Low-voltage formation lights

Anti-collision beacon

UHF/Tacan

Type: Day fighter and close-support aircraft.

Engines: Two 13,668lb (6,200kg) Chengdu WP-7 afterburning turbojets.

Dimensions: Not known but assumed wing is similar to MiG Ye-152A (span 29ft 5.1in, 8.97m); length about 70ft (21.3m); wing area (Ye-152A) 304sq ft (28.2m²).

Weights: Not disclosed, but loaded must be similar to Ye-152A at 31,305lb (14,200kg).

Performance: Similar to Ye-152A which had a maximum speed (clean, high altitude) of 1,550mph (2,500km/h) or Mach 2.35; high-altitude range of 152A was 1,430 miles (2,300km).

Though a purist might describe this strikingly long tube-like fighter as a warplane of the past rather than of the future, it is included here because until 1984 it was known in the West only in the form of vague reports. These reports, to which were assigned the NATO name "Finbank", suggested that the J-8 was a 1970s design being groomed for production in the 1980s. It was inevitably associated with the Rolls-Royce Spey engine, for which the People's Republic took a manufacturing licence, and said to incorporate technology (swing wings were assumed) from the MiG-23 supplied from Egypt in 1976. In fact the design was completed in China prior to 1965, and it is doubtful if any of the production J-7s was completed later than 1970. Despite this it remains one of the fastest combat aircraft currently flying, and certainly merits its treatment here after for so long being unknown.

When the Chinese came to Moscow as MiG customers in 1957 (the first manufacturing licence, for the MiG-19SF, was signed in 1958) they visited the MiG OKB (design bureau), and as well as the initial purchase of the MiG-15UTI, MiG-19 they showed intense interest in what was then being urgently developed as the next MiG production fighter, the Ye-66, soon to enter production as the MiG-21. This was in the process of being transferred to China when the political break came in 1960. No MiG-21 licence had been signed nor had the complete set of manufacturing drawings and other documents been transferred, so the Xian J-7 finally emerged as a true "Chinese copy".

During their stay at the MiG OKB the Chinese naturally learned of the bureau's other prototypes which had not been accepted for production, notable examples being the I-3, I-7 and Ye-150 families. All were tailed deltas larger and more powerful than the MiG-21, and most had even higher flight performance. The I-7K had demonstrated 1,586mph (2,553km/h), easily outpacing every other military aircraft of its time (January 1957), and the Ye-150 of 1959 combined this flashing speed with what was claimed to be "true all-weather operation", using "an improved sight system". All these fighters had enormous inlet centrebodies, much bigger than those of any MiG-21 and larger even than that of the later Su-11 interceptor, though not all had the radar (prototypes of the Uragan series) actually installed. The final model in this group of large MiGs was the Ye-152A, which also carried two very large AAMs of a type which, like the aircraft, was not built in quantity (NATO name "AA-4 Awl"). The Chinese were offered the whole weapon system, and what clinched the deal was the fact that, unlike all its many predecessors, the 152A was twin-engined, and used the same engine type as the MiG-21F. This appeared to offer a useful next generation to follow the MiG-21 on the Chinese production lines.

Production drawings for the Ye-152A had not been produced, so the Chinese recognised that they had another copying job on their hands. It appears that the actual Ye-152A remained in the Soviet Union, and really all the Chinese had were some test results, details of the Ye-152A airframe and drawings of such parts as the landing gears. There was an embargo on any technology transfer on the radar. Thus, in parallel with drawing the Chinese Xian J-7, a large team was put on creating the nearest thing pssible to the Ye-152A, starting in about 1962. Lacking the radar, the nose centrebody was made smaller, which in turn enabled the nose itself to be of considerably smaller diameter, giving the pilot a rather better view ahead. The canopy was that of the original J-7, a single-piece moulding hinged at the front to protect the pilot during ejection. The fuselage was largely redesigned and made significantly longer. The vertical tail was greatly increased in chord, reflecting the MiG development of that surface on the successive MiG-21s, while the twin canted ventral fins were made longer and shallower.

As this was written, no details had emerged on when the J-8 prototype flew, but it was probably in the middle of the 1960 decade. Subsequently the J-8 was further developed, with twin NR-30 cannon and underwing pylons for two bombs, rocket pods, CAA-1 (Chinese-built K-13A "Atoll") or Harbin-built AIM-9B Sidewinder AAMs. After producing what appears to have been a small number, the design was then again modified, most notably by fitting the later type of MiG-21 cockpit enclosure with a fixed windscreen and hinged rear canopy of conventional form (not used as a windbreak on ejection). These later J-8s also have pylons at the wingtips plumbed for large, and therefore heavy, drop tanks (this may have been a feature of the original model). Certainly, with a substantial internal fuel capacity and four or possibly even six external tanks the J-8 must have a ferry range considerably greater than the limit for any MiG-21, though whether adopting this larger twin-engined fighter can be considered cost/effective is arguable.

It is possible that when the People's Republic took a licence for the Rolls-Royce Spey in 1975 it was studying a twin-Spey J-8, among other possibilities, because such an aircraft with a redesigned fuselage would have been little more of a problem than the J-8 had been originally. Certainly no such aircraft was built, and the plan to put the Spey into production was abandoned. Lack of engines has been given as one reason for the small number built.

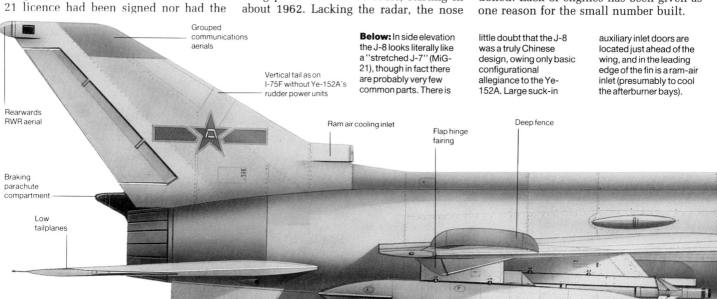

Grouped communications aerials

Vertical tail as on I-75F without Ye-152A's rudder power units

Rearwards RWR aerial

Braking parachute compartment

Low tailplanes

Deep, widely spaced ventral fins

Ram air cooling inlet

Flap hinge fairing

Deep fence

Below: In side elevation the J-8 looks literally like a "stretched J-7" (MiG-21), though in fact there are probably very few common parts. There is little doubt that the J-8 was a truly Chinese design, owing only basic configurational allegiance to the Ye-152A. Large suck-in auxiliary inlet doors are located just ahead of the wing, and in the leading edge of the fin is a ram-air inlet (presumably to cool the afterburner bays).

Right: One of the best photographs available of a J-8 actually in service with the People's Republic air force. The extraordinary length ought to betoken large internal fuel capacity, and increased range is probably the only thing this aircraft can offer in comparison with the MiG-21. Other aspects of performance might even be inferior.

Below: Seen from above the J-8 does not look so grotesquely long because the fuselage has considerable width. Nevertheless there is no room for fuel between the engines, the only additional internal capacity (compared with contemporary MiG-21s) being in the greater length of tankage outboard of the inlet ducts after the latter have swept inboard behind the cockpit. The wing is appreciably larger than that of the single-engined fighter and thus may provide room for fuel.

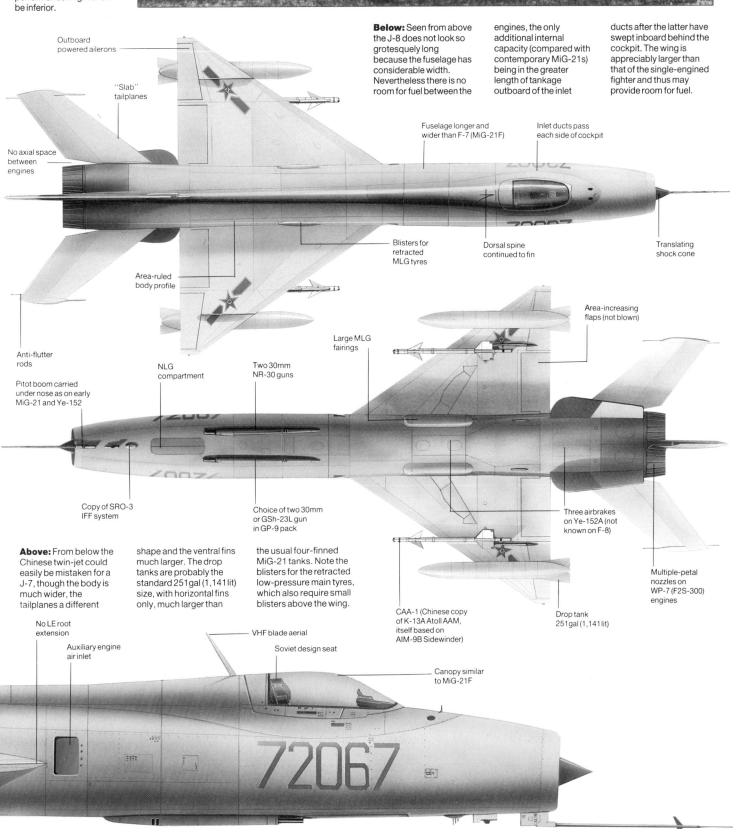

Outboard powered ailerons

"Slab" tailplanes

No axial space between engines

Anti-flutter rods

Pitot boom carried under nose as on early MiG-21 and Ye-152

Area-ruled body profile

Copy of SRO-3 IFF system

NLG compartment

Two 30mm NR-30 guns

Choice of two 30mm or GSh-23L gun in GP-9 pack

Fuselage longer and wider than F-7 (MiG-21F)

Inlet ducts pass each side of cockpit

Blisters for retracted MLG tyres

Dorsal spine continued to fin

Translating shock cone

Large MLG fairings

Area-increasing flaps (not blown)

Three airbrakes on Ye-152A (not known on F-8)

Multiple-petal nozzles on WP-7 (F2S-300) engines

CAA-1 (Chinese copy of K-13A Atoll AAM, itself based on AIM-9B Sidewinder)

Drop tank 251gal (1,141lit)

Above: From below the Chinese twin-jet could easily be mistaken for a J-7, though the body is much wider, the tailplanes a different shape and the ventral fins much larger. The drop tanks are probably the standard 251gal (1,141lit) size, with horizontal fins only, much larger than the usual four-finned MiG-21 tanks. Note the blisters for the retracted low-pressure main tyres, which also require small blisters above the wing.

No LE root extension

Auxiliary engine air inlet

VHF blade aerial

Soviet design seat

Canopy similar to MiG-21F

72067

STOVL/VSTOL PROJECTS

Type: Tactical close-support fighter and reconnaissanca aircraft.
Specification: None finalised.

VTOL (vertical takeoff and landing) can be achieved by using powered lift in any of 16 different ways. The actual lifting device may be anything from a helicopter rotor, via a tilting propeller and a large fan to a plain jet engine (turbofan, turbojet or rocket). Thrust may be vectored by having separate lift and propulsion systems, or the slipstream may be deflected (by large flaps, for example), or the engine may be bodily tilted or fitted with rotating jet nozzles. Of all the 16 possible forms only the simplest, that in which a single engine is used with rotating nozzles to give thrust vectored over a total angle of some 100°, has ever gone into combat service. In the Soviet Union the Yak-38 (or 36MP, NATO "Forger") combines such an engine with two additional turbojets used purely for lift.

Everything in aviation is a compromise. Among shortcomings of the simple single vectored engine configuration are: the engine is over-large for cruising flight (though no more so than the engines of the latest air-combat fighters, which have roughly the same ratio of thrust to weight in the clean condition); the turbofan with side-mounted vectored nozzles is not well suited to flight at high supersonic Mach numbers; and it is difficult to find an aircraft configuration that does not have shortcomings in drag, or engine/wing performance, or weapon carriage, or some other major area. Such supposed deficiencies have been given much publicity, while little has been said of the equally large advantages of all jet-lift aircraft in that their fundamentally different way of flying has a profound effect on combat deployment, flexibility, survivability and safety.

Early in the century Thomas Alva Edison wrote, "The airplane won't amount to a damn until they get the machine that will act like a hummingbird, go straight up, go forward, go backward, come straight down and alight like a hummingbird. ..." Such

statements by famous inventors certainly need not be taken as Gospel truth, but there is no doubt that Man's overriding concentration on what can be called conventional aeroplanes has diverted attention from the "humming-birds". In general, the CTOL (conventional takeoff and landing) aircraft is more efficient in cruising flight than any VTOL, on a strict basis of ton-miles per gallon of fuel. This is fine in peacetime, the only serious drawback of the CTOL being its inability to stop before landing, which in bad weather or very poor visibility has not infrequently resulted in a crash. In wartime the CTOL is virtually a non-starter,

because they can be destroyed on the ground before their user knows he is at war.

Quite apart from this fairly basic fact, the ability of the VTOL or STOVL (short takeoff, vertical landing) aircraft to operate from a small mobile platform on land or sea gives it extra flexibility. Though the budgets allocated have been miniscule, and far too small to interest, say, the US Congress, British Aerospace has been refining the Skyhook and SCADS concepts for operating STOVL aircraft from almost any ship.

It is a scarcely credible fact that in 1985 no new families of advanced STOVL aircraft were being developed in the West.

Above: Dating from 1977, this McDonnell Douglas idea was acceptable because, instead of actually trying to avoid airfields, it merely added canards and part-vectoring nozzles in order to use a little less runway. The notion that airfields are by far the most deadly spots on our planet is taking time to sink in.

Below: For combat aircraft to be in fashion today they must require either airfields or large carrier decks with catapults and arrester gear. Anything that might survive in warfare, such as this General Dynamics E7 project, is rejected because it might suffer "penalties" – in the eyes of military policy makers, at least.

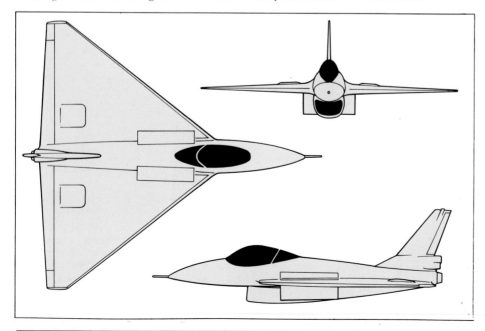

Above: Artist's impression of the E7 (shown also at left). Diverter valves direct the F110 engine to blast down through the vertical lift ducts which, by entraining fresh air from above, greatly augment the original mass flow and lift force. This supersonic deck-launched interceptor would not need a carrier, or an airfield, and for that reason it remains on paper – except for this small NASA model, which is seen in the vertical-lift mode.

Officials from the USA and Britain met in Washington in February 1984 to talk about "a supersonic short takeoff and vertical landing fighter" for the year 2000. NASA Deputy Administrator Hans Mark said the aircraft would be "a follow-on to the technology that produced the Harriers". This is very good news indeed, because without such an aircraft the Western air forces will soon have no viable or survivable airpower, but the programme is being emphasised as a long-term one "in its early planning stages".

Meanwhile, in Britain, where this technology was invented, not only has the RAF dropped any STOVL AST (Air Staff Target) but British Aerospace's STOVL design team at Kingston has been politely told to soft-pedal its P.1214 and similar jet-lift projects because Britain's official next-generation fighter is the FEFA, for which the Warton-designed EAP is a demonstrator prototype. The author's comment is, "That's fine, just so long as we never actually get involved in a war."

By far the leading partners in any Anglo-US project for a supersonic STOVL combat aircraft, British Aerospace at Kingston and McDonnell Douglas at St Louis, are at present jointly producing the Harrier II as the AV-8B for the US Marines and Harrier GR.5 for the RAF (see separate entry). As far as published studies are concerned, the two partners have very different ideas about a next-generation machine. Of course, STOVL is to be preferred to VTOL because if a short run is available – say 400ft (122m) – the load of fuel and weapons that can be carried is greatly increased, compared with the VTO limit. If a ski ramp slope is available at the end of the run the benefits are much greater still. Of course, the lift from a wing at the end of a short run depends critically on the wing, and one of the original minor drawbacks of the Harrier was that the wing was sized for high-speed low-level attack rather than for air combat. In general all next-generation studies have larger wings, roughly in the same size class as those of CTOL fighters.

In fact, when it is realised that tomorrow's STOVL fighter is very like a CTOL except for its configuration and vectoring capability, the wing area, flight controls and engine thrust being closely similar, it can be seen that the CTOL is almost wickedly inflexible in being rigidly tied to runways or fully equipped carrier decks.

Out of many Kingston projects since 1980 the P.1214-3 is the only one to have been publicly illustrated. Details of its engine installation remain under wraps, but the engine is a Pegasus successor with three nozzles and plenum-chamber burning (PCB), which is exactly akin to afterburning in a turbojet but instead of the extra fuel being burned downstream of the turbines it is burned in the fresh air compressed by the fan. Thus the velocity and energy of the upstream (so-called cold) nozzles is greatly increased. Bench testing by Rolls-Royce has demonstrated increase in cold-nozzle thrust of about 100 per cent. so the thrust of the whole engine is boosted by about 50 per cent (because about half the total thrust previously came from the front nozzles). Thus, in the case of the Pegasus at about 22,000lb (9,979kg) thrust, the front-nozzle thrust might be increased by PCB from around 11,000lb (5,000kg) to 16,500lb (7,500kg), raising the thrust of the complete engine to 27,500lb (12,500kg). PCB handling and ignition problems have been explored at simulated high altitude and high-supersonic speed, and no special difficulty has arisen. This greatly enhances the prospects for supersonic STOVL aircraft, and certainly a PCB Pegasus seems not only the obvious but almost the only possible powerplant for studies now in hand at BAe and McDonnell.

There is still the choice of three nozzles or four. Indeed, the author has suggested in an accompanying sketch a supersonic STOVL with a single nozzle, which eliminates pitch/roll/yaw problems resulting from turning moments imparted by multiple nozzles. The main disadvantage of a single nozzle is that it would normally be associated with a turbojet, or a turbofan of low bypass ratio, and this might burn more mission fuel than a Pegasus-type engine of high bypass ratio. Rolls-Royce did much work on single-jet VTOL engines in the

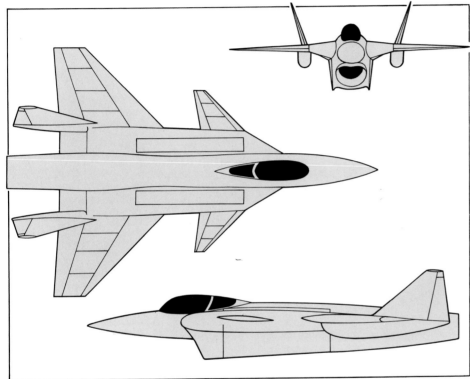

Above: Also working on ejector lift is de Havilland Canada, which has been getting augmentation of 50 to 100 per cent. This supersonic STOVL combat aircraft by DHC dates from 1983, and the basic arrangement of engine, valve and twin lift ducts is exactly the same as in the E7 opposite. The work began in 1968 and has now reached the stage at which, if money were available, a full-scale model could be tested in the NASA Ames 120ft × 80ft (36 × 24m) tunnel. Model testing has been "very satisfactory".

Below: BAe's P.1214-3 is probably the "most experienced" STOVL project in the world. The team has been told to stop; official policy is to need airfields.

1960s, notably on the RB153, and there is no technical difficulty in putting a VTOL nozzle downstream of a high-temperature afterburner. This might be the ideal arrangement for a future supersonic STOVL aircraft, and would eliminate losses due to the side nozzles and scrubbing of the fuselage skin.

The P.1214-3, however, would have a three-poster configuration, with two PCB front nozzles and a single central nozzle at the rear. The position of the rear nozzle is roughly indicated by the suggestion of the jet in the illustration. The engine is fed by an F-16 type inlet, and in this particular P.1214 there are forward-swept wings (see Grumman X-29 entry on later page) and a distributed tail looking like two Harrier Trainer tails with tailplanes on the outboard sides only. The tail booms are convenient for the main gears and for weapon carriage, and the general impression is of a plausible machine with tremendous manoeuvrability. It could doubtless recover to base with one tail missing, and as designers learn to link digital control systems into the aircraft trajectory in more sophisticated ways we could see aircraft of this kind extracting slightly more of the multiple capabilities that are theoretically to be had from all aircraft. For example, loss of a wing in flight could be countered automatically by swivelling the front nozzle on that side to

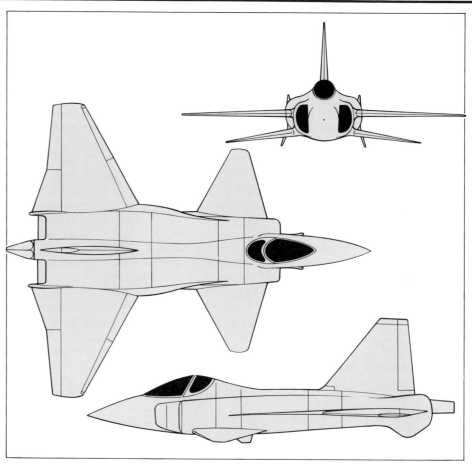

Below: Any British STOVL engineer would have a feeling of *déja vu* on seeing the McDonnell Model 279-3, because in so many respects it resembles the Hawker P.1154RN which was cancelled in 1965. Instead of a conventional tail it would have a large canard, which would probably give greatly enhanced combat manoeuvrability (at least in CTOL aircraft, which cannot Viff their total installed thrust). This stainless-steel high-speed tunnel model was used for pressure plotting and aerodynamic force research. Rolls-Royce are participating in both the Model 279 studies and in PCB research, an obvious augmentation method for supersonic STOVLs. The 279-3 would have a span of 36.9ft (11.2m) and length of 56ft (17.0m).

Above: This Fairchild AFT (advanced fighter technology) concept has a canard so big it is almost a tandem-wing configuration. This is a good layout for many STOVL arrangements, such as the tandem fan (used in the TF120 opposite), ejector duct and use of separate lift jets, "Forger" style. The main engines have two-dimensional vectoring nozzles.

the correct angle downwards. In the final landing, of course, loss of a wing is of no consequence, because the wings are not lifting.

In contrast the McDonnell Douglas Model 279 family are rather more conventional lower-risk projects which in the main form (279-3) utilise a regular Pegasus of the four-poster type, though greatly uprated by increasing the airflow and fitting PCB to a maximum of 36,900lb (16,738kg). All the 279s are canards, with around 45° sweep on the leading edges of the large canard and the aft-mounted main wing. Various forms of supersonic inlet have been studied, the 279-3 being shown with lateral centrebody inlets like a Mirage. A bigger version, the 279-4, would have MiG-25 type inlets feeding two engines each with two nozzles with crossover ducts as proposed for the stillborn twin-Spey P.1154RN in 1964. Downstream in all versions is a normal rear fuselage but vertical tail only.

A further similarity to the P.1154 is that, as in the big BS.100 engine that would have powered that supersonic STOVL (so short-sightedly cancelled in 1965 and replaced by the Phantom!), the engine(s) of the 279 have nozzles rotated from the equatorial level down to the flanks. Here the overall flow patterns are better, especially in low-altitude hover in which the jets impinge on each other not far below the aircraft and

thus prevent the formation of a powerful rising hot gas column in the centre. It would be extremely rash to predict that the "future Anglo-American supersonic STOVL" will be a 279 or derivative, but this looks more likely than anything else.

Several jet-lift schemes are probably non-starters, despite their having one or two major advantages. The fan-in-wing idea, flown on the Ryan XV-5A from May 1964, is one. Another is probably the augmentor jet idea in which lift jets were arranged to entrain a much greater flow of fresh air from above. First tested on the Lockheed XV-4 Hummingbird and later the basis of the General Dynamics E-series studies (such as the E-7 for deck-launched intercept, with an F110 engine and huge diverter valve) and the Rockwell XFV-12A, the only supersonic V/STOL actually built in the USA and a severe disappointment.

The use of batteries of purpose-designed lift jets, strongly pushed by Rolls-Royce 25 years ago, is now seldom discussed, and the RALS (remote augmented lift system) also seems to have few adherents, though this scheme for blasting compressor bleed air out of a fuel-burning auxiliary thrust nozzle has much to commend it. Superficially the most attractive arrangement of all is to use pivoted main engines, which can be bodily rotated to provide thrust in the desired direction. It enables a perfectly designed supersonic engine installation,

with straight-through flow and variable inlets and nozzle, so that the final aircraft need have no "penalties" worth mentioning. There is an obvious severe problem of control if an engine were to be lost in the vertical lift mode, unless the aircraft was such that the engine(s) were on the centre-line, and the pilot and other items offset to one side. A centreline tilting engine aircraft might well be an all-wing stealth design.

Two of the most promising schemes are the tandem fan and hybrid fan, in which the fan airflow can be diverted down for lift or passed to the core downstream in normal flight. In the vertical lift mode the core needs its own auxiliary inlet system. The Vought TF-120 was a Navy deck-launched interceptor with tandem-fan propulsion and auxiliary inlets in the top of the fuselage.

Of course, not all studies for future jet-lift machines are fighters. Three interesting published studies funded by US industry, the US Navy and NASA are the Grumman 698, Lockheed cross-duct VTOL and LTV V-530, all of which are handy-sized proposals for aircraft able to fly ASW, AEW, COD, SAR and similar missions from the helicopter platforms of surface vessels. Grumman uses tilting engines, LTV tandem fans and Lockheed vectored thrust with cross-linking in the event of engine failure. The Lockheed even has a nose towbar for a steam catapult!

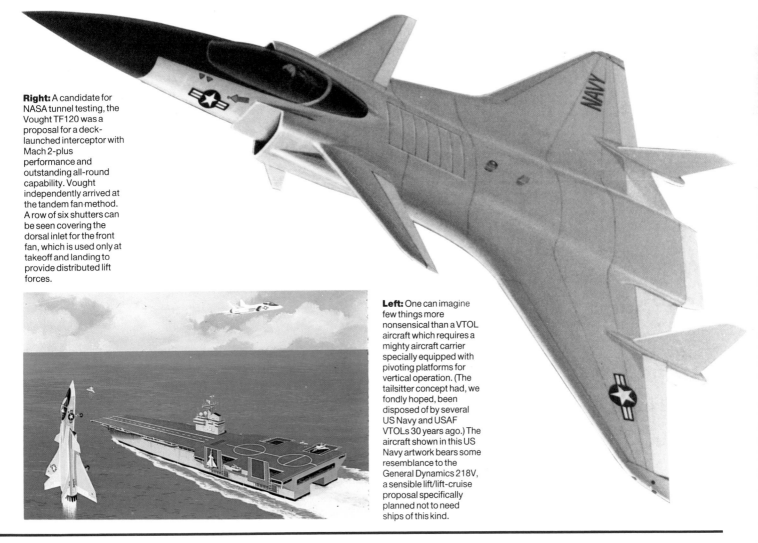

Right: A candidate for NASA tunnel testing, the Vought TF120 was a proposal for a deck-launched interceptor with Mach 2-plus performance and outstanding all-round capability. Vought independently arrived at the tandem fan method. A row of six shutters can be seen covering the dorsal inlet for the front fan, which is used only at takeoff and landing to provide distributed lift forces.

Left: One can imagine few things more nonsensical than a VTOL aircraft which requires a mighty aircraft carrier specially equipped with pivoting platforms for vertical operation. (The tailsitter concept had, we fondly hoped, been disposed of by several US Navy and USAF VTOLs 30 years ago.) The aircraft shown in this US Navy artwork bears some resemblance to the General Dynamics 218V, a sensible lift/lift-cruise proposal specifically planned not to need ships of this kind.

SUKHOI
SU-25 "FROGFOOT"

Type: Close-support (and probably reconnaissance) aircraft.

Engines: Two turbojets or turbofans in the 10,000lb (4,535kg) class.

Dimensions: (Estimated) span 50ft 10in (15.5m); length 47ft 6in (14.5m); height 16ft 9in (5.1m); wing area 400sq ft (37m²).

Weights: (Estimated) empty 17,000lb (7,711kg); loaded (forward airstrip) 28,000lb (12,700kg), (maximum) 36,050lb (16,350kg).

Performance: (Estimated) maximum speed (SL, clean) 546mph (880km/h); combat radius (load and mission profile not stated) 345 miles (556km).

First detected in satellite pictures in 1977, this "AX" style attack machine was originally dubbed Ram-J as one of a long list first spotted on test at Ramenskoye test centre. Later it received the NATO name "Frogfoot", though names beginning with "F" were reserved for fighters. Even stranger, it has for five years been agreed in the West that the true VVS (air force) designation is Su-25, though odd numbers were always reserved for fighters only. Possibly the explanation is that odd numbers are now indiscriminately allocated to small frontline jets, although "Fencer" has an even number (24) and the swing-wing "Fitter" family include both odds and evens (17, 20 and 22, all VVS examples having the odd number).

Be that as it may, the Mujaheddin tribesmen in the Afghan hills fear this aircraft as much as any other Soviet weapon. Operating in the closest partnership with Mi-24 helicopters, small groups of Su-25s (occasionally single examples) have repeatedly demonstrated their ability to carry 20 to 30 separate stores, or hundreds of 57mm rockets, and to deliver these with great accuracy against the most difficult targets.

Above: One of the few photographs of "Frogfoot" to become available in the West. The first Warsaw Pact air force known to receive the type was Czechoslovakia's. The Su-25 has also served alongside large numbers of "Hind" helicopters with the Soviet and/or "puppet" Afghan air forces.

Predictably, the Su-25 has shown exceptional ability to absorb battle damage, and as this was written in spring 1985 it is not thought that any Su-25 has been brought down by Mujaheddin fire.

The basic aircraft strongly resembles the Northrop A-9A, the losing finalist in the USAF AX competition won by the A-10). It is about the same size and flies the same missions, though the American requirement was strongly polarized around defence against oncoming armour. Features include twin unaugmented engines, which could well be R-25s (fitted, with afterburner, in late MiG-21s). The author's estimate for thrust given above is higher than the "5,620-9,000lb" (2,549-4,082kg) commonly published in Western circles. The engines are installed under the wing roots in nacelles which angle downwards from inlet to nozzle. The nose resembles the "ducknose" of the MiG-27, the pilot having a good view ahead and down. No radar is normally fitted, but one may expect FLIR and/or laser or TV for weapon guidance. Guided attack missiles can be carried, as well a K-13A, R-60 or similar dogfight AAMs for self-defence. All the photographs so far seen suggest a typically comprehensive RWR and ECM installation, and various types of chaff and, more often, flare dispensation have been shown in newsreels.

Like the US AX aircraft the Su-25 was apparently designed around a very powerful gun, for use against hardened targets such as armour. It is on the ventral centreline; there has been speculation as to whether it is internal or podded, but an eminently logical arrangement would be to equip the aircraft to receive either of two large recessed installations, one the gun and ammunition and the other an advanced multisensor reconnaissance pallet. Most Su-25s have been seen with either four or five pylons under each wing. The tip pods appear to be ECM jammers. No stores have been positively identified under the wide fuselage and inlets, though (despite the presence of the main landing gears) there should be no difficulty in carrying loads in this location.

Of course, details of the accompanying artwork are still to some extent provisional, but the general form of this formidable machine has been well known for several years. Its nearest Western counterparts are the AM-X and A-10A, the Soviet type falling somewhere between them. The author finds many reasons for estimating the engine thrust at around 10,000lb (4,535kg), even though the estimate for gross weight is much lower than that of the A-10A. There is no doubt that this is no sluggish weapon platform but a notably agile aircraft which when engaged by guns frequently manages to dodge. When clean it has been observed to make zoom climbs out of sight in a clear sky, and even with all pylons loaded the low-altitude turn radius appears to be respectable, though extreme manoeuvres are then avoided. Total weapon load is estimated by DoD at 8,820lb (4,000kg), though it is difficult to see why the figure has been pitched so low.

Production is centred at Tbilisi (Tiflis). Deliveries began in about 1980, and again one is bemused at the low estimates emanating from the Pentagon for numbers built. The official DoD view was that "about 75" had become operational by April 1984. There have been several recent instances of single Soviet plants approaching 75 aircraft per month! The figure could hinge on the definition of "operational". There must have been something like 75 Su-25s in Afghanistan alone.

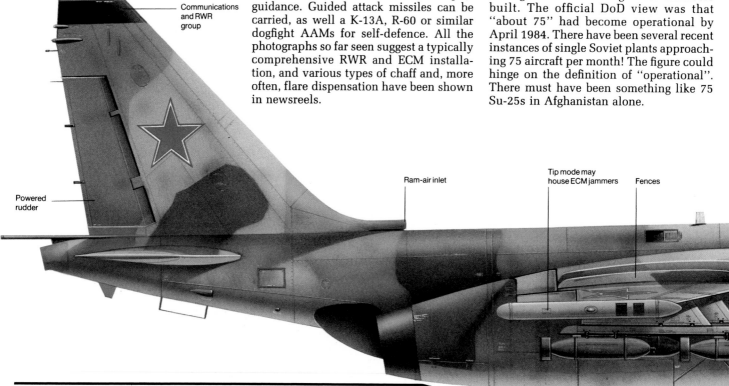

Communications and RWR group

Powered rudder

Ram-air inlet

Tip mode may house ECM jammers

Fences

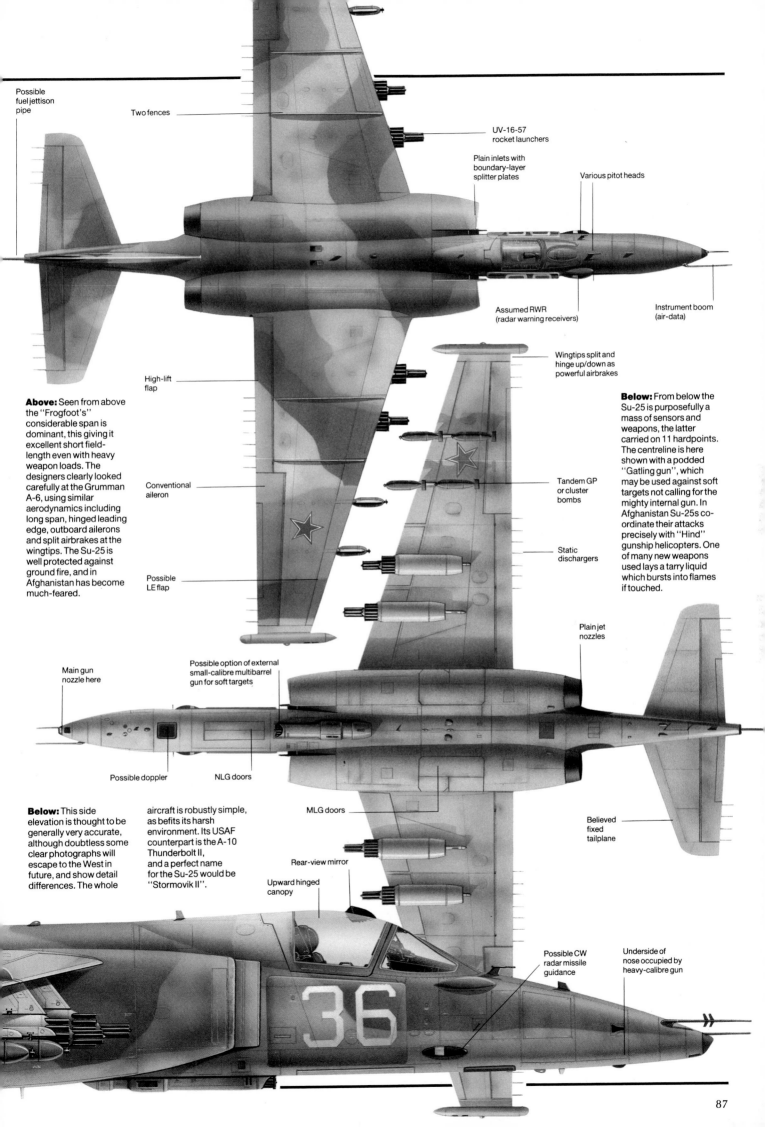

Possible fuel jettison pipe

Two fences

UV-16-57 rocket launchers

Plain inlets with boundary-layer splitter plates

Various pitot heads

Assumed RWR (radar warning receivers)

Instrument boom (air-data)

High-lift flap

Wingtips split and hinge up/down as powerful airbrakes

Conventional aileron

Tandem GP or cluster bombs

Static dischargers

Possible LE flap

Plain jet nozzles

Main gun nozzle here

Possible option of external small-calibre multibarrel gun for soft targets

Possible doppler

NLG doors

MLG doors

Believed fixed tailplane

Rear-view mirror

Upward hinged canopy

Possible CW radar missile guidance

Underside of nose occupied by heavy-calibre gun

Above: Seen from above the "Frogfoot's" considerable span is dominant, this giving it excellent short field-length even with heavy weapon loads. The designers clearly looked carefully at the Grumman A-6, using similar aerodynamics including long span, hinged leading edge, outboard ailerons and split airbrakes at the wingtips. The Su-25 is well protected against ground fire, and in Afghanistan has become much-feared.

Below: From below the Su-25 is purposefully a mass of sensors and weapons, the latter carried on 11 hardpoints. The centreline is here shown with a podded "Gatling gun", which may be used against soft targets not calling for the mighty internal gun. In Afghanistan Su-25s co-ordinate their attacks precisely with "Hind" gunship helicopters. One of many new weapons used lays a tarry liquid which bursts into flames if touched.

Below: This side elevation is thought to be generally very accurate, although doubtless some clear photographs will escape to the West in future, and show detail differences. The whole aircraft is robustly simple, as befits its harsh environment. Its USAF counterpart is the A-10 Thunderbolt II, and a perfect name for the Su-25 would be "Stormovik II".

SUKHOI
SU-27 "FLANKER"

Type: All-weather interceptor and multirole fighter/attack aircraft.
Engines: Two advanced afterburner jet engines each in the 30,000lb (13,600kg) class; Tumanskii R-31 has been suggested.
Dimensions: (Estimated) span 47ft 7in (14.5m); length, excluding probe 69ft (21m); height 18ft (5.5m); wing area 690sq ft (64m²).
Weights: (Estimated) empty 33,000lb (15,000kg); loaded (air-to-air mission) 49,600lb (22,500kg); maximum on attack mission 77,200lb (35,000kg).
Performance: (Estimated) maximum speed (high altitude, air-to-air mission) 1,555mph (2,500km/h) or Mach 2.35; combat radius (high air-to-air mission) 715 miles (1,150km).

Certainly likely to prove one of the world's outsanding combat aircraft of the rest of this century, this aircraft was first seen in satellite imagery in 1980. Designation Ram-K was applied, and at first it was thought to have a variable-sweep wing. Gradually, as it became better known, it was recognised as the same TsAGI shape as the MiG-29 on a much bigger scale, thus exactly repeating the MiG/Su history with tailed deltas. The NATO name "Flanker" was announced in 1982 together with the supposed actual designation of Su-27, though it is now obvious that these "Soviet designations" are often invented ones, generally stemming from Washington, and cannot be relied upon. Satellite imagery, however, probably can be relied upon, though it is often tricky to interpret. It is reproduced here, together with the author's own interpretative comments.

If, as the author believes, the Su-27 had a VG wing, this puts renewed emphasis on its multirole capability. Previously it had been regarded almost entirely as an all-weather interceptor, and it is said to have a normal armament in this role of "eight

AAMs", which are now said to be of the new AA-10 type. This AAM is unknown in the West, where not even vague guesses at numerical values have appeared. It is said to have "medium range', but as the current notion of "long range" (for the so-called AA-9) is 12.5 miles (20km) at low level rising to 25 miles (40km) at high altitude we may as well ignore such Western non-sense. For comparison, the commonest Western medium-range AAM, Sparrow, has an announced range of 62 miles (100km), while the long-range Phoenix can be used over distances "greater than 124 miles (200km)". For some reason that has never been explained, all Western estimates of Soviet air-to-air missile ranges, like aircraft weapon loads and most other numerical parameters, are pitched at about half (in some cases one-quarter) of what would appear sensible and reasonable. The objective may be to improve morale in Western armed forces or merely create a general impression that the Russians are techically backward, but whenever the truth comes out it has a most unfortunate effect. Certainly the Indians, who will soon have MiG-29s in their air force, are trying very hard indeed to get Soviet AAMs as well "because they are so much better than the ones available from Western sources". The man who said that knew his Western

missiles well, and there is no reason to doubt that he also knew the available Soviet ones.

Of course it will probably be a long time before the Su-27 comes on to the export market. When it does, its price will probably prove a deterrent to some third-world countries, because there is no doubt that this is a big, very powerful, superbly equipped multimission fighter that lacks nothing that could possibly be provided with 1970s technology. Full look-down shoot-down capability against very low altitude targets can be taken for granted, and BVR (beyond visual range) missiles were available in the Soviet Union long before they were in the West, though such capability is presented as something only now becoming available with such aircraft as the Su-27. Some Su-27s may be deployed by air-defence regiments, but so versatile a machine is far more likely to be found in Frontal Aviation. In the attack role a typical load is said to be 12 bombs of 1,102lb (500kg) size. Another obvious capability would be a large multisensor reconnaissance pallet or pod, as would additional bad-weather sensors for weapon delivery and precision navigation. An inflight-refuelling probe may well be fitted, and data links with Awacs-type aircraft would seem logical, though this generation of Soviet aircraft can operate autonomously and, if necessary, without any radio or radar emissions whatsoever.

The Su-27 has been named as the type most likely to equip the new giant carrier, believed to be named *Kremlin*, fast completing at Nikolaiyev. A swing-wing machine would be particularly suited to carrier operation, though the one does not confirm the other. Su-27 production is at Komsomolsk, in the Far East, which since 1938 has also been the location of the main Su OKB (design bureau), titular head of which is E. A. Ivanov.

Above: The only US satellite photograph of an Su-27 so far released is believed to show a prototype, which almost certainly had VG "swing wings". The production aircraft is universally considered to have a fixed wing roughly similar to an F-15 wing but with tip AAM launchers. The latter have not been shown in the three-view drawing as they are still a matter for debate. This prototype clearly had none fitted.

Below: This side elevation suggests an Su-27 looking faintly like an enlarged F/A-18 Hornet, though with better understanding this configuration will obviously have to be modified. In particular the inlets are still vertically unknown, and it could be that the wing is mounted higher, the upper surface being unbroken except by a dorsal spine behind the canopy. The laser under the nose is, of course, a mere guess.

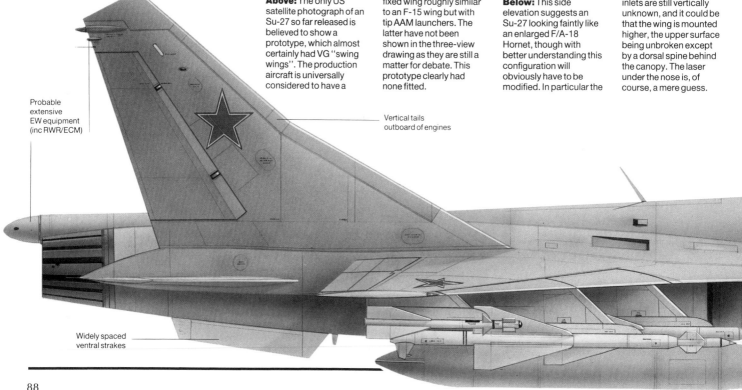

Probable extensive EW equipment (inc RWR/ECM)

Vertical tails outboard of engines

Widely spaced ventral strakes

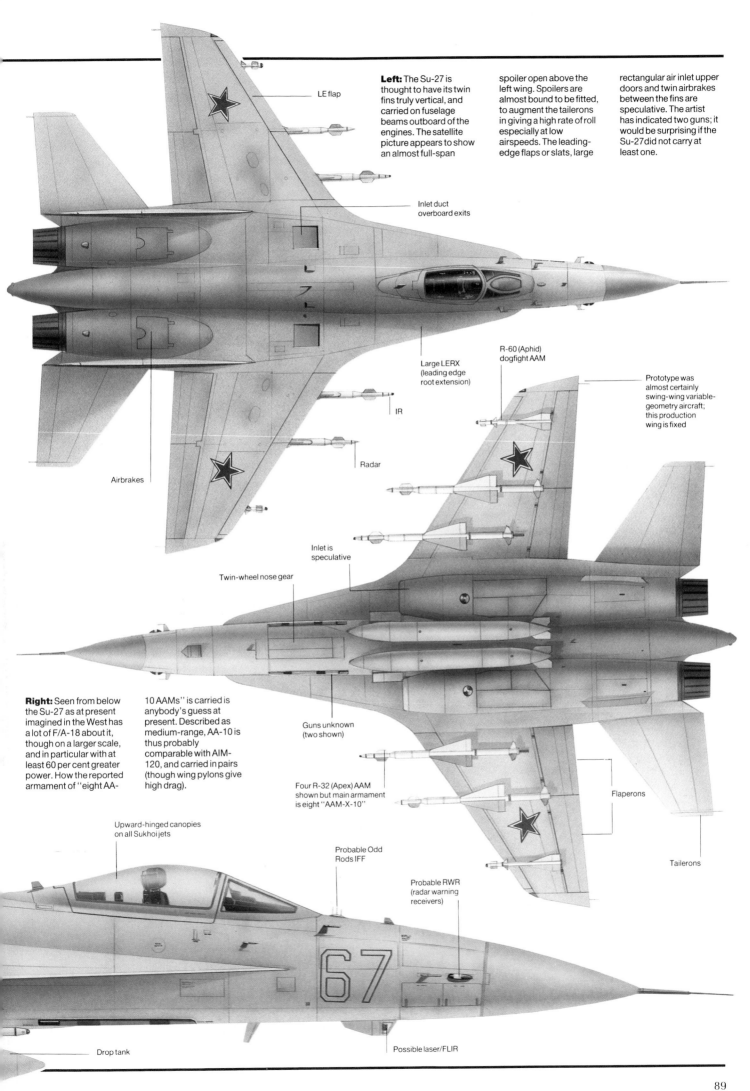

Left: The Su-27 is thought to have its twin fins truly vertical, and carried on fuselage beams outboard of the engines. The satellite picture appears to show an almost full-span spoiler open above the left wing. Spoilers are almost bound to be fitted, to augment the tailerons in giving a high rate of roll especially at low airspeeds. The leading-edge flaps or slats, large rectangular air inlet upper doors and twin airbrakes between the fins are speculative. The artist has indicated two guns; it would be surprising if the Su-27 did not carry at least one.

LE flap

Inlet duct overboard exits

Large LERX (leading edge root extension)

IR

Radar

Airbrakes

R-60 (Aphid) dogfight AAM

Prototype was almost certainly swing-wing variable-geometry aircraft; this production wing is fixed

Inlet is speculative

Twin-wheel nose gear

Guns unknown (two shown)

Four R-32 (Apex) AAM shown but main armament is eight "AAM-X-10"

Flaperons

Tailerons

Right: Seen from below the Su-27 as at present imagined in the West has a lot of F/A-18 about it, though on a larger scale, and in particular with at least 60 per cent greater power. How the reported armament of "eight AA-10 AAMs" is carried is anybody's guess at present. Described as medium-range, AA-10 is thus probably comparable with AIM-120, and carried in pairs (though wing pylons give high drag).

Upward-hinged canopies on all Sukhoi jets

Probable Odd Rods IFF

Probable RWR (radar warning receivers)

67

Drop tank

Possible laser/FLIR

ADVANCED TACTICAL FIGHTER (ATF)

Type: Advanced multirole fighter.
Engines: Two augmented turbofans (JAFE) with vectored nozzles.
Dimensions: Not yet decided.
Weights: Gross weight probably about 40,000lb (18,000kg) air combat or 80,000lb (36,000kg) attack mission.
Performance: Maximum speed (clean, high altitude) in the region of Mach 2 (1,323mph, 2,128km/h); combat radius highly variable but comparable to F-15.

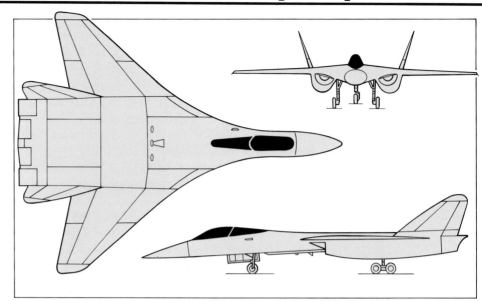

ATF and its associated JAFE (Joint Advanced Fighter Engine) are the kingpins of the entire future of the US Air Force, alongside the B-1B and ATB in the strategic sphere. ATF will be a totally new design, in no way derived from any of today's excellent USAF aircraft. Trying to decide what the USAF wishes to buy has proved difficult, however.

The point must be made that, rightly, the USAF compares itself with its most likely enemy, the Soviet Union. Unfortunately, while the USAF publishes in the utmost detail not only what it does but also what it plans to do in the distant future (such as ATF), the Soviet Union publishes very little except what it wishes to have known. This at once makes comparative assessments somewhat one-sided. In 1976 a review of Soviet aerospace technology noted that "... this is now changing. New fighter versions, and probable new designs, are introducing look-down shoot-down

capability". The review went on to discuss Soviet BVR (beyond visual range) AAMs. Even earlier Western writers had commented on the new freedom of action and initiative being cultivated throughout all the Soviet armed forces, and especially in tactical aircraft cockpits. As early as 1969, and possibly before, we read such statements as "The old philosophy of rigid central control is on the way out; individual initiative is not only permitted but encouraged." Yet, almost beyond belief, the same "news" is still being trotted out as

Above: This three-view of the Rockwell International proposal also depicted below, shows one of the more recent ATF-type illustrations. All actual ATF submissions are classified, and pictures broadcast by some of the seven competing airframe companies (dating from 1983-4) most certainly do not show any of the true ATF submissions.

Below: This ATF-style fighter by Rockwell International would have a span of 47.43ft (14.46m) and length of 60.17ft (18.34m). Aerodynamic and stealth considerations result in a blended wing/body form, with twin underslung engines whose nozzles have 2D (ie, up/down) vectoring to reduce field length and enhance manoeuvrability. Note gun in the left wing root.

if it were just dicovered. No description of any modern Soviet fighter is complete without noting that it has "look-down, shoot-down capability with BVR missiles", as if this was something new, while the March 1985 edition of *Air Force Magazine* opens a major article on the USAF with, "Soviet air-to-air tactics and training are slowly drifting away from total pilot dependence on rigid command and control. . . ."

If this really does reflect our knowledge of the competition, how ever can the ATF be specified correctly? It will not be lost on many impartial observers that what is commonly done is to contrast USAF ATFs and other as-yet unbuilt machines with the latest known Soviet types. But the latter are already in service, mostly in large numbers; what any fighter designer would like to do is design something better than the best on his opposite number's drawing board, not the best on the combat-ready flightline. Unfortunately ATF designers have to work in the dark and try to meet requirements which are continually changing and are generally out of date.

ATF is probably the biggest single project in the entire Aeronautical Systems Division of USAF Systems Command. So far the customer has confined himself to funding numerous local research programmes likely to have a favourable impact on the eventual ATF, ranging from the complete propulsion system (which cen-

tres on the Joint Advanced Fighter Engine) down to details of new systems, avionics and structural techniques. From the late 1970s Systems Command could see how future fighters could be made with newer airframes, more advanced aerodynamics, advanced composite structures, digital data networks linking every part of the aircraft, integrated defensive and offensive avionic systems, new low-consumption engines and scores of other seemingly desirable features.

The manufacturers lost no time in producing fabulous artwork showing future fighters mainly characterized by their "supercruise" design (ie, they could cruise at supersonic speeds). Behind it all the need for high T/W (thrust/weight ratio) and high SEP (specific excess power) was deemed essential in order to win a close manoeuvring dogfight (something the

author would have thought an outnumbered NATO would have tried to avoid at all costs, but which insistently appeals to the USAF). Had anything actually have gone ahead in, say, 1980, it might have been a grave error, because if the pictures were to be believed what the designers were working on were fighters longer than the SR-71, heavier than the F-111, shattering the sky with flame, smoke and radar waves and in one case actually drawn with leading edges glowing red-hot with kinetic friction at Mach 5.

Fortunately the real studies were rather different, and closer to what might actually survive in war both on the ground and in the sky. Two qualities determine this survivability: stealth and powered lift. Gradually these came to dominate the overall ATF requirement, despite the entrenched opposition of diehards who cannot bring themselves to understand that the quickest way to get an aeroplane wiped off the map is to put it near a known airfield in wartime. Indeed, this self-evident truth is still very far from being universally accepted at Systems Command, even yet, but during the past two years one timid toe has been stuck in the powered-lift water by ordering McDonnell to build a STOL F-15 with canards and 2-D nozzles able to vector in the vertical plane to give thrust, lift or braking after landing. As this is written the official "party line" on ATF is still that it will "have STOL capability", and i?

Below: This Grumman model shows a rather more complex approach than the big-wing Rockwell. Obvious features include the long body fully available for fuel and (one hopes) internal missiles, between the widely spaced engines with 2D vectoring nozzles. The powered canard is also clear enough, but the advanced aerodynamics lie in the wing. Just discernible are white lines, marking hinges, drawn across the giant leading-edge droop flaps and broad trailing-edge flaps. This configuration would be highly suitable for one of the most promising of the STOVL arrangements, the tandem fan. The additional (front fan) inlets would be in the upper surface of the main inlets just ahead of the front spar.

pressed to be more explicit the answer may be elicited that "it will be able to takeoff and land between the craters of a bombed runway". Fortunately for the USAF this lunatic idea, which assumes that the rest of the airbase, and the aircraft thereon, will be left carefully intact, was by spring 1985 becoming seen for the nonsense it is, and – for the first time – the USAF absolutely refuses to be drawn on what sort of ATF it thinks it wants.

To recap on the programme itself, Fairchild Republic were sadly eliminated, and current study contracts each for just under $1 million, are held by Boeing Military Airplane Co., GD, Grumman, Lockheed, McDonnell Douglas, Northrop and Rockwell. General Electric and Pratt & Whitney are working on the JAFE knowing that they will share the eventual propulsion responsibility. The JAFE will have to be not only more compact than previous engines in the 25,000-30,000lb thrust (11 to 13t) class, but have much lower fuel consumption, 40 to 60 per cent fewer parts, be "three times as reliable as those in the current inventory" (a few years back this demand might have looked easy) and be designed to fly 6,000 TACs (total accumulated cycles, each representing a typical fighter mission) while even the most advanced F100 engines are now being built for 4,000 TACs. These are very severe demands indeed, especially when it is remembered that 2-D vectored nozzles are still a very immature concept.

Only two years ago one company had a monopoly in the supply of USAF fighter engines, and for the Navy's dedicated fighter as well. Now it has a keen rival, pressing it hard. P&W and GE will be marked according to the financial warran-

Above: One of many ATF-type Boeing pictures, this "supercruise" warplane is clearly configured for sustained cruising and manoeuvring at Mach numbers well into the supersonic region. There are shielded inlets to the engine pods, which have unvectored nozzles, and a long internal weapon bay in the blended fuselage.

Below: Another view of the Rockwell fighter. In this artwork the engine inlets can be seen, showing one of the more popular approaches to the problem of getting good inlet performance, even at high angles of attack (for example in sustained turns) whilst trying to improve stealth qualities. Note black EW areas on the wing roots.

ties offered with their production ATF engines. According to Systems Commander Gen Lawrence A. Skantze this is "good business . . . that provides high-tech leverage to the future force, but with a unit price that is affordable and wrings out every ounce of aerospace industry production genius". One is reminded of the keen battle by Rolls-Royce to sell the RB211 into the L-1011 in 1967-68 which resulted in the collapse of the firm three years later. Both P&W and GE are portions of giant corporations, but too keen a competiton could just

prove anything but "good business".

As for the ATF study contracts, these are going ahead but the schedule is being deliberately allowed to slip. The next step is the demonstration/validation phase, when real money begins to be spent, but in December 1984 the DSARC (Defense Systems Acquisition Review Council) "requested additional data" before permitting the programme to proceed to this next step. Widely heralded as "a setback", this seems in the author's view to have been a godsend, because it is a last chance to try to get

Above: This Grumman fighter would have side inlets with semicircular centrebody aerodynamics leading above the low-mounted canard and wing to engines with 2D vectoring nozzles shielded against IR-seeking SAMs. The canards are close-coupled and at the same level as the variable-camber wing.

commonsense priorities right and avoid wasting billions on useless aircraft that either will never get off the ground or else never get back on to it in one piece.

It should be self-evident that ATF is the one opportunity we have in the West to start afresh with a fighter that, instead of just looking nice in a brochure, will actually provide real airpower for the West. It is a time for a sweeping away of preconceived notions, and a fresh start on a low-observables aircraft difficult to see by eye, by radar or by IR, not aurally noisy, without noticeable emissions of its own and able to operate for sustained periods without ever going near any known airfield. All this calls for good design, but not for any technology not already familiar. And there is no reason why a near-invisible fighter that never goes near an airfield should not be a superior fighting aircraft after it has taken off.

Of course, while the various study contractors have been prolific in publishing exciting pictures of old-technology fighters, of the kind needing a paved runway and with radar and infra-red signatures rather like a blast furnace, not a glimmer has leaked out about the kinds of fighter that Skantze and his 53,000 people are actually studying. We may be sure that the sudden hold called by DSARC last December is being put to good use in establishing—perhaps by brute force, in the face of closed minds — as proper subjects for discussion those previously regarded as

hot potatoes, or politically difficult, such as whether the USAF dare actually make its ATF a jet-lift STOVL, something laughed to scorn ever since the Hawker P.1127 of 1960. There has never been the slightest suggestion that Britain should have even the smallest crumb in this potentially vast programme, and everything possible is being done to edge out such outstanding USAF suppliers as Marconi Avionics and Martin-Baker, yet somehow the very idea of using the thrust *already installed in the aircraft* to lift it off the ground and back on again, as well as thrust it forward has been more than USAF could digest.

It remains to be seen whether commonsense will prevail, but at least the Mach 5 fire-breathing monsters look rather less likely. Several spokesmen have added "low" or "greatly reduced" observables to the list of ATF attributes, while the Commander of TAC, Gen Jerome F. O'Malley, recently said, "We are not necessarily looking for a big fighter; we want to keep the size at an affordable level." All of which is good news, because obvious things are often overlooked. What is still surprising is that O'Malley and the Commander of USAFE, Gen Charles L. Donnelly Jr, told a Symposium of the Air Force Association that it is, in their view, important to design the ATF "as an air-superiority vehicle unencumbered by multirole features". O'Malley, for example, said, "Air superiority has been, and always will be, the linchpin of combat operations. . . ."

This is a rigidly held bit of USAF doctrine, and because of this it is rigid NATO doctrine as well, yet the author has never been able to understand it. If NATO were going to move eastward, air-superiority fighters would be essential, to clear the

enemy fom his own heavily defended airspace. But the scenario is the other way round. The Bad Guys are seen as coming West, and trying to engage their hordes in a series of individual dogfights seems the worst possible kind of defence. Even with perfect IFF it is possible to get "own goals", and the MiG-29 is not going to be an easy opponent to score over in much better than one-for-one. The obvious better answer seems to be 100,000 SAMs, and to keep one's own aircraft as far as possible out of harm's way for at least the first day or two.

One fervently hopes that the sheer nonsense uttered by so many USAF leaders, not only in the 1960s and 1970s but in the 1980s, will eventually have to be replaced by some evidence that human brains are being applied to what is in any case a major challenge. For Gen Donnelly to comment that only rapid runway and taxiway repair capability can meet the need of aircraft to "flow" around airbases, moving to shelters and hangars for refuelling and rearming, shows how utterly divorced from reality the USAF has become. And his comment that STOL aircraft "lack the capability of conventional designs" because "the Harrier, the only STOL in the US inventory, really can't go against a MiG-25 or MiG-29" is almost beyond belief. Gen Donnelly perhaps knows that the Harrier was designed 25 years ago, with no thought whatsoever of flying fighter missions, at a time when manned military aircraft as a class were almost taboo in Britain, and it was a major achievement to get this extremely small subsonic machine built at all. It would be a disaster for the West if such utter nonsense were to have any influence on what the USAF simply must have for the 1990s.

FUTURE BOMBERS

The Russians have a deserved reputation for being logical and methodical. They work out what military hardware they will need and go ahead and build it, uninfluenced by capricious whims of what may happen, in any particular year, to be fashionable. It is for this reason that, during the four years 1977-81, the large bomber remained an ongoing concept and not a mere dinosaur ready for the museum.

Like the fixed-wing carrier, the bomber was found all over the world. Today it is a "rare bird", found only in the Soviet Union, USA, China and France. China is a special case, a mighty nation content to move ahead at what may seem to Western eyes a slow pace yet which involves enormous numbers of people in deepseated changes. A small force of H-6 (Tu-16 "Badger") bombers with free-fall nuclear or conventional bombs sounds like the technology of the 1950s rather than the 1980s, but it is all-Chinese and quite a step

on from a bullock-cart. It would be logical for the very rapidly growing Chinese army of qualified engineers and technologists gradually to acquire a national design capability which in the next century will become formidable.

As for France, this proud nation has never for a moment doubted that it must have a powerful and diverse nuclear deterrent based in submarines, in land silos and delivered by bombers. The bomber element, handled by the Mirage IVA, has been slowly run down, but 18 aircraft are being rebuilt by the Armée de l'Air's Atelier Industriel de l'Air at Clermont Ferrand to IVP standard, carrying the ASMP supersonic cruise missile with a range of 62 miles (100km). The first IVP, not quite up to definitive standard, was delivered for service tests in March 1985. IOC (initial operational capability) is due in 1986, and these 18 aircraft will remain combat-ready into the 1990s. Of course, the ASMP will

have been deployed previously on the Mirage 2000N, and if you are on the receiving end it is academic whether the missile was originally hung under something called a fighter or something called a bomber.

Nomenclature has always been a problem in the West where combat aircraft are concerned. The fault is chiefly that of the mass media, which have never heard of attack or close-support aircraft, avoid the word tactical and think bombers died in World War II. It follows that if it is a combat aircraft it must be a fighter; if it is not a fighter, it gets called a fighter just the same. In the USA in the early 1960s the name trouble spread right through the Pentagon,

Below: Though the non-blended engine pods look crude this forward-swept strategic aircraft has structural, aerodynamic and weapon features that at first glance appear very attractive. Another name for it would be "subsonic bomber". A few changes could make it stealthy.

with the result that the TFX (Tactical Fighter Experimental) remained the F-111 long after it ceased to have any fighter capability, though the crews still like to use the word despite the fact that bombing of one sort or another is what it is there for. There is some kind of finely drawn demarcation line that suggests to the media that aircraft on one side are fighters and aircraft on another are bombers. Size and weight do not enter into it; all F-111s are far heavier than the Mirage IVA or IVP, but the fact they have a fighter designation clouds the issue.

It is evident that there is little demand for exciting artwork showing possible future bombers. In the 1970s a few companies, such as Rockwell, issued the occasional picture to keep the pot boiling but never used the supposed outmoded word "bomber" (the FSW concept reproduced here was presented as "strategic FSW aircraft". The SAC star-spangled band

appeared on its tail, as it also did on a contemporary painting with the cryptic title "laser aircraft in flight", showing that not even bomber defensive turrets can yet be regarded as obsolete.

This is odd, because bomber turrets have been in production in the Soviet Union right up to the present, the almost universal armament in all the different turret versions being twin 23mm cannon. High-power lasers are generally regarded as one area where the Soviet Union is ahead of the West, yet if the Western drawings are to be believed the new "Blackjack" is the first Soviet bomber not to have a turret!

Back in the 1950s some observers, especially in the British government, said that the ICBM made the bomber obsolete. Then it was remembered that armies, ships and many other targets can move, so it was planned for the RAF to get TSR.2 (which could fly recon missions as well, all very hard for an ICBM to do). The RAF was

eventually told to give up any pretensions at deterrence, or any interest in strategic targets, but the two superpowers still recognise their need for bombers despite their possession of powerful strategic missile forces. Yet in summer 1977 President Carter cancelled the B-1, saying that the USAF would use cruise missiles instead. His presentation of the cruise missile as a new invention was ludicrous; quite sophisticated ALCMs were developed in World War I! The fact still remains that, to a much greater degree than the ICBM or SLBM, the ALCM can reprogramme itself in flight to avoid previously unknown defences, study the target, assess the (possibly completely changed) situation and take on-the-spot decisions on which target to go for. Basically similar vehicles can fly reconnaissance missions.

As it is much easier with such small vehicles to achieve almost perfect stealth qualities the writing does appear to be on the wall for the manned bomber. The author recently asked a USAF bomber crew to explain what they could do that no pilotless vehicle could do. After along and heated debate, which at times almost became acrimonious (because the chaps felt they were being "got at") the answer seemed to be a vague belief that six human brains and six pairs of eyes still count for quite a lot. Most readers would agree, but the Northrop ATB is likely to prove the last of the manned bombers. But faced with the lesson of Britain's policy in 1957 such a prophecy could well prove, in its turn, to be mistaken.

Left: Assembly of a B-1B at Rockwell's Palmdale facility. This impressive machine has taken over 20 years to materialise yet, because it has been constantly updated, it remains competitive. Northrop is now hard at work on the ATB, perhaps the future B-2, with full stealth design.

Below: When the wing of this slew-wing bomber is pivoted round flush with the top of the box-like fuselage it becomes a wingless flying fuselage, with good stealth qualities. In contrast, tomorrow's Northrop ATB has virtually no fuselage and gains in stealth by being all-wing.

ADVANCED TECHNOLOGY BOMBER (ATB)

Type: Advanced technology bomber.
Engines: Probably two unaugmented turbofans.
Dimensions: Likely to be much smaller than B-52 or B-1 but larger than FB-111.
Weights: Empty possibly 70,000lb (31,750kg); maximum perhaps 200,000lb (90,700kg).
Performance: Unlikely to be supersonic; combat radius probably at least 3,000 miles (6,400km).

The figures given above are pure guesses. They may be very wide of the mark, and in fact the US media have got in the habit of describing the ATB as a 180-ton (ie, 360,000lb, 163,300kg) aircraft. It has been suggested it is powered by four F101s, like the B-1B, a suggestion the author receives with total disbelief.

To start at the beginning, the formative years of this aircraft were cloaked in secrecy, nothing being published until the "stealth" programme was revealed in late 1981. It was then announced that Northrop Corporation *had already been awarded* contracts totalling $7,300,000,000 to develop an Advanced Technology Bomber to serve as the SAC next-generation bomber after the B-1B. The first ATB prototype is to fly in November 1987. Other companies named as working in the programme are BMAC (Boeing Military Airplane Co.), LTV

Aerospace & Defense and General Electric Aircraft Engine Business Group. The partners are just the ones one might have expected, though of course they are the tip of the iceberg. ATB has since been the biggest single aircraft programme in the Western world, and embraces a very large number of associate contractors and specialist suppliers. It is so important it has a Deputy all to itself in Aeronautical Systems Division at USAF Systems Command, which exerts management on behalf of the customer.

This completes available fact on the ATB, apart from the official entry in a list of Aeronautical Systems Division projects "Advanced manned penetrating bomber employing low-observables technology, with an IOC in the early 1990s". Beyond these stark facts lies a colossal wealth of interesting change in the design of military aircraft which ought to have been predictable at any time in the past 40 years (indeed, to anyone in an official position in Britain, 50 years).

Stealth technology, which incorporates low-observables (LO), means that the entire design of the aircraft is made so that it is very difficult to see at any EM wavelength. The emphasis is strongly on radar wavelengths, but optical (light) invisibility, IR (heat) and other wavelengths are almost equally important. It is impossible to modify an aeroplane into a stealth aeroplane; trying it on a B-52 would not work, and be much more expensive than starting afresh. The expected replacement for the B-52 was the B-70 (RS-70), but this was never put into production because by the time it was ready the idea of Mach 3 at high altitude no longer offered any advantage or

security. Next came the B-1, and here again the emphasis at first was on Mach 2 at high altitude. Major redesign took place and today the B-1B carries heavy loads of "iron bombs" and ALCMs, in place of the original nuclear bombs, and flies at 500mph (800km/h) at the lowest possible altitude. It also has extremely comprehensive defensive electronic systems and large areas specially shaped or skinned with RAM (radar-absorbent material) to reduce the RCS (radar cross-section). Thus, whilst forgetting about the once important demand for supersonic speed, the B-1B has been made roughly one-tenth as "observable" as the B-1A, which itself was only one-tenth as "visible" to radar as a B-52!

This reduction of radar cross section (RCS) to 1 per cent of that of the aircraft it is replacing is good, and totally without precedent. This vital factor was given extraordinarily low priority in the past. The B-52 had roughly double the RCS of its predecessor the B-47, and the final model, the B-52H, roughly doubled it again. Maybe it was thought SAC would never fight against any nation equipped with radar? Certainly, the B-1B is a major step forward, but when President Reagan announced its go-ahead in 1981 he had been advised that, as a modified version of a very old design, it was miles away from a 1981 "clean sheet of paper" bomber. Hence the ATB, which will probably become the B-2 in due course.

A few observers, recalling Northrop's pioneer work with all-wing strategic bombers in 1941-49, have surmised that the company might have been picked because this is an excellent stealth shape. Certainly the Northrop B-35/B-49 families were

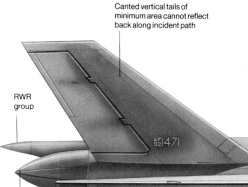

Canted vertical tails of minimum area cannot reflect back along incident path

RWR group

2-D vectoring nozzles masked in side view

Radar altimeter is only (vertical) emitter

ROCKWELL
B-1B

Type: Strategic bomber and cruise missile (ALCM) carrier.
Engines: Four 30,000 (13,600kg) class General Electric F101-102 augmented turbofans.
Dimensions: Span (fully spread) 136ft 8.5in (41.67m), (fully swept) 78ft 2.5in (23.84m); length 147ft 0in (44.81m); height 34ft 0in (10.36m); wing area 1,950sq ft (181.2m²).
Weights: Empty about 172,000lb (78,000kg); maximum 477,000lb (216,365kg).
Performance: Maximum speed, clean (low level) over 600mph (966km/h), (high altitude) 825mph (1330km/h) or Mach 1.25; combat radius (high altitude) 3,600 miles.

One views the B-1B with uniquely mixed feelings. With a baseline budget of $20,500 million in FY81 dollars, the B-1B is at last providing SAC with some modern and probably penetrable muscle. It at last takes the pressure off the old B-52s and allows courageous belief in their penetrative capability to be abandoned and instead enables them to serve their twilight years as ALCM carriers and in the anti-ship role. The full force of the 100 B-1Bs will completely transform SAC and restore the concept of the strategic Triad, composed of ICBMs, SLBMs and bombers. The other side of the coin is that the B-1 has been 23 years in coming, is the end-product of an outrageously long period of specification, argument, discussion, evaluation and

policy-change, and finally is entering service in a form that tries to bridge a basic design of the 1960s with the demands of the next century. In particular, it is much bigger than the optimised 1980s design to fly the same missions, and is in no sense a true stealth design.

This is not to deny that the stealth qualities of the B-1B are about two orders of magnitude better than the B-52, and in fact remarkably good for so large an aircraft whose design originally paid little heed to this requirement. As noted previously in

Right: A B-1A prototype, distinguished by its pointed tailcone, flying at relatively high level with wings at maximum sweep. The European 1 camouflage will probably be replaced by ferrite-derived stealth-quality "iron ball" skin.

amazingly advanced aircraft with superb stealth qualities, though of course this was not thought of at the time. Apart from the obvious facts that the ATB will be as small as possible, as clean as possible, and specially designed to minimise observ- ability, it is not easy to be dogmatic, and certainly not about its appearance. One sketch by the author was based on the possibility of supersonic cruise, but this is difficult to achieve without pumping out high-rate IR energy. A slower ATB, with well shrouded cool engines, would be a little more like the earlier "flying wing" Northrops, and would probably enable size to be reduced for any given combat radius.

Certainly the 180 ton guess is, one hopes, at the upper end of what makes sense; the bigger the ATB, the greater its observabi- lity, especially by IR. There is no reason to claim, as has been reported, that even a 180-ton aircraft is "too large for current or near-term CFC technology"; carbon-fibre composites, like Kevlar and many other fibre-reinforced materials, are just the thing for the ATB, which will use lots of them. We may certainly expect it to have an advanced flight-control system enabling it to overcome deficiencies in natural stabi- lity. Vertical tails are no longer necessary; indeed there was no fin on the first North- rop XB-35!

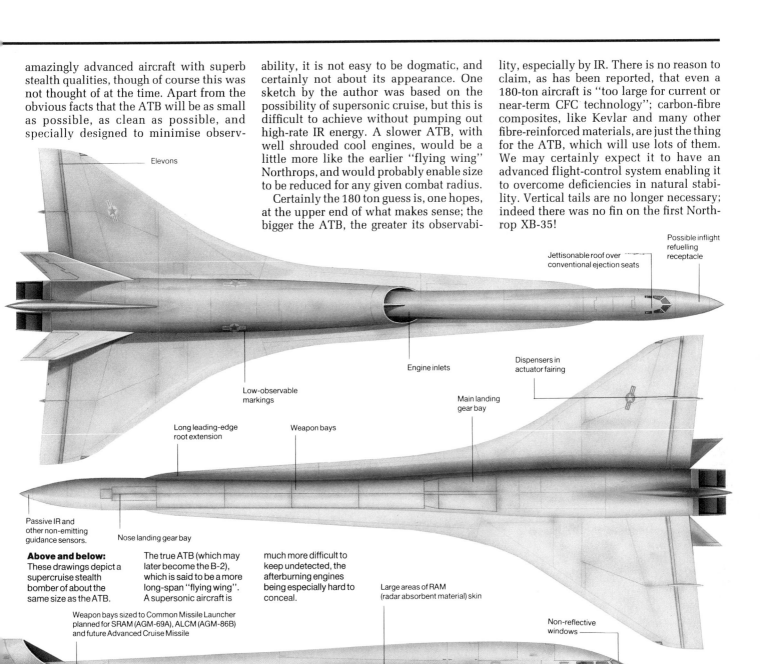

Elevons

Jettisonable roof over conventional ejection seats

Possible inflight refuelling receptacle

Engine inlets

Dispensers in actuator fairing

Low-observable markings

Main landing gear bay

Long leading-edge root extension

Weapon bays

Passive IR and other non-emitting guidance sensors.

Nose landing gear bay

Above and below: These drawings depict a supercruise stealth bomber of about the same size as the ATB.

The true ATB (which may later become the B-2), which is said to be a more long-span "flying wing". A supersonic aircraft is

much more difficult to keep undetected, the afterburning engines being especially hard to conceal.

Large areas of RAM (radar absorbent material) skin

Weapon bays sized to Common Missile Launcher planned for SRAM (AGM-69A), ALCM (AGM-86B) and future Advanced Cruise Missile

Non-reflective windows

this book, the B-1 was originally designed to fly at Mach 2 at high altitude (though the primary mission was low-altitude penetration), and some of the larger modifications introduced when the original four prototypes were flying (1974-77) were made possible when it was realised that Mach 2 was of no interest. Among the changes were replacement of a complex crew-escape capsule by four ordinary ejection seats, simplification of the engine inlets and the nacelles and overwing fairings were also simplified. Curiously, when these changes were announced, in 1975-76, the reason given was pure financial economy, possibly to appease the programme's numerous critics at that time. Another interesting feature is the tremendous emphasis placed in the first half of the 1970s on the B-1's ability to scramble quickly from an airfield about to be hit by an enemy SLBM or ICBM warhead. If anything this is today even more important, but is soft-pedalled.

A go-ahead had been expected in 1976, for SAC service in 1978. Instead argument raged about whether or not "bombers" were obsolete, and – unquestionably against the advice of the Joint Chiefs of Staff – President Carter delayed a decision until the end of FY77, on 30 June 1977, and then announced that there was a new weapon called a cruise missile. This had suddenly transformed the effectiveness of the B-52; the B-1 was therefore no longer needed and would not be put into production. It was a statement fully worthy of British authorship, though contrary to the many British political cancellations Carter did permit some B-1 test flying to continue. In fact the USAF and Rockwell, as well as their main associate contractors, used the next few years to advantage in making the B-1 a much better aircraft. Major changes included a tremendous increase in internal fuel capacity, with corresponding increase in strength of the landing gear; great increase in the numbers and variety of

weapons that can be carried, with a movable fuselage bulkhead in the forward weapons bay and the addition of rows of external stores stations beneath the fuselage; optional weapons-bay tanks; and, most important of all, dramatic improvement in stealth characteristics both by modifying the airframe and the on-board defensive electronics systems.

Below: Informative view of the aft radome of No 4 B-1A, which differs from the production bomber. The vortex generators around the rear fuselage and fin are prominent, as are the completely unshielded (non-stealth) engine nozzles.

External appearance of the bomber hardly changed, and in fact it returned close to the original by elimination of the long dorsal spine. The only significant changes in appearance were the blunt rounded tailcone and obliquely slanting engine inlets. Another item that matured significantly after the Carter cancellation was the F101 engine, which was greatly refined into the F101-GE-102.

In October 1981 a totally new spirit of national confidence enabled President Reagan to announce that 100 of the improved bombers, designated B-1B, would

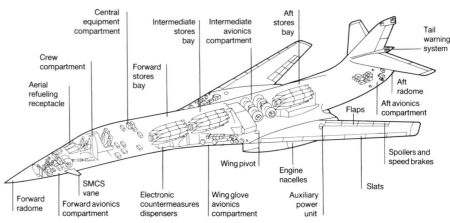

Above: Highly simplified diagram showing disposition of major equipment items in the B-1B. Each of the three stores bays is shown with a rotary dispenser, for a total of 24 SRAM missiles. The electronic countermeasures dispensers which appear to be beneath the forward stores bay are, in fact, beside it in the most forward part of the wing root. The large box ahead of the main landing gears is the titanium wing carry-through box, which carries the wing pivots and also acts as a fuel tank. The circular objects in the wing-glove avionics are ECM antennas.

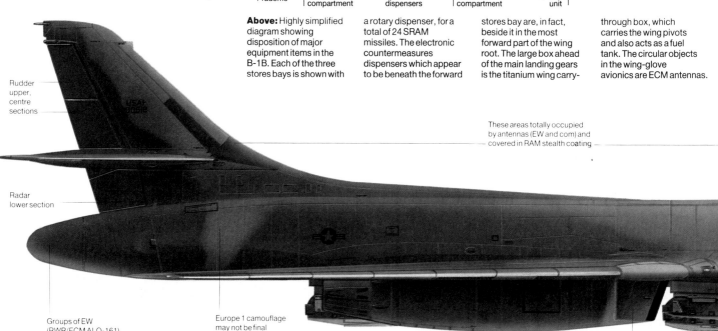

Rudder upper, centre sections

Radar lower section

Groups of EW (RWR/ECM ALQ-161) equipments face aft

Europe 1 camouflage may not be final colour scheme

These areas totally occupied by antennas (EW and com) and covered in RAM stealth coating

Plain subsonic inlets

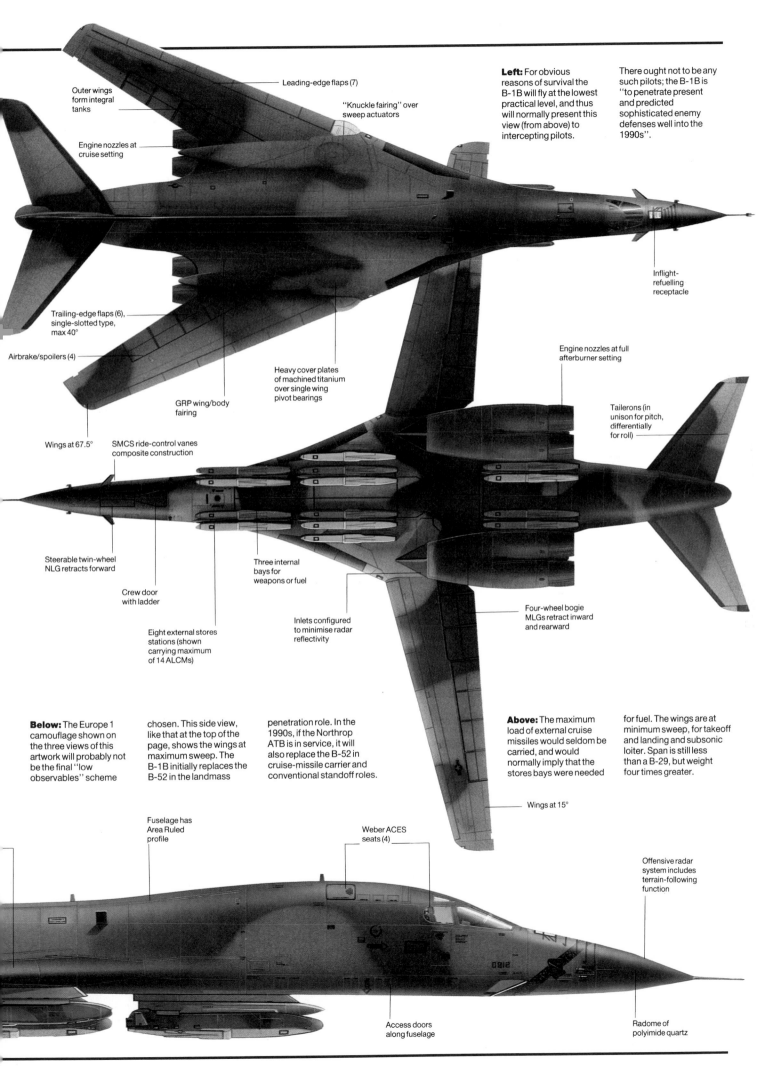

Leading-edge flaps (7)

Outer wings form integral tanks

"Knuckle fairing" over sweep actuators

Engine nozzles at cruise setting

Left: For obvious reasons of survival the B-1B will fly at the lowest practical level, and thus will normally present this view (from above) to intercepting pilots.

There ought not to be any such pilots; the B-1B is "to penetrate present and predicted sophisticated enemy defenses well into the 1990s".

Inflight-refuelling receptacle

Trailing-edge flaps (6), single-slotted type, max 40°

Airbrake/spoilers (4)

Heavy cover plates of machined titanium over single wing pivot bearings

GRP wing/body fairing

Engine nozzles at full afterburner setting

Tailerons (in unison for pitch, differentially for roll)

Wings at 67.5°

SMCS ride-control vanes composite construction

Steerable twin-wheel NLG retracts forward

Three internal bays for weapons or fuel

Crew door with ladder

Inlets configured to minimise radar reflectivity

Four-wheel bogie MLGs retract inward and rearward

Eight external stores stations (shown carrying maximum of 14 ALCMs)

Below: The Europe 1 camouflage shown on the three views of this artwork will probably not be the final "low observables" scheme chosen. This side view, like that at the top of the page, shows the wings at maximum sweep. The B-1B initially replaces the B-52 in the landmass penetration role. In the 1990s, if the Northrop ATB is in service, it will also replace the B-52 in cruise-missile carrier and conventional standoff roles.

Above: The maximum load of external cruise missiles would seldom be carried, and would normally imply that the stores bays were needed for fuel. The wings are at minimum sweep, for takeoff and landing and subsonic loiter. Span is still less than a B-29, but weight four times greater.

Wings at 15°

Fuselage has Area Ruled profile

Weber ACES seats (4)

Offensive radar system includes terrain-following function

Access doors along fuselage

Radome of polyimide quartz

be bought for SAC service from 1986. Subsequent contracts enabled the former No 2 prototype to handle B-1B stability/control, flutter and weapon system tests (but this stalled and crashed in August 1984 after loss of control at low level in circumstances never to be repeated). The former No 4 was also brought in to complete development of the offensive and defensive electronics, which far transcend anything seen in any other combat aircraft – in the West, at least.

Rockwell and partners really hustled on the first B-1B, and instead of flying it in March 1985 got it out of the door at Palmdale in September 1984 and into the air on 18 October. The first SAC delivery, to Dyess AFB, was due in June 1985, and this base now expects to achieve IOC in 1986, almost a year ahead of the original schedule. Rockwell is due to deliver about four aircraft per month from the Palmdale assembly plant, these being received by Dyess, Ellsworth, Grand Forks and McConnell AFBs, the 100th and last in 1988. Ellsworth will have two squadrons of 16 aircraft each, but most bases will have only one, plus supporting KC-135s or KC-10s. Programme cost (rather more than the baseline figure given previously) is currently on-budget at $28,400 million, or some $40,000 million including all supporting services.

During its low-level penetration the B-1B would have the wings partly or wholly swept, the maximum angle being reached at full speed in the most heavily defended area – this despite the great increase in IR emission from the engines in afterburner. At a rough estimate the B-1B RCS (radar cross section) is 1 per cent as large as that of a B-52H, compared with 5 to 10 per cent for the B-1A prototypes. A special subsystem called SMCS (Structural Mode Control System), previously LARC (low-altitude ride control), senses vertical and lateral accelerations of the nose caused by turbulence and automatically damps the motion out by commanding deflections of two small foreplanes (originally the third rudder section was used as well). This extends structural life and improved crew comfort; indeed some form of ride control is essential for all high-speed attack aircraft of the future.

To fly its mission successfully the B-1B uses both an OAS (offensive avionics system) and a defensive avionics system, each bigger and more advanced than anything previously attempted in the West. The prime contractor for the OAS is BMAC (Boeing Military Airplane Co,), and remarkably enough several of its elements are derived from those fitted to the F-16, one of these being the Singer Kearfott INS. There have to be plenty of unavoidable emissions, three emitters being the radar altimeter, doppler and TFR (terrain following radar), the latter being part of the main APQ-164 multimode nose radar which, again very unexpectedly, is derived from the F-16's APG-66 radar, a small aircooled radar of low power but in the B-1 modified with a phased-array aerial (antenna). Much

Top: The first production bomber as it might be seen by an enemy defender on the ground, wings part-swept.

Above: The No. 4 B-1A, partly to B-1B standard, arriving in England in 1982 for the Farnborough airshow.

Below: An amazing "kit layout" of B-1 stores, including nuclear and conventional bombs and ALCM and SRAM missiles. Several of the stores have never been publicly identified. A typical conventional load is 128 Mk 82 bombs.

bigger and more costly, the defensive electronics are the responsibility of Eaton AIL Division and centre on AIL's vast ALQ-161 system, developed for the original B-1 programme and now considerably upgraded and augmented.

Though the B-1 was a completed design just too early for the entire aircraft to be linked into one digital databus, a single bus does integrate all elements of the ALQ-161, and these extend to almost every part of the aircraft. The main task of the ALQ-161 is to detect, locate and jam enemy air-defence radars, the first and most basic task of any defensive electronics system. Comprehensive Elint (electronic intelligence) missions by specially equipped aircraft and satellites continuously attempt to monitor Soviet "threat" systems – such as were all activated during Korean Flight 007's penetration of Far East Soviet airspace in 1983 –

Above: Wings fully forward, the first B-1B displays its smooth contours which are accentuated by the

Europe 1 camouflage scheme. The first production aircraft flew in October 1984, six months ahead of schedule.

and each new emitter waveform and characteristic is then incorporated in the ALQ-161 threat library, the computer storage and programs being designed for easy and repeated updating. This updating also extends to the actual jamming techniques used to confuse the defences. Details are classified, but the ALQ-161 system includes a large number of Northrop computer-controlled jammers and Raytheon phased-array aerial installations. The latter are either flush with the aircraft skin or beneath it, and an exceptional proportion of the surface area of the B-1B is composed of GRP (glass-reinforced plastics) which is a dielectric material

transparent to most EM waves. Extreme engineering skill is needed to allow the internal jammers to "see" out clearly whilst at the same time absorbing or diverting incoming radar signals from outside, which must not under any circumstances be merely reflected back along the incident path.

Despite the fact that it is now in squadron service the ALQ-161 system is so large it hardly stays the same for two days together. The main operating elements are packaged into (as this is written) 131 line-replaceable units, of which about 35 are aerials (antennas). Installed weight of these units is around 5,200lb (2,400kg), to which must be added the weight of cabling, displays and controls; an idea of cable weight is given by the news that during early system design it was found that, while the preferred sub-system arrangement added to the LRU "black box" weight, it *saved* 750lb (340kg) of cabling!

When the B-1 was originally designed the longest item of ordnance to be carried was the AGM-69 SRAM (short-range attack missile), with a length of 14ft 0in (4.27m). The ALCM (air-launched cruise missile) was at that time planned to be the same length, to fit the same rotary launcher, resembling a giant revolver cylinder, which accommodates eight missiles and could fit inside one weapon bay of the B-52. The B-1 was designed with three weapon bays each able to accommodate one of

Below: First production aircraft on systems test. It retains the quick-getaway button on the nose gear which, hit by

the first man to reach it, brings the whole aircraft to takeoff readiness, with engines running and all systems live.

these rotary launchers as an alternative to other loads. What threw a major spanner into the works was the decision to stretch the ALCM to increase its range to 1,550 miles (2,500km), the resulting AGM-86B having a length of 20ft 9in (6.32m). In turn this demanded a longer rotary dispenser which cannot fit in the original triple B-1 weapon bays. The result is an untidy modification which links the front and centre bays into a single volume with a length of 31ft 3in (9.53m) with a movable bulkhead between them. Should it be desired to carry ALCMs internally the bulkhead is moved to accommodate a single launcher with up to eight ALCMs. This is all that can be carried internally.

On the other hand it is still possible to carry three launchers loaded with 24 SRAMs, one in each bay. Other internal load options include 12 B28 or B43 thermonuclear bombs, 24 B61 or B83 bombs, or in a conventional role up to 84 Mk 82 (nominal 500lb/227kg) or 24 Mk 84 (nominal 2,000lb/907kg) GP bombs, all on rotary launchers. Along the underside of the fuselage are hardpoints for eight large stores ejector racks on which can hang an additional 14 ALCMs or SRAMs, eight B28s, 14 B43s/B61s/B83s or Mk 84s, or a further 44 Mk 82s.

The total load of, for example, 38 Mk 84 bombs – which actually weigh well over the nominal 2,000lb figure, so the actual

Above: The B-1B prepares to have a High-Speed Boom thrust into its open receptacle. White lines are for the guidance of the boom operator. The ideal tanker would have direct side-force control to hold station.

Below: A similar scene to that above, but with standard low-observable markings. Note also the instrumentation boom ahead of the radome, which will not be fitted to production B-1Bs. On many missions the B-1B will need no tanker.

load is much greater than 76,000lb (34,475kg) – does not represent any kind of absolute limit, either on grounds of structural strength or available takeoff distance, but is unlikely to be increased. Given a choice, however, a B-1 designed today would have more or larger internal weapon bays in order to eliminate the need for external stowage which both reduces penetration speed and increases radar cross section. There is no provision for external fuel, though long-range auxiliary tanks can be installed in each of the weapon bays after removal of any weapon rotary launchers. There is a flight-refuelling receptacle for a Flying Boom type tanker in the top of the aircraft nose, immediately ahead of the extremely large curved windshield.

In combat service with SAC the expected primary assignments of the B-1B squadrons will be to demonstrate the capability to mount major nuclear or conventional attacks on enemy heartlands, or on any other strategic land targets. Nothing has been said about carrying multisensor reconnaissance pallets, and as this book was written there was no requirement for this capability which is now handled virtually entirely by satellites. However, the B-1B is

Above: The real OAS (Offensive Avionics System) operator station is classified, but this Boeing mock-up's displays are real, and show in great detail hostile threat types and locations, and ECM management.

Below: First production B-1B on its first flight on 18 October 1984. SAC expects to have a 15-aircraft squadron operational by late 1986, by which time production should be four per month. The 100th and last should be delivered in 1988.

stated to have secondary maritime roles, including minelaying, long-range maritime surveillance and ASW (anti-submarine warfare) patrol. Clearly, while minelaying presents few problems and could be carried out with unprecedented accuracy, the ASW mission would require a total rethink of the on-baord systems and sensors. The author regards this as an odd statement in view of the limited number of 100 B-1s being deployed in all, and the fact that one converted for ASW patrol means removal from SAC's force structure of an extremely costly aircraft specially designed to penetrate defended airspace. Perhaps the comment on suitability for ASW patrol was meant to refer to about the year 2020?

Since late 1983 there has been a small but noisy group in US industry, and possibly within SAC, which would like to see a further 100 B-1s purchased in a direct follow-on, if necessary taking money from the ATB budget to pay for them. These aircraft would, it is suggested, be B-1Cs with further structural and systems redesign to increase penetrability, the main change being major modifications to shape and materials and further use of RAM (radar-absorbent materials) coatings in order to give the B-1C stealth characteristics not far short of those of the definitive ATB. There appeared in spring 1985 to be no likelihood of this plan being adopted.

TUPOLEV
BLACKJACK

Type: Strategic bomber and missile launcher.

Engines: Apparently four large augmented jet engines (see below).

Dimensions: (Estimated) span (fully spread) 172ft (52m), (fully swept) 110ft (33.75m); length 166ft (50.6m); height 45ft (13.75m); wing area 3,875sq ft (360m²).

Weights: (Estimated) empty 250,000lb (113,400kg); maximum 590,000lb (267,620kg).

Performance: (Estimated) maximum speed, clean (high altitude) said in West to be Mach 2.1 (1,390mph, 2,235km/h); maximum combat radius with full weapon load (presumably hi-lo-hi profile) 4,535 miles (7,300km).

Existence of a giant new Soviet bomber was rumoured in the late 1970s, and – to the amazement of almost everyone, because one imagines it must have been a politically contrived leak – in late 1981 a satellite image taken on 25 November of that year, showing a prototype of the new bomber parked at Ramenskoye test centre was published in Western media apparently with the full blessing of the US Department of Defense. This was the first time such a reconnaissance picture had been published – for obvious reasons they are normally highly secret – and it showed the new bomber parked near to two Tu-144 or 144D SSTs. This enabled a very accurate calculation to be made of the new bomber's size, yet oddly the published figures have varied over ridiculously large amounts ever since, at first down, then very sharply up and in 1984 back again, but still at a level larger than the original guesses. Why this is strange is that assuming absence of perspective, quite justifiable over a small target area seen from satellite distance of over 100 miles (161km), it should be possible to estimate the bomber's dimensions well within 1 per cent. The figures given are the latest.

Of course it is without question that the DoD now has numerous other satellite images, taken from different angles, and it is not impossible that these later aircraft may be of different sizes. Originally

dubbed Ram-P, the new bomber was given the NATO reporting name "Blackjack", and it is assumed to be a product of the Tupolev OKB, though so far the justification for doing so seems shaky, to put it mildly. With a programme like this nothing would be subcontracted outside the Soviet Union, and assembly is expected to take place in a gigantic new complex at the Kazan GAZ (state aviation factory), the biggest of all the many new or extended factories being completed during the period 1984-86.

Whereas the Tu-22M or Tu-26 "Backfire" was a derived design, originally based on the Tu-22 "Blinder", the new and much larger bomber is a totally fresh design. Yet the wing pivots are at least as far outboard as on the Tu-22M, the fixed inner "glove" portion of the wing has an area roughly as great as that of the swinging outer panels, and aerodynamically the new bomber seems little better than its predecessor except for a greater leading-edge sweep and much greater wing root chord. Why Mach 2.1 should have been considered desirable is uncertain.

At once the point must be made that we in the West (other than Pentagon analysts) are groping in the dark. All we have are a single fuzzy digitally transmitted image of a real prototype and a rash of Western artists' impressions, whose reference appears to have been the B-1 rather than the "Blackjack". In due course, of course, we shall see the aircraft in the air and learn what it is really like.

For the record the author's original 1981 estimates included a length of 188ft 8in (57.5m) and spread span of 174ft (53m), but a guessed maximum weight of 390,000lb (180 tonnes). The current Western guess at the weight is very much greater, though the weapon load is estimated at a mere 36,000lb (16,330kg). This presupposes a tremendous fuel capacity, which would have been feasible on the original size estimates but simply does not tally with the "current" size (said to be only "13 per cent larger than the B-1" instead of the previous guess of "40 per cent").

To wrap up the guesses with the author's

firm belief that it is lighter yet bigger than the official estimates, there remains the question of engines. The simple answer would be "four Backfire" engines, these being assumed to be the same 44,090lb (20,000kg) Kuznetsov NK-144 augmented turbofans as fitted to earlier Tu-144s. Later Tu-144s have Koliesov single-shaft turbojets giving increased range, and a further complicating factor is the series of world records gained by a mysterious aircraft called "Type 101" in July 1983. Aircraft 101 was described as a tailless delta with four 44,090lb (20,000kg) "Type 57" turbojets in underwing nacelles; it set many long range records, with heavy payloads, at speeds up to 1,262mph (2,032km/h), or Mach 1.91. Aircraft 101 also carried a 30-tonne (66,140lb) payload to 59,711ft (18,200m). There is no reason to conclude that Type 101 is "Blackjack", but it is a possibility, despite the description as a tailless delta. Regarding the tail, the 1981 satellite picture appeared to show a long Concorde-like tailcone projecting far behind the tail, and tailplanes with marked anhedral, none of which appear in Western artwork.

Another inexplicable Western statement is, "If the engines are mounted in pairs inside divided underwing ducts, as on the Tu-144, the gap between the ducts will determine the type and size of weapons that 'Blackjack' can carry."

Above: The single satellite image printout, dating from November 1981, on which all public "Blackjack" analysis has been based. Also shown are two of the fleet of Tu-144 (or 144D) transports, which though no longer used by Aeroflot are almost certainly being put to some useful purpose. One may have been the enigmatic "Aircraft 101" which on 13 July 1983 set the first of 14 world class records including Mach 1.91 round a 1000km circuit with 30-tonne (66,140lb) payload. It could well fly surveillance missions.

Entire fin probably devoted to communications, RWR, VOR and other antennas

Upper and lower rudders

Probable fuel tanks along fuselage

Probable aft ECM

Possible APU inlet

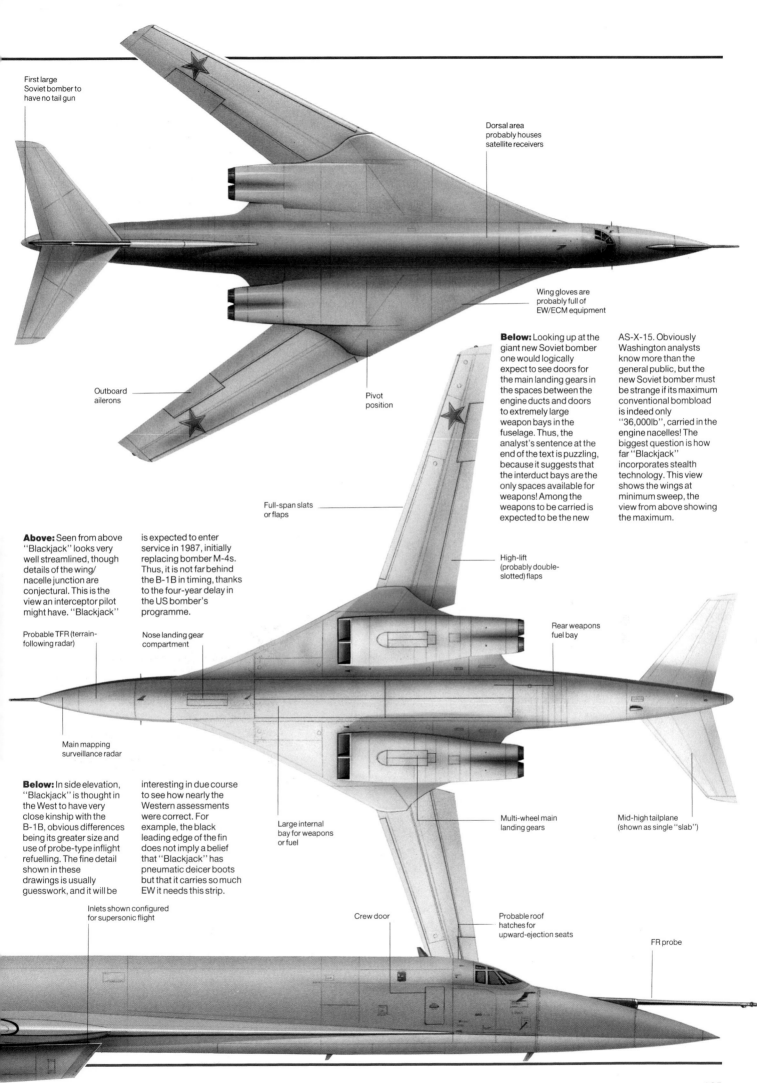

First large Soviet bomber to have no tail gun

Dorsal area probably houses satellite receivers

Wing gloves are probably full of EW/ECM equipment

Outboard ailerons

Pivot position

Below: Looking up at the giant new Soviet bomber one would logically expect to see doors for the main landing gears in the spaces between the engine ducts and doors to extremely large weapon bays in the fuselage. Thus, the analyst's sentence at the end of the text is puzzling, because it suggests that the interduct bays are the only spaces available for weapons! Among the weapons to be carried is expected to be the new AS-X-15. Obviously Washington analysts know more than the general public, but the new Soviet bomber must be strange if its maximum conventional bombload is indeed only "36,000lb", carried in the engine nacelles! The biggest question is how far "Blackjack" incorporates stealth technology. This view shows the wings at minimum sweep, the view from above showing the maximum.

Full-span slats or flaps

Above: Seen from above "Blackjack" looks very well streamlined, though details of the wing/nacelle junction are conjectural. This is the view an interceptor pilot might have. "Blackjack" is expected to enter service in 1987, initially replacing bomber M-4s. Thus, it is not far behind the B-1B in timing, thanks to the four-year delay in the US bomber's programme.

High-lift (probably double-slotted) flaps

Rear weapons fuel bay

Probable TFR (terrain-following radar)

Nose landing gear compartment

Main mapping surveillance radar

Below: In side elevation, "Blackjack" is thought in the West to have very close kinship with the B-1B, obvious differences being its greater size and use of probe-type inflight refuelling. The fine detail shown in these drawings is usually guesswork, and it will be interesting in due course to see how nearly the Western assessments were correct. For example, the black leading edge of the fin does not imply a belief that "Blackjack" has pneumatic deicer boots but that it carries so much EW it needs this strip.

Large internal bay for weapons or fuel

Multi-wheel main landing gears

Mid-high tailplane (shown as single "slab")

Inlets shown configured for supersonic flight

Crew door

Probable roof hatches for upward-ejection seats

FR probe

FUTURE HELICOPTERS

The future of combat helicopters was, and largely still is, bound up in the US Army's LHX programme. This is not to suggest that the world market is waiting to buy whatever LHX is selected – though a sizeable proportion of it probably will do so – but to emphasise that this programme, far more than all others combined, will decide the kinds of vertical-lift aircraft used in land and sea warfare well into the next century. Indeed, one could also add "air warfare" because, following the example of the scout (ie, recon) aircraft of 1914-15, today's helicopters are learning how to shoot each other down.

The LHX is divided into two distinct missions, one called U for utility and the other called SCAT for scout/attack. The objective is to buy one basic type of vehicle in two forms, one tailored to each mission. An obvious example from a previous generation is the Bell "Huey", built in capacious utility forms with a large cabin and few weapons and also in the gunship Cobra forms with tandem armoured seats in a slim fuselage bristling with weapons. But the LHX search has gone much wider, and for several years important research centres and the US industry have been working on a broad front to see what kind of airborne vehicles might best fly the missions. As this is an Army programme it does not include such duties as ASW search/strike or anti-ship operations, but it does embrace almost every kind of overland mission other than bulk cargo and heavy lift. The Army expects to buy at least 4,000 LHXs, as explained later.

The reason the programme is so important is that the technology has now reached the point at which the wealth of possible kinds of LHX causes its own problems. Conventional helicopters are understood and quite capable, but inevitably limited in agility, speed, range and many other aspects of performance, and their very large rotors, which tend to be visible to enemies even when the rest of the helicopter is hidden "hull down" behind cover, can now be instantly identified by radars because of their characteristic blade frequency. Some alternatives seem much more attractive on the grounds of speed, agility, survivability and cruising efficiency (which equates with greater range).

One of the most attractive alternatives is the ABC (advancing blade concept) contra-rotating rotor system, fully explored by Sikorsky and the US Army at speeds over 300mph (482km/h). Perhaps even better is another scheme investigated by the same contractor, the X-Wing, which is good for 345mph (556km/h). A completely different scheme is Bell's tilt-rotor, extensively tested on the XV-15 and now to be used on the V-22 transport, described in the next section; this is good for almost 400mph (644km/h). There are many other schemes which offer the helicopter's advantages without its severe restrictions, yet one of the most significant announcements in the history of combat aircraft was that by the US Army earlier in 1985 that the LHX would be a helicopter. In other words, all the clever and attractive new schemes are, at present at least, not as good as the conventional helicopter!

Some 20 years ago metal or wooden rotor blades started to be replaced by lighter, more efficient fatigue-free blades made of fibre-reinforced composites; and complicated articulated hubs with dozens of oil-lubricated bearings were replaced by simpler hubs, either with elastometric bearings needing no attention or with no bearings whatever, the blade roots being flexible. Today the US Army has extended composite structures to embrace the whole airframe of a helicopter, Bell and Sikorsky having built complete ACAP (Advanced Composite Airframe Program) helicopters which promise to be lighter, cheaper, simpler, safer, maintenance- and fatigue-free, and harder to see by radar. New helicopters made in the traditional way with light-alloy airframes are already out of date, and will soon find their markets diminishing.

The same is true of on-board systems. Digital data highways are absolutely essential, and an unexpected British MoD research contract awarded in 1983 to Westland Helicopters requires the company to demonstrate data looms of optical fibres, transmitting the signals by coding the coherent light passing along the fibres. Systems of this nature, because of their extremely high frequency and data rate, can transmit information at millions to billions of times the limiting rates possible with traditional electrical conductors or even coaxial cables. Helicopter subsystems, linking navigation, weapon-aiming and steering sensors to new kinds of cockpit display, are among the most exciting and rapidly developing areas of modern technology, the main hold-up in development – as in all other forms of advanced technology outside the Soviet Union – being a desperate shortage of qualified people able to fill thousands of vacancies.

Predictably the major helicopter pro-

Below: In the original 1961 US Army LOH (light observation helo) contest Bell and Hughes got big orders and Hiller got nothing. Today the new Hiller company has relaunched a totally revised version as the RH-1100M Hornet. Claimed to be the cheapest light attack machine in its class, it draws a global experience with the 5-seat civil FH-1100. Powered by an Allison C20 of 420hp it is seen here with TOWs and a nose-mounted TOW sight.

ducers are already finding it increasingly difficult to sell their products worldwide because of the rapid growth of licence construction and, since 1980, in the establishment of new helicopter industries with design capability. Though at first the products of these industries may not be fully technically competitive, they are indicative of gradually shrinking markets for the handful of famous helicopter builders who once competed only with each other. Recognising this such alert builders as Aérospatiale and MBB now have major stakes in some of these newly emergent helicopter industries. Where this is impossible, as in India, the best that the established builders can do is collaborate in design and provide specialist parts, as in the new ALH programme.

The following entries are the most important of which details are reliably known in spring 1985. Such very important new Soviet combat helicopters as the Kamov "Hokum" and Mil "Havoc" were still little more than names outside the Soviet Union, and the only illustration purporting to be of either was a "Havoc" which had clearly been traced over a distorted picture of the AH-64 Apache!

Above: By the time this book appears flight testing should have begun of the Sikorsky RSRA (described later) in its X-wing form. The very special rotor is locked in the position shown and the helicopter becomes an aeroplane!

Below: Sikorsky's other radically new helicopter is the XH-59A ABC (advancing blade concept) coaxial machine, seen here on US Army test. Capable of over 300mph (482km/h) it is judged ready for production.

EUROCOPTER HAP/HAC/PAH

A basic feature of the Eurocopter programme is the development of the three distinct versions. In terms of planned numbers the most important is the German model, the PAH-2. This is almost bound eventually to be developed with an MMS (mast-mounted sight), but in spring 1985 it still had the sight systems low in the nose, forcing the helicopter to expose itself before it can set about combat operations. This machine seats the pilot above and behind and the copilot/gunner in the forward cockpit, where he can manage the sights and weapons. The weapon wing is mounted well forward and would normally carry eight HOT missiles on the inboard attachments and either two twin Stinger missile boxes or Thomson-Brandt 68-22 rocket launchers (22 tubes of 68mm calibre) on the outers. As in many battlefield helicopters the Stingers would be carried for self-defence in the air/air role. Exact details of the nose sight are still being worked out, but it will include a FLIR and large-aperture magnifying optical sight;

low-light TV and/or laser designation are likely to be added alongside. The sight is of course stabilised to take out helicopter attitude-change and vibration, to give a clear target image under all conditions including battlefield smoke.

The French counterpart of PAH-2 is HAC-3G (anti-tank helicopter, 3rd generation). The most obvious difference between the two helicopters is that HAC-3G has an MMS above the main rotor, giving a perfect view of the target area without exposing the helicopter other than the main rotor. The French ALAT (light aviation of the army) has specified that the pilot should sit in the front cockpit and the copilot/gunner in the rear. The MMS normally serves the back-

seater's cockpit display, while the pilot also has a PNVS (pilot's night vision system) in the nose to assist in night and bad-weather navigation at extremely low altitudes. No details have yet been published of the navigation aids that will be carried, though the main mission computer(s) will almost certainly store all necessary battlefield waypoints as in other helicopters in this class.

The HAC-3G is likely to have the same "wings" as PAH-2, though the weapon fit may not be identical. In terms of timing this is the last of the three versions, and according to 1985 published information the prototype HAC-3G (No 07) is not due to fly until January 1993. By this time the

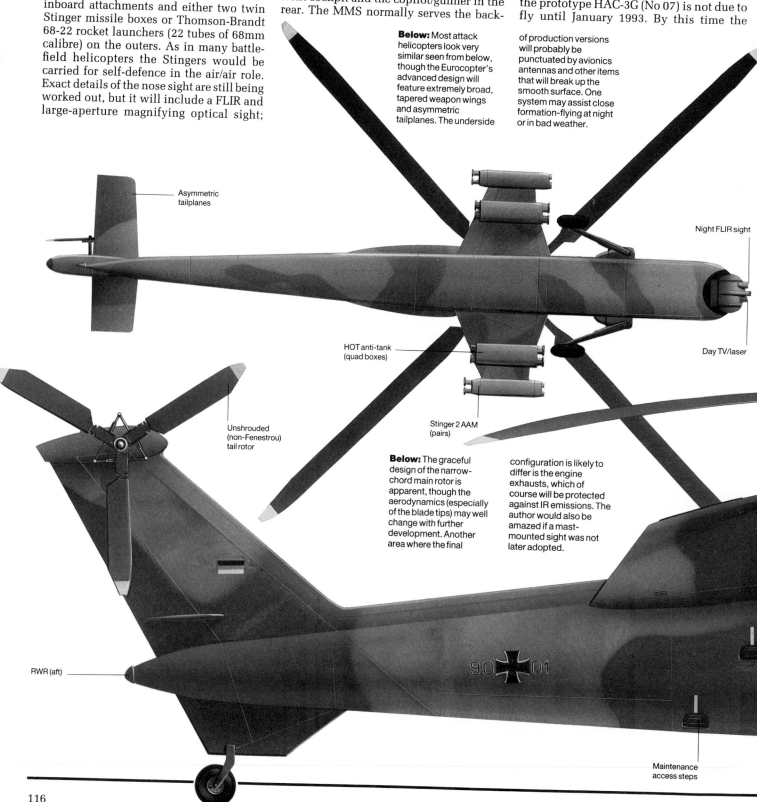

Below: Most attack helicopters look very similar seen from below, though the Eurocopter's advanced design will feature extremely broad, tapered weapon wings and asymmetric tailplanes. The underside of production versions will probably be punctuated by avionics antennas and other items that will break up the smooth surface. One system may assist close formation-flying at night or in bad weather.

Asymmetric tailplanes

Night FLIR sight

HOT anti-tank (quad boxes)

Day TV/laser

Stinger 2 AAM (pairs)

Unshrouded (non-Fenestrou) tail rotor

Below: The graceful design of the narrow-chord main rotor is apparent, though the aerodynamics (especially of the blade tips) may well change with further development. Another area where the final configuration is likely to differ is the engine exhausts, which of course will be protected against IR emissions. The author would also be amazed if a mast-mounted sight was not later adopted.

RWR (aft)

90 01

Maintenance access steps

116

planned ATGW-3 (anti-tank guided weapon, 3rd generation) ought to be in production by EMDG (Euromissile Dynamics Group). This completely new high-speed missile will be of the "fire and forget" type, and totally different in technology from HOT (which in 1985 is becoming obsolescent). It is thus expected that by the time HAC-3G enters ALAT service its normal anti-tank armament will comprise four ATGW-3s on each inboard wing pylon. The ALAT expects to deploy 140 HAC-3Gs, compared with 212 PAH-2s for the German army.

Third of the variants so far planned is the French ALAT's HAP (Hélicoptère d'Appui et de Protection). This is in many respects considerably different from the specialised anti-tank versions, because to fly its armed escort and fire-support missions it will have a powerful chin turret armed with a GIAT AM 3078 gun of 30mm calibre, with belt feed from a rear magazine. The weight of this installation is balanced by moving the weapon wings rearwards, to a position

well aft of the rotor hub. Among the external weapons to be carried are two quadruple boxes of Matra Mistral close-range IR-homing AAMs (instead of Stingers) and two Thomson-Brandt 68-22 rocket launchers, all carried on the outer (wingtip) attachments only. Sights and sensors are again not fully determined, but in this helicopter they are to be grouped in the cockpit roof immediately ahead of the main rotor pylon. Planned production of the HAP is to be 75, the first prototype (No 04) being due to fly in December 1987.

This prototype is to fly in France at roughly the same time as No 03 makes its maiden flight at MBB in West Germany. These December 1987 flights will start the

development of the operational versions of this helicopter, but development of the basic machine will begin in about September 1987 with prototypes 01 and 02. These will be unarmed machines and will be used to help develop the engines, rotor system and basic on-board equipment and systems. A total of seven development prototypes is planned. This number might be increased if further variants should be called for. The point must be made, however, that none of the helicopters of this family can offer any significant capability not already present in the Italian A 129, and thanks to its earlier start the A 129 is much cheaper and will be in operational service before the first Eurocopter flies.

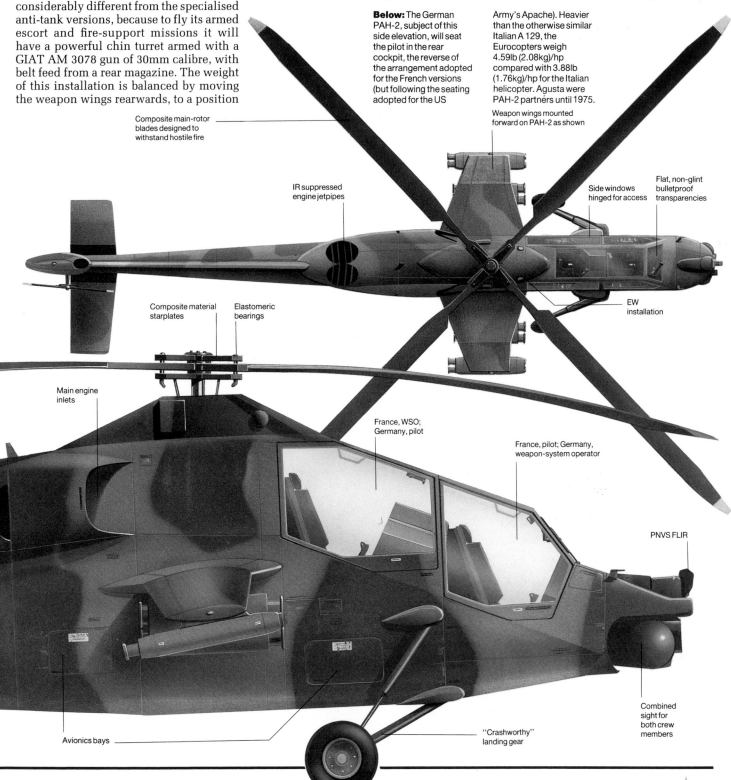

Below: The German PAH-2, subject of this side elevation, will seat the pilot in the rear cockpit, the reverse of the arrangement adopted for the French versions (but following the seating adopted for the US

Army's Apache). Heavier than the otherwise similar Italian A 129, the Eurocopters weigh 4.59lb (2.08kg)/hp compared with 3.88lb (1.76kg)/hp for the Italian helicopter. Agusta were PAH-2 partners until 1975.

Composite main-rotor blades designed to withstand hostile fire

Weapon wings mounted forward on PAH-2 as shown

IR suppressed engine jetpipes

Side windows hinged for access

Flat, non-glint bulletproof transparencies

Composite material starplates

Elastomeric bearings

EW installation

Main engine inlets

France, WSO; Germany, pilot

France, pilot; Germany, weapon-system operator

PNVS FLIR

Avionics bays

"Crashworthy" landing gear

Combined sight for both crew members

HINDUSTAN AERONAUTICS LTD
ALH

Type: Utility and multirole helicopter.
Engines: Two turboshaft engines, either 965shp Turboméca TM333B or 1,050shp P&WC PT6B-35E.
Dimensions: Not yet finalised (spring 1985).
Weights: Empty about 4,244lb (1,925kg); maximum 9,039lb (4,100kg).
Performance: Maximum cruising speed at SL 169mph (270km/h); range at SL with 1,543lb (700kg) payload and 20min reserve 248 miles (400km).

Like aircraft industries all over the world, HAL (Hindustan Aeronautics Ltd) is steadily growing up and taking on wider responsibilities. The Bangalore Complex's Helicopter Division, under K. N. Murthy, has many years' experience building basically Aérospatiale machines under licence. Some six years ago it began studying the design of an indigenous ALH

(Advanced Light Helicopter), and by 1980 had decided that this should be a machine in the 4-ton class with two turbine engines, to be developed in three basic versions, one for the Indian Air Force, another for the army and a third for the navy. In due course a civil version is also expected to be produced, but the emphasis at present is entirely on military versions.

Since 1981 overseas partners have been sought to underpin the design and development of what is by any standard a major challenge. No modern helicopter has ever been developed in Asia outside the Soviet Union; not even Japan has produced a machine of its own design. In 1983 MBB of West Germany agreed to collaborate , and the MBB BO 108 design is already being used as the basis for the ALH. The point must be made that MBB is already collaborating with Kawasaki of Japan in the development and production of the BK

117, and as the two helicopters are in exactly the same class it is remarkable that the Indian agreement has gone through.

The four-blade main rotor has CFRP (carbon-fibre reinforced plastics) blades, with power folding at least in the naval version. The hub is likely to be metal, rather than of composite construction. The fuselage will be mixed metal and composite, and will incorporate a typically capacious cabin seating up to 16, not including the two in the cockpit. The engines are above the cabin, and the fuel in four tanks under the floor. The tricycle landing gears have fully retractable single wheels, the main units being pivoted to short stub wing sponsons to achieve adequate track.

Clearly this is intended to be an all-can-do helicopter, because despite its enormous cabin it is being developed in an armed version with a 30mm Hughes Chain Gun in a chin turret, and carrying up to

KAMOV
"HOKUM"

Type: Probably, multirole armed and air-combat helicopter.
Engines: Not known but believed to be two 2,225shp Isotov TV3 turboshaft engines.
Dimensions: Not known, but main rotors may be similar in diameter to those of Ka-27/Ka-32, which are 54ft 11.4in (16.75m); no definite dimensions known.
Weights: Said in Washington to be "in 12,000lb (5,443kg) class".
Performance: Combat speed probably at least 186mph (300km/h), reported in DoD "Soviet Military Power" 1985 to be 217mph (350km/h), and range to be 155 miles (250km).

Though existence of this helicopter was reported in the West in summer 1984, almost a year later hardly anything was known about it, and the only artist's impression published was a sketchy side view in the 1985 DoD "Soviet Military Power". Apart from the fact that it is apparently designed by the Kamov OKB (experimental construction bureau) and is in the flight-test stage, almost everything else is supposition. Even the NATO code-name of "Hokum" may perhaps refer to a different helicopter. As all previous Kamov helicopters have used the superimposed coaxial rotor layout it has been assumed

that "Hokum" is also of this family, and combined with the suggested weight, and the belief that it has a two-man crew, the inference is that it is an air-combat derivative of the Ka-27/Ka-32 "Helix" series.

It would be logical to mate the existing powerplant group, transmission and co-axial rotors of these well-established shipboard helicopters with a slim tandem-seat fuselage to create a formidable air-combat helicopter which could carry guns, AAMs and other weapons. It could fly from ships with units of the AVMF (Soviet naval air force), but similar machines could also fly various missions connected with land

MIL
Mi-28 (?) "HAVOC"

Type: Believed to be air-combat helicopter.
Engines: Believed to be two 2,200shp Isotov TV3 turboshaft engines.
Dimensions: Diameter of main rotor believed to be same as Mi-24 (estimated 55ft 9in, 17.0m); length of fuselage (estimate) 57ft 1in (17.4m).
Weights: (Estimate) empty 17,640lb (8,000kg); maximum 24,250lb (11,000kg).
Performance: (Estimate) maximum speed 220mph (354km/h); combat radius 149 miles (240km).

The 1984 edition of the US Department of Defense booklet "Soviet Military Power" contained a crude drawing (traced over an AH-64 Apache, so far as one could tell) labelled "Mi-28 Havoc". The existence of a slim-bodied Mil gunship had been suspected for a long time, and prototypes may have been under test for years. Now it appears that the helicopter given the NATO name "Havoc" is nearing operational service. If the number is 28 it suggests a primary role other than air-combat,

though possibly the rule that fighters always receive odd numbers does not apply to helicopters.

Little is known about "Havoc", though *Jane's All the World's Aircraft* suggests that it actually more closely resembles the Lockheed AH-56A Cheyenne than an Apache. One would expect to find a tandem stepped cockpit followed by a slender fuselage and, probably, engines, rotors and tail similar to the Mi-24. This would be a wholly logical, if not obvious, development. Such a helicopter would have outstanding flight performance (the large-cabin Mi-24 already holds various speed records at speeds up to 228.9mph, 368.4km/h) and also outstanding man-oeuvrability, even when heavily loaded with weapons. A "Havoc" could fly all the missions flown by "Hind" versions except those requiring transport of a squad of troops. It would combine tremendous weapons capability in air/air and air/ground roles with improved survivability and probably the highest speed of any

combat helicopter currently in service.

In April 1985 the US Department of Defense issued its annual review of "Soviet Military Power", but the artwork is still highly speculative. The drawing of an Mi-28 "Havoc" is far better than the crude outline of 1984 but can almost certainly be relied upon to be pure invention. The very large single-barrel gun is nothing like any Soviet weapon previously known and appears to be of some 30mm calibre. The enormously bulky nose looks more like a World War II bomber than a modern gun-ship helicopter, and perhaps the oddest thing of all is that nothing except the main rotor seems to bear the slightest commonality with the Mi-24. Why almost everything proven and reliable should be totally altered is not explained.

Armament is not yet reliably known, but in the colour art at right the weapon wings are carrying four-tube anti-tank missile boxes (believed to be a modified AS-6 Spiral) and two tubes of close-range AAMs. The gun is turret-mounted and trainable.

eight TOW or HOT anti-tank missiles. The naval version is expected to undertake minelaying among many other duties. Normal equipment is expected to include weather radar or radar for battlefield surveillance or anti-ship targeting or for ASW operations. Maximum payload is to be 2,205lb (1,000kg) internal or 2,866lb (1,300kg) slung externally. All versions will have provision for a rescue hoist, and comprehensive avionics for all-weather operation are planned. In spring 1985 it was expected that the first prototype would fly in "1985 or 1986", and the simpler utility models might be in service by 1988.

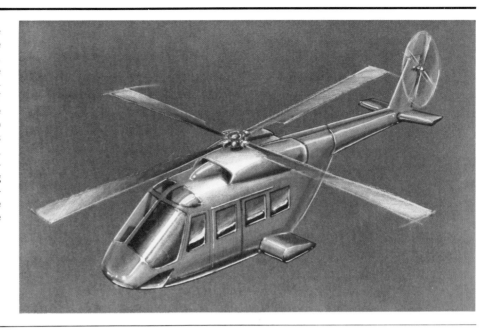

Right: This impression was the only illustration of ALH to become available by spring 1985. It was prepared by the partner company, MBB. It is surprising that the Rolls-Royce Gem is not a candidate engine, as it is both modern and experienced, with a proven combat record.

warfare. One of the main shipboard advantages of the coaxial Kamovs has been compact overall dimensions, but Sikorsky has used a similar form of rotor – in a very different and more advanced form – to create helicopters able to manoeuvre like a fighter at speeds exceeding 300mph (482km/h). There is no point in speculating further on "Hokum", whose characteristics will become better known in due course. Apart from the DoD's figures quoted under performance, the only thing it has said of the new helicopter is that it "will give the Soviets a significant rotary-wing air superiority capability".

Below: This drawing is based on that which appears in the 1985 edition of the US Department of Defense "Soviet Military Power". Some aspects of the shape cannot be correct, but it does confirm that the only parts which may be common to "Helix" are the engine/rotor system. The apparent cylinders under the engines may be weapon pods, and the shape like a barrel in front of the swept fin may be an endplate fin on a tailplane. Landing gears retract.

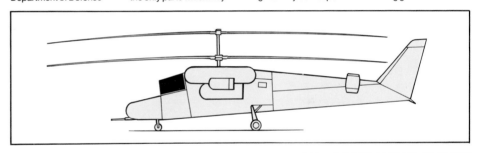

Below: An illustration from the 1985 edition of "Soviet Military Power" showing the US Department of Defense version of "Havoc" in Afghanistan.

Right: There has been much speculation as to the number of main rotor blades; the artist has shown only four, though recent analysis indicates there could be five.

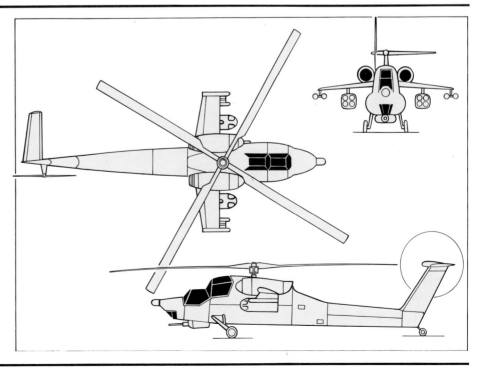

Type: Two versions, SCAT and Utility.
Engines: Two 1,200shp T800 turboshaft engines (contractor to be selected).
Dimensions: Not yet finalised.
Weights: Maximum to be 8,000lb (3,630kg).
Performance: Required speed (SCAT) 170 knots (196mph, 315km/h), (Utility) 160 knots (184mph, 296km/h).

The US Army's LHX (Light Helicopter Experimental) programme is intended to decide the baseline SCAT (scout/attack) and utility helicopters which will be standard types far into the next century. The Army alone expects to buy at least 4,500 of the two versions, and the winner will be in a good position to become the dominant builder of light helicopters throughout the non-Communist world. It is hardly surprising that each of the major US helicopter builders has since 1983 striven to win the mighty LHX programme to the exclusion of everything else. Major helicopter builders outside the USA have shown intense interest but have no chance

of being considered in any role except possibly as a licensee of winning designs.

From the start of the programe the Army has been clear that the ROCs (required operational capabilities) exclude a single winning design. The utility machine, called LHX-U, will replace the UH-1 "Huey" in all its transport versions, carrying a crew of two and a squad of 6/8 troops. No armament is required other than a light machine gun fixed to fire ahead or mounted on a pintle in the doorway, but the LHX-U obviously has to be capable of rescue using a hoist, casevac using stretchers, light cargo missions with loads carried internally or slung, and also in due course it is certain to fly EW missions laden with Elint, Comint, jammers and similar specialised avionics. The Army needs 2,408 of this version, costing $5 million each.

The LHX-SCAT (scout/attack) will replace the various AH-1S and related versions of the HueyCobra as well as the UH-1M and, eventually, the OH-58D which itself will continue joining the Army

until 1991. This version will have a slim single-seat fuselage, and almost all its payload will comprise sensors and weapons. The number needed in the pure "gunship" attack role is 1,100, with 1,027 more required to fly scout missions, at $8 million each.

At the start of work by industry on LHX contractors were encouraged to explore every technical solution that appeared to offer promise. Among these were the Bell/Boeing Vertol tilt-rotor VTOL (see V-22 described later), Sikorsky ABC (advancing blade concept) and X-rotor/wing, Hughes Notar (No Tail Rotor) and various even more unconventional schemes. In almost every case the unconventional approach offered escape from the fairly rigid limitations on flight performance imposed by the conventional helicopter. The tilt-rotor aircraft looked particularly attractive because it was quite compact, potentially highly manoeuvrable and could fly at 350mph (563km/h) with cruising efficiency much better than any helicopter, which equated with greater range and pay-

load. Yet, after studying the prospects, the US Army decided in early March 1985 to disallow all unconventional approaches and insist upon submissions of conventional helicopters only.

This is a decision of the most profound importance. The reason behind it is simple enough. The ROC figures laid down by the Army can be met by conventional helicopters, and so there is no point in going for more advanced solutions which appear bound to involve higher technical risk and increased acquisition and life-cycle costs. In the words of the LHX Program Manager, Brig-Gen Ronald K. Andreson, "We feel we can reach our goals without the higher risks involved with the more unconventional technical solutions. Our goals for the LHX include a significant enhancement in survivability and a significant increase in capabilities – but not at a boundless cost." At first glance this all sounds sensible and will go down well with the US Congress which votes the money.

At the same time, this is not just another helicopter but a programme that will

Left: A Boeing-Vertol impression of an LHX operating in the SCAT role. The MMS feeds in distance and direction of two ground targets, which are at once engaged by missile and gun, while chaff/flares fired below give protection. The pilot's view is synthetic, generated by sensors which cannot be blinded by lasers or adverse weather.

Above: Disqualified from being an LHX candidate, the Bell BAT (Bell Advanced Tilt-rotor) was expected to be the fastest offering, at 350mph (563km/h), and with the impressive range of 2,415 miles (3,887km). Its weapons would have been exposed just before firing. Reasons given for rejecting "unconventional" configurations are explained on this page.

Below: This Sikorsky X-wing bears DARPA/Navy titles, but a similar configuration has been studied for the LHX programme, using a rebuilt Sikorsky S-72 for research. As explained in the X-wing entry later in this book, it is not certain that the X-wing configuration may not be admitted. Certainly it could outperform any coventional helicopter.

Above: Broadly conventional, except for Notar design, the Hughes Helicopter bids have a good chance of winning. This is one of several versions with small swept wings, some carrying missiles on the tips. This is the sort of thing the Army wants, but figures must be guaranteed.

determine the kinds of aerial vehicles used not only by the US Army but by all Western armies for perhaps the next 30 years. A conventional helicopter, with one main rotor and either a tail rotor or (as explained later) a Notar tail boom, imposes rigid limitations on speed, cruising efficiency and payload for any given installed power. By pulling out all the latest technology it is possible to do perhaps 10 per cent better with the engine and 5 to 10 per cent better with the helicopter, whilst greatly reducing maintenance needs and improving reliability and survivability. But by switching to a different technology the margins can easily exceed 100 per cent. What happens if the 1986 edition of "Soviet Military Power" includes pictures of red-starred tilt-rotor or stopped-rotor machines, or jet-lift STOVLs to fly these missions? At one stroke the LHX decision could look an error of colossal magnitude. This is a risk the US Army is prepared to take, and it will soon be irrevocable.

So far as is known all main contractors are still fighting hard to win: Bell, Boeing Vertol, Hughes Helicopters and Sikorsky. It would appear highly likely that the next stage will be for these to team into two pairs each pushing one joint submission. This has already happened with the engine industry, where three new 1,200hp turbo-

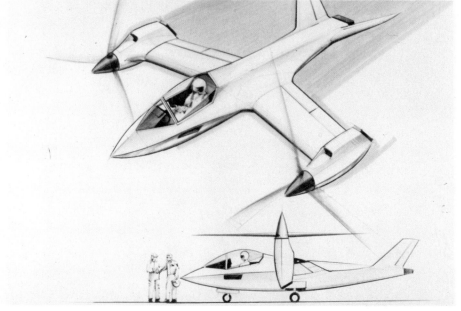

Above: One of the Bell tilt-rotor projects, studied for at least the SCAT mission until disqualified. SCAT missions can be flown by single-seaters, though an advanced cockpit is needed. Note body chine and blended wing root.

shaft candidates are being promoted by Allison/Garrett, Avco Lycoming/Pratt & Whitney and General Electric/Williams. The Army has insisted that, no matter which of the three teams wins the award (for an engine to be designated as the T800) both partners will be qualified from the start in what is called dual-source supply. Thus, throughout the entire life of the LHX, the engines could be bought from either partner, thus maintaining razor-sharp competition between them. Exactly the same policy seems certain to be applied to the helicopter itself. As Bell/Boeing are already teamed on the V-22, they will probably collaborate again on LHX, leaving Hughes and Sikorsky as the rival team. Hughes/Sikorsky would take some knocking of heads together, but it does not look impossible.

There is little point in speculating on the various conventional helicopter submissions being studied by the Army in

Above: Acceptable as a "conventional" helicopter, this Bell study shows evidence of stealth design and attention to minimising emissions. Weapons and landing gear are carried internally, and the tail rotor is shrouded.

spring 1985, but the Hughes Notar concept certainly features on one. A subsidiary of the giant McDonnell Douglas since early 1984, Hughes Helicopters received an Army contract in 1981 to investigate its idea for eliminating the familiar tail rotor, normally fitted to counter main-rotor torque and also provide yaw (directional) control. Part of the funding was provided by DARPA (Defense Advanced Research Projects Agency), which has also underpinned several other new technologies for inclusion in the LHX.

The Notar idea reduces noise and vulnerability, which might be particularly important in flight at extremely low altitude; and it would also eliminate casualties to people on the ground caused by walking into tail rotors or being struck by blades from a tail rotor which has come into contact with the ground or other obstruction. Instead of the tail rotor, the rear shaft drives a fan which blasts compressed air from a narrow slit along the lower left side of an enlarged tail boom. The resulting circulation causes a powerful side force similar to that from the tail rotor and, like the rotor, it automatically varies with engine power to counter the varying torque from the main rotor. A small rotary nozzle at the tip of the boom blows in any chosen direction to give yaw control. Notar could well be a feature of the eventual LHX, no matter which candidate helicopters win the production contracts.

The weight of the LHX, in both versions, is expected to be 8,000lb/3,630kg (plus or minus 500lb/225kg). Anything under 7,500lb (3,400kg) will not be competitive because it will be deficient in range, payload or other variables, while anything over 8,500lb (3,855kg) will simply be disqualified as too heavy. An indication of the kind of performance expected is afforded by looking at some helicopters from the past. The S-55 weighed about 7,000lb (3,175kg) and had 600hp. The S-61 (Sea King) weighs 21,500lb (9,750kg) and has 2,400hp. The LHX will pack 2,400hp into an 8,000lb helicopter, and so ought to fly rings round any other rotorcraft of any conventional type. The calculated risk that the US Army is now taking is that nobody else is going to do even better with a VTOL machine of some unconventional type.

FUTURE TRANSPORTS

Lockheed's evergreen C-130 Hercules, still finding customers after more than 30 years, was the classic design which at last put together all the things that today seem obvious requirements and yet are taken for granted. Among them are: a single strong floor for the payload, at a convenient (so-called truck-bed) height above the ground, and horizontal instead of steeply sloping; an unobstructed interior with width and height adequate for the items that need to be carried; pressurization and air conditioning; high flight performance, and in particular STOL capability; high-flotation landing gear able to operate from soft or rough surfaces without digging in or flinging stones or other debris at any part of the aircraft; the ability to carry large numbers of paratroops and despatch them safely in very tight sticks; provision of a rear ramp door so that heavy trucks, palletized freight and other bulky loads can be put straight on board; and design of this ramp door so that it can be opened in flight for heavy dropping of cargo and then closed to restore the low-drag external shape. Until the C-130 came along most military transports lacked more than half of these "obvious" features.

When the C-130 was young propellers were needed both for STOL and for long range operation. By 1960, however, the turbofan had shown that jets can fly long ranges, and today the high bypass ratio fan

Above: NASA's Augmentor Wing research aircraft was a DHC-5 Buffalo rebuilt with Spey turbofans with not only vectored nozzles but also giant pipes ducting fan air to the exceedingly powerful flaps. Though it had a short-span wing the AWRA could fly at 41 knots (46mph, 76km/h), and could easily operate from an airship 1,500ft (450m) long. This technology has not been put to use.

Right: Boeing's YC-14, part of a programme planned to replace the C-130, was the first and by far the biggest and most impressive of all USB (upper-surface blowing) aircraft. Here one of the two YC-14s is seen in reverse thrust. Nobody has yet explained why USB has found no production application, despite the fact that, on paper, it is easily the most powerful STOL system for efficient military airlifters.

Left: Careful study of the Japanese Asuka research transport shows that the wing boundary-layer control systems are very different from anything previously published, which probably explains the very long delay in getting this machine out of the factory door. It is a further application of the USB method first tested, with just two engines, on the YC-14 pictured above. Of course, the ideal USB aircraft would have engines from wingtip to wingtip.

Right: The caption which Tass news agency wrote for this photograph of the first takeoff by the Soviet An-72 in December 1977 explained how the USB principle worked. Yet subsequently O.K. Antonov diverted attention from USB, explaining that he put the D-36 turbofans above the wing to avoid ingesting debris on rough airstrips.

engine is taken for granted in all long-haul transports, military and civil. In due course, however, the UDF (unducted fan) or propfan will almost certainly put visible propeller blades back into fashion, though they will be contra-rotating and look like scimitars. So far this important new propulsion technology has not yet percolated down to the military procurement machine, and it is a strange reflection on changed priorities that such new ideas are likely to go into service first with the airlines, where the pressure of competition overcomes reluctance to accept risk. The air forces, on the other hand, are less aware of "competition" than they are of the need to go for low-risk, low-cost solutions that will avoid accusations of waste, mistakes or misuse of funds. The new propulsion technology may get on to the airlines by 1991 and into the air forces by 1995.

Indeed, when one studies the biggest new military transport now being developed in the West one is struck by its apparent ordinariness. The McDonnell Douglas C-17 is in fact much more ordinary than the Boeing YC-14 of 1976. The YC-14 was, with the McDonnell Douglas YC-15, a candidate aircraft to replace the C-130 in the AMST (Advanced Medium STOL Transport) programme. Both the YC-14 and YC-15 looked rather like bigger versions of the C-130, but their powered high-lift systems were entirely different. The Boeing aircraft used USB (upper-surface blowing), in which the entire efflux from a large turbofan (a GE CF6-50) was blown from a flattened nozzle across the upper surface of the wing. If this was done when the flaps were lowered it was demonstrated that the transonic sheet of air would remain "attached" to the upper surface and curve sharply down across the depressed flaps. By this means the entire engine flow, plus a large flow of entrained fresh air, could be expelled off the trailing edge of the wing almost vertically downwards, giving up to five times as much lift as a conventional wing of this size.

The entire AMST programme was abandoned, the C-130 being retained in production, but USB remained the most impressive fixed-wing powered lift system in the world, and in the NASA Boeing QSRA (Quiet Short-haul Research Aircraft) even better results were achieved, a higher proportion of the wing (originally a C-8A Buffalo) being blown by the four F102 engines. Today, Japan's National Aerospace Laboratory is extremely slowly converting a Kawasaki C-1 military cargo aircraft into the Asuka QSTOL (Quiet STOL) research transport, a slightly larger machine than the QSRA with four Japanese FJR710 engines of 10,800lb (4,900kg) thrust each. In theory USB is better than any other STOL system, but despite Boeing's demonstration of it the customers have stayed away. In the Soviet Union the Antonov design bureau used the same technique in the An-72 and An-74. These have D-36 engines of 14,330lb (6,500kg) thrust and are roughly in the same weight class as the Japanese machine described on a later page.

What is at least as strange as the lack of

use made of USB is the selection of the externally blown flap (EBF) scheme for today's C-17. The EBF concept was explored in the YC-15, which had large heat-resistant flaps made mainly of titanium. The four engines were slung close beneath the wing so that they could blast straight into the lowered flaps. In principle EBF cannot rival USB; it is fundamentally less powerful as an augmented-lift system. On such grounds as cost and reliability both methods proved acceptable, and they are probably equally tricky in the case of an engine failure during a maximum-performance takeoff. Why the EBF method was picked for the very important C-17 has not been explained. Perhaps the fairest assessment is that EBF offers slightly lower risks and costs than USB, and the C-17 is not so much a true STOL transport as a long-runway machine fitted with very powerful externally blown flaps which cut the field length roughly in half, to around the 3,000ft (914m) level.

In the true VTOL class at the opposite end of the scale of size and capability, the V-22 (originally JVX) promises to be an aircraft of tremendous attractiveness and versatility. This is not for the customer who wants to bring in an armoured division but for the customer who wants the speed and efficiency of the aeroplane to be combined with the brief capability of VTOL or hovering. In the hovering mode the helicopter is

Below: BAe idea for a possible FIMA (Future International Military Aircraft) on which most major European aircraft companies are collaborating. Unusual features of this interpretation are the 1960-style engines and absence of visible STOL design features.

more efficient, so for the offshore or mountain rescue mission, where possibly half the flight time is in the hover, the helicopter will probably be the preferred answer. The V-22 is not for prolonged hovering but for rising off a pad – in a forest clearing, or city centre or on the fantail of a

Below: More than 30 years ago Bell flew the XV-3 with tilting rotors mounted on the tips of a fixed wing. Now the concept is at last about to bear fruit in the V-22 Osprey, developed jointly by Bell and Boeing Vertol. Here Marine Ospreys are engaged in an assault exercise.

ship for example – and then flying at 373mph (600km/h) over great distances and with a load which, by comparison with most VTOL aircraft, is considerable. Indeed, it is not too much to claim that the V-22 family is a new kind of flying machine. Just as the high bypass ratio turbofan fills the gap between the turbo-prop and the turbojet, so does the tilt-winger fill the gap between the helicopter and the aeroplane.

The amazing thing is that it is not new. Tilt-wingers have been flying 30 years, but despite doing all that was asked of them they have all eventually made their last flight – always in a vague research programme without any obvious objective in view – and been consigned to the "boneyard". Now at last, thanks to Bell Helicopter's demonstration of capabilities with the XV-15 prototypes, the US armed forces have all become enthusiastic that this is the way to go. The point must be made that a tilt-rotor machine is not a helicopter but an aeroplane whose very large propellers can be pivoted round to pull it upwards when necessary instead of along.

Several transport type aircraft appear in the next section of this book, dealing with various research aircraft whose results are likely to impinge on future warplanes. They cannot be included here because there is doubt as to whether their technology will be put to use, and even less

certainty that it will be used in future military transport aircraft.

The RAF has long had an obvious need for a strategic airlifter able to fly between Ascension and the Falklands. Opening the runway at March Ridge makes a major difference to the situation in that the Falklands terminal can now accept any kind of transport and not just the C-130. What has been lacking is any aircraft suitable to fly logistic supply missions on this route. The ex-British Airways L-1011-500 TriStars have the range but are civil passenger liners. The C-130 has a more suitable cargo hold, though very restricted in cross-section and load limit, but lacks the range. If the MoD had any money it would buy several C-5 Galaxies powered by RB211-524D4 Upgrade engines. The result would be a world-beater, with improved takeoff field length and easily able to carry its maximum payload non-stop between the islands, or between Ascension and the UK. Unfortunately it remains a pipe-dream, and by the year 2000 several times its cost will have been spent on umpteen thousand air refuellings of wholly unsuitable aircraft.

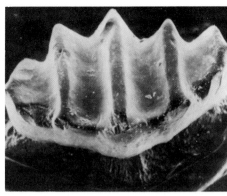

Above and below: NASA is doing many tests to see if skin friction drag can be cut by covering all the non-laminar parts (more than half the total surface of any aircraft) with microscopic grooves which help control small-scale turbulent flow. The concept of what are called riblets (shown cut in a metal skin, below) was identified before Soviet research showed similar grooves in the skin of fast sharks (above left). Above right is Nature's confirmation of the riblet concept, a shark's dermal denticle shown at 3,000 times magnification.

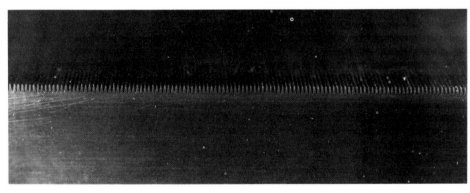

Below: Having hitched its wagon to the star of direct EBF (externally blown flaps) the USAF will probably have to live with the choice for the next 30 years. Foreplanes that lift are better than tails that thrust downwards, but even so the C-17 will be a most valuable aircraft.

ANTONOV
An-124 "CONDOR"

Type: Strategic airlift transport.
Engines: Four 51,650lb (23,430kg) Lotarev D-18T turbofans.
Dimensions: Span 240ft 5.8in (73.3m); length 228ft 0in (69.5m); height 72ft 2.1in.
Weights: Empty 390,000lb (177,000kg); maximum 892,857lb (405,000 kg).
Performance: Maximum cruising speed 537mph (865km/h); takeoff run (max wt) 3,937ft (1,200m); landing run 2,625ft (800m); range 3,100 miles (5,000km) with 330,700lb (150,000 kg) payload.

One of the few major gaps in the Soviet aviation inventory was for many years a large high bypass ratio turbofan engine, in the 25-ton thrust class. This made it impossible to build a large strategic jet to replace the An-22 Antei (NATO "Cock"), the last of which was delivered in 1974. By the late 1970s the Lotarev engine bureau was well advanced with the D-18T engine, and this was almost certainly the pacing item in the development of the enormous An-124.

In many ways the An-124 Ruslan (a famed giant in Pushkin) resembles the USAF C-5A, having the same demand for low footprint pressure. The wings are

much bigger, and carry more fuel (about 220 tons) than any other aircraft. The cargo hold is fractionally shorter at 118ft 0in (36m) but wider (20ft 11.9in, 6.4m) and higher (14ft 5.23in, 4.4m), and maximum payload is significantly greater at 330,688lb (150 tonnes), as against 118 tonnes. On the example flown to Paris in

Above: Three An-124s flew between 26 December 1982 and mid-1985. An efficient and impressive machine, it incorporates extensive composites and new alloys in its structure, and its 20 main tyres are soft enough for operations from all normal land surfaces. The giant cherry picker, parked by the crew door airstairs, can easily be taken on board; so can any Soviet mobile weapon. In the upper deck at the rear is a pressure cabin for 88 passengers.

BELL/BOEING VERTOL
V-22 OSPREY

Type: Multirole VTOL transport.
Engines: Two 5,800shp turboshaft engines (type and contractor not yet selected).
Dimensions: Diameter of main rotors/propellers 39ft 4.4in (12.0m); span (measured between rotor centrelines) 46ft 7in (14.2m); length (excluding guns, probes, etc) 57ft 11in (17.65m); height (rotors vertical) 20ft 8in (6.3m).
Weights: (Not finalised) VTOL maximum 43,800lb (19,865kg); STOL maximum 55,000lb (24,945kg).
Performance: Maximum cruising speed 374mph (601km/h); other details see below.

It was in 1973 that Bell announced that it had been selected by NASA and the US Army to fly two tilt-rotor VTOL research aircraft. Bell, with many other companies, had built such machines since the early 1950s. The award led to two XV-15 research aircraft which as well as proving the concept of a tilt-rotor VTOL also flew many simulated military missions, including some from US Navy ships because the Navy also added funding from 1979.

The XV-15s did outstandingly well in all manner of challenging assignments far beyond anything attempted previously with aircraft of this configuration. Their layout puts two engines and geared rotors on the tips of a wing pivoted to the fuselage, with a high-speed shaft linking the gearboxes so that flight is possible with either engine out. With the wing vertical the aircraft can rise vertically; following a transition cycle lasting about 12 seconds the wing reaches the normal horizontal position in which the aircraft is in all respects

an aeroplane, though with very large propellers. In this mode the flight control system drives aeroplane flight control surfaces, whereas in the hovering or VTOL mode the control system drives through hub swashplates to give full cyclic/collective control via the rotor blades.

By 1980 all the US services were enthusiastic, and the Advanced Vertical Lift (or JVX) programme received the go-ahead in December 1981. Bell teamed up with Boeing Vertol to win the JVX programme (whatever it might prove to be) and as no other company responded to the RFP

Above: Artist's impression of Marine Corps Ospreys operating in the assault role. Despite long and successful tests with the two small XV-15s the tilt-rotor concept is still to a large degree an unknown quantity. All the US services have high hopes of it, and potential export customers, including Australia and Japan, are discussing purchase.

Right: Seen here in tactical camouflage about to come to the hover, the XV-15s were small (3000hp) research prototypes which demonstrated not only versatility but also unexpected reliability during many kinds of simulated military mission. This was the second aircraft, N702. Without the XV-15s, the JVX would never have happened.

Above: Though previously illustrated the opening nose caused great surprise when one An-124 was flown to Paris in 1985. The landing gears variously steer or castor, and also kneel to tilt the floor or adjust sill height. Front and rear doors are opened with hydraulic power from APUs in both main-gear fairings. The An-124 has digital quad-redundant fly-by-wire flight controls, and quadruple inertial navigation systems (INSs) feed the navigation displays.

1985 there was no roller conveyor system, but two 10-tonne electric travelling cranes covered the whole length of the interior. At the rear of the upper deck, accessed from the main hold, was a passenger cabin with 88 seats; forward of the wing, aft of the flight deck, were areas for relief crew.

A most important feature of the An-124 is its relaxed-stability design, made possible by quadruplex digital (not analog, as reported elsewhere) FBW (fly by wire) flight control system, which even has a fifth emergency channel feeding direct to the power units driving the surfaces, which are all split into two equal halves. The flaps are true Fowlers, and they help bring normal operating field length down to 3,900ft (1,200m). At maximum landing weight the Ruslan can stop in 2,625ft (800m) even on icy surfaces. Pressures of all 24 tyres can be adjusted in flight, and the aircraft can kneel to adjust sill height and floor angle.

Production of the "Condor" will almost certainly considerably exceed the 55 of the An-22, and the numbers will probably be divided between the VTA (air force transport aviation) and Aeroflot (civil fleet). In emergency all Soviet aircraft are immediately available for war purposes, but in peacetime the Aeroflot examples would be used for opening up major resources in Siberia and other republics where surface transport is virtually non-existent. "Condor" can probably carry all Soviet ICBMs and the SS-20 mobile long-range missile system as a complete package.

(request for proposals) the Bell/Boeing team won automatically. Since then the JVX programme has grown almost daily; in March 1985 the aircraft was renamed V-22 Osprey, and a total of 932 initial Ospreys are planned for all four US armed services.

Biggest and most urgent customer is the Marine Corps, which wants 552 MV-22As. These are mainly assault transports, carrying 24 armed troops or a cargo load of 5,760lb (2,613kg). The troops must be carried 127 miles (205km) at low level, with a 40min loiter, followed by a repeat of the whole round-trip mission, plus 20min reserve without using the air refuelling capability. The cargo load is merely to be taken on a 230 mile (370km) round trip.

The USAF wants 80 CV-22A transports able to carry an F100 (F-15 fighter engine) or to fly 12 special-mission troops over 800 miles (1,300km) with unrefuelled return.

BELL/BOEING VERTOL V-22 OSPREY

This long range calls for extra tanks in the sponsons, other versions having wing fuel only. Wing fuel suffices for the basic ferry mission, which is California to Hawaii (2,415 miles/3,887km), with a 35mph (56km/h) headwind on a tropical hot day with 10 per cent reserves. The Navy wants an initial 50 HV-22A Ospreys, one mission for this version being to depart from a parent ship, fly 529 miles (851km) on an even hotter (30.5°C, 103°F) day, loiter 15min while picking up four rescuees from the sea and then bring them back, all at low level, on internal fuel. The Army version will be similar to the MV-22A, and a total of 231 are required, but not until 1995. This ground total of 913 for the US military customers is expected to double at least, ignoring sales to civil or foreign customers.

Almost every dimension of the Osprey has been virtually dictated by some rigid operational requirement, or by the need for at least 12in (0.3m) blade clearance beside the fuselage, or for bulky cargo to miss the tail, or because of the size of ship decks or many similar variables. Detailed simulations, and XV-15 experience suggests that this new machine will be delightful and exciting to fly. The XV-15 was flown through fighter-type manoeuvres, pulling high g, and also flown sideways and backwards, and been dived at 400mph (644km/h), landed in crosswinds at various forward speeds down to zero, flown along rugged contours, and used for weapon aiming, carriage of slung loads and used for

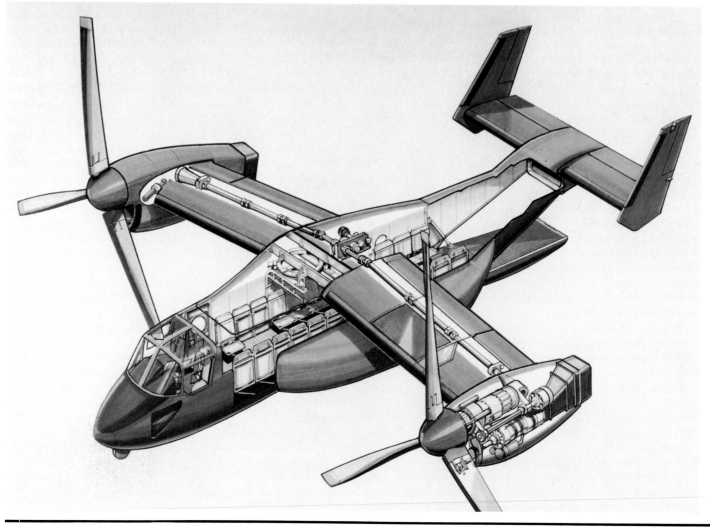

Left: During its evaluation by the US Navy and Marine Corps this XV-15 made 54 takeoffs (five of them rolling) and landings aboard the LPH USS *Tripoli*. Pilots judged it "easier than a helicopter". In particular, the small tilt-rotor showed convincingly that it is a practical combat vehicle.

Below: A joint Bell/ Boeing Vertol drawing of the V-22 Osprey in its basic utility transport form. The original plan was to fly V-22 prototypes with the interim General Electric T64-717 engine of 4,855shp, but it is still anyone's guess which company (or team) will get the V-22 engine.

countless other tasks. To take just one example, there is no control jerk when one rotor suddenly gets in ground effect over a deck while the other is blasting on to nothing.

One of many remarkable features of the Osprey is its unprecedented use of carbon-fibre composite, to a total of more than 60 per cent of the basic aircraft weight. One carbon item is a huge ring on which the wing is mounted; as soon as the aircraft is parked with engines off a hydraulic system

takes just 90 seconds to fold the rotors and rotate the wing around its mounting ring until the whole aircraft is a compact box-like shape.

Very comprehensive all-weather avionics and EW/IRCM systems will be standard. On the other hand, to keep within a total budget of $2,400 million the planned basic armament of a nose gun and self-defence Sidewinder AAMs has temporarily been omitted. As the sums involved must be trivial there is no doubt

these weapons, and others, will eventually be restored. Moreover, because of the almost universal use of CFRP structure there is considerable stretch available in today's V-22 Osprey. By 1990, with 8,000shp engines, it will be one of the most important of tomorrow's warplanes.

This is one of the few examples in recent years of a possible future airliner riding entirely on the back of a military programme.

Right: The first XV-15 (N702), this time in civilian colours in the forward-flight mode. From this picture it will be obvious that failure to rotate the engines to the vertical attitude would be hazardous, because the propellers would strike the ground. The production V-22 Osprey will have 38ft (11.6m) propellers

Below: The second XV-15, N703, transitioning from forward flight to the hover. There is an opening in the engine cowl in line with the wing in cruising flight. SPECO double ballscrew actuators rotate the engines on the fixed wing. The latter is swept slightly forward for balance reasons.

Type: Heavy airlift transport.
Engines: Four 37,600lb (17,055kg) Pratt & Whitney PW2037 (possibly to be designated F114) turbofans.
Dimensions: Span 165ft 0in (50.29m); length 170ft 8in (52.02m); height 53ft 6in (16.31m); wing area 3,800sq ft (353m^2).
Weights: Empty (fully equipped) 259,000lb (117,480kg); maximum 572,000lb (259,455kg).
Performance: Cruising speed (high altitude) 512mph (823km/h); combat radius with 140,800lb (63,865kg) payload on outward sector only, no refuel at destination, 2,190 miles (3,520km).

Though the AMST (Advanced Medium STOL Transport) competition involving YC-14 and YC-15 aircraft was allowed to fade away, the US Air Force still considered it needed to augment and update its airlift capability, and in 1979 decided to invite completely new designs in a category larger than the AMST, with the ability to carry outsize cargo which can at present be airlifted only by the C-5 Galaxy. The CX programme was therefore launched, and requests for proposals were issued in October 1980. On 29 August 1981 the McDonnell Douglas submission was announced the winner, but shortly afterwards a proposal by Lockheed-Georgia for the restart of C-5 Galaxy production was accepted, and in 1982 funding was authorised for 50 new C-5Bs. The C-X programme carried no production commit-

ment, but in fact McDonnell Douglas continued to receive funding for development of the C-17 aircraft and has lobbied hard for full-scale engineering development. The company's Long Beach facilities virtually completed tunnel testing in 1984 and has also introduced numerous update features, particularly in the two-man flight deck. By late 1984 sustained Air Force pressure was beginning to win through, and at last the funding for Fiscal Year 1985 was increased sufficiently for formal start of fullscale engineering development, and this was approved in March 1985.

The plan is to buy 210 C-17s for the Military Airlift Command inventory. The first is to fly in 1989, IOC (initial operational capability) has slipped one year to 1992 and the whole force should be operational in 1998. R&D is estimated to cost $4,015 million and procurement $35,000 million, representing the extremely high price of $186 million per aircraft. One reason for the high price is that it is quoted in "then year" dollars over the period 1985-98. Prices quoted in 1998 dollars might on inflation alone be at least three times today's prices.

Though it incorporates the latest technology throughout its systems the C-17 is basically a conventional aircraft, similar to the commercial DC-10 in size, weights and power but totally different in payload provisions, manoeuvrability and STOL performance. Of course, no aircraft of such weight with 1980s technology could be a

STOL in the rigorous sense of the word; the C-17 is merely designed to operate from unsurfaced strips much shorter than major runways and to make steep (5°) approaches in the worst weather. Routine operation into 3,000ft (914m) strips is a basic design objective, and thus the C-17 promises in one vehicle to carry the heaviest and bulkiest loads both on intertheatre (strategic) missions and, without unloading, also on intratheatre (tactical) missions.

The point should be made, however, that with maximum payload of 172,200lb (78,110kg) the actual landing run is 3,000ft (914m), and it is close to this value with reduced payloads; on published figures landing distances are at least as long as for the C-5B, though Gen Bernard Rogers, Supreme Allied Commander Europe, testified before Congress, "There's no question that the C-17 has a greater flexibility for various types of airfields on which we'd like to use it than does the C-5".

Little has been said concerning structure, beyond the fact that it is warranted for a 45,000h combat life, with landing gears guaranteed for 10 years at specified intensive use levels. The wing has a deep supercritical section, no dihedral and is tapered on the leading edge. Large supercritical winglets are fitted, and movables include full-span slats and enormous flaps using a refined EBF derived from the YC-15 arrangement. The flaps are double-slotted (often incorrectly called Fowler type), are heat resistant and swing down to any angle

Below: This illustration gives an impression of how the C-17 will look when it emerges in 1989. Some details, such as the wingtip winglets and rear-fuselage ventral strakes, may change in the intervening years. The PW2037 engines, previously used only in some Boeing 757s, are installed well ahead of the wing but high up, so that on landing they blow straight back into the double-slotted trailing-edge flaps, which pivot aft on single faired hinges (unlike the Fowler flap which runs out from beneath a fixed housing). All engines have directed-flow reversers which discharge ahead and upwards only, thus avoiding scrubbing on the ground with consequent debris ingestion. These reversers will be deployable in flight as well as on the ground.

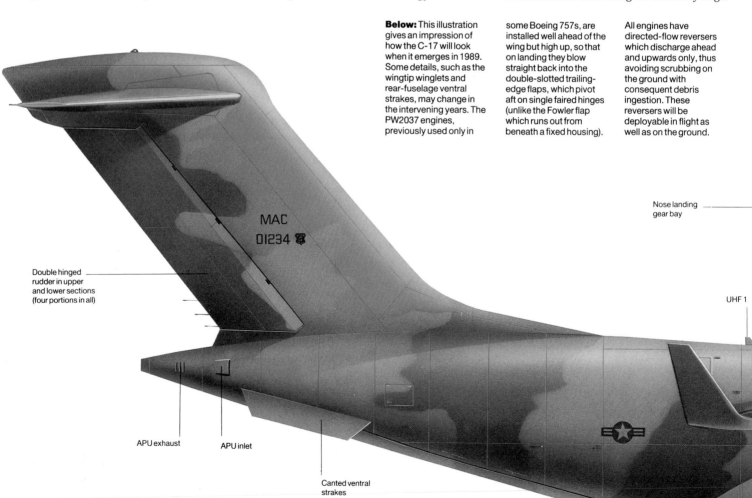

Double hinged rudder in upper and lower sections (four portions in all)

Nose landing gear bay

UHF 1

APU exhaust

APU inlet

Canted ventral strakes

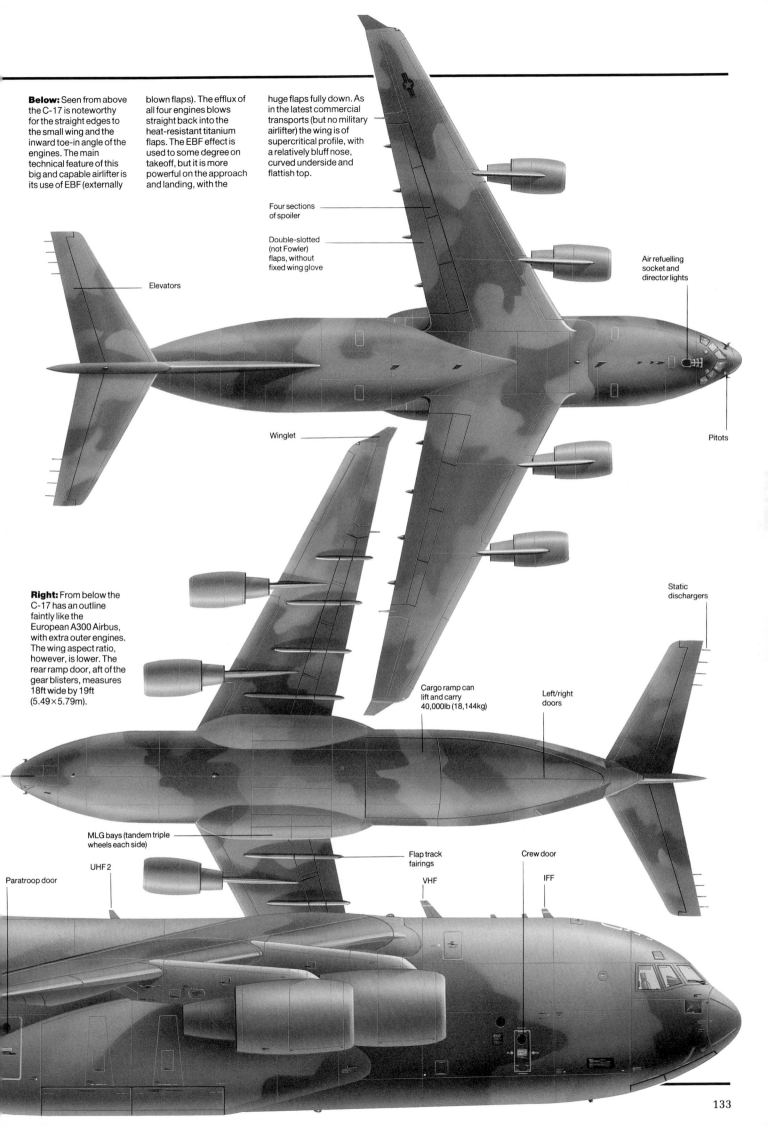

Below: Seen from above the C-17 is noteworthy for the straight edges to the small wing and the inward toe-in angle of the engines. The main technical feature of this big and capable airlifter is its use of EBF (externally blown flaps). The efflux of all four engines blows straight back into the heat-resistant titanium flaps. The EBF effect is used to some degree on takeoff, but it is more powerful on the approach and landing, with the huge flaps fully down. As in the latest commercial transports (but no military airlifter) the wing is of supercritical profile, with a relatively bluff nose, curved underside and flattish top.

Elevators

Four sections of spoiler

Double-slotted (not Fowler) flaps, without fixed wing glove

Air refuelling socket and director lights

Pitots

Winglet

Right: From below the C-17 has an outline faintly like the European A300 Airbus, with extra outer engines. The wing aspect ratio, however, is lower. The rear ramp door, aft of the gear blisters, measures 18ft wide by 19ft (5.49×5.79m).

Static dischargers

Cargo ramp can lift and carry 40,000lb (18,144kg)

Left/right doors

MLG bays (tandem triple wheels each side)

Flap track fairings

Crew door

Paratroop door

UHF 2

VHF

IFF

selected by the crew. Though the mean temperature of the efflux from the PW2037 is low (much cooler than the YC-15 engine) the flaps are of heat-resistant titanium. Details of flap schedules for each flight regime have yet to be worked out, but the EBF powered lift will be used both for slow airdrops and also for short landings. Routine short landings involve the afore-mentioned steep approach, with engines at high power blowing through the flaps; ground effect cushions the high sink rate and immediately the oleos are compressed the engines go into reverse, the reversers blowing diagonally upward around the top of each nacelle only, thus avoiding debris ingestion.

Compared with the C-5 the cargo hold is much shorter but similar in cross-section. Width is 18ft (5.5m), 1ft (0.3m) less; height is the same at 13ft 6in (4.1m) except for a reduction to 12ft 3in (3.7m) under the wing. Length of the main floor is 69ft (21m), but the 19ft (5.79m) rear loading ramp is stressed to bear a load of 40,000lb (18,144kg). Overall length of the C-5 hold is 144ft 8in (44.1m), and there is a full-section door at each end, but the rear ramp is limited to 15,000lb (6,800kg). It would have been simple to raise the C-17 flight deck and carry the payload through to a

Below: A fine impression of low-altitude paratroop exercises with a C-17, some time after 1990. Up to 102 paratroops can be carried, dispatched through rear doors on each side. Airdrop speed at this height can be as low as 132mph (213km/h). SL cruise is 403mph (648km/h).

Above: A C-17 departing from a battle zone airstrip. Yellow outlines mark the crew door and, high up, two of the four emergency exits. Not visible is the SKE (station-keeping equipment); on the C-130 the antenna is housed under a "pillbox" above the fuselage.

Right: A 1985 artist's impression of C-17s operating in the field. The near machine is landing, with double-slotted flaps blown by the engines set at high power. For Fiscal Year 1985 the US Congress allocated $123 million for continued C-17 development. Note AH-64 and OH-58D.

nose door, as in the C-5, but this was not requested. The floor is covered with 25,000lb (11,340kg) tiedowns, and there are naturally inbuilt loading systems. The illumination sets a new brilliant standard, and a basic feature of the C-17 is that, as far as possible, it carries with it everything needed for role changes.

For example there are 54 paratroop seats along the sidewalls, each of which can be pulled and locked into an inboard position which leaves room for the paratroop backpacks. Static lines carried on board can be rigged in two minutes. Above the rear (upward-opening) section of cargo door are stowed another 48 seats which can be installed to form back-to-back rows down the centre providing for 102 paras in all. Also stowed on board are 12 stanchions, each supporting four stretchers (litters). To convert to the casevac role the 12 stanchions can be unloaded and secured in place in about 3min.

Using EBF the airdrop speed can be as low as 132mph (213km/h), or it can be considerably more than twice this speed. Even at 25,000ft (7,620m) drops can still be made as slow as 150mph (241km/h). Unit loads up to 55,000lb (24,945kg) can be dropped, far more than for other US airlift transports. It would be possible, for example, to load

three IFVs (Infantry Fighting Vehicles) and airdrop all three. Most vehicles can be loaded in two side-by-side rows. The entire cargo area can be managed by a single loadmaster, and this includes all role-change tasks, loading/unloading of outsize cargo and airdrops.

The flight deck uses sticks instead of yokes or wheels, and the primary flight instruments will be multicolour function displays (MFDs) and HUDs. Should all these modern items fail "we'll still have a C-130 cockpit left", in the words of William Casey, C-17 project pilot. Everything possible will be done to increase automation, computer storage of such data as characteristics of every load item or the desirable parameters in taking fuel from any USAF tanker, provide system redundancy and reduce human workloads. At the same time it is strange that this $186 million truck should not have either auto-landing provision nor an area-navigation system. In view of the fact that it will not spend all its life flying established airways, with known waypoints, nor call only at major airbases, these deficiencies are fairly certain to be rectified in due course.

Of course the air refuelling socket is compatible with a Flying Boom tanker; it is located in the roof of the flight deck. Flight

controls, tied into the digital bus system linking all parts of the aircraft, are basically conventional. There are four spoiler/lift dumper sections ahead of each flap, outboard ailerons, a tailplane with elevators, and upper and lower sections of double-hinged rudder, exactly as on the smaller YC-15. The nose gear has twin wheels, while the main gears comprise four legs each carrying a transverse row of three wheels which rotate through 90° to lie fore/aft along the unpressurized blisters on each side of the circular-section fuselage. Main gears are stressed for a no-flare landing with a sink rate of 16.5ft (5m)/s, though as noted earlier tunnel testing shows that sink is almost arrested by ground effect.

In a nutshell the C-17 promises to offer, at a high price, airfield capability at least as good as a C-130 combined with the cargo unit size and mission range of the C-5. To a high degree this long-range airlifter will avoid the need for any trans-shipment, but will be able to deliver anything needed in a theatre at the very point where it is needed. Britain's RAF will have cast covetous eyes on the C-17, because with a very slight stretch in span, Rolls-Royce 535E4 engines and some trivial system changes it is just what is needed to provide long-range airlift, notably to the Falklands.

NAL
ASUKA

Type: STOL research transport.
Engines: Four 10,800lb (4,900kg) MITI/NAL FJR710-600S turbofans.
Dimensions: Span 100ft 4.7in (30.6m); length (excluding prototype probe) 95ft 1.7in (29.0m); height 33ft 7.35in (10.245m); wing area 1,297sq ft (120.5m²).
Weights: (Estimated) Empty about 55,000lb (25,000kg); maximum 85,320lb (38,700kg).
Performance: (Estimated) Cruising speed 373mph (600km/h); maximum range 1,036 miles (1,668km).

For a dozen years the Japanese National Aerospace Laboratory has been developing a QSTOL (quiet STOL) research aircraft. The main result of this effort so far has been the reconstruction of a Japanese Air Self-Defense Force Kawasaki C-1. This short-haul cargo machine was originally powered by two JT8D engines in underslung pods, and despite having very limited payload/range capability is a well-established JASDF type. The selected C-1 has been subjected to many modifications including the following: removal of the engine pods

and addition of four high bypass ratio turbofans in closely spaced nacelles ahead of and just above the inboard wing; replacement of the inner flaps by special USB (upper surface blowing) flaps; addition of bleed-air BLC (boundary-layer control) along wing leading edges and ailerons, to improve handling at very low airspeeds;

Below: The much modified C-1 turned-Asuka with all engines installed. First flight was planned for autumn 1985.

The Asuka QSTOL is not intended to be a production aircraft but is for research into upper surface blowing.

SOVIET
WIG/EKRANOPLAN

Type: Wing in ground-effect ("wingship").
Data: See below.

Since 1965 there have been repeated tales of large Soviet surface-skimming craft called "Ekranoplan", a surface-effect vehicle having features akin to aeroplanes, hydroplanes and ACVs (Hovercraft). There are many small examples of such craft, including examples built in the USA, Federal Germany and Soviet Union. Some have been called ram-wings or ram-wing aircraft, some ground-effect aircraft, while Stephan Hooker has formed a Wingship Society (and collated a vast amount of published information). All evidence available suggests that in the Soviet Union such vehicles are in military and commercial service in numbers, while outside the Soviet Union little has been produced except paper studies.

The Soviet name comes from *ekran*, a

screen or shield, and *plan*, a lifting plane (for gliding). There are said to be such craft in many sizes and configurations, but the illustrations show a typical configuration. This Ekranoplan is about 100ft (30m) in span, 200ft (61m) long and probably weighs about 550,000lb (250 tonnes), considerably more than an aeroplane of similar wing size and installed horsepower. The main propulsion is a turboprop at the top of the T-tail; it could be an NK-12M engine in the 15,000shp class. Once this is opened up the craft accelerates ahead, still floating on the water. Jets from two auxiliary engines at the front are directed under the wing and build up a cushion pressure under it, trapped by the lowered flaps and the side-wall surfaces at the tip which project down into the water. The growing lift causes the craft to rise clear of the water, the forward speed then building up rapidly. At cruising speed the tip sidewalls are clear of the

water, the flaps up and the bow jet engines switched off. The lift from the wing keeps the vehicle just clear of the highest waves. Cruising speed is estimated at 150-250 knots (173-288mph, 278-463km/h).

Compared with a free-flight aeroplane the WIG or Wingship is claimed to be much more efficient, with very little induced drag and with a lift/drag ratio around 23-25 compared with about 16. A Hooker Wingship proposal is for a 5,000-ton craft with a span of 250ft (76m), length of 460ft (140m) and propelled by 20 turbofans each of 84,000lb (38 tonnes) thrust each coupled by secondary liquid-metal loop into a central nuclear reactor. This vehicle would have almost a trimaran layout, the main lift being provided by the amidships wing with a span of 180ft (54.9m) and underside of the central rear hull. At cruising speed of 400kt (460mph, 740km/h) the engines would be at one-quarter thrust.

addition of tailplane slats, enlarged elevators and large double-hinged upper and lower rudders; strengthening of the fuselage and landing gear; and installation of a digital flight control system with a stability augmentation subsystem.

Apart from the extremely impressive QSRA (a DH Canada C-8B Buffalo completely rebuilt by Boeing with four F102 engines), the Japanese QSTOL is the only fully engineered USB aircraft so far built, and it makes use of all the experience gained with the QSRA and Boeing's pioneer (and much larger and more powerful) YC-14. The project has taken much longer than planned. First flight was to have taken place in Fiscal Year 1984, which ended on 30 June 1984, but had still not taken place as this was written almost a year later. The part-completed Asuka (named after a former capital of Japan) was exhibited in October 1983 with the inboard engines only installed. In early summer 1985 the start of flight trials was reported to be imminent.

It is hoped that the QSTOL will take off over a 35ft (10.7m) screen in a distance of 2,230ft (680m), and land over such a screen in a distance of 1,575ft (480m), touching down at 83mph (133km/h). The objective is to provide data for the design of a civil/military aircraft in the 150-seat class able to operate from airstrips only 2,625ft (800m) in length. Such an aircraft would need engines of greater power, and in any case the brochure thrust of the locally developed FJR710 engine is 11,243lb (5,100kg), rather more than the nominal value assumed for QSTOL flight test purposes and given above.

The US concept is clearly applicable to fighters and other future warplanes, as well as to transports. The sketch at right shows current thinking, and such a configuration would tie in well with the requirements of stealth design.

Above: USB involves mounting the main engines so that they can blow back across the wing. The NASA QSRA (Quiet Short-haul Research Aircraft) has the same engines as a BAe 146 but is an ultra-STOL machine.

Below: Boeing's proposal for using USB technology in a fighter/attack aircraft. Such integration of engine power and wing lift is bound to result in aircraft far more agile and flexible in operation than cruder machines.

The Wingships are aimed at commercial objectives, but Soviet examples appear to be highly warlike. They are said to handle many missions including beach assault and resupply, ASW, anti-ship (using SS-N-22 sea-skimming missiles of 137-mile/220km range) and many other duties, unaffected by mines, torpedoes, tides, sea state or underwater obstructions.

Mating of a WIG with an ICBM launch tube is proposed (drawing at right) because it has obvious attractions. This is just one suggested configuration. There is no public evidence of military WIG/Wingships.

Right: This three-view is typical of those purporting to show the "Soviet WIG". Large and capable, it would have a payload much higher than that of a conventional aircraft. The folding column is a suggested ICBM (SS-20) launcher, which could be reloaded without having to return to base, though probably such missiles would not be fired whilst airborne. This is a class of vehicle ignored by Western designers.

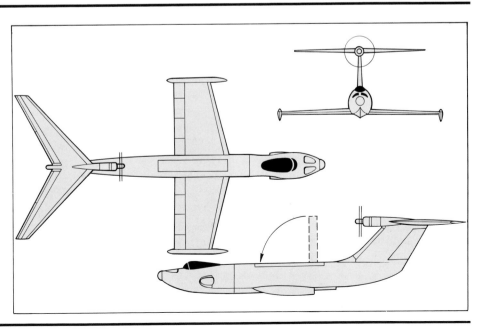

RESEARCH PROGRAMMES

Far from all looking alike, warplanes are today more diverse than at any previous time. All over the world many hundreds of aircraft are being used to help develop the warplanes that are not yet in service, or not yet off the drawing board. Most of this motley research fleet are concerned with seemingly mundane tasks such as perfecting flight control systems, avionics, engines, weapons and weapon delivery subsystems, navaids and secondary power systems. A few have more fundamental tasks, such as helping develop new shapes, new structure and new ways of changing shape in flight. Some of these will greatly influence the combat aircraft of the next century, either by enabling fundamental improvements to be made in aircraft of

traditional form or by underpinning the design of completely new kinds of aircraft.

Some of the "completely new" species of warplane are actually extremely old, but have either faded from the scene (like the airship) or never really made much impact (like the drone or RPV). There are entries in this section which examine the prospects for both. There could hardly be two more contrasting types of aircraft, and a third contrast is provided by Microlights, some of which are also described in this section. All three are utterly unlike the popular conception of a combat aircraft.

This fact certainly does not disqualify them from consideration, but outside the Soviet Union it often seems extremely difficult for the people in positions of execu-

tive power to sweep the cobwebs from their minds and take decisions objectively. Instead, they tend to be gripped by emotional or political considerations which make sensible decisions extremely elusive. The following are examples of common Western thinking:

1. We have a pretty well fixed overall budget, so there's no point in trying to "save money"; if we succeeded in finding cheaper solutions we'd have our budget cut next year.

2. Vectored-thrust V/STOLs are a British idea, so we don't want to consider them seriously; our official position has always been that we reluctantly can't afford the penalties of using such inferior airplanes.

3. On the question of the RPV or drone,

Right: Carbon fibre is black, and so are the primary load-bearing structures of tomorrow's fighters. Here a complete wing box for a Harrier II is seen in the forward-looking McDonnell Douglas plant at St Louis.

Above: A Lockheed Solar HAPP (high-altitude powered platform) orbits silently, converting sunlight into electric power to drive propellers. These intriguing craft have much in common with man-powered aircraft, but fly much higher and for months at a time. But are they useful, survivable and reliable?

Below: Drag chutes pull back the massive air-cushion transporter used to get a USAF F-15 into the air from its base, which the kind enemy has merely pockmarked with a few bombs! How the F-15 gets back does not seem to be in the brochure, which also overlooks the fact that the base (and men and F-15s) would not exist.

Below: One of the most exciting new shapes in the sky, the Grumman X-29 prototypes just might be the precursors of a new family of super-agile and super-efficient fighters with forward-swept wings. Previously structurally unattainable, such wings are almost impossible to add as a modification. Maybe Europe's rivals should wait?

our planning staffs of thousands have decided that there are far too many unanswered questions, so we are organizing a multi-billion dollar investigation to see how such vehicles might best be integrated into a mix of manned and unmanned surveillance platforms some time in the next century. . . .

4. As for lighter-than-air craft, we don't have a budget for this right now, but maybe, provided we can make it appear that we invented the idea, we might manage to create a study programme costing enough to make it worth doing, but it could not lead to anything in the inventory this side of year 2000.

5. The usage of Microlights by the military deserves very careful study. (Thinks: we'll have a lot of fun with these things.) At the same time our official position is that out airpower is based on colossal concrete runways, and we expect to spend zillions on methods of repairing craters quickly, providing huge air-cushion transporters and generally preserving mobility on airfields after attack. If these microlights should prove operable without runways this would seriously weaken our posture, and even make it more difficult to justify expenditure on airfields, so we probably ought to ensure that we don't find genuine combat tasks where Microlights might show to advantage.

6. The anti-gravity plane, which can remain airborne indefinitely without consuming fuel or emitting any radiation, is seen as a major threat by important elements in our industry. We cannot overlook the fact that to adopt it would at a stroke have a serious effect on much of our current infra-structure, base organization and support services, and would require major changes in operational methods, and it is calculated that these penalties would outweigh any theoretical advantages. . . . In any case, any procurement decision would obviously have to be delayed until all our major contractors could offer similar competitive aircraft. We could then have a multi-year study phase, a multi-year project-definition phase and then maybe a multi-year fly-off evaluation, to make absolutely certain the airplane we were buying is right for our requirements before we permitted large funds to be voted on long-

lead items for any production examples.

Of course, these quotes are "tongue-in-cheek", but hardly a day goes by without a fresh press release that appears to be a duplicate of one issued 20 or 30 years previously. Soon after Northrop bought the Radioplane Co. in 1952 it produced an internal report analysing the pros and cons of using recoverable or expendable drones for photo reconnaissance. In 1962 the Big Safari programme run by USAF Logistics Command produced a mammoth analysis of the same subject (and it was one of many that addressed themselves to just this topic). In 1985 we find the Secretary of the US Air Force telling Congress that "a question to be answered" is whether or not reconnaissance RPVs should be recoverable or expendable. Doubtless we shall have further rediscoveries of the same question in the next century.

EFFECTS OF TECHNOLOGY CHANGES

Technology never stays the same for two consecutive days. This makes each fresh report or recommendation obsolete before

it can be issued. An analysis of military uses of the airship in 1910 would have come to different conclusions from one written in 1945, and this in turn would differ tremendously from one written today. Modern airships, as yet unbuilt, could far surpass every capability of their predecessors, but they would emerge into a perilous world filled with methods of detecting and destroying aerial vehicles from great distances, which would make the military airship a non-starter were it not itself able to deploy defence techniques

that are quite new and improving daily.

This rapid technological change dramatically reduces the value of an old assessment. Until the 1960s there was not much of a problem. A new kind of aircraft could be designed, built and tested inside a year, so one could be fairly sure that its basic conception would not be invalidated before it could get into service. An accompanying bar chart graphically illustrates the Convair B-24 Liberator programme, and contrasts this with today's B-1B, its direct successor as the main advanced

Right: Should RPVs be recoverable? If they are they usually descend by parachute, but Lockheed's Aquila is recovered by flying (under infra-red guidance) into a Dornier net, swiftly lowered to keep a low profile.

technology strategic bomber of the USA today. The difference hardly needs emphasising. Today's programme has been repeatedly crippled by taking so long that the requirements and the technology have overtaken it.

Why has the B-1B taken so long? The most truthful answer would probably be, "Because tens of thousands of dedicated people wanted to get it right." Americans, like Russians, have an aversion to making large-scale mistakes, which in the former country lead to media exposure and Congressional investigations and in the other automatically lead to career termination if not imprisonment. There is thus every reason to plan with great care.

All the evidence we have suggests that the development timescales of future weapon systems are going to become longer rather than shorter. An indication of the changing timescales for fighters is afforded by examination of progress with the USAF ATF programme. All the planning for the ATF is being done now, and the current demo/validation phase is imminently leading to a firming up of concepts, specifications and actual design proposals. All this for a fighter estimated to reach operational service "in the mid-1990s". Some research aircraft, such as the HiMAT, X-29 and MAW/F-111, ought to provide information reading across directly to the ATF. So too will countless less obvious investigations into advanced engines, structures and systems which will all ensure that the ATF will be more reliable, more maintainable, longer lived and more effective in all conditions than its predecessors.

But it is easy to have so many trees that the wood gets overlooked. We are told the ATF will have "greater supersonic manoeuvrability ... supersonic persistence ... greatly increased combat radius". Clearly the USAF has already forgotten the lessons of the F-111, which was killed as a fighter by the same demands. And it is suffering agonies reluctantly accepting that ATF may have to "take off between craters 1,500ft apart". Let us hope that this is being done to deceive the enemy and that the USAF really does understand that long before the mid-1990s airfields of known location will be places that combat aircraft just never go, except in peacetime. But where are the research aircraft to support an ATF that will actually survive until Day 2 in a future war?

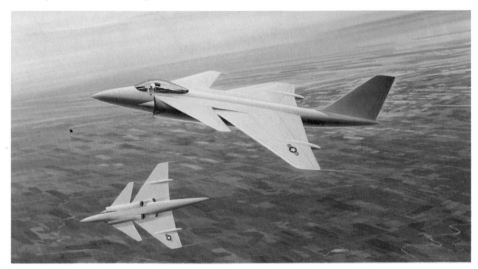

Left: It seems self-evident that, in any field of human endeavour, progress results from sustained effort. In contrast Britain has restarted PCB (plenum-chamber burning) research, essential for supersonic successors to the Harrier, after having dropped it in 1965 on government orders! This special test rig is almost all we have as a basis on which to try to build an air force survivable in modern war.

Above: McDonnell's Model 279-3 is one of many ideas for a supersonic successor to the Harrier. Such an aircraft would not only survive by never being parked where the enemy thought it was, but also by having combat manoeuvrability far superior to anything possible by crude fighters with plain fixed jetpipes. Its PCB engine (Pegasus next generation) has four nozzles; three is a good alternative.

Below: A uniformed USAF project engineer alters an ATF by a stroke of a light pen. Such a change costs nothing, but when squadrons are ready to take off a change would cost millions to billions. The "ATF shape" is typical of what is currently fashionable; and we should not poke fun at it because at least it has 2-D vectoring nozzles, while in Europe the EAP and Rafale have plain fixed holes, which ought to have gone for ever.

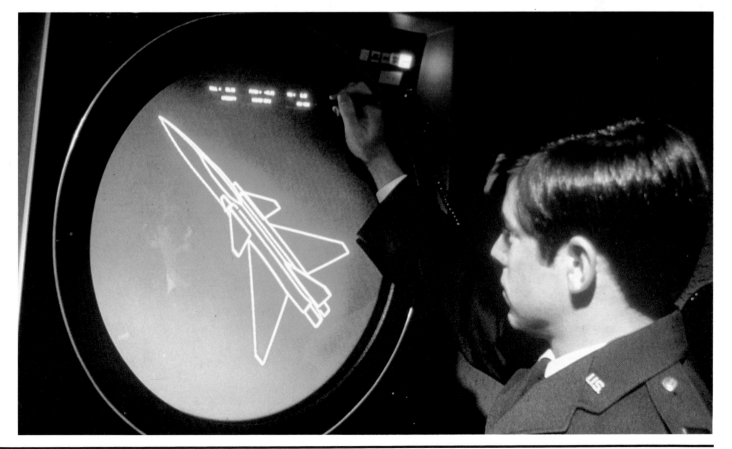

AIRSHIPS

Type: Chief mission would be radar surveillance?
Data: None finalised.

Non-rigid airships, commonly called blimps, were used in large numbers by the US Navy in World War II, doing tremendous work on ASW patrols mainly in the North Atlantic and Caribbean. In the 1950s the sizes of US Navy non-rigids grew until the final ZPG-3W series were 403ft (123m) long and had a buoyant volume of over 1.5 million cu ft (42,475m^3). Two 1,525hp Wright Cyclone piston engines gave a speed of 90mph (145km/h), and it was possible to fly missions lasting a week while carrying the same enormous surveillance radar system as the PO-2W (later EC-121K Warning Star) Super Constellations. The Navy had already decided airships were becoming archaic and the fleet was inactivated in 1961.

This was the last military use of airships. In the 1970s various individuals came to the conclusion that it ought to be possible to build airships so much superior to anything done in the past that they would not only be commercially viable but would enable transport prices for containers and bulk cargo to be reduced. Interest centred on large ships able to lift 100 or more loaded ISO containers (standard 8ft×8ft×40ft/2.44m×2.44m×12.2m), picking them up and depositing them not at docks or rail yards or other trans-shipment points but at the exact places needed – literally a door-to-door service over intercontinental distances. It was considered that new composite structures, advanced gas turbine engines, all-weather avionics, helium lifting gas and modern navaids would result in airships able virtually to go anywhere and do anything, at extremely competitive costs. Cruising speed might be in the region of 100mph (161km/h).

So far, while the idea has in no way been discredited or disproven, backers have failed to come forward with the money. This, of course, means nothing; there are plenty of other investments that are much easier to assess and promise to yield much quicker profits.

On the other hand several companies have produced a range of small non-rigid airships, filled variously with hydrogen, helium or hot air, some of which have been sold as commercial products used for fun, advertising or, in very few instances, some form of surveillance. Plans exist for heavy-lift airships, for lifting and positioning heavy or bulky loads but without moving them over large distances.

Meanwhile Airship Industries, the British subsidiary of an Australian company, is leading the drive to find military, naval and other warlike applications for its range of Skyship non-rigids which in all

Below: A remotely pointed camera pod was one of several sensors flown under Skyships 500 and 600. Even the existing Skyship 600, a baby by the standards of a bygone era, can carry all the sensors so far requested, except for the largest high-power surveillance radars.

important respects are similar to the US Army and Navy blimps of the mid-1930s. Envelope structural design, shape, tail configuration and construction, gondola design and propulsion system are all practically identical to the non-rigids of 50 years ago, but with the important advantage of such new materials as Kevlar fibres for cables and reinforced composites, Fibrelam plastics laminates, GRP and CFRP mouldings in any desired size, and completely new polyester envelope fabrics

Below: A small surveillance radar being tested inside Skyship 500. Airship Industries has designed Skyship 5000, with 66,000lb (30 tonne) payload, to undertake US Navy battle group AEW cover, RN offshore patrol vessel duties, ASW, and mine countermeasures.

treated to resist UV (ultraviolet) embrittlement in years of bright sunlight and with gasproof inner films weighing very little. It goes without saying that today's avionics eliminate bad-weather navigation and handling problems.

Today Airship Industries is collaborating with such major radar suppliers as Ferranti and Westinghouse in mating large surveillance radars with future Skyships. Considerable experience has already been gained using the 181,977cu ft (5,153m^3) Skyship 500 and the 235,400cu ft (6,666m^3) Skyship 600, which are broadly similar and are powered by twin Porsche piston engines (respectively of 204hp and 270hp each) driving ducted propellers which can be vectored about a transverse axis to thrust from 90° upwards to 120° downward. Skyship 600 has a disposable load of 5,511lb (2,500kg) and cruises at 60mph (96km/h). Equipment carried has included Omega, ADF, VOR/ILS, a stabilised MEL Marec surveillance radar, IR surveillance, a high-resolution camera pod and FBL (fly-by-light) flight controls. In an evaluation by the French navy a two-man inflatable boat, stabilized by air fins, was lowered 150ft (46m) to the sea, starting its 30hp engine just before reaching the water.

Airship Industries is planning Skyships of up to 2.5 million cu ft (70,000m^3), powered by twin turbocharged diesels for 10-day missions and reversing twin vectored propulsors driven by turboprops for dash speed of 105mph (167km/h), and for powerful manoeuvring control. A 10-day mission would burn about 14,300lb (6,500kg) of fuel, leavig about 71,000lb (32 tonnes) available for mission equipment. This fits in well with the giant Westinghouse phased-array radar expected to meet a US Navy BSAS (Battle Surveillance Air Ship) programme and the wide spread of sensors needed for the Royal Navy OPV-3 (Offshore Patrol Vehicle 3) study, which was originally expected to be a ship but may well turn out to be an airship.

Obvious features of the airship that are unavailable from other vehicles are endurance limited basically by the crew's food supplies (and food, crews and other items can readily be transferred whilst on station), the ability to hover at, say, 10,000ft (3,000m) while burning very little fuel, almost unlimited payload volume and thus, by implication, the ability to carry enormous radar reflectors inside the envelope. For example, the use of a radar scanner 330ft (100m) long would give definition better than any planned SAR (synthetic aperture radar) without the need to build up the picture from small elements sent out in a timed sequence as if from an imaginary reflector of the same size.

There are still big unanswered questions. How vulnerable are 1990s airships going to be to severe weather (such as microbursts and windshear), and to the attentions of the enemy? How safe are they when moored in Force 10 winds? The many years of US Navy experience suggest that there are no insuperable problems, and we could be on the verge of a big airship comeback.

Left: Letting down a two-man inflatable assault boat from Skyship 600 whilst undergoing trials with the French Aéronavale. This airship, which has been busy since first flight in March 1984, has a cruising speed (50 per cent power) of 60mph (96km/h) and reduced-speed endurance of 55h. The "fly by light" flight control system is a major advantage in handling during prolonged sorties in adverse weather.

Above: Another picture taken during an evaluation of Skyship 600 by the French Navy, showing the assault boat at speed after being lowered by the airship. This is one of an essentially limitless range of tasks which airships can perform. So far the Western world's leading potential customer is the US Navy, which has carried out extensive studies and in December 1984 organised a conference.

BOEING
E-6

Type: Long-endurance communications relay aircraft.
Engines: Four 22,000lb (9,979kg) CFM International F108-100 turbofans.
Dimensions: Span 145ft 9in (44.42m); length 152ft 11in (46.61m); height 42ft 5in (12.93m); wing area 3,050sq ft (283.4m²).
Weights: Empty about 155,000lb (70,300kg); maximum classified but probably 325,000lb (147,420kg).
Performance: Typical transit speed 512mph (825km/h); patrol conditions about 248mph (400km/h) at 29,000ft (8,840m); endurance, see below.

It is by chance that this aircraft follows the entry on airships, because commonsense suggests that an airship is a better lifting device than a massive jet aeroplane when the requirement is merely to hold a radio relay station at a chosen place in the sky. In fact the E-6, like its near-relative the E-3 Sentry, can orbit at some 29,000ft (8,840m), which is getting on for three times a comfortable on-station height for typical non-rigid airships (though Zeppelins in 1917 dropped heavy bombloads from 25,000ft/ 7,620m, so one cannot be dogmatic). Airship protagonists claim that above 10,000ft (3,000m) a law of diminishing returns sets in, and one pays heavily for not much real gain in radio horizon. Of course, the whole purpose of putting a communications relay station high in the sky is usually to "see" further to the line-of-sight horizon, but in the case of the E-6 it is survivability.

The E-6 Tacamo (Take charge and move out) is to replace the EC-130Q Hercules as the US Navy's radio link between the US President, or other national command authority, and submerged Trident ballistic missile submarines on station ready to fire.

There is no way messages can be transmitted from Washington, Norfolk or other Naval HQ direct to a submerged submarine on the other side of the globe. It can be done with airborne relay stations. The full Navy force will comprise ten EC-130Qs and 15 new E-6s, all operational by 1993 when the 14th and last Trident submarine will commission. Eight E-6s will be deployed with the US Pacific Fleet and the other seven in the Atlantic/Mediterranean. At all times one E-6 in each area will be on station, one on standby alert and another on ready alert.

The E-6 is one of the most expensive aircraft ever bought by the US Navy. It has an airframe generally similar to the E-3 but retains the 707-320C large freight door for installation and removal of giant communications systems and consoles, as well as the drum of 26,000ft (7,925m) of special wire with a 90lb (41kg) weight on the end

BOEING
767/AOA

Type: ICBM detection technology demonstrator.
Engines: Either two 47,800lb (21,682kg) P&W JT9D-7R4D or 47,900lb (21,727kg) GE CF6-80A turbofans.
Dimensions: Span 156ft 1in (47.57m); length 159ft 2in (48.51m); height 52ft 0in (15.85m); wing area 3,050sq ft (283.3m²).
Weights: Empty about 200,000lb (90 tonnes); maximum probably 345,000lb (156,490kg).
Performance: Cruising speed about 500mph (805km/h); patrol speed probably about 300mph (482km/h); orbit altitude about 38,000ft (11,580m); time on station at least 12h.

One of the strangest paradoxes of the modern world is that the Soviet Union has far more intercontinental and submarine-launched ballistic missiles (ICBMs and SLBMs) than all other countries combined, as well as comprehensive ABM (anti-ballistic missile) installations, while the Western nations on which the awesome ICBMs are targeted have no ABM systems and nothing planned. Substantial sums have been voted to continue research into how the West might be defended, but there is no plan actually to construct any defence.

Biggest of the post-1975 contracts for ABM work was one awarded by the US Army to Boeing in July 1984. Valued at $289.4 million, it calls for the demonstration of how extremely sensitive IR sensors could be used in a future ABM system to detect and track incoming RVs (re-entry vehicles) fired by hostile ICBMs. One of the basic problems in any ABM system is getting the earliest possible warning of an

attack and then distinguishing the deadly RVs, containing the warheads, from clouds of chaff, decoys, flares and other false targets all intended to dilute the defences. Precisely how the IR sensors would separate the RVs from the decoys has not been made public; the enormous sensors, probably more sensitive than any previously constructed, are being supplied by Hughes Aircraft. (IR sensing is described later under NASA.)

It is expected that for the demonstration the IR detectors will be mounted in a giant upper lobe "doghouse" built on a Boeing 767. This aircraft has particularly good high-altitude capability, and the intention is to install the associated cryogenic cooling systems (probably using liquid nitrogen and liquid helium) on the main deck under the sensors. Aft on the main deck,

BOEING/NASA
F-111/MAW

Type: Mission-adaptive wing research aircraft.
Engines: Two 18,500lb (8,390kg) Pratt & Whitney TF30-3 augmented turbofans.
Dimensions: Span (variable with sweep angle) up to 63ft 0in (19.2m); length 75ft 6.5in (23.03m); height 17ft 0.5in (5.19m); wing area (max) 525sq ft (48.78m²).
Weights: Empty about 46,500lb (21,092kg); maximum originally 91,300lb (41,400kg) but unlikely as MAW to exceed 76,000lb (34,474kg).
Performance: Maximum speed (high altitude) over 1,320mph (2,124km/h), (low altitude) about 912mph (1,468km/h).

BMAC (Boeing Military Airplane Company) has since 1979 been working under a USAF contract trying to achieve one of the true advances of human flight: make a wing flexible in profile, like a bird's. In the past wings have been able to change their profile (cross-section aerofoil shape) only in crude ways, by moving pivoted or track-mounted slats, ailerons and various kinds of leading- or trailing-edge flap. The fixed part of the wing remains rigid metal, and so do the so-called movables, there being sudden discontinuities at the joints or hinges. What aerodynamicists have always wanted to do has been to make a wing smoothly flexible, so that at all times its profile would be close to the efficient ideal shape. The reason this has never been done is that it is too difficult. If a wing has to stay on in fighter manoeuvres, there is no way it can also be made flexible, like the wing of a bird.

One of the first small advances towards the shape-changing wing came when Boeing fitted enormous leading-edge slats to the 747 "Jumbo" with glass-fibre skins;

when the captain selects slats the skins bend to preserve a smooth leading-edge profile with no kinks. But it is a far cry from that to the MAW (Mission-Adaptive Wing), which BMAC has designed and fitted to NASA's F-111 research aircraft, originally an early F-111A No 63-9778. The outer pivoted "swing wings" have been completely redesigned so that each has a slim rigid main box, on which the wings pivot, and completely flexible leading and trailing sections. These sections have flexible skins and complex internal mechanisms, driven by powerful actuators tied in to a digital FBW (fly by wire) control system integrated with the F-111's basic flight control system. Most of the skins are laminated glass-fibre plastics, and prolonged testing was needed to prove that the skins would stand up to millions of bending reversals, and survive transonic hail, birdstrikes and which serves as the main VLF communications aerial (antenna). On station the E-6 orbits ceaselessly around the weighted end of the wire not far above ground level vertically below. Signals sent out at 200kW power are received by a buoyant wire aerial towed by each submarine. ESM, satellite communications and other devices are in wingtip pods. Each E-6 has an endurance of 16h, but will normally be repeatedly refuelled and kept on station 72h at a time. One of its classified systems is an ERCS (emergency rocket communications system) which presumably can retarget or destroy a Trident SLBM after launch. Each E-6 carries two on-board crews.

Right: Unlike the mass of special EC-135/RC-135 versions the E-6 has F108 engines. Here the domestic area with bunks can be seen forward, the SSBN communications centre amidships and the high-power radio and antenna section at rear.

where passengers sit in other 767s, is the Honeywell data-processing system, which together with sensor equipment by Aerojet Electro Systems and extensive signal processing and analysis consoles, will demonstrate the required target detection and tracking capability.

The AOA (Airborne Optical Adjunct) is just one of several research programmes intended to provide data for a future ABM system, should such a system ever receive approval. The 767/AOA will not furnish data until about 1988-89, and no ABM system could actually protect Western countries until well into the next century.

Right: The 767/AOA will have a giant "doghouse" with two unique optical sensors, Aerojet's in front and Hughes' behind. The on-board data processor will hand target data to ground-based radars. What is lacking is any will to create ICBM defence.

other harsh usage without fatigue or sudden failure.

The MAW can flex itself to increase wing efficiency in subsonic cruise or in supersonic flight, or slow-speed flight for landing, give direct lift control allowing the pilot to change flight level suddenly without changing attitude, change shape for manoeuvres, and alleviate gust loads.

Right: A MAW model in a tunnel at USAF Arnold Engineering Development Center. Boeing is running late, first flight having been due in 1982.
Below: Testing the flexible MAW before pivoting it to the USAF/NASA F-111.

Type: Forward-swept wing technology demonstrator.

Engine: One 16,000lb (7,258kg) General Electric F404-400 augmented turbofan.

Dimensions: Span 27ft 2.44in (8.29m); length, excluding probe 48ft 1in (14.66m); height 14ft 9.5in (4.51m); wing area 188.84sq ft (17.54m²).

Weights: Empty 13,326lb (6,045kg); maximum 17,303lb (7,848kg).

Performance: Maximum speed (high altitude) over Mach 1.6, current test programme goes to 1.5 (992mph, 1596km/h).

The unique X-29 (Grumman Model 712) is possibly going to have a greater effect on the design of future air-combat fighters than any previous research aircraft in history. For the first time it is enabling the calculated advantages of the forward-swept wing (FSW) to be realised in practice. It has been known for almost 50 years that the FSW offers the theoretical advantages of rearward sweep in delaying transonic drag rise, plus large benefits in reduced stalling speed, improved low-speed handling, virtually stall-proof flight characteristics and, it was believed, the ability to make fighters smaller and thus both faster and more agile for any given installed power.

Metal FSW aircraft would either have had their wings torn off from aeroelastic divergence in manoeuvres (because with an FSW the deflection of the wing under load increases the load acting on it) or would have had to be so heavily constructed as to negate any advantages. Grumman Aerospace, NASA and others all appreciated that modern composite structures are sufficiently strong, rigid and light to make an FSW fighter feasible. DARPA (Defense Advanced Research Projects Agency) funded the X-29 programme, and Grum-

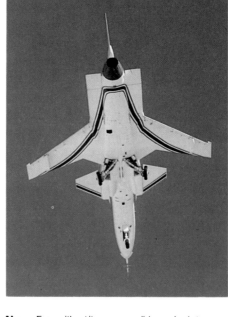

Above: Even without its company colour scheme the X-29As would be striking-looking aircraft. Here the No. 1 machine is seen from below, possibly coming in to land at Dryden, with gear and flaperons down. Pilots have said suddenly seeing the FSW flying is disconcerting.

man built the Model 712 using the front end of an F-5, the main gears and surface power units of the F-16, and F-18 engine and many other off-the-shelf parts to save cost. What is totally new is the aerodynamic shape, structure and movable surfaces.

The wing has an inner structure of EBW (electron-beam welded) titanium and light alloy. On top are fixed upper and lower skins which are one piece from tip to tip and are made from CFRP (carbon-fibre reinforced plastics), each skin being made up of 156 layers at the thickest points well inboard. This wing is so stiff yet light that it can have a high aspect ratio for high

efficiency, with a forward sweep angle at quarter-chord of nearly 34°, yet resist the colossal bending loads of violent high-speed flight manoeuvres. The leading edge is fixed, but the trailing edge comprises full-span flaperons. These have one-quarter of the wing chord, and each is double-hinged into front and rear sections. Thus the wing can be given powerful variable camber, ranging from a full-up (rear section) position, through an almost neutral cruise setting to a down-curved manoeuvre setting and finally a fully down position for very high-AOA flight at low speeds and for landing. It has been shown that the wing comes close to a theoretically fully flexible VC (variable camber) wing, such as the Boeing MAW described earlier, without the MAW's complexity.

Other movable surfaces include the rudder, two trailing strake flaps behind the extended wing root trailing edge, and the canards. The latter have one-fifth the area of the wing and are close-coupled, and powerfully driven by the triply redundant flight control system as the primary control in pitch. Under most conditions they generate lift, trimming out tail-up moments and enhancing manoeuvres while at the same time having strong interactions with the wing which benefit both the canard (by effectively doubling its moment arm) and the wing (the canard downwash postponing stall at the wing root). The X-29 has RSS (relaxed static stability) yet so far the flight controls have fully borne out tunnel testing and simulations showing outstanding control and agility. Even at the most impossible AOA the X-29 cannot stall and retains impressive roll control.

The first flight was on 14 December 1984 at the NASA Dryden Center/Air Force Flight Test Center. Grumman completed four flights and then in March 1985 turned the aircraft over to the Air Force for sub-

Below: Three-view of the X-29 (also designated X-29A). The main wing box structure, here outlined (visible in carbon-black colour in the picture at upper right) is made as a single piece from tip to tip. For its size it is probably the strongest and stiffest aircraft component in history, yet light in weight. Its interior is metal.

Right: The No. 1 X-29 in the NASA Dryden circuit, with gear and flaperons down, and the tail-end trailing flaps up to retrim the aircraft. By June 1985 most flight-test results were encouraging, though many tasks remained unexplored. Grumman have said there are plans to conduct flight tests with wing-mounted dummy missiles.

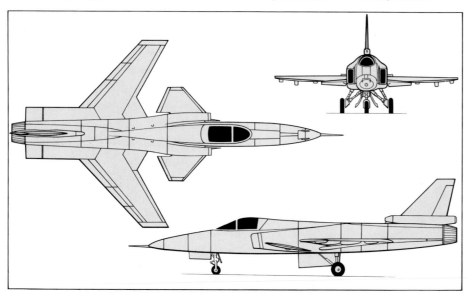

sequent testing by a rota system using pilots from NASA and the USAF. Testing by March 1985 had begun to explore the digital reversionary mode – a backup mode using fewer sensors and separate computer software – and the analog reversionary mode which eliminates the main digital system entirely. It is thought that there could never be a failure in sensors, digital subsystems or the analog backup that would embarrass the pilot or put the basically unstable aircraft at risk. So far the X-29 has shown itself exceptionally reliable, experiencing virtually no snags, and a remarkable feature of Flight 1, maintained on subsequent missions, was that the fuel burn was 300lb (136kg) below prediction.

The big question is whether data can come in fast enough from just two X-29s (No 2 had not flown as this was written) to influence the ATF (Advanced Tactical Fighter), a planned supercruise interceptor and other future USAF programmed combat aircraft. If predictions continue to be fulfilled, the FSW appears likely to become the standard form of wing for agile air-combat fighters. It also has much to offer attack aircraft, because its high aspect ratio can reduce induced drag and improve cruise lift/drag ratio, resulting in enhanced range and/or greater weapon load. Whether or not a variable-sweep FSW is possible is uncertain; the author believes that the current fixation on variable camber rather than variable sweep is a mere passing fashion, and that in due course pivoted outer wings will be back in favour. The question is whether they will pivot aft or forwards?

Left: This picture taken at Grumman's plant during erection of the first X-29 gives some idea of the test gear and auxiliary supplies needed in the manufacture of a prototype. The F-5 nose had previously flown with the USAF. The mascot on the right inlet duct was not airworthy.

HELICOPTER RESEARCH PROGRAMMES

In recent years virtually all the research helicopters known to exist have been American. Some have been concerned with exploring new kinds of rotor, or even the long-sought "stopped rotor" concept, while two of the most recent have demonstrated the use of modern fibre-reinforced composites in primary airframe structures.

Potentially the most significant of the research helicopters illustrated here is the Sikorsky S-72 RSRA (rotor systems research aircraft). Originally flown with a conventional (S-61 Sea King) rotor system, the S-72 then sprouted fixed wings, an

aeroplane tail and two powerful turbofan engines (TF34s of the type which power the S-3 Viking ASW aircraft). After testing as a compound helicopter the main rotor was then removed and the S-72 flown as an aeroplane at speeds up to 301mph (485km/h).

By far the most difficult step is the installation and test of a rotor system that can be slowed down and stopped in forward flight. Most helicopters rely on the fact that the airspeed of the rotor blade is much higher than that of the helicopter, so each blade leading edge stays a leading edge

right round each complete revolution. A slowing-down blade on a high-speed helicopter has the problem that each leading edge intermittently becomes a trailing edge, and vice versa; moreoover, one side of the rotor would experience zero or negative airspeed and would give no lift. The only solution, first demonstrated at Farnborough, England, in 1964, is to use blades of symmetric section (so that leading and trailing edges look alike) and then blast high-pressure air from full-span slits to control the circulation around the blade. Credit should also be given to Kaman Aero-

Below: Looking up at a hypothetical ABC (advancing-blade concept) attack helicopter of the kind seen for years on Sikorsky drawing boards. Such a machine could have outstanding performance, and prolonged testing of the XH-59A (fitted with two

Pratt & Whitney J60 booster turbojets) gave excellent results and no severe problems. What is still not clear is whether the US Army's insistence on "conventional helicopter technology" for the vitally important LHX programme rules out the use of the ABC technology.

Propeller jet would be deflectable in horizontal and vertical planes

Two 36ft (10.97m) composite rotors

Turret M197 three-barrel gun

Weapon boxes (various fits including FFARs, guns, Hellfire, TOW, Stinger)

Below: In side elevation this proposed ABC technology LHX looks like what it is: an attack/ scout helicopter significantly faster and more agile than those flying today. The artist based his drawing on the proposed Sikorsky XH-59B, which would combine the proven counter-rotating ABC

rotors with a redesigned rear drive train to a ducted tail propulsor. There is no drive torque to be cancelled, and the tail propulsor could confer speeds exceeding 300mph (482km/h). A broadly similar arrangement, but with a conventional rigid main rotor, was used in the cancelled AH-56.

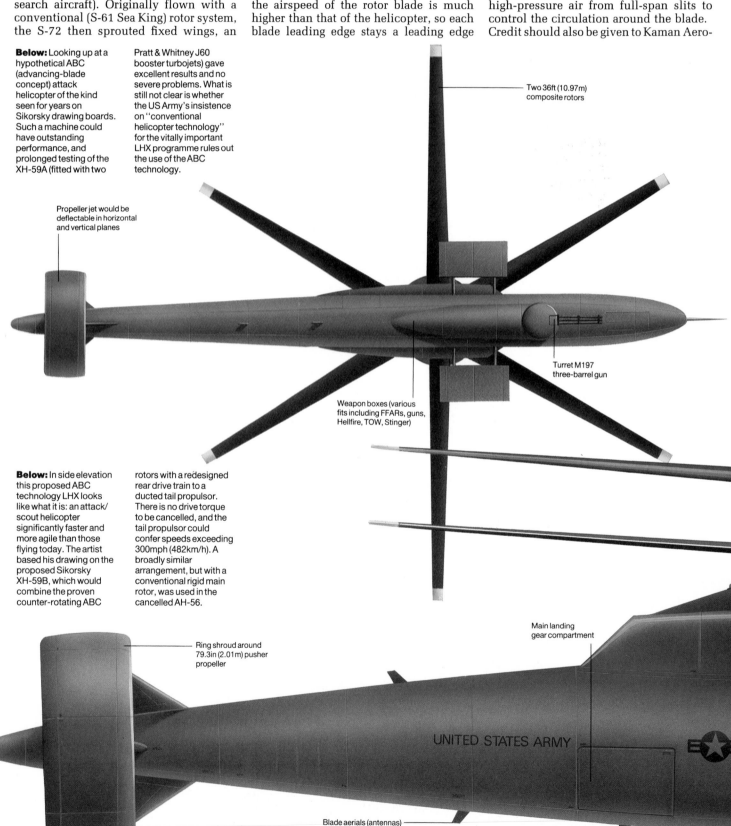

Main landing gear compartment

Ring shroud around 79.3in (2.01m) pusher propeller

UNITED STATES ARMY

Blade aerials (antennas) for VHF/UHF/Tacan

Left: Otherwise known as the RSRA (rotor systems research aircraft), the Sikorsky S-72 combined the conventional rotor system of an S-61 Sea King with a wing, twin TF34 turbofan engines and a new flight-control system. The landing gears were the same as on the Northrop F-5E. With the main rotor removed it flew at 301mph (485km/h). It might lead to the X-wing.

space, which with Navy funding pioneered the circulation-controlled rotor with a modified HH-2D in 1975-85. Lockheed has also researched this potentially important new technology.

Sikorsky now have to take the idea further, under a 1984 contract for $77 million by DARPA (Defense Advanced Research Projects Agency) and NASA, which calls for one S-72 to be rebuilt for the final phase of the X-wing programme. The idea is that the rotor should be slowed down, using modulated air bleed through the full-span slits to maintain lift and roll

Below: Looking down on the hypothetical ABC attack/scout helicopter, notable for the almost perfect streamlining of its two rotor hubs. The directions of rotation are indicated. Possibly, if this technology were admitted for the LHX, the definitive three-blade rotors would have broader-chord blades with greater taper from root to tip. Of course, the suggested armament is purely notional, and one feature of such fast helicopters would be greater attention to streamlining than on the relatively sluggish military helicopters flying today.

Clockwise rotation (seen from above)

IR suppressed engine exhausts

Mast mounted sight (MMS)

The MMS might house all sensors

Anti-clockwise rotation

Bearingless hub

High-speed engine would have stealth features

Pilot

Copilot/gunner

Alternatively, duplicate or additional sensors could be in the nose

RESEARCH HELICOPTERS

control, and finally bring it to rest in what is called the X-wing mode (because the stopped four-blade rotor forms an X-shaped wing). All the ejected air would then issue from the rearward-facing slits, while lift would be provided by the X-wing and the fixed auxiliary wing, propulsion being provided solely by the two TF34 engines. In early 1985 Sikorsky envisaged the X-wing rotor blade as having an effective length of 28ft (8.5m) and chord of 36in (0.91m). The rotor is expected to fly on the S-72 in 1986, to be stopped at 196mph (315km/h) and to make possible speeds up

Left: Most of this helicopter will be recognised as the Sikorsky S-72 RSRA. The rotor system, however, is the radical new X-wing "stopped rotor" concept. The 55ft (16.76m) rotor has four broad sharp-edged blades blown at the edges by compressed air. Flight testing began in 1985, and could lead to a helicopter with three times the speed and range of the best conventional helicopters.

Below: The underside view of this hypothetical X-wing helicopter looks conventional, apart from the staggering fact that the rotor would not be rotating! The blades are shown with parallel chord, but in practice they would probably be tapered. Note the internal weapon bays and general fine streamlining.

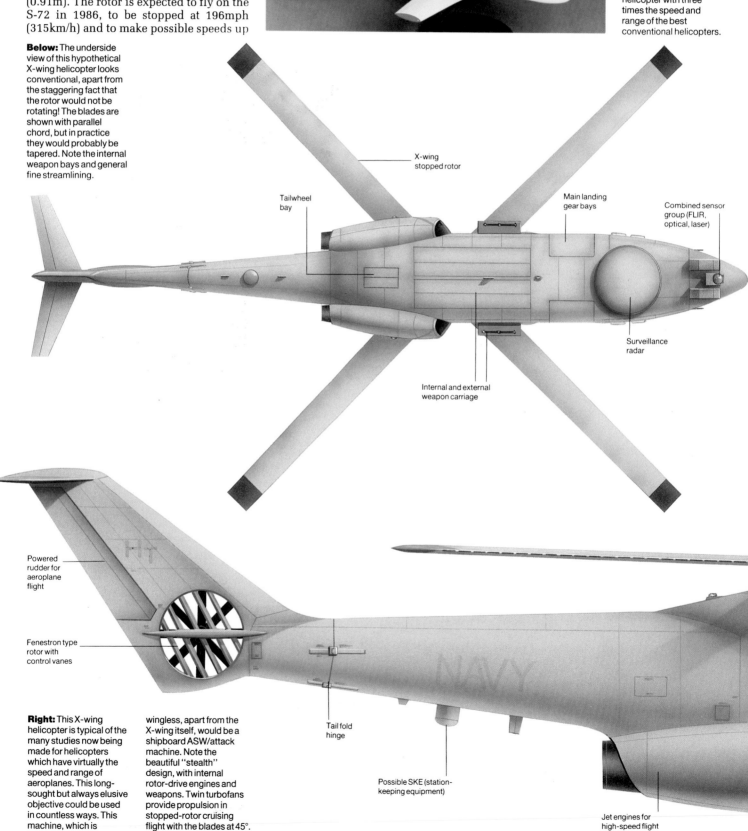

X-wing
stopped rotor

Tailwheel
bay

Main landing
gear bays

Combined sensor
group (FLIR,
optical, laser)

Internal and external
weapon carriage

Surveillance
radar

Powered
rudder for
aeroplane
flight

Fenestron type
rotor with
control vanes

Tail fold
hinge

Possible SKE (station-
keeping equipment)

Jet engines for
high-speed flight

Right: This X-wing helicopter is typical of the many studies now being made for helicopters which have virtually the speed and range of aeroplanes. This long-sought but always elusive objective could be used in countless ways. This machine, which is wingless, apart from the X-wing itself, would be a shipboard ASW/attack machine. Note the beautiful "stealth" design, with internal rotor-drive engines and weapons. Twin turbofans provide propulsion in stopped-rotor cruising flight with the blades at 45°.

to 518mph (833km/h). If the stopped-rotor can at last be made to work it would revolutionize helicopters, more than doubling maximum speed.

Sikorsky's other fundamental research helicopter, the S-69, is less revolutionary but unlike the X-wing has already demonstrated significant advances. By using superimposed coaxial helicopter main rotors of advanced design, with stiff hingeless blades, the ABC (advancing blade concept) overcomes one of the basic problems encountered as soon as a helicopter tries to fly fast. The difficulty is that the "retreating" half of the main rotor disc, where the blades are moving backwards, generates progressively less lift. When the speed of the helicopter is roughly the same as the speed of the mid-point of each blade due to its rotation then the average blade airspeed round the retreating part of the disc becomes zero. No lift is generated on that side, and the helicopter tends not only to fall like a stone but also to roll over.

With the ABC coaxial rotors there is no problem; lift remains strong on both sides of the helicopter, and testing by the US Army with twin J60 booster turbojets has reached 276mph (445km/h), and over 300mph (482km/h) in a shallow dive, with excellent flight control at all times. A basic feature of the ABC rotor is that its blades are extremely rigid. Normally flexible blades would not withstand the severe inflight bending forces and would collide catastrophically. An XH-59B has been proposed, but not yet funded, with ABC rotors on a new fuselage with a ducted tail propeller.

Yet another Sikorsky research helicopter is the Shadow (Sikorsky helicopter advanced demonstrator of operator work-

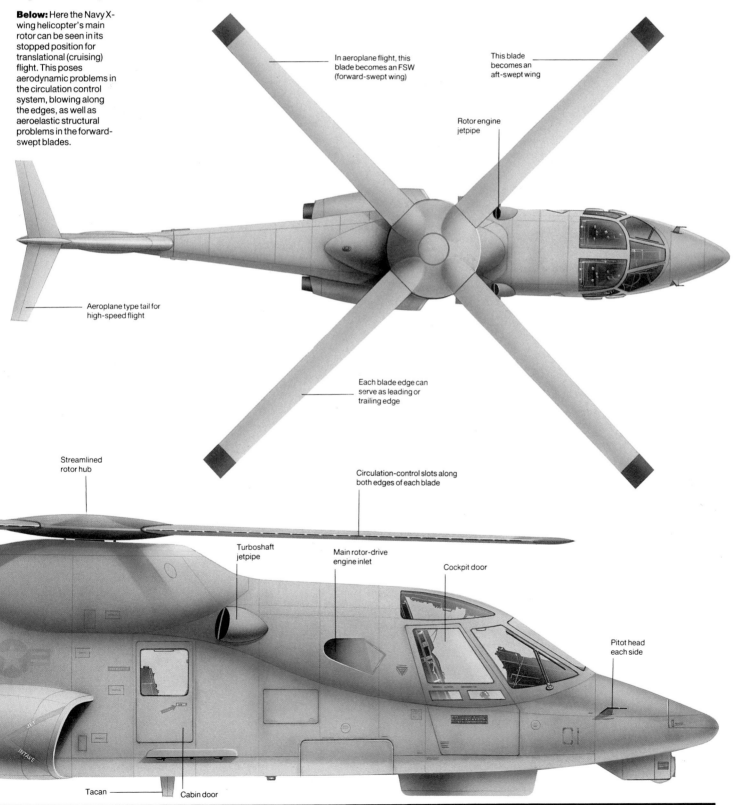

Below: Here the Navy X-wing helicopter's main rotor can be seen in its stopped position for translational (cruising) flight. This poses aerodynamic problems in the circulation control system, blowing along the edges, as well as aeroelastic structural problems in the forward-swept blades.

In aeroplane flight, this blade becomes an FSW (forward-swept wing)

This blade becomes an aft-swept wing

Rotor engine jetpipe

Aeroplane type tail for high-speed flight

Each blade edge can serve as leading or trailing edge

Streamlined rotor hub

Circulation-control slots along both edges of each blade

Turboshaft jetpipe

Main rotor-drive engine inlet

Cockpit door

Pitot head each side

Tacan

Cabin door

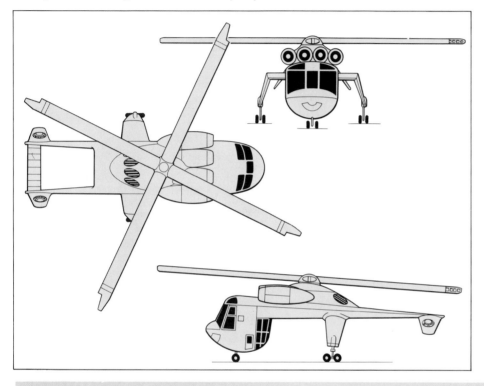

RESEARCH HELICOPTERS

load). A modified S-76, it has a new single-seat cockpit built on the front to demonstrate how best to arrange displays and controls for the LHX/SCAT (see earlier pages).

Sikorsky and Bell have both built ACAP (Advanced Composite Airframe Program) helicopters to demonstrate the extensive use of composite materials to save 22 per cent in weight and 17 per cent in manufacturing cost. Both contractors handsomely exceeded these numerical requirements, Bell (and associate Grumman) using mainly Kevlar and glass while Sikorsky

(and associates LTV and Hercules) used mainly graphite. Neither the Bell D292 nor the Sikorsky S-75 is seen as a production helicopter but as a proof of concept that will enable fibre-reinforced composites to account for perhaps 85-95 per cent of the structure of future helicopters.

Hughes Helicopters has a potential lead over its rivals with the Notar (no tail rotor) programme, discussed in the LHX entry. The company is convinced it can result in superior helicopters, and most of its future military and civil projects feature it. All published artwork shows the use of a full-

length slit along the underside of the tail boom to generate the required offset force to counter the torque needed to drive the main rotor, as well as a controllable series of exit vanes (various arrangements have been suggested) at the tip of the tailboom to provide yaw and directional control. A suggested Hughes LHX has no "tail" at all, whereas a suggested future civil Model 500E seven-seater has a twin-finned tail.

In the early days of helicopter technology there was enthusiasm for tip drive in which the main rotor is driven by thrust applied at the tip. The tip can carry a self-

Left: Provisional three-view of the Hughes HLH (heavy-lift helicopter). The giant rotor is shown with blades aligned parallel to the helicopter longitudinal and transverse axes in the head-on and side views, but in the plan view it is slightly rotated to reveal "fuselage" detail. The four gas turbines have no shaft drive to a rotor gearbox, but instead supply a high-energy flow of compressed hot gas which drives the rotor blades round from their tips. Thus there is no drive torque reaction, other than the very small friction in the main-rotor bearings. The angled tail rotors are purely for pitch/yaw attitude control.

Right: The proposed Hughes HLH. With rotor powers in the over-20,000hp class tip drive is unmatched in saving total installed weight.

contained ramjet or pulsejet, or it can be provided with a thrust unit supplied with air, hot gas or an air/fuel mix for combustion at the tip. Tip drive is particularly attractive in the largest sizes, where elimination of the main gearbox can save much more than the combined weight of the engines. Today there is less enthusiasm for tip drive, but it is far from dead, and Hughes Helicopters has completed extensive tip-drive research for HLH (heavy-lift helicopter) concepts, under contract to the David Taylor Naval Ship R&D Center. An accompanying illustration shows a pro-posed Hughes HLH with a 185ft (56.4m) rotor with a blade chord of 10ft (3m), to carry an enormous gas flow to tip jets, and with circulation control at frequencies higher than blade-rotation frequency to reduce vibration. Such a helicopter could airlift a 54-ton M1 Abrams battle tank.

In the Salamander book "An Illustrated Guide to Future Fighters and Combat Aircraft" details are given of another research helicopter used by Hughes Helicopters to develop its Notar (no tail rotor) scheme. This replaces the usual tail rotor by compressed air ejected from a thin slit along the tail boom, which causes airflow round the boom generating the necessary side force. A rotating air jet at the tip of the boom provides variable side thrust for yaw control.

An artist's impression below shows a civilian Notar helicopter, and the concept might be used in the LHX programme as described on earlier pages. Notar design is expected to result in reduced noise and vibration, and to be especially advantageous in helicopters flying NOE ("nap of the Earth") missions, at the lowest possible height above ground.

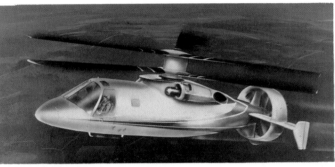

Left: Nearing completion at Fort Worth, the Bell ACAP (Advanced Composite Airframe Program) is now flying together with another ACAP built by Sikorsky (the S-75). The Bell D292 is shown with a Model 222 rotor, but was to fly in 1985 with the Model 680 composite bearingless rotor.

Below: The Bell D292 was designed purely as a structural exercise, but might lead to an all-composite production helicopter. It came out weighing 22.7 per cent less than an equivalent metal helicopter and cost 23.2 per cent less to build. It would carry four people.

Top: The proposed XH-59B, which would be a logical next step beyond the extremely successful XH-59A ABC (advancing blade concept) machine. Twin 1,700hp T700 engines would drive the coaxial rotors and a ducted tail propeller. It would be for attack, SAR and electronics missions.

Above: Hughes Model 500-derived Notar (no tail rotor) helicopter. The US Army has confirmed Notar is admissible for the Hughes LHX submissions, not being sufficiently radical to be disqualified from the vital next-generation Army helicopter. It would be extremely quiet.

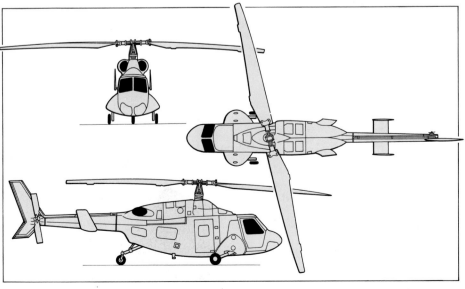

153

LOCKHEED
HAPP

Type: High-altitude VLEA (very long endurance aircraft).
Engine: Solar power train of very low power (see below).
Dimensions: Span might be 304ft 6in (92.8m).
Weights: Empty and maximum would be virtually identical, at possibly 3,000lb (1,361kg).
Performance: Cruising speed at 60,000-70,000ft (18,000-21,000m) must be greater than expected winds; endurance typically one year (design target).

There are many clear applications for an aircraft which can carry a modest payload to a height of perhaps 70,000ft (21,000m) and then hold station for weeks, months or years (if necessary relaying data to an Earth receiver station). In 1974 Lockheed Missiles & Space Co. teamed up with Astro-flight Inc. to demonstrate a limited-capability VLEA (very long endurance aircraft) to DARPA (US Defense Advanced Research Projects Agency). Since then LMSC has been working for NASA Langley on what are called HAPPs (high-altitude powered platforms).

To be useful a HAPP must be robust enough to survive launch and climb through the dense lower atmosphere, light enough for the wing loading to be well below 1lb/sq ft (4.9kg/m²) and have high enough loiter speed to maintain its assigned station in the face of any atmospheric disturbance or wind. The only known form of power source is electric propulsion drawing current from solar panels covering large areas of the airframe. A typical installed power/weight ratio is 0.005hp/lb (0.003kW/kg). Either silicon or gallium arsenide cells can be used, the former having various problems (such as brittleness), but being simpler to fabricate than the complex GaAs cells. The power generated by the solar panels in the daytime has to be enough both to hold station, hold altitude and also store energy in batteries to fly the HAPP during the night.

There is no particular magic about flight

Below: How does a solar-powered aircraft fly at night? Answer: by storing surplus energy during the day. A HAPP could have a computer to set its outer wings to the best angle to capture sunlight in daylight. At night the outer wings would be hinged horizontal to achieve the greatest loiter efficiency. It would be better to retract or jettison landing gears.

LOCKHEED
HTTB

Type: High-technology testbed STOL transport.
Engines: Four 4,680ehp Allison 501-D22A turboprops.
Dimensions: Span 132ft 7in (40.41m); length 106ft 1in (32.33m); height 38ft 3in (11.66m); wing area (before modification) 1,745sq ft (161.12m²).
Weights: (Before modification) Empty 74,629lb (33,851kg); maximum 175,000lb (79,380kg).
Performance: Cruising speed up to 374mph (602km/h); takeoff data significantly better than C-130/L-100.

Throughout the 35-year life of the C-130 Hercules programme Lockheed has been studying ways of improving the aircraft additional to the modifications introduced by natural development with newer engines and improved avionics. Most of the studies have centred on ways of improving field length and slow-flying capability. Two study programmes have been taken further, and it seems extraordinary that so far the various STOL Hercules possibilities have failed to reach the production line.

First of the two major rebuilds was originally the seventh C-130B, USAF 58-0712, which in 1959 was rebuilt as the C-130BLC (Boundary Layer Control), with two extra T56 engines in underwing pods driving compressors to blow over the flaps and ailerons, and with increased-chord rudder and elevators. Later designated NC-130B, it flew with Systems Command and NASA, proving controllable at 60mph (97km/h) and landing in 1,400ft (427m). A cynic might say it was so effective that the customer lost interest.

Undeterred, Lockheed-Georgia continued STOL studies, and in the absence of interest by the military decided to fund a demonstrator with its own money, assisted by such suppliers as Hamilton Standard, Menasco, Allison, Garrett, Bendix, Collins, Honeywell, Litton, Northrop and Texas Instruments. Starting with a commercial L-100-20, the intermediate-length version, the HTTB (high-tech testbed) was first given a very advanced and comprehensive data sensing, analysis and display system, which includes long sensor probes ahead of the wingtips very similar to those used on several earlier C-130s used for STOL tests. Root extensions were added ahead of the fin and tailplane prior to the start of flight tests in June 1984. Subsequently a major high-lift system is being installed including multi-slot track-mounted flaps and outer-wing leading edge flaps. Details of the progress of HTTB flying had not been published in spring 1985, but it would be really strange if this aircraft was regarded as a mere research tool to gather data. Allison has a 5,250shp T56 in production and several growth versions (some using modules from the T701 turboshaft for the Boeing Vertol XCH-62 described previously) offering up to 8,000shp. Most of the elements appear to exist for a dramatically upgraded STOL C-130, carrying bigger loads out of or into much smaller airstrips.

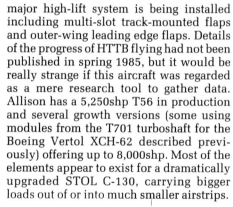

Left: Bearing in mind that the C-130 flew over 30 years ago it seems ridiculous to regard it as a "warplane of the future", but current research looks like making it so. The HTTB is supported by Allison, Hamilton Standard, Garrett, Menasco, Bendix, Collins, Honeywell, Bendix, Litton, Northrop, Texas Instruments and other companies.

Right: Even in take-off configuration the HTTB looks very much like any other C-130. Only in its detail design and performance is this a new aircraft, and it is likely to have a major long-term effect on the future of the C-130 programme. Remarkably, though it was designed in 1952-3, the C-130 is still hard to beat, and with HTTB engineering design changes it could remain in production into the next century.

levels of around 65,000ft (19,500m), but throughout most of the world wind speeds at this height band are low enough to make a HAPP especially attractive. LMSC has refined HAPP structural methods using large amounts of standard graphite/epoxy tubing joined at integral gussets and clam-shell fittings of the same material. The only viable night storage system appears to be to use surplus daytime current to electrolyse water into hydrogen and oxygen; each night these gases are then recombined in a fuel cell to generate electricity. Radiators to dissipate the inevitable heat generated have to be carefully designed to radiate into the near-vacuum around the HAPP. Total power-train efficiency is likely to be about 56 per cent.

In 1985 LMSC were confident that, with current technology a HAPP can be put on station for a year or more, with high reliability, at any Earth latitude. The company hope that an R&D HAPP can be put on station in the 1980s to underpin the design of future operational platforms.

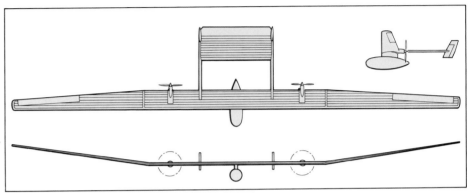

Right: Largest of the LMSC HAPP designs in the original DARPA-funded study had a span of 304ft (92.8m), though structural advance enables this figure slightly to be increased. Blue areas are solar cells.

Below: Three-view of the same HAPP proposal.

155

HI-SPOT

Type: High-altitude platform.
Engine: Long-endurance, low power (see text).
Dimensions: Length in the region of 500ft (152m); diameter about 100ft (30m).
Weights: Empty, possibly about 17,000lb (7,711kg); loaded less than 18,000lb (8,165kg).
Performance: Maximum speed, probably about 10mph (16km/h) airspeed; operating height 70,000ft (21,400m); endurance on station 100 days.

Although the high-altitude Hi-Spot is a most unusual form of warplane concept, its inclusion here certainly is graphic proof of the amount of attention that such aircraft are attracting in the USA (and probably in other advanced countries).

This class of vehicle is the unmanned platform able to loiter at great height for very long periods. The primary missions of such platforms are surveillance in all its forms, and many of the tasks they can perform are military and would continue during hostilities. Some VLEAs (very long endurance aircraft) are similar to sailplanes with low-power engines (see previous page). Hi-Spot is basically an airship, of novel character.

LMSC (Lockheed Missiles & Space Co) studied Hi-Spot (HIgh-altitude Surveillance Platform for Over-the-horizon Targeting) under contract to the US Naval Air Development Center at Warminster, Pennsylvania. It would have a very light but stiff and strong envelope of special fabric woven with fibres of Kevlar and Tedlar. There would be very little "airframe" apart from the envelope, which would be stabilised by being slightly pressurised. The filling gas would probably be hydrogen, and the propulsion system would be hydrogen fuelled.

The onboard power would be needed to maintain control and attitude/direction during the climb up from the parent ship or other launching base. On-station power would be needed only to counter winds, which can be brought close to zero by automatic computer control of launch altitude to minimise air movement. (Solar power is also easy to apply to an airship, because of the large area of envelope available.)

Hi-Spot could handle air/sea surveillance 24 hours per day, communications relay, OTH (over the horizon) targeting for friendly weapon systems, and many other military tasks. Payload could be 550lb (250kg) of various electronics, and studies are in hand on physically enormous but extremely light radar antennas.

Right: Interest in Hi-Spot platforms has become so great that now an Associaton for Unmanned Vehicle Systems has been formed in Washington DC. Such vehicles, both heavier and lighter than air, are likely to play an increasing role in future military affairs.

MBB RESEARCH

By far the largest aircraft company in Federal Germany, MBB has built mainly collaborative or licensed designs, except for its helicopters. Two of its current flight research programmes are aimed at proving advanced flight control systems for future fighter and transport type aircraft. Despite the possibility of detailed "mathematical modelling" and computer simulations there is no substitute for actual flight test to provide the degree of confidence needed for future aircraft designs.

The MBB military Aircraft Division, at Ottobrunn, Munich, has for five years been using a modified Lockheed F-104G (originally built by MBB's predecessor companies) in a long-term CCV (control-configured vehicle) research programme. The most obvious external modification is the addition of a destabilized canard surface on a pylon above the forward fuselage. Flying in Phase IV of the test programme, in 1984-85, has been carried out in a neutrally stable regime. The digital autopilot uses the existing CCV computer, with automatic jerkless switchover to direct FBW (fly by wire) control on any axis where the pilot input exceeds a preselected limit. Extensive work was completed in mid-1985 to perfect not only the flight-control software but also the ability to fall back in emergency on purely mechanical flight control, using different control laws.

Another research programme being flown with Starfighter 98+36 (originally in Luftwaffe service as 23+91) is development of a laser INS (inertial navigation system). The ring laser gyro has no moving parts and offers improved reliability and great accuracy. Two gyro types were flown, one from Litton/Litef and the other from Honeywell, carried in a bright orange belly pod together with the measurement and data system.

MBB's Transport Division at Bremen and Lemwerder is converting a VFW 614 short-haul transport (a product of an MBB-merged company) for outstanding fundamental research for the DFVLR, the federal aerospace research establishment. The twin-turbofan transport, distinctive for its overwing Rolls-Royce M45H turbofan engines, is to renew flight trials in 1986 as the ATTAS (advanced technologies testing aircraft system). Among other tasks it will test and evaluate integrated digital flight controls, new navaids and MLS (microwave landing systems), test systems by inflight simulation, and study aerodynamic questions including the behaviour of boundary layers and airflow over fast-acting flaps. The entire aircraft flight controls are new, including direct lift wing controls, and the flight deck is packed with special sensors, monitors, instrumentation and displays.

Of course, MBB has its sights set firmly on the EFA (European Fighter Aircraft). It has done much work of is own (TKF90, JF90), and is looking forward to playing its full role in a multinational programme. The Federal German need is urgent, like that of Britain.

Right: The MBB CCV F-104 has proved an excellent vehicle for research into advanced fighter flight-control systems. Like the BAe unstable Jaguar it explores flight conditions well beyond the permissible boundary of any current fighter such as the Mirage 2000. The orange box under the fuselage houses a laser inertial gyro inertial navigation system.

Below: From this angle the MBB CCV F-104 looks almost like two aircraft in formation. The canard and its support fin destabilize the aircraft in both pitch and yaw, and instability is enhanced by up to 1,323lb (600kg) of ballast in the rear fuselage. MBB's Phase IV flight programme ended in mid-1985. Further work is awaiting the European Fighter Aircraft decision.

MICROLIGHTS

Modern microlight aircraft generally belong to one of two classes, those with flexible wings and those with rigid wings. The latter can be more efficient aerodynamically, but they lack the capability of being rolled and folded for transport and for storage in a small space, and many cannot compete with the rugged strength and rough-weather tolerance of the former. The most popular form of microlight is the flex-wing trike, a combination of a flexible wing, often an actual hang glider, with a three-wheeled frame on which is mounted the seats, engine and propeller. There is no tail unit, the tips of the swept wing and the reflex of the trailing edge providing longitudinal stability. The rigid-winged microlights tend to have tail units, and most use conventional aerodynamic flying controls instead of the simple weight-shift system of in-flight control used by the flex-wings.

The advantages of microlights include extremely low first cost, very low operating cost and insurance, and fuel consumption usually well below that of a family car (on the basis of fuel burn per unit distance travelled). Almost all are to some degree foldable, roadable and easily storable. Their drawbacks include maximum speeds below 100mph (160km/h), maximum range below 200 miles (322km) unless extra fuel tanks are clipped in, and a susceptibility to the effect of strong winds on the flight plan. Some of the latest flex-wing trikes can cope with surprisingly high wind speeds, but gust factors have to be monitored carefully and gusty winds averaging over 25mph (40km/h) should be avoided. Today's microlight aircraft are not inherently dangerous or structurally weak: some are

Above: Typical of tandem two-seaters, the Chargus (Pegasus Transport Systems) Panther tandem tourer, has a first cost, complete, of under £4,000. Modern microlights are modular, and it is possible within a few minutes to change a wing to a differently equipped trike unit.

fully aerobatic, and most are stressed to +6g/−4g. However, as with the low kinetic energy machines, built before 1914, severe weather can cause difficult problems, particularly when landing or taxying, or even after landing.

No major adoption of Microlights has been announced by a military customer, but many types have been evaluated for various purposes including covert surveillance with silenced engines. The following are some military models currently on offer:

Canada: Ultraflight Lazair, in Surveillance Special form; two 9.5hp or 30hp engines, 4h endurance (sold to police departments).

France: Aéronautic 2000 Baroudeur, one engine of 24, 25, 43, 50 or 52hp, 3h endurance; Baroudeur M with four anti-tank rockets evaluated by French para regiments in 1983.

NASA RESEARCH

As the USA's federal research agency concerned with all forms of aerospace technology, NASA conducts a vast range of research projects, some indirectly or directly of benefit to future military aircraft. One of the larger aircraft research programmes is the MAW (mission adaptive wing) described earlier under Boeing/NASA. Future military spacecraft, such as described later, will benefit from a test programme at Dryden Flight Research Center in which an F-104 is testing advanced flexible reusable surface insulation "tiles", which are flown under high dynamic pressures up to 1,100lb/sq ft (5,370kg/m^2).

NASA has carried out a vast amount of research into sensors operating at various wavelengths, some ostensibly for civil purposes but which have obvious military applications. The Boeing 767/AOA is likely to draw upon a tremendous background of NASA work on IR sensing looking both down (in Earth resource surveys, for example, but applicable to ICBM launch detection) and upwards (in IR astronomy but equally applicable to detection and tracking of ICBM re-entry

vehicles). Current IR mapping of landscapes, especially through cloud and smoke, is a major task of the NASA Lockheed ER-2 (TR-1 type aircraft) operated by Ames Research Center. Upward-looking IR research has been done with U-2, Learjet and C-141 StarLifter aircraft, the C-141 having a very large sensor for detection and tracking of "celestial objects" which could

Above: NASA AD-1 slew-wing research aircraft flying from Ames Research Center. Powered by two Microturbo engines, the AD-1 largely confirmed NASA's belief, based on earlier tunnel testing and computer analyses, that a future 1,000mph (1,600km/h) oblique-wing airliner "might achieve twice the fuel economy of more conventional supersonic transport aircraft". Here the wing is in an intermediate setting at about 45°. At sufficiently high speed the wing can be aligned fore and aft.

Left: Firing Luchaire 89mm rockets from an Aeronautic (Zenith-Aviation) Baroudeur on trials at CEV Cazaux in November 1984.

UK: The twin-seat dual-control Pegasus SkyEye is currently under evaluation as a cheap reconnaissance vehicle easily air transportable for out-of-area operations. Its wing has been developed from the high performance Solar Typhoon hang glider, winner of the 1984 European Open, and spans 34ft (10.4m), has an area of 190sq ft (17.6m^2), and an aspect ratio of 6.15. Various engine options are available, typical being a Rotax 447 providing 40hp at 6,500rpm, a climb rate with one occupant of over 1,000ft per minute (305m/min), and a ceiling above 20,000ft (7,000m). Among the other roles for which the Pegasus aircraft are being adapted is the use of a SkyEye variant as a transport for hand-held precision guided munitions (PGM) such as those which would be used against armoured vehicles.

Mainair Mirac (Microlight Recon Aircraft), is based on standard Mainair 2-seat trike units (50hp engine) with provision for infantry kit, communications and light weapons; Kevlar armour optional, and package can be airdropped and quickly rigged for flight.

USA: Austin Hawk, 32hp engine giving 3.3h endurance at 60mph (96km/h), equipped for battlefield missions at minimun height with four underwing weapons attachments for anti-tank rockets, machine guns, grenade launchers, smoke canisters and many other loads.

CGS Hawk, 48hp engine, achieved a 400-aircraft sale to Israel in 1984 but these were mainly for agricultural use by Kibbutz.

Left: Previously used for the research into truly supercritical wings, NASA's fly-by-wire digital F-8 Crusader is shown here as it may later look with an oblique wing. A feasibility study in 1983 showed exciting results with a new composite aero-elastically tailored oblique wing, in many ways related to that of the X-29. In a joint NASA/Navy programme it is planned to make about 40 flights of the oblique-wing F-8 in 1986-87. Phase 2 of the programme will determine potential operational capabilities.

of course include hostile RVs and read straight across to today's US Army AOA programme.

One of the strangest aircraft in the sky, the AD-1 is the only slew-wing aircraft known to be flying at present. Built for NASA by Ames Industrial Corporation, the AD-1 is a slender single-seater powered by two baby turbojets – French Micro-turbo TRS 18-046 of 247lb (112kg) thrust each – and with a one-piece wing pivoted above the fuselage at its mid-point so that it can be set to any desired angle relative to the fuselage. Some companies have proposed the slew, or scissor, wing as a possible configuration for a transonic low-level attack aircraft with stealth characteristics, the attack being made with the wing retracted and relying on body lift only.

NASA is also using a B-57 to investigate violent atmospheric gusts, of the kind believed to have caused structural failures, and an F-106 to penetrate storm cells and gather data on intense rain, turbulence and lightning strikes for future composite-structure aircraft.

RAM-M

Type: Ultra-high-altitude (supposed reconnaissance) aircraft.
Engine(s): No information.
Dimensions: Unofficially said to be slightly larger than TR-1 (which has span 103ft/31.39m and length 63ft/19.2m).
Weights: Not known, but maximum may be greater than TR-1 limit of 40,000lb (18,144kg).
Performance: Operating speed unlikely to be as high as 500mph (805km/h); operating height probably about 90,000ft (27,430m); endurance, probably comparable to 12h of TR-1.

In early 1982 an apparently slightly garbled report of uncertain origin referred to Ram-M as another in the long list of new Soviet aircraft types seen on satellite imagery on Ramenskoye test centre, near Moscow. The description varied slightly in different publications picking up the story, but all

ROCKWELL
HiMAT

Type: Remotely piloted agile research vehicle.
Engine: One 5,000lb (2,268kg) General Electric J85-21 afterburning turbojet.
Dimensions: (As built) Span 15ft 7.25in (4.755m); length (incl probe) 22ft 6in (6.86m); height overall 4ft 3.6in (1.31m).
Weights: Empty 2,645lb (1,200kg); max 3,370lb (1,528kg).
Performance: Max speed 1,060mph (1,710km/h, Mach 1.6); landing speed 207mph (333km/h); average flight duration 30min.

Rockwell built two HiMAT (Highly manoeuvrable aircraft technology) RPRVs (remotely piloted research vehicles) to explore the limits of flight manoeuvre possible with existing structures and propulsion. The two aircraft were made remotely piloted partly to make them smaller but chiefly in order to exceed the g limits at present considered reasonable for human pilots. The sustained positive acceleration to which the HiMAT airframe was designed is 12g. The aircraft was designed in modular form to facilitate subsequent modification in shape, and the introduction of different control surfaces, 2D vectoring nozzles of varying forms and wings of different (supercritical) profile.

The basic HiMAT has a swept wing at the rear with vertical endplate fins and carrying the outward-canted fins on beams projecting aft alongside the engine nozzle. Above the inlet is a large swept flapped canard with dihedral. Various arrange-

Above: Two engineers of Rockwell International's Military Aircraft Division (as then) pictured with the first HiMAT in 1977, before it was painted. The overall black colour shows the high proportion (over 90 per cent) of exterior skin made of graphite fibre composite. The first HiMAT was delivered to NASA on 7 March 1978.

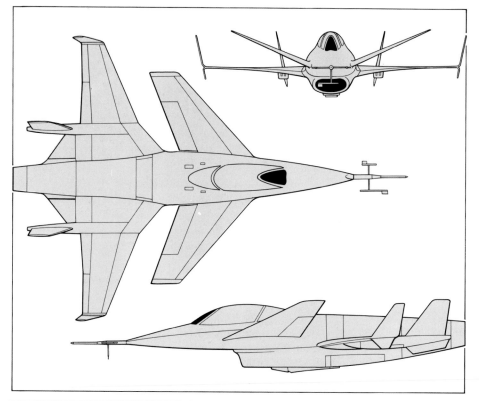

Left: Three-view of the HiMAT research RPVs as originally built. The canard foreplanes are relatively enormous, with area comparable with that of the wings. The artist has drawn the relative-wind vanes as they appear in the photograph above.

Above: Parked at Edwards (Dryden Research Center), waiting for its parent B-52, this HiMAT has the pitch/yaw vanes on its nose probe at arbitrary angles. In the air they align themselves with the relative wind. One canard elevator is down.

were agreed that Ram-M is a high-altitude reconnaissance aircraft in the class of the Lockheed U-2 and TR-1, but with twin fins. Some reports added that the fins were carried on twin tail booms, and a common extra embellishment was that the tailplane bridged the tops of the fins.

The Soviet Union's first high-altitude jet reconnaissance type was Yakovlev's Yak-25RD (NATO "Mandrake") which set altitude records with various loads at heights to 67,113ft (20,456m). One of this RV (Russian initials for record height) family is in the VVS (Soviet air force) museum at Monino. All had an unswept wing of 21.5m (70ft 6.5in) span and most were single-seaters.

In view of its political pre-eminence and apparent lack of other work it would be logical for "Ram-M" also to be a Yakovlev design, but this is speculation.

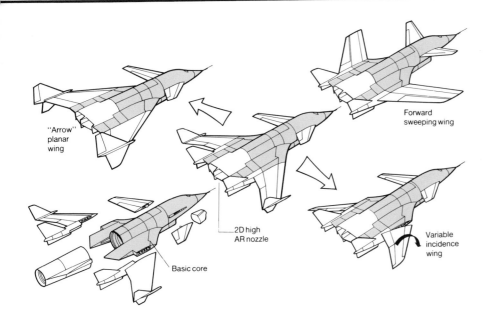

"Arrow" planar wing

Forward sweeping wing

2D high AR nozzle

Basic core

Variable incidence wing

ments of leading and trailing wing flaps, canard power and other movable surfaces were used during the test programme by NASA Dryden Flight Research Center and the USAF. Though independent takeoffs were possible it was usual to carry the HiMAT under a B-52 to 45,000ft (13,716m), for a much longer mission time. The pilot was usually on the ground, though backup control could be exercised by a safety pilot in a supersonic chase aircraft, usually a TF-104G Starfighter.

The flight programme investigated a wide range of control configurations, control system dynamics, composite structures, aeroelastic tailoring (also a feature of the man-rated X-29) and interactions of close-coupled canards, wings, winglets and fins. Roughly double the combat manoeuvrability of the F-15 or F-16 was repeatedly demonstrated, and in general results at least equalled the design goals. It had been intended to go on to test different configurations, but funding was terminated at the close of the 1983 flight programme. Data were still being analysed in 1985, and it is just possible that an additional test programme may be required. In any case, the HiMATs have demonstrated manoeuvrability that no manned fighter is likely to equal until the next century.

Above: The original plan was to use the two basic HiMATs as "core vehicles", to which could be added different types of variable feature at minimum cost. The idea was to test contrasting main wings, canards, tip or tail surfaces and controls, engine inlets, jet nozzles (particularly including 2-D vectoring nozzles) and many radical control features. High AR in the middle sketch means high aspect ratio, the nozzle being a letter-box slit. In addition to the features illustrated NASA hoped to fly wings with powerful variable camber, and deformable outer wings with self-trimming qualities. No reason has yet been given for the lack of progress.

Above: A HiMAT in combined NASA/USAF markings being taken to release height under a NASA NB-52 (whose side proudly lists its numerous "mother ship" missions). The pylon adapter incorporates a tank for JP-5 fuel.

Right: A HiMAT with slightly different features pictured from a manned chase aircraft formating with it over the Mojave desert. Later the remote pilot would lower the skid landing gears and fly the HiMAT all the way down to the strip.

REMOTELY PILOTED VEHICLES

During the past 30 years many hundreds of types of RPV have found military sponsorship, and some dozens of basic families have been deployed in numbers. Some are genuine RPVs in that they are controlled directly by a human pilot on the ground or in another aircraft. Others, known as drones, have pre-programmed guidance. A few have various forms of missile type homing guidance to seek and hit a target, and these are basically slow-flying missiles. Some RPVs are supersonic, many are subsonic jets and the majority are low-cost propeller machines. Some are used as targets, or as vehicles to test the detection and tracking capability of defence systems. A very large number fly reconnaissance, surveillance or target designation missions, in connection with land or sea warfare. A minority, discussed here, carry warheads and are a particular species of small warplane. So far the remotely piloted air-combat fighter has not emerged, though it is a favourite subject for discussion.

PAVE TIGER

Most important attack/harassment RPV in the West is the Pave Tiger programme, a USAF programme whose prime contractor is Boeing Military Airplane Co. Pave Tiger is a simple low-speed machine with a glassfibre airframe which folds into a tight box. Here it can be stored without maintenance for ten years, remaining instantly

Below: Diagram of Boeing Pave Tiger. The entire front half of the 7ft (2.12m) fuselage is occupied by mission sensors and equipment. The engine burns about 1 US gal (0.83gal) per hour. Typical endurance is 8 hours, with sensor payload roughly as shown (less with ECM and warhead).

Below: The Boeing "Pave Tiger" has USAF designation CGM-121A and has now been developed into the Brave-200 for commercial sale (Brave coming from "Boeing robotic air vehicle"). The plastics-composite airframe has canard elevators and roll spoilers.

ready. A standard 8ft×8ft×20ft (2.44× 2.44×6.1m) container houses 15 Pave Tigers, each with electric starter and zero-length launcher.

When a mission is to be flown the Pave Tiger is selected, the door jettisoned, the launcher extended, the wings unfolded, rudders and canard elevators unlocked, gasolene (petrol) fuel added in seconds, electric power connected, the RPV checked

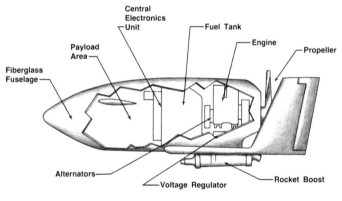

Below: A high-speed class of RPV, the Northrop BQM-74C RECCE is a version of an established RPV target.

Flying at 610mph (982km/h) at up to 40,000ft (12,190m), its TV camera zoom lens is controlled by remote pilot.

Below right: ADS Skyeye. Bigger than Pave Tiger, typical endurance is 8.5h with 77lb (35kg) payload

out, the mission programme fed in, engine started and boost rocket fired. The QRC (quick reaction capability) of only a few seconds is a severe requirement. Melpar E-Systems is a contractor for guidance, which can be pre-programmed, remotely piloted or self-homing on the target. Non-nuclear warheads can be quickly replaced by ECM or sensor packages. Pave Tiger has a 28hp Cuyuna engine, span of 8ft 5in (2.56m), launch weight of up to 280lb (127kg) including boost motor, and endurance 8h at 115mph (185km/h).

INTERNATIONAL RPV PROGRAMMES

Other RPVs used (or intended) for attack missions include:

Brazil: CBT BQM-1, with a large swept wing and rear tail and dorsal 67.5lb (149kg) locally developed turbojet, giving endurance of 45min at 525mph (845km/h).

Germany: Dornier Mini-RPV, a glass-fibre tailless delta with pusher 24hp engine giving 3h endurance at 155mph (250km/h), used for many duties including anti-radar or anti-tank operations with a warhead, using IR homing or passive or active radar homing.

MBB PAD (Panzerabwehrdrone), with cruciform horizontal and vertical wings for turns without banking, with "several hours" endurance at 155mph (250km/h), and like Pave Tiger with 20 PADS instantly ready in one container.

Italy: Several RPVs in the Meteor Mirach system have attack capabilities, including the Mirach 100 (253lb, 115kg, Microturbo turbojet; 528mph, 850km/h) and the

Mirach 600 (twin 750lb, 340kg, turbojets; 690mph, 1,110km/h). The Aeritalia G222 Quiver can carry six Mirach-100s on wing pylons.

South Africa: The National Dynamics Eyrie (52hp pusher) can carry rocket rails under its rhomboidal wings for recoverable attack missions, using remote piloting with a forward-looking TV camera.

Sweden: The small (1.6hp) FOA Skatan

(Magpie) can be used in a "kamikaze" attack role, though normally its task is battle recon/smoke/ECM/designation.

UK: Eyrie AX flying wings can carry a warhead, the 3m (9ft 10in) version having a range of over 1,243 miles (2,000km).

USA: DS offers several R4E SkyEye models equipped for attack, the most important being the R4E-30 (30hp pusher) with provision for launching 2.75-in (70mm) rockets, Viper rockets or smart weapons, endurance of 8h being claimed with 50lb (22.7kg) weapon load.

All the E-Systems Melpar RPVs can fly expendable strike missions, these types being the E-75, E-90, E-175 and E-260. The intermediate 18hp E-175 has a range of 300 miles (482km) with a 40lb (18kg) weapon load.

Fairchild Republic's ATM (Advanced Tactical Mini-drone) has various payloads including a Chaparral warhead; level speed can reach 225mph (362km/h) on 18hp, and range 375 miles (603km).

Teledyne Ryan delivered almost 7,000 of the numerous models of Firebee I, and current BQM-34S versions have wing pylons which can carry 500lb (227kg) bombs, Maverick missiles or bomblet dispensers. Speed is 690mph (1,112km/h) and range up to 796 miles (1,282km). The wealth of control subsystems available includes active seeker terminal guidance, but in most Firebee attack missions the RPV itself is a weapon carrier and is recoverable.

V/STOL RESEARCH

Since the mid-1970s the US Navy, together with NASA, has funded considerable research into V/STOL jet aircraft to fly a wide range of shipboard missions. Known generally as the A-series of studies, they were seen as combining helicopter basing flexibility with aeroplane speed (though not attempting to rival the Sea Harrier on either count). Typical missions suggested included ASW, AEW, Awacs, SAR, amphibious assault close support, amphibious assault transport, casevac, COD and ship resupply, vertrep (vertical replenishment), air-defence AAM launch, reconnaissance and anti-ship attack.

None of the A type designs is still active, but work on similar concepts continues and such aircraft might in the 1990s mature as successors to the V-22 Osprey. Three of the 1980-vintage proposals are illustrated here to show contrasting methods of providing the required powered lift.

GRUMMAN MODEL 698

Grumman's Model 698 was the smallest of the three because of the limited lift available from the suggested twin GE TF34 turbofans, each rated at 9,275lb (4,207kg). Clearly, liftoff weight could not exceed about 18,000lb (8,165kg) for vertical take-off, whereas using the same engines the Lockheed S-3 can take off along a deck or catapult at 52,539lb (23,831kg). The 698 would have been based on the Mitsubishi MU-2M twin-turboprop, with substantial modifications. The original wing turbo-props would be replaced by the twin TF34 turbofans, mounted on the fuselage so that for VTOL they could pivot upwards. Grumman patented a method of providing control at low airspeeds by vanes in the jet nozzles plus guide vanes in the inlets. In forward flight the digital FBW (fly by wire) control system would drive spoilers on the gull-shaped wing and movable surfaces on the T-tail.

Grumman estimated a speed of 575mph (925km/h) for the 698, as well as a time of only 2.5min to climb to 30,000ft (9,144m). In the transport role a payload of 3,000lb (1,361kg) could be delivered to an airstrip 1,400 miles (2,253km) distant, while in the attack mode a weapon load of 2,000lb (907kg) could be delivered against a target at a radius of 600 miles (966km) with return on internal fuel. Grumman became particularly interested in AEW capabilities, using conformal radar with the aerials (antennas) forming major parts of the airframe, without modifying the external shape. On one mission it would be possible to cover 900,000sq miles (2.83 million km²) and feed data on 2,000 targets to a parent ship, the 300 highest-priority targets being displayed in the aircraft.

LTV V-530

LTV (Vought) have a 30-year history of jet-lift studies, the arrangement selected for the V-530 being the tandem fan (see description later). The engines were to be turboshafts in the 5,000shp class, mounted

Above: Prolonged testing of the Grumman 698 took place at the NASA Ames Research Center in California. The programme was sponsored by NASA, the US Navy and Grumman Aerospace. This full-scale model took part in "live" tests, here on hot-gas reingestion.

Right: This three-view of the Vought (LTV) V-530 shows the integration of efficient lift/cruise engines into a high-lift airframe that has been a keynote of the company's research for 25 years. Many companies believe the tandem-fan scheme to be most promising.

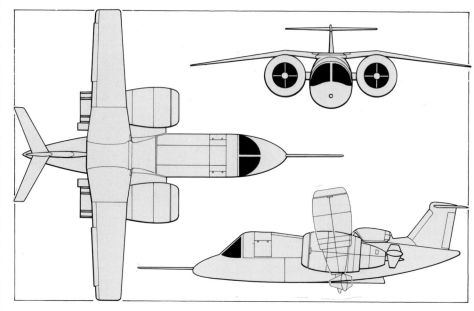

Above: Three-view of the proposed Grumman Model 698, in which turbofan engines were to be pivoted on each side of the fuselage. Span was to be 36ft 6in (11.13m), span (wings folded) 16ft (4.88m) and length 40ft 8in (12.4m). An advantage over the V-22 was higher cruising speed.

Below: A Grumman 698 shown operating in the rescue role, carrying out a "snatch" of a downed aviator whilst flying at about 30 knots. Such operations require computer control with a sensor-reflective target. In any case it looks as if the V-22 Osprey has been chosen.

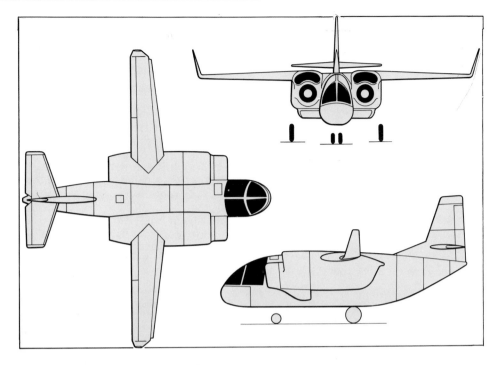

Left: Another Navy jet-lift proposal, Lockheed's V/STOL based on the cross-duct propulsion system. It attempts to achieve V/STOL with a degree of engine-out safety.

Below: Another previously unpublished three-view, in this case of the Lockheed aircraft shown left. Heat-insulated pipes would transfer gas from one side of the aircraft to the other, outer wings being conventional.

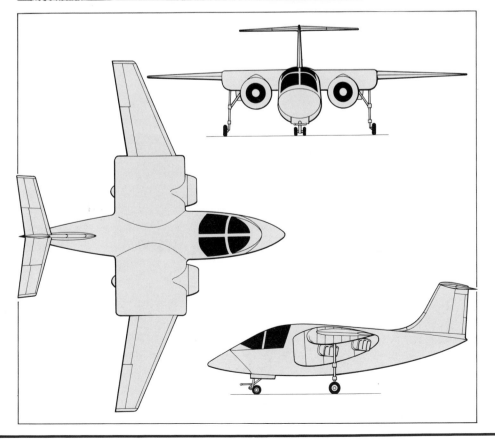

close on each side of the 50ft (15.24m) fuselage. The engines would be connected by a cross-shaft to enable either to fly the aircraft in the event of failure of the other. Each would drive a forward extension shaft on which would be mounted the tandem fans, far enough apart for each fan to have its own independent inlet duct system (one at the front of the engine nacelle and the other a rectangular inlet above the nacelle ahead of the leading edge of the wing). Fan diameter was to be 51in (1.3m). The tandem-fan scheme uses large valves to divert the front-fan delivery vertically downwards for VTOL, the rear (core) jet having its own vectored nozzle. Several engine and aircraft companies have a high opinion of the tandem fan, and believe it may yet become the favoured system once the notion of jet lift becomes more generally accepted.

The V-530 would have had a fixed wing of 58ft 10in (17.93m) span, and takeoff weight could have been up to 45,000lb (20,411kg), depending on mission requirements. Cruising speed would have been about 400mph (644km/h), and range with maximum payload of over 8,000lb (3,630kg) would have been about 1,000 miles (1,610km). The model shows the planned standard V-530 with a large 21ft (6.4m) cabin for troops or cargo, but in the pure attack role a slim body would have been preferred, with external weapon carriage.

LOCKHEED V/STOL

Newest of the US Navy projects illustrated here is the May 1984 Lockheed-California artwork showing a jet V/STOL with a cross-duct propulsion system. Dornier of West Germany was the first to fly a jet VTOL cargo type machine, with a Pegasus (Harrier-type) vectored turbofan under each wing, plus pods of lift jets. There was no connection between the Do 31E engines, and failure of either would have resulted in uncontrollable roll. Lockheed seek to overcome this by following the philosophy of the twin-Spey P.1154RN and ducting half the thrust of each engine to the opposite side of the aircraft. The artist has shown the four lift jets evenly disposed around the aircraft centre of gravity. There are various ways of arranging the cross ducting, but sudden failure of one engine would normally take out the jets from two diagonally opposite corners. The result would be a loss of height but no tendency to pitch or roll.

This particular Lockheed proposal is intended for conventional flight from carriers at overload weights (the artwork shows a cat towbar on the nose gear). The integration of engine power and lift with circulation around the thick inboard wing sections is claimed to be much more efficient than plain wing-hung vectored engines alone, and Lockheed hope that this scheme will prove to be the best next-generation V/STOL to follow the V-22 Osprey in many shipboard missions, possibly from about 1995.

SPACE WARFARE AIRCRAFT

At the most basic human level, preparations for warfare in space evoke strongly contrasting emotions. Some protesters take the view that Man, having done his best to pollute and destroy his own planet, ought not to broaden the region in which his weapons can operate. Others adopt a contrary stance, and consider that the best place for any future conflict, nuclear at least, is in outer space, rather than on Earth itself.

Renewed impetus to the debate has stemmed from President Reagan's March 1983 SDI (Strategic Defense Initiative), popularly called "Star Wars", which called for research into several new military capabilities in space, notably the ability of US satellites and spacecraft to destroy enemy long-range ballistic missiles, and to shoot back at an attacking ASAT (anti-satellite) weapon. In both the USA and Soviet Union research and development of military space systems, including weapons, has been on a large scale for 25 years. The effort has involved the development of many kinds of satellite, for reconnaissance, geodesy/mapping, communications, sur-

face navigation and meteorology, and for a very broad range of specific capabilities which have increasingly been directed towards survivability in nuclear environments. This book deals with "warplanes" in the broadest sense, and this excludes most military space activity, fascinating as it is (the subject is covered in other Salamander books, including *The Intelligence War, Advanced Technology Warfare,* and *Space Technology).*

However, the vehicles variously called aerospace planes, shuttle orbiters, Hotol launchers, TAVs (transatmospheric vehicles) and STSs (space transportation systems) certainly do come within the purview of this book. Where these differ from previous space launchers is that they are reusable. It happens that the Wright Brothers' *Flyer* of 1903 was designed to

make repeated flights, and we have taken reusability for granted in subsequent aircraft. But space launchers were initially developed from ballistic missiles, which are not required to be reusable. Any objective study would regard as obvious that any transport system designed to place payloads in outer space is bound to be large and costly, and therefore ought to be designed to be used more than once.

Elsewhere in this book the point is made that future warplanes will be forced eventually to manage without airfields or any other immovable form of airbase. This means that they will have to become airborne without any significant horizontal accelerating run. In the case of space operations the changing scenario is pulling vehicle design in opposite directions. Past space launchers have all been VTOLs, but

Below: Just one of dozens of ideas for US military aerospace planes, this artwork shows a USAF Shuttle-type orbiter thundering into the air on a reusable heavy-lift aeroplane. The latter uses USB and air-cushion technologies. Ironically British schemes of 25 years earlier (English Electric/Shorts PD.17) used VTOL platforms to lift aircraft out of forests.

Right: This Mach 12 recon aircraft, which could have external-combustion propulsion, was suggested to the US Congress in December 1983 by McDonnell Douglas. Able to operate from "today's airfields", such a machine could orbit at a height of 1,250 miles (2,000km), and in addition would probably be very stealthy. Europeans might ask "Why not collaborate?"

of a peculiarly costly and inefficient type. On the one hand they are used once only. On the other they need large fixed launch sites, so from the point of view of basing they are just as vulnerable as conventional runway-dependent aircraft. The new breed of Hotol (horizontal takeoff and landing) launchers merely exchange massive launch pads for runways, and so from the aspect of vulnerability in war are at least no worse off than their predecessors.

The first military aerospace plane was designed for traditional launch by an upright rocket, even though it was to land like an aeroplane. The lifting-body research vehicles were not in any sense intended for operational use, and were carried aloft by B-52s. Today's Shuttle Orbiter lifts off in the traditional vertical manner, boosted by two gigantic SRBs (solid rocket boosters) and riding on an even bigger cylindrical tank of liquid oxygen and liquid hydrogen. The huge tank and the SRBs are all jettisoned when spent, but the SRBs are recovered for reuse. The only part of the Shuttle system thrown away on each mission is thus the tank and, while it is the

biggest single item in the system, it is also by a wide margin the cheapest.

Thus the Shuttle, which is designed to airline standards of maintenance and repeatable operation, breaks totally new ground in reusability and thus in cost per launch, or per unit mass delivered to orbit or other space destination. Where it falls short as a military transport system is in the long time needed to prepare for each launch, and the susceptibility of each launch to delay caused by hurricanes or other severe weather. To be of military value a system invariably has to be ready and available, whenever the force commander wants to use it. It is largely for this reason that the USAF is looking at TAVs that promise the same kind of availability as any other CTOL (conventional takeoff and landing) system. Vulnerability at its

base is one of those hard questions that is not being ignored. At present several contrasting takeoff systems are being studied.

Meanwhile, Britain has plenty of ideas but not the slightest intention of making anything, while France is going flat out for a Shuttle which duplicates the existing US Shuttle techniques, but with the main applications commercial rather than military. The Soviet Union has traditionally followed the philosophy of ''make it bigger'' in space as in all forms of strategic rockets and missiles. There has never been an evident lack of payload capability, and in spring 1985 there were reported to be a new outsize conventional space rocket (quite different from the G-1-e of 1969), a small aerospace plane and a large Shuttle system all well advanced in flight development.

Below: Fishing a ''Soviet aerospace plane'' test vehicle from the Indian Ocean in March 1983. One imagines that the Royal Australian Air Force P-3C crew who took the photograph knew what was happening and where splashdown would be – oceans are rather large for chance meetings! Vehicle colours were black and white. No official Soviet reports were released.

Right: Computer graphics picture of Hermès in orbit, with payload doors open. Now that France has decided to copy the US Shuttle there seems no chance of bringing that country into a more sensible programme for a later-technology vehicle such as the BAe Dynamics Hotol. Indeed, nationalism today far overrides such matters as technical assessment.

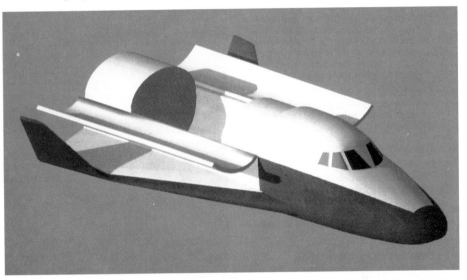

HOTOL

Type: Conventional-takeoff aerospace plane.

Engines: Variable-geometry ducted rockets fed with liquid hydrogen fuel and either liquid oxygen or (at low altitudes) atmospheric air. Takeoff thrust 246,900lb (112,000kg).

Dimensions: Span 65ft 6in (20m); length 249ft (76m); fuselage diameter 18.7ft (5.7m).

Weights: At takeoff (excluding trolley) 441,000lb (200t); at landing 92,590lb (42,000kg); payload up to 15,430lb (7,000kg).

Performance: Takeoff speed 334mph (537km/h); orbital velocity 17,670mph (28,435km/h); landing speed 196mph (315km/h).

BAe has long recognised that Europe is doomed in space in the long term if it relies upon expendable launchers such as Ariane 5, and also that it is impossible to beat US Shuttle developments by copying the first-generation Shuttle on a smaller scale. For success there has to be a dramatic new development, and HOTOL (horizontal takeoff and landing) is unquestionably this.

It is a one-stage-to-orbit aerospace plane, which on paper cuts the cost of putting payloads in low orbit by a factor of five, and to geosynchronous orbit by half (even allowing for use of current upper stages).

Most of the Shuttle-diameter fuselage is the liquid hydrogen tank, on the nose of which are canard controls for atmospheric

flight. Behind this is the payload bay, which could resemble a 66-seat section of BAe 146 or A320 fuselage. Next comes the Lox tank, with the engines at the rear. The fuselage rides on Concorde-like wings, with the engine air inlet underneath. Most upper skin is titanium, but the underside is refractory metal.

Takeoff is from a trolley to avoid the need for a massive undercarriage. Takeoff run is typically 7,500ft (2,290m), well matched to today's airports. Vertical acceleration never exceeds 1.4g in entering the 24° climb. Mach 1 is passed in 2min, commercial airspace is cleared at 40,000ft (12,200m) in 4.5min, Mach 5 at 85,300ft (26,000m) is reached in 9min and orbital velocity at 295,000ft (90,000m). Main

HERMÈS

Type: Manned reusable space transport vehicle.

Engine: Hermès vehicle will have its own high-energy liquid rocket engine(s) controllable from the cockpit; for launcher see below.

Dimensions: Not finalised, but smaller than NASA Shuttle Orbiter.

Weights: At liftoff, probably in the region of 132,000lb (60,000kg).

Performance: Orbital, ie 17,500mph (28,200km/h) plus.

In early 1983 the ESA (European Space Agency) initiated a study for a European shuttle-type reusable launch vehicle. Most

of the funding (£7 million total) was provided by France and West Germany. Just two years later, in February 1985, France's CNES (national space agency) pre-empted this study by announcing the Hermès manned shuttle programme. It stated that it was putting Aérospatiale and Dassault-Breguet in head-to-head competition for the prime contract. Full presentations were called for in April, so that a decision on the prime contract could be taken in the summer (it was expected to be announced at the Paris airshow in June). France planned to take a 50 per cent share in the programme, including the prime vehicle contract, assembly and test. Other Euro-

pean nations were to be invited to contribute the other half, with participants to be chosen by the end of 1985.

The main purpose of Hermès, like the ESA study which preceded it, is to avoid Europe and other countries being totally dependent on the NASA Shuttle for placing large payloads into low Earth orbits (the European Ariane non-reusable launch vehicle already has an outstanding track record with somewhat lighter payloads). The uprated Ariane 5, with new engines including the high-energy HM60 of 202,320lb (91,772kg) thrust in upper stages, is planned to be the launch vehicle. Thus the only reusable part of the Euro-

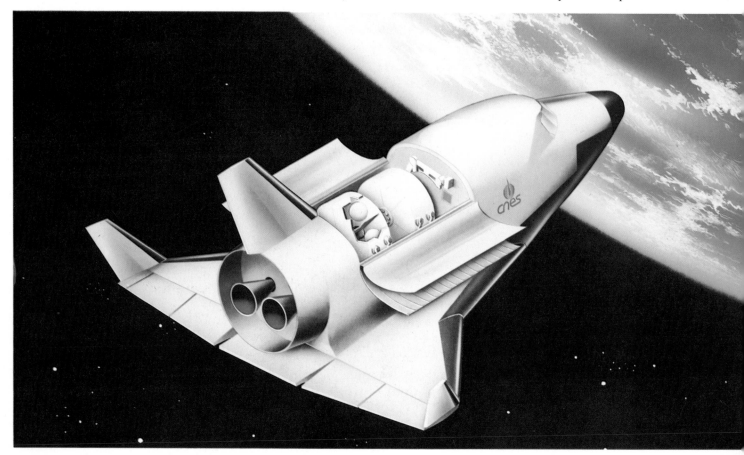

propulsion is shut down, the OMS (orbital manoeuvring system) being used for flight control.

On an airline flight a ballistic trajectory soon takes HOTOL to its destination. Sydney, Australia, takes 45min, but allowing for full air-traffic procedures 67min might be total elapsed time. On space missions a 50h sortie might be typical, coasting up to a height of 185 miles (300km). Re-entry at some 80° AOA is slower than for the Shuttle, and the landing procedure simple. Wet-runway groundroll is 6,000ft (1,800m).

Right: HOTOL lifts off at AOA of 4°, with lift coefficient of 0.75. L/D ratio would be 6.5 in subsonic flight and 4.5 supersonic. These values are over twice that of the American Space Shuttle.

---

pean space transport system as at present conceived will be the winged vehicle itself, which is unlikely to cost more than an Ariane 5.

For a programme as challenging as this it would be strange if CNES were really to pick one of the two French competing companies and reject the other; a joint development would have seemed a better answer. More serious for Europe, thanks to France's dynamic outlook and willingness to take decisions, the European shuttle programme will hardly be a "European" programme but a French programme in which certain other countries are permitted to participate.

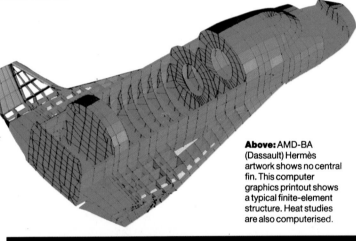

Above: AMD-BA (Dassault) Hermès artwork shows no central fin. This computer graphics printout shows a typical finite-element structure. Heat studies are also computerised.

Below: Aérospatiale's proposed Hermès cockpit. All such illustrations show two pilots side-by-side, with a hand controller on each seat-arm, and four more seats in a row behind. Aérospatiale's Aircraft Division is making a major contribution with input from the flight deck of the A320. Many main electronic displays, and even the sidestick controllers, are very similar to those of the new transport. The basic concept, however, is identical to the US Shuttle.

Left: Artist's impression of a Hermès in low orbit. CNES is the French national space organization, which so far is the only apparent customer. Aérospatiale and AMD-BA have issued contrasting artwork: so far there is no joint design.

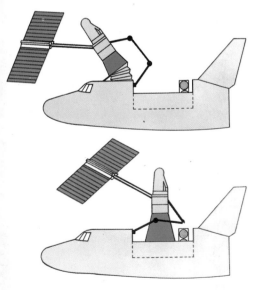

Above: In the Hermès proposal the payload bay, manipulator arm and overall procedures would be exactly as in today's Shuttle Orbiter. In the upper sketch a flexible airlock tube provides a crew passage between the Orbiter and a payload. In the lower view the satellite is in the payload bay, requiring remote manipulation or spacesuit access by extra-vehicular activity.

SPACE CRUISER

Type: Manned space vehicle to research military capabilities.
Engines: Numerous (eg, 16) high-energy liquid propellant rocket engines, plus very small attitude-control thrusters.
Dimensions: Length (1985 concept) 26ft 6in (8.08m); base diameter about 5ft (1.5m).
Weights: Loaded about 10,000lb (3,050kg).
Performance: Required to orbit, ie 17,500mph (28,200km/h) plus.

The manned Space Cruiser was not funded as this was written in mid-1985, but the budget required is so modest that it may soon get the go-ahead. The original survey phase was costed at $60,000 and DARPA (Defense Advanced Research Projects Agency) assigned this phase to DCS Corporation, of Alexandria, Virginia, with a request that the contractor should study 170-200 military, industrial, scientific and other potential uses.

The Space Cruiser is seen by DARPA as a natural successor to the X-series of aircraft which carried out research in the atmosphere. It would be extremely simple, the current configuration being a hypersonic-profile cone for minimum drag on launch and climb through the atmosphere. Launch could be on top of a rocket boost vehicle (of which many types are currently available), or carried to high altitude under a B-52 or above a 747, which would reduce mission cost still further.

Obviously such a vehicle must have propulsion systems with multiple restart capability, for "flight" in space in any desired direction and with any necessary trajectory change. Owing to the high speeds involved major changes in trajectory would demand large energy input and quickly exhaust the limited supply of propellant. Nothing has been said about on-board power, and this would depend on mission endurance (which looks like being hours rather than

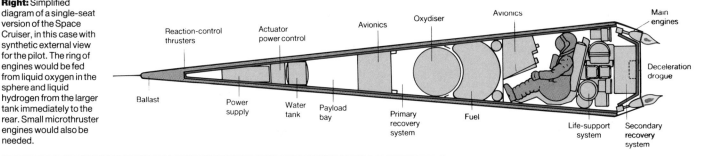

Right: Simplified diagram of a single-seat version of the Space Cruiser, in this case with synthetic external view for the pilot. The ring of engines would be fed from liquid oxygen in the sphere and liquid hydrogen from the larger tank immediately to the rear. Small microthruster engines would also be needed.

Labels: Reaction-control thrusters · Actuator power control · Avionics · Oxydiser · Avionics · Main engines · Ballast · Power supply · Water tank · Payload bay · Primary recovery system · Fuel · Life-support system · Secondary recovery system · Deceleration drogue

SPACE TRANSPORTATION SYSTEM

Type: Reusable manned, winged aerospace launch vehicle.
Engines: Launched vertically by two SRBs (solid rocket boosters) as described below; Orbiter has three SSMEs (space shuttle main engines) as described below.
Dimensions: Span 78ft 0.68in (23.79m); length 122ft 0.2in (37.19m); length of assembled system at launch 184ft 2.4in (56.14m); wing area 2,690sq ft (249.91m^2).
Weights: Empty production Orbiter about 149,700lb (67,900kg); liftoff (loaded Orbiter) usually about 238,000lb (108 tonnes); launch weight of whole system (typical) 4,503,033lb (2,042,576kg); typical landing weight 212,000lb (96,162kg).
Performance: Orbital, ie speed over 17,500mph (28,200km/h); nominal landing speed 208mph (334km/h).

The STS (Space Transportation System), managed by NASA (US National Aeronautics and Space Administration) is the world's first reusable space launch system. Studies dating from 1967-68 led to a major meeting in 1969 at which 30 technical papers were presented on Shuttle design. The configuration picked at first looked like a stumpy flying boat with straight (ie, conventional unswept) low-mounted wings. By 1970 a broad tailless delta shape had been substituted, but budgetary restrictions forced the Orbiter to be reduced in size. The colossal tanks for liquid oxygen and liquid hydrogen propellants were removed, the liquids being accommodated instead in a giant ET (external tank). The delta-winged booster was replaced by two plain SRBs, one attached on each side of the ET. Air-breathing turbojet engines were eliminated, forcing the Orbiter to fly through the atmosphere and down to the runway without propulsion, making it the world's heaviest-ever glider. This increased payload, and more weight was saved by eliminating the crew launch escape system.

President Nixon approved the STS in January 1972. The possibility of raising the number of missions that could be flown by large space launchers from 1 to something approaching 100 was obviously going to have a very large effect on cost per unit mass placed in orbit. So far the pricing has been to fix levels as high as the market will bear, but already these levels are much less than half those for one-shot launchers, and so far as is known the USAF pays prices similar to those charged to the many commercial customers.

Major contracts were let in 1972-73: prime contractor for the Orbiter is Rockwell International, for the SRBs Morton Thiokol and for the ET Martin Marietta. Each SRB is 149ft 2in (45.46m) long, weighs 1,292,000lb (586,051kg) in steel-cased form (slightly less for the filament-wound pattern introduced in late 1985) and blasts off with 3.3 million lb (1,497,000kg) thrust. Each SRB nozzle is vectorable to provide trajectory control during the early part of the mission, the enormous multi-ton nozzle swivelling in flexible bearings under the force of two hydraulic actuators, all tied into the main FBW control system via the autopilot. The SRBs burn out after about 2min, whereupon they are jettisoned (thrust away by four 22,000lb/10,000kg separation motors at the front and four more at the back), deploy a stabilizing drogue parachute and then a large triple-canopy main chute.

Above: USAF Shuttle flights will all start (and, on present planning, finish) at Vandenberg AFB on the Pacific coast. Orbiter *Enterprise* is seen here in early 1985 while it was being used to check out the Vandenberg space site systems under construction.

Right: In chronological order the first five Orbiters are: OV-101 *Enterprise*, OV-102 *Columbia*, OV-099 *Challenger*, OV-103 *Discovery* and OV-104 *Atlantis*. Here *Challenger* lifts off for 41-B mission (1st "human satellite") on 3 February 1984.

weeks). The crew would comprise a pilot and possibly a second person. Both would wear a space suit, eliminating the need for an on-board life-support system. An "open cockpit" has been studied, but a transparent dome may be added to enhance micrometeorite protection.

DARPA estimate that an early go-ahead would enable a Space Cruiser to be in orbit in calendar year 1988. Provision for payloads would be made in the hinged nose and in the centre of the engine ring at the rear. Initially the payload would be for research, but DARPA – eager to see this seemingly cost/effective project launched – comment that the Space Cruiser could become "an operational mission-oriented vehicle".

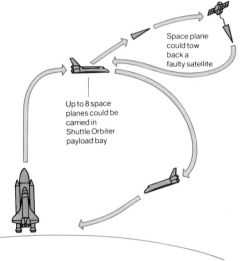

Below: As at present conceived the Cruiser would not have lift/drag ratio adequate for "flight", and airfield landings would be impossible. In this type of mission the vehicle self-launches from above a carrier aircraft and climbs to orbit; after its mission it re-enters by itself and is finally recovered to ground by a parachute system. The USA has no experience of recovering manned craft on land, and oceanic recovery would probably result in hardware deterioration.

Space plane would go anywhere a satellite could go

Space plane slows as it re-enters atmosphere, and deploys a parachute

Space plane could be flown back to base from 60,000ft (20,000m)

Right: In this alternative scheme the Cruiser is taken near to orbital parameters by a Shuttle Orbiter. After completing its mission the Cruiser would (probably under automatic control) rendezvous with the Orbiter and be secured by the latter's manipulator arm, which would return it to the cargo bay for the flight back to Earth. Elimination of the re-entry protection and parachute system might be foolhardy, however, because for various reasons the Shuttle Orbiter might not make the recovery.

Space plane could tow back a faulty satellite

Up to 8 space planes could be carried in Shuttle Orbiter payload bay

Recovered from the ocean, the SRBs are refurbished and are expected to be good for 20 launches. The ET carries 1,361,936lb (617,774kg) of liquid oxygen and 227,641lb (103,257kg) of liquid hydrogen; because of its lower density the hydrogen fuel tank is much larger than the Lox tank. The complete filled tank, thickly insulated to minimise boiloff of the intensely cold liquids, weighs 1,655,600lb (750,980kg). This tank supplies the SSMEs, and is jettisoned about 8min from liftoff, at a height of 68 miles (109km), just before orbit insertion. The ET is not recovered.

The three SSMEs, prime contractor for which is Rockwell's Rocketdyne Division, are identical high-pressure oxygen/hydrogen engines fully controllable over the range 65-109 per cent of rated power, if necessary direct from the cockpit. The SSMEs are currently cleared for 55 flights, using airline maintenance and overhaul procedures, and in 1985 were in the process of being recertificated to 120 per cent rated power to allow for future growth in Shuttle capability. Thrust rises from 417,300lb (189,287kg) per engine at liftoff (sea level) to a rated 512,000lb (232,243kg) each in vacuum conditions.

A particular feature of these SSMEs is their high operating pressure; for example the 77,310hp liquid hydrogen pump delivers at 7,040lb/sq in, and the combustion pressure in the chamber is 3,260lb/sq in. Qualifying the SSMEs was one of the biggest tasks in the development of the STS, because for the first time giant rocket engines, one of the most intense and con-centrated sources of power known to Man, have been certificated just like an airline engine for direct control from the cockpit on numerous repeated flights. So far there is every indication the 55-mission design life will be met if not exceeded.

The Orbiter is outwardly a simple tailless delta, notable for its extremely bluff shape, rounded leading edge (swept over the inboard section at 81°) and flat underside. The airframes are built mainly by Grumman (wings) and GD Convair (fuselage), and are basically conventional aluminium structures. Each wing carries two elevons, while the Fairchild Republic vertical tail carries two-section rudders which split open to act as speedbrakes. The gap between the wing and elevons is faired by heat-resistant hinged panels of titanium

Left: The ability of men to operate untethered in space is an important part of Shuttle Orbiter missions. It was first demonstrated by

Astronauts Robert L. Stewart (seen here) and Bruce McCandless on the 41-B mission, testing two MMUs (Manned Manoeuvring Units).

Below: OV-099 *Challenger* photographed in orbit on 18 June 1983 from Shuttle Pallet Satellite SPAS-1, which it had

itself placed in orbit. Still in the cargo bay can be seen two larger shrouded payloads, Telsat Canada Anik C-2 and Indonesian *Palapa B1*.

Above: Astronaut Stewart forming a satellite by himself at distances up to 320ft (97.5m) with no umbilical. The nitrogen-powered

MMUs performed well on this first free-flying mission, on which the Astronauts spent more than 12 hours outside the Orbiter.

and Inconel (high-nickel alloy) sandwich.

Every other part of the airframe, except the special flight-deck windows, is covered in a special thermal protective coating, made up of various kinds of tiles designed to match the stresses and temperatures encountered by each region. The leading edges and nose are RCC (reinforced carbon/carbon), a composite made up of strong carbon fibres in a carbon matrix, and this is designed for re-entry temperatures of 1,430°C.

The crew compartment, which provides a "shirtsleeve" environment, has three levels. At the highest level is the cockpit with dual controls. Behind are seats for one or two mission specialists. On the middle level are three more seats, bunks, hygiene station, galley, electronics bays and various other items including the airlock leading to the payload bay. For rescue missions the bunks can be replaced by three more seats. The lowest level houses the ECS (environmental control system) and crew equipment stowage.

The Shuttle Orbiter is intended for delivering payloads of up to 65,000lb (29,484kg) to orbital height of 115 miles (185km) due East, 32,000lb (14,515kg) into 115-mile polar orbit or 25,000lb (11,340kg) to a 311-mile (500km) orbit at 55° inclination. Payloads, of which there can be several on each mission, are carried in a large central bay, 60ft (18.29m) long and about 15ft (4.57m) diameter. The bay is covered by two 60ft (18.29m) structural doors, made of graphite/epoxy honeycomb sandwich, each door carrying on its inner side space radiator panels, the forward (30ft/9.14m) half of each radiator being hinged and deployed in space. A retractable manipulator arm is mounted at the front on the left, and a second arm can be mounted on the right if needed for that mission. The arm carries a TV camera, and several other cameras are carried including a colour one in the crew compartment looking aft from the payload controls.

NASA SPACE TRANSPORTATION SYSTEM

In space the Orbiter is controlled by a comprehensive array of smaller rocket engines. At the rear are the two Aerojet OMS (Orbital Manoeuvring Subsystem) engines, each burning nitrogen tetroxide and monomethyl-hydrazine and rated in space at 6,000lb (2,722kg) each. These can move the Orbiter to a higher orbit. The RCS (Reaction Control Subsystem) has 38 motors each rated at 870lb (395kg) and six small vernier thrusters each rated at 24lb (10.9kg), all made by Marquardt and burning the same propellants as the OMS engines. Primary electric power generation is effected by three fuel cell systems each of which combines liquid hydrogen and liquid oxygen to generate up to 12kW of DC power. Honeywell provide the 4-channel redundant FBW flight-control and engine-control subsystem.

Development and initial use of the STS has been entirely a NASA affair, the launches being made in an easterly direction from KSC (Kennedy Space Centre) at Cape Canaveral, and landing being initially at Edwards AFB and subsequently back at Kennedy. Almost all the hundreds of payloads already launched, or booked, from Kennedy are civilian ones, either for NASA or for commercial or scientific customers. A very small proportion are military, mainly for the USAF and in no case of a sensitive nature. The USAF has built its own Shuttle launch complex on the Western Test Range at Vandenberg AFB, California, which is specially equipped for launching payloads into the polar or high-inclination orbits needed for global sur-

Above: Spaceflight gives a brilliant yet detached view of our planet. This photograph taken by ESA Spacelab 1 Metric Camera shows one of Earth's saddest regions, Somalia's war-torn and hungry Horn of Africa. Time 04.45GMT on 3 December 1983 (STS-9).

Below: With its tiling showing obvious signs of its searing re-entry, OV-102 *Columbia* is seen landing at Edwards in April 1981 after its first 36-orbit flight STS-1. Today NASA flights land back at KSC and Air Force missions will land back at Vandenberg AFB, at 208mph (334km/h).

veillance missions. (In general, a rough approximation is that a satellite launched at an inclination of, say, 76°, will cover the globe between 76°N and 76°S parallels of latitude; most USAF recon firings have been at an inclination of about 96° to give total coverage.)

Vandenberg's most southerly launch complex, originally designed for the cancelled Titan IIIM/MOL (Manned Orbiting Laboratory) is SLC-6, almost 20 miles (32km) from the most northerly Minuteman III training silo. Here the complex was resurrected and completely rebuilt for the USAF Shuttle launches. SLC-6 LE-1 became fully operational in 1985, and work is proceeding on SLC-6 LE-2 less than a mile (about 1km) away to provide a second Shuttle facility. Firings from Vandenberg are likely to be almost due south. Most military missions require great orbital heights, and to take care of this NASA developed various upper stages such as the IUS (Inertial Upper Stage), developed by Boeing with CSD propulsion by large and small solid motors, and the SSUS (Spinning Solid Upper Stage), developed by McDonnell Douglas with Morton Thiokol propulsion, and another McDonnell Douglas booster, the PAM (Payload Assist Module). These can take payloads up from the orbiting Shuttle vehicle to geostationary height of about 22,300 miles (35,890km) or beyond.

At the conclusion of each mission USAF Orbiters will recover to land on the existing Vandenberg AFB runway. An Orbiter Facility has been built close beside this runway, which is in North Vandenberg AFB, north of the Santa Ynez river. The refurbished Orbiter will then be towed by road out of North Vandenberg, across the public "corridor" serving the beach, enter South Vandenberg and on for a distance of about 12 miles (20km) before regaining SLC-6. Here it will be rotated to the vertical attitude and mated with a new ET, with perhaps the original pair of SRBs attached on each side.

Not surprisingly, the USAF is retiring all its one-shot launch vehicles. In a major speech in January 1985 President Reagan called for increased use by the USAF of the STS, and announced evaluation of Block 2 Shuttle vehicles with expanded capabilities (perhaps including extended duration in orbit). He also announced a return to one-shot launchers, including the Titan 34D-7 and a very large new super-booster for the SDI programme. These will be important by the 1990s, but are far removed from the content of this book.

Above: Future Shuttle Orbiters will partner various expendable ballistic vehicles, such as Titan 34D, in placing US Air Force satellites in orbit. Here an artist in 1982 depicts two Agena-based USAF satellites being exchanged. Thirty per cent of Shuttle activities are military.

Below: A 1984 illustration from NASA (KSC) showing an Orbiter servicing the triangular (Delta) space station, one of several candidate designs for the 1990s. With Orbiters the cost and difficulty of building such stations is reduced by at least an order of magnitude.

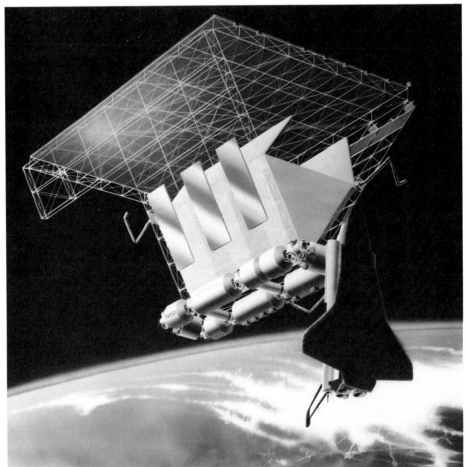

SOVIET AEROSPACE PLANE

Type: Fully mission-oriented manned, winged aerospace vehicle.
Engine(s): No information, but launched by ballistic rocket (see below) and provided with comprehensive thrusters for control of trajectory and attitude.
Dimensions: (US estimate) Span 39ft (12m); length 50ft (15.2m).
Weights: (US estimate) at least 33,000lb (15,000kg).
Performance: Orbital, ie 17,500mph (28,200km/h); plus mission endurance unlikely to exceed one or two days.

Called the Reusable Spaceplane, or Aerospace Plane, by Western analysts, this reusable vehicle is quite different from the big shuttle-like transporter, and is certainly not intended for mere transport of materials to space. Bearing a degree of affinity with the much earlier US X-20 Dyna-Soar and lifting-body vehicles, and almost identical to the original (1968) US Shuttle Orbiter in configuration, it appears to be a programme being carried through by the Soviet Union to provide what might suddenly become an urgently needed capability. Probably, like the USAF TAV, it is at present without any obvious missions, though if its launch system were to be changed it could become the basis of the first "combat spacecraft" or "space fighter".

The test craft seen so far are intended to prove the configuration and control system. These manned single-seat vehicles (at least the first two of which were probably flown without a human pilot) are estimated to be about one-third of full size. Gaudily striped to show up against an ocean background, they have been fired four times, with details as given in an accompanying table.

The launch vehicle being used for these sub-scale tests is a refurbished missile, of the type known to NATO as SS-5 Skean. The first two shots each took the test vehicle about 1.2 times round the Earth to re-enter and splashdown in the Indian Ocean, south of the Cocos Islands. On the second flight the entire recovery was photographed with great clarity by the crew of a Royal Australian Air Force P-3C Orion. The aircraft's presence must have been fortuitous, because no advance knowledge of the mission can have been gained, and the 90-odd minutes of the test could not have sufficed to vector the Orion to the exact point of recovery.

The photographs showed a lifting-body vehicle with very large diagonal surfaces serving as both wings and fins, with aerodynamic controls. An additional smaller fin was mounted above the centreline. Areas subject to severe heating on re-entry, such as the bulged forward sections of the wing/body blended region, were seen to be covered with thermal tiles each about 6in (152mm) square. Recovery was obviously by parachute, and after splashdown the vehicle floated high in the water. It is not known whether the four shots have all been made by the same test vehicle.

The full-scale space plane has repeatedly

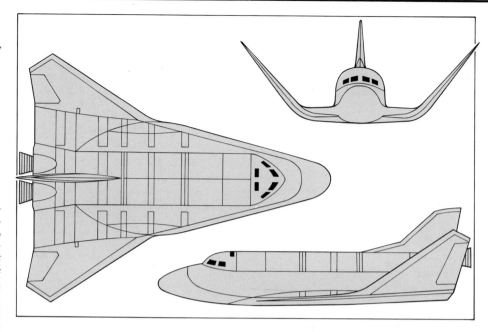

Above: This three-view drawing is based chiefly on the photograph at right. One area that is almost unknown is its propulsion; the DoD sketch below shows a row of three main engines and no others, inside the blunt trailing edge of a wing of wedge profile. The trailing edge is certainly blunt, and the overall configuration strongly resembles that originally selected for the NASA Shuttle Orbiter in 1968.

Right: The aerospace plane test vehicle having been hauled from the Indian Ocean after the second orbital test. Obviously the picture shows a small-scale version of the manned vehicle. It appears to be some 9ft (2.7m) long, and the Western estimate for payload in orbit on all its four flights so far was 2,205lb (1,000kg). At least there is no chance of confusing the full-scale vehicle with the larger Soviet "Shuttle Orbiter".

PUBLISHED TEST FLIGHTS

Mission	Launch centre	Launcher	Date	Splashdown
Cosmos 1374	Kapustin Yar	C-1 (SL-8)	3 June 1982	Indian Ocean
Cosmos 1445	Kapustin Yar	C-1 (SL-8)	16 March 1983	Indian Ocean
Cosmos 1517	Kapustin Yar	C-1 (SL-8)	27 December 1983	Black Sea
Cosmos 1614	Kapustin Yar	C-1 (SL-8)	19 December 1984	Black Sea

been illustrated in the US Department of Defense review *Soviet Military Power* alongside what looks like a stretched F-1-m medium launch vehicle (derived from the ICBM known to NATO as SS-9 Scarp), together with the DoD figures of 1,300,000kg (2,865,961lb) liftoff thrust and 400,000kg (881,800lb) liftoff weight. Of this weight about 33,000lb (the actual US estimate is 15,000kg+, 33,070lb+) is the spacecraft. The latter is expected to be the same shape as the models, and may have a crew of two or even three, depending on the mission.

According to a report in the US periodical *Aviation Week & Space Technology* (7 January 1985) the full-scale vehicle is expected to be launched by "the Soviet's new medium lift SL-X-16 booster". Clearly an enlarged F-1 series rocket, the SL-X-16 was said to be undergoing checkout at Tyuratam launch centre prior to its first flight. In mid-1985 US observers expressed surprise that the new booster appeared not yet to have flown. This means a flight of the manned space plane is unlikely before 1986.

Roald Sagdyeyev, a space expert and member of the (Soviet) Academy of Sciences, is reported to have said (at the time of Cosmos 1614), "We are still not really certain about the economics of such a reusable spacecraft." This statement is curious on several counts. As commented earlier, the Soviet Union has seldom in the

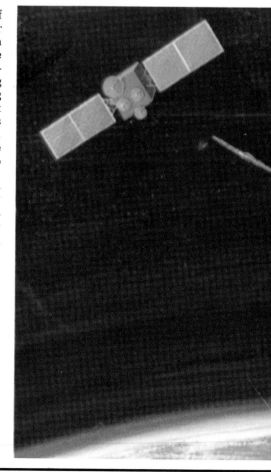

past shown much concern for cost when it wanted to acquire a capability or a weapon. Second, Sagdyeyev's statement appears to contradict colleague A. Y. Skripko (see entry on Soviet "Shuttle") who said it was hoped to cut the cost of getting mass into orbit to "one-tenth that of the US Space Shuttle". If the Soviet Union are "not really certain" about the economics of reuseable space launch systems then the figure of one-tenth appears even more unlikely of attainment than before.

Probably the eminent scientist's statement was intended to divert attention from the importance attached by the Soviet Union to the ability to "fly" in space, and also to generate the (unquestionably mistaken) impression that the so-called Reusable Space Plane is merely for transport, and is cost-sensitive. Of course it may be merely a differently shaped Shuttle-type transporter, but on the evidence so far available it looks much more like a rather simple TAV, of the kind now being studied by the USAF.

Left: Like the three-view drawing, this sketch purports to show the full-scale manned Aerospace Plane. Taken from the 1985 edition of the official DoD assessment *Soviet Military Power*, it depicts the vehicle firing at a hostile satellite, a task of which such a craft would be entirely capable if suitably armed. There can be no blast effects in space, but it would be foolhardy to come so close to hardware that was about to explode; even small fragments could cause damage.

SOVIET SHUTTLE ORBITER

Type: Reusable space transport vehicle.
Engines: US reports claim that the vehicle is launched by two large strap-on boost motors using liquid propellants, plus a large central liquid oxygen/liquid hydrogen booster which (unlike the US Shuttle) has its own main engines. Total liftoff thrust (US estimate) 8.8-13.2 million lb (4-6 million kg). The orbiter itself is thought to have only small trajectory control engines.
Dimensions: (US estimate) Span 78ft (23.5m); length 105ft (32m); length of assembled vehicle at liftoff 223ft (68m).
Weights: Total at liftoff 3,300,000lb (1,500,000kg); vehicle weight delivered to 119 miles (180km) over 209,500lb (95,000kg), including Shuttle payload of 66,000lb (30,000kg).
Performance: Orbital, ie 17,500mph (28,200km/h) plus; landing speed about 173mph (278km/h).

Ever since the start of the US Shuttle programme it has been rumoured that the Soviet Union was developing a similar reusable system, and this was to some degree confirmed when Soviet Science/Technology Attaché in Washington, Anatoli Y. Skripko, announced not only that his country was considerably reducing the cost of placing materials in orbit but that the Soviet goal was to cut costs to "one-tenth those of the US Space Shuttle".

No photographs have appeared in the West showing the big Soviet Shuttle-type vehicle, but since 1984 a seemingly detailed drawing of the assembled vehicle ready for launch has appeared in the annual US Department of Defense review *Soviet Military Power*. Further information has become available as a result of US satellite reconnaissance of the Ramenskoye test airfield. This is the biggest centre in the Soviet Union for experimental flying, and several years ago the decision must have been taken to follow the US procedure with the Shuttle Orbiter and carry out initial atmospheric flight and landing tests after carrying the vehicle aloft mounted on a

large parent aircraft. The choice fell on the Myasishchyev M-4 strategic bomber, one of which was greatly modified with a twin-finned tail. This facilitated mounting the Soviet orbiter on top, with a long pointed tail fairing projecting past the position previously occupied by the bomber's original vertical tail.

All was set for the start of testing in early 1983 when, according to American reports, the M-4/Shuttle combination "slid off the runway" and sustained damage. Why this occurred, or what damage was sustained, can only be conjectured. Almost unbelievably, if US reports are to be accepted as factual, nothing more appeared to happen for 18 months, until the vehicle was again seen at Ramenskoye in late 1984. Even in mid-1985 the start of flight testing using the M-4 carrier aircraft had not been announced by US intelligence, though the 1985 edition of *Soviet Military Power* contained an artist's impression of a take-off. This drawing clearly showed the end-plate fins/rudders of the M-4 canted

Right: Space buffs will recognise several of the sources of inspiration for the artist who drew this "Soviet space station of the 1990s" for the 1985 *Soviet Military Power*, published by the US Department of Defense. In the background the Soviet Shuttle-type orbiter is standing off, presumably to deliver a fresh crew and housekeeping supplies. Though fanciful, such artwork has an important underlying basis of fact, and it helps to crystallise understanding. It matters little now whether the shapes and details have been guessed wrongly; time will put that right.

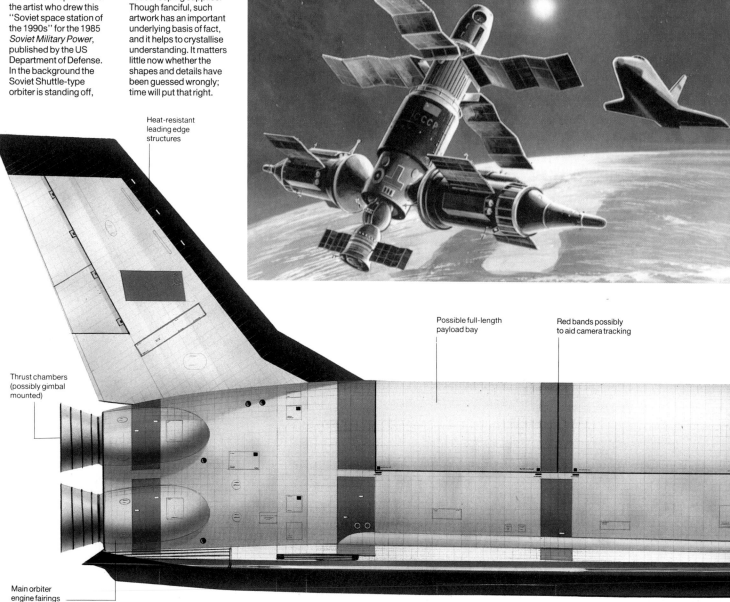

Heat-resistant leading edge structures

Thrust chambers (possibly gimbal mounted)

Main orbiter engine fairings

Possible full-length payload bay

Red bands possibly to aid camera tracking

inwards, earlier sketches showing them vertical.

As for the Soviet reusable orbiter, this is normally drawn as a near-copy of the US Shuttle vehicle. It is drawn as slightly smaller (though weight and payload are estimated to be the same) and in particular it is thought to have no main engines. Thus, unlike the US Shuttle Orbiter which has large bulges over the two upper (of three) main engines, the Soviet orbiter is thought to taper off sharply to a group of small trajectory-control engines at the tail. When mounted on the M-4 this rather stumpy rear section is hidden inside the gigantic aerodynamic tailcone fairing, which is said to have several small fins (presumably to stabilize it after separation). Some idea of the size of this fairing is given by the US statement that the streamlined orbiter riding on the M-4 is almost as long as the bomber, which has a length of 162ft (49.4m); without the fairing the length is only about 105ft (32m) as reported above.

Of course, while the Soviet Union pro-

claims that the NASA Shuttle is totally military in character, it describes its own reusable vehicle in neutral and technical terms. Common sense teaches us that the Soviet "shuttle" will be used for a wide range of purposes, many of which will be military. It is not possible to assess accurately the capabilities of the Soviet space transport system because so little is known about it, but what little is known suggests that (as reported by the USA) it is merely a close copy of the existing US Shuttle. This could never come close to fulfilling the prophecy of Mr Skripko that the Soviet objective is to cut payload-to-orbit costs by 90 per cent. Though a copy of the US Shuttle could have a fly-by-wire control system, as part of a digital integrated bus system, and might have a rather newer airframe than the US orbiter, improvements of this nature could never make anything like a 10:1 difference in mission costs.

All the evidence we have shows that when responsible Russian spokesmen make public statements they should be

taken very seriously. Skripko may have been misreported; certainly, there are few people in NASA or USAF Space Command who would not be prepared to go on record as describing Skripko's figure of "one-tenth the cost of the Shuttle" as impossible, and by a wide margin. In any case, history also shows us that, whenever the Soviet Union perceives a required capability, such as a reusable space launch system, it is totally disinterested in what it costs.

The point could be made that the choice of large liquid-propellant boosters and tank-mounted main launch engines are all in direct contrast to the low-cost features of the US Shuttle, the only expendable part of which is the bare tank shell. Apart from the changed configuration, recovery of undamaged boosters from land would be much more difficult than from the ocean. All these differences make the "one-tenth" figure look even less likely.

Early assessments of Soviet work are sketchy. Space, however, is already an area of USSR/USA co-operation.

Below: Another drawing based on *Soviet Military Power 1985*, this shows the large Shuttle vehicle assembled on what is (fairly confidently, we are told) believed to be its launch vehicle. So far the Soviet Union has not attempted coastal launching and ocean recovery of large boost motors (this Shuttle uses three).

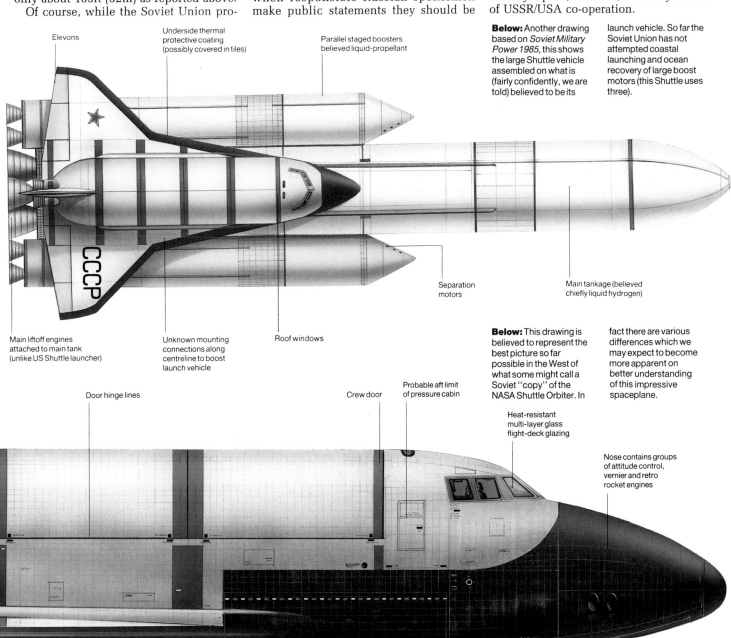

Elevons

Underside thermal protective coating (possibly covered in tiles)

Parallel staged boosters believed liquid-propellant

Main liftoff engines attached to main tank (unlike US Shuttle launcher)

Unknown mounting connections along centreline to boost launch vehicle

Roof windows

Separation motors

Main tankage (believed chiefly liquid hydrogen)

Door hinge lines

Crew door

Probable aft limit of pressure cabin

Heat-resistant multi-layer glass flight-deck glazing

Nose contains groups of attitude control, vernier and retro rocket engines

Below: This drawing is believed to represent the best picture so far possible in the West of what some might call a Soviet "copy" of the NASA Shuttle Orbiter. In fact there are various differences which we may expect to become more apparent on better understanding of this impressive spaceplane.

Data cannot yet be quoted meaningfully, but:

Type: Trans-atmospheric vehicle (many missions envisaged).
Engines: Many possibilities, but favoured solution is multiple liquid oxygen/liquid hydrogen rocket engines, under pilot control.
Dimensions: Span in the region of 60ft (18.3m); length in the region of 120ft (36.5m).
Weights: Usually put in bracket 1.0-1.5 million lb (453-680 tonnes).
Performance: Maximum speed Mach 29 (19,200mph, 30,850km/h); landing speed 150mph (240km/h).

The concept of a Trans-Atmospheric Vehicle (TAV), or Aerospace Plane, goes back to before World War II. Such a vehicle would take off (by one of many possible methods), climb away into outer space and there carry out various kinds of mission, using rocket thrust to change trajectory. With its mission completed it would plunge down through the atmosphere and revert to the status of an aeroplane, using aerodynamic controls to bring it back to a conventional landing. (Or the TAV could takeoff, "fly" out of the atmosphere and back into it and be anywhere on Earth 90 minutes later.) This sounds very like the mission of the Space Shuttle, but the latter is specifically a transport system. The TAV would not be used to carry items to locations in space, but would be used for reconnaissance, space warfare and almost any other kind of military mission, over global ranges.

The first aerospace plane, which was never built, was Ed Heinemann's Douglas D-558-3, or Model 671, designed in 1953-54 for Mach 9 at 700,000ft (6,000mph/9,700km/h at 213,000m). Next came the NAA X-15, which made many flights in the 1960s to Mach 6.72 at up to 354,000ft (4,534mph/7,297km/h at 108,000m). Even earlier than these vehicles, which were really aeroplanes designed for hypersonic Mach Numbers, there had been many paper studies including most notably the farsighted Sänger-Bredt vehicle of 1938-42 which was popularly called the "antipodal bomber" because it could skip in and out of the upper atmosphere to drop a bomb on the other side of the Earth. The Sänger-Bredt study was picked up in 1949 by Chien Hsueh-Sen at Caltech, and also pushed by Walter Dornberger, former German general and military boss of the A4 (V-2) rocket, who at Bell Aircraft urged the USAF to research the boost/glide concept. Boeing received a contract, for the RoBo (rocket bomber), but this was overtaken by an ambitious plan to build a manned boost/glide vehicle which became designated X-20 Dyna-Soar (from "dynamic soaring"). The USAF sent out the RFP (request for proposals) on 1 January 1958, and Boeing's team, headed by George Stoner, won this potentially giant programme.

Dyna-Soar was not a very big vehicle, with an almost pure delta (triangular) wing of 35ft (10.7m) span. The tips of the wing swept up to become fins and rudders. The underside was flat, as if it had been belly-landed on sandpaper. On top was a chunky 45ft (13.7m) fuselage, cut off at the back as if by a cleaver. Dyna-Soar was to be launched vertically by a Titan III rocket, and then skip in and out of the atmosphere at Mach numbers up to 25. At the end of what might be a long mission the vehicle would re-enter the atmosphere, travel long distances at Mach 4 and finally slow to 130mph (209km/h), drop its landing gear and land like any other aeroplane. After Maj Y. Gagarin's manned flight in April 1961 there was renewed pressure behind US space programmes, but Dyna-Soar fell between two stools. It was reaching far out to a new kind of capability. The money was wanted for simple short-term manned orbital flights, and for the colossal Apollo programme to put men on the Moon. Boeing reassigned Stoner as manager of the gigantic Saturn V for the Apollo programme. The USAF, having no clear military "mission" for Dyna-Soar, fought a losing battle for it. This extremely advanced example of what was later to be called an Aerospace Plane, was reduced to the status of a mere research project. The United Nations then said space was for peaceful purposes only; this was NASA's task. Dyna-Soar was cancelled on 10 December 1963.

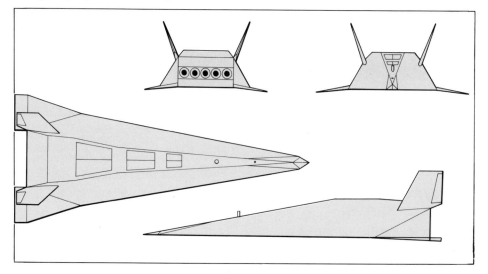

Above: A possible future TAV. Testing with Asset vehicles over 20 years ago solved problems of flight at Mach 18 to 28, using a metal radiator shield to reflect heat back into space. Today the TAV programme has many new structural, material, propulsion and systems developments, but the shape is dictated almost entirely by aerodynamic and re-entry considerations. As in the NASA Shuttle Orbiter, the underside suffers the severest heating.

Below: Sensors sprout from the open cargo bays of a TAV drawn by a McDonnell Aircraft artist and cleared for publication by the US Air Force. This TAV would "be capable of flight in and out of the atmosphere at speeds up to Mach 25. It could routinely travel to any point on the Earth in under two hours". Such vehicles would clearly play a major role in any fully developed SDI kind of capability, whether for recce or attack missions.

During the final two years of the Dyna-Soar programme the USAF Aeronautical Systems Division managed a parallel study called the Aerospace Plane. This was another concept without a clear military mission, but which was undertaken because it had suddenly become possible. It was to be a Hotol (horizontal takeoff and landing) vehicle which began as a single-stage to orbit craft with rocket engines and matured with air-breathing engines as well, probably scramjets (supersonic-combustion ramjets). Martin Marietta built a full-scale wing/fuselage test structure.

Among many related research projects of the 1960s were the Asset (Aerothermo-dynamic/elastic structural systems environmental test) vehicles built by McDonnell to explore re-entry "corridors", and the MRRV (manoeuvring re-entry research vehicle) which is not quite completed. The USAF and NASA also flew a series of lifting-body research aircraft: the X-24A and B, M2F3 and HL-10. Carried aloft under a B-52, they relied on body lift on their subsonic or supersonic recovery back to a normal landing, paving the way to the Shuttle (described separately).

Next the USAF Flight Dynamics Laboratory contracted with GD and Rockwell in the AMSCTI (advanced military space-flight capability technology identification) programme which investigated critical technologies in various types of ground- or air-launched systems. In 1983 this was followed by a study by three of the Boeing companies (Aerospace, Military Airplane and Commercial Airplane) on the aero-dynamic problems of subsonic launch, for example from above a 747. Boeing has also built a test specimen representing a TAV fuel tank wall in a high-temperature superalloy.

This test panel is needed because, whereas the Shuttle Orbiter is a civilian spacecraft, the USAF TAV has to meet

Above: US Air Force artwork showing a TAV riding on its expendable propellant (liquid oxygen/ liquid hydrogen) tank, carried aloft by an E-4B. The latter has a large "doghouse" dorsal fairing over the special space communications systems needed for TAV missions.

stringent military requirements. One of these is quick reaction time; it has to be ready for a mission within minutes (if possible at any time of day or in any weather at the launch site). The thermal tiles used as heat insulation on the Shuttle are not acceptable, and the TAV will have some form of refractory metal airframe possibly derived from the X-15, hence the Boeing test panel. There are very many detail design or constructional features of the Shuttle Orbiter that would not be carried across to a TAV, which would have to have

Below: An alternative launch method being studied is use of an aeroplane-type launch vehicle acting as little more than a powered landing gear to help acceleration and to support the TAV during its ground run. This five-engined launcher has no pilot but, with special powered high-lift systems, would be recoverable. The TAV is much more bluff-nosed than that shown opposite, being tailored for pure military oriented space missions.

almost pushbutton readiness (the figure for planning has been 5min) with extremely high reliability.

In a major policy statement on 25 February 1985 President Reagan expanded USAF space capabilities sharply, calling for increased Shuttle utilization, development of a new Saturn-5 class heavy launcher (mainly for Strategic Defense Initiative missions), purchase of Titan 34D-7 boosters as alternatives to Shuttle Orbiters to avoid any hold-up caused by a Shuttle pad accident, and development of the TAV to fly high-priority National Security missions. The latter are still ill-defined, though numerous speakers have hinted that TAVs would replace the SR-71 in strategic reconnaissance missions, cruising at Mach 29 at 45 miles (72.4km) height, and follow the ATF as the USAF "fighter" for the early part of the 21st century. The author will leave readers to draw their own conclusions regarding the cost, effectiveness and base vulnerability of squadrons of TAV "fighters".

Suffice to say the climate of opinion in the USA today is to ignore United Nations resolutions saying "space is for peaceful purposes", and to proceed to develop whatever military space capability is felt necessary. Phases I and II of the TAV study are complete, technology identification for ground-launched and air-launched TAV systems is proceeding at GD and Martin Marietta, and by the end of the 1980s it should be possible to take final decisions.

At present TAV is seen as yet another — and probably the most costly — system rigidly tied to fixed air force bases. Provided the enemy refrains from interfering, TAV could be launched at short notice, with reconnaissance sensors, warheads or other loads, to reach any point on Earth within 90min (reduced in 1984 from a previous figure of 120min).

In Phase I, started in May 1983, there were 14 TAV concepts. Battelle Columbus sifted these and selected six which have been further refined in Phase II, conducted by Science Applications Inc. Later in 1985, following elimination of several schemes and careful evaluation against advanced aircraft and other alternative systems, surviving TAVs will move into the next phase, leading to a decision on FSED (full-scale engineering development) in 1991.

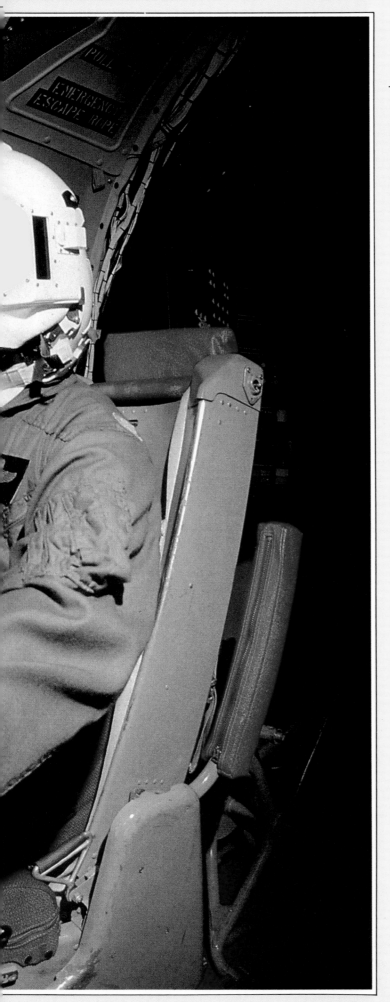

PART TWO

SYSTEMS OF THE FUTURE

Some aircraft are mere airframes wrapped around incredible systems whose complexity is equalled only by their price. Most systems concern avionics (aviation electronics) nature, but this chapter also addresses itself to the vital question of propulsion. Future engines will play a crucial role in both the central requirements of future warplanes: the need to do without airfields and the need to be invisible and silent. Of course, proliferating systems make invisibility and silence difficult.

AIRCRAFT DESIGN

From 1913 until roughly 50 years later the designer of combat aircraft took it for granted that the customer wanted ever-higher flight performance. With the coming of jet propulsion new vistas of speed were opened up, so that aerodynamicists had to find new shapes to exploit the new possibilities. As noted in the section on propulsion it was widely thought that ramjets would become widely used on supersonic fighters, and combat aircraft were designed for flight Mach numbers up to at least 3.7 (2,446mph, 3,936km/h). By the late 1950s the military customer was becoming unsure of the way ahead. Britain led in the belief that manned combat aircraft were entirely obsolete, and that all future wars would be waged by missiles. This helped to release funds for the new generation of intercontinental silo-launched and submarine-launched missiles (curiously, having cancelled its fighters and new bombers, Britain then cancelled its silo missile and bought a submarine missile from the USA). The quest for speed in manned aircraft continued, however, and in 1955-59 the USAF, with limited extra funding by the Navy, even sponsored a colossal programme for so-called "zip fuel" – a high-energy ethyl borane mixture which would have multiplied both the logistics and maintenance problems of every combat unit using it. But times were changing.

The missile proponents did not replace fighters but for a while the US Navy sponsored an AAM with a range exceeding 100 miles (161km), and calculted that with such weapons the fighter merely needed to carry them into the sky somewhere above the fleet it was protecting. In August 1959 Rear-Admiral Bob Dixon, head of BuAer, testified to Congress that zip fuel was no longer needed because in future fighters did not need to fly fast.

This was one of the major discontinuities in combat-aircraft design. Another was the gradual realisation in the 1950s that jet engines could lift aircraft straight off the ground, and by 1960 this had led to frantic enthusiasm for jet VTOLs. The subsequent history is one of the most extraordinary in the whole history of human conflict. Whereas in the early 1950s the vulnerability of airfields dominated NATO aircraft procurement – so that, for example, the very first multinational contest for a new NATO warplane was for a light tactical strike fighter that could operate away from known airfields, a competition won by the Fiat G91 – by the early 1960s the vulnerability of airfields had become almost a taboo subject, and the need to disperse into the countryside something either not discussed or firmly squashed as highly undesirable.

The full story may never be told, but American (and in particular USAF) influence had by 1962 come down firmly

Below: An F-16B at Edwards prepares to pick up the cable in the All-American Engineering MAG (mobile arresting gear) which is standard equipment in the USAF. Highly developed, MAG is just one of many items of infrastructure that work in peacetime when the airfields exist.

against jet-lift VTOL, or rather STOVL. It may have been that the USAF had its eyes squarely on its new tactical fighter, the TFX, which was supposedly not only going to fly rings round everything else but also carry enough fuel to fly 3,455 miles (5,560km) without air refuelling. It was this range requirement which did more than anything else to eliminate the TFX (F-111) as an air-combat fighter, and also for practical purposes eliminate an unenforced requirement for STOL off-base operation. A further factor in establishing the USAF's stance on STOVL may have been that most of the pioneering, and available engines, had come from Britain; this made it "a

foreign idea" and thus extremely hard to view objectively.

For whatever reason, the USAF rather suddenly ceased to pay any public attention to the vulnerability of its airfields. It continues to this day to pour billions into programmes for fragile aircraft which, on delivery, are parked on the very spots on the planet which are more heavily targeted by missiles than any others in history.

This amazing attitude has so far prevented the development of any survivable Western airpower. Instead the emphasis has been squarely on the ability to operate intensively and reliably for many years at minimum cost. This objective, which is reasonable enough provided the aircraft are never actually needed, has placed demands on the aerospace industry at least as great as those in the days when the emphasis was on flight performance. It must be remembered, in reading this Section, that today's buzzwords are reliability, maintainability and affordability. But the USAF, whose objectives and attitudes have a gigantic effect on all other air forces (even, or perhaps one might say especially, in the Soviet Union), continually sets its sights on the stars. Today it has thousands of civilian and uniformed staff looking at the ATF and TAV, potentially the biggest warplane projects of all time. One cannot help wondering if the astronomic sums they will consume might not be better spent in creating airpower that could last until Day 2 of a future war.

PROPULSION

In November 1944 farsighted Roy Marquardt set up a company in California to make ramjet engines. Such engines are popularly called "flying stovepipes", because they are little more than a carefully profiled duct, into which air is rammed in at the front, compressed highly by virtue of the engine's speed through the sky, and after passing through a white-hot combustion chamber is expelled at the rear as a propulsive jet. Almost the only moving part is the fuel pump, which in fact has to pump a lot of fuel. It looked as if ramjets would be needed by the thousand, not only for missiles but also for supersonic warplanes.

It never happened that way. Though ramjets are beginning to find a sustained market in the cruise and anti-ship missiles of the post-1990 period, there has never been a ramjet-engined aircraft squadron. The only way the scene could change would be for future fighters to be driven round the war area on large trucks equipped with a launch catapult. The fighter could then be propelled by simple, cheap and almost troublefree ramjets. It would be lighter and more agile than any fighter with complex and weighty gas turbine engines, but it would have to fly under constant digital control – for example to ensure that air-inlet conditions were always within the ramjet flight envelope – and recovery back on to the launch catapult would require not only the same automatic control but also a foolproof method of slowing the fighter from about 150mph (240km/h) to zero in the length of the launcher. At first glance it sounds a hare-brained scheme, but if a Hellfire missile can consistently be put through a target bull's eye there is no reason why a fighter cannot be homed at the correct angle on to a mobile launch/recovery ramp. Most of the technology for such a system exists today, and if it works in sunshine it would work at night or, as the Americans put it, "in weather". A detail point is that modern canard fighters can land in a fairly flat attitude; another detail is that the only landing gear needed would be simple wheels for ground mobility, preferably with drive from an APU so that the aircraft can taxi in any direction without changing its attitude or running its main engine(s).

Such a fighter has a lot going for it; indeed almost all the new features are pluses, and the only negative feature is that we have not done it before. The idea is radical but potentially safer than traditional operation from a runway, quite apart from the vital consideration of survivability in war. How do we generate the energy for the launch, and absorb the incoming fighter's energy on landing? There appear to be at least 12 methods worth looking at, and it must be borne in mind that it is desirable to avoid the use of large quantities of hypergolic (spontaneously reactive) liquids, and also to minimise the mass of fast-moving hardware other than the fighter. (In launching "V.I" flying bombs a heavy piston left the ramp along with the missile and had to be retrieved from about 1,000ft (300m)

Above: While GE and Pratt & Whitney fight for the lead in ATF propulsion, SNECMA in France is the first company in Europe to run a next-generation fighter engine. The M88 is a two-spool turbofan almost as powerful as the M53 (Mirage 2000 engine) but much lighter.

Below: Instead of going the whole hog with thrust vectoring US designs feature 2-D (rectangular two-dimensional) nozzles which can direct the jet diagonally up or down. This can give modest gains in field length and manoeuvrability. (PW model shown.)

away, unacceptable for any modern system.

This idea is put forward to emphasize that new thinking is needed. There will be no shortage of people eager to point out that the launcher must be almost as long as the "cat" on a carrier, and that therefore the vehicle must be large. Others will doubt the reliability of a landing procedure that requires such precision, but this is almost the least of the problems. For 25 years we have lived with people whose immediate reaction to jet STOVL fighters has been to point out the percentage "penalties" supposedly suffered. The same people will be only too eager to pick holes in any new idea

that lets fighters escape from 10,000ft (3km) of immovable concrete!

For the moment, however, the world's warplanes – apart from a handful of Harriers and "Forgers" – are tied to airfields, and to conventional jet engines. Many Soviet aircraft still use turbojets, but almost all modern Western combat aircraft use turbofans. The Mirage 2000 is a special case, because this aircraft was so heavily biassed towards highly supersonic flight that its engine is almost a plain turbojet. The M53's bypass ratio is extremely low, and it has a single shaft, yet despite these features it is extremely heavy for its power. Another engine with a low bypass ratio is

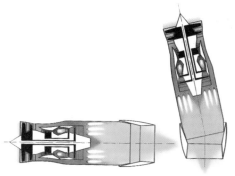

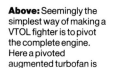

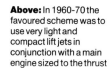

Above: Seemingly the simplest way of making a VTOL fighter is to pivot the complete engine. Here a pivoted augmented turbofan is shown with additional small-angle vectoring in the nozzle. In practice tilting engines pose problems in basic aircraft stability and control.

Above: An alternative scheme is ejector-jet lift by piping compressed air from the main engine to a separate lift duct near the nose. Here ejector jets induce a much larger flow of fresh air from above, thereby getting lift much greater than could be achieved by the bleed air alone.

Above: In 1960-70 the favoured scheme was to use very light and compact lift jets in conjunction with a main engine sized to the thrust requirement in cruising flight or combat. Having to carry spare lift jets more than cancels out gains from reducing the size of the main engine.

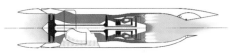

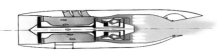

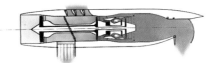

Above: The hybrid fan is regarded by Rolls-Royce as one of the better schemes for supersonic fighters, such as the Vought V-120 study. It removes any problems due to the transition from jet-borne to wing-borne flight. The front nozzles could retract in cruising flight.

Above: A related scheme is the tandem fan, in which a different method is used to shut off the core from the front fan and feed it from a dorsal inlet. This scheme has also been studied by Vought for supersonic US Navy fighters. It promises to minimise the "V/STOL penalty".

Above: RALS (remote augmented lift system) has been studied by GD and Grumman. Rolls-Royce say that bleeding air to a separate fuel-burning lift jet is bound to reduce STO performance and cannot smoothly vector the thrust during the vital transition from jet lift to wings.

the General Electric F404, used in the F-18 and Gripen, and this is a two-shaft engine with an outstanding record (like most current GE engines), with perhaps the fastest spool-up to full power of any fighter engine in history. Nearly all current combat engines have two shafts, but the Turbo-Union RB199, used in the Tornado, has three. Subject to years of sniping by commercial rivals, like the Tornado itself, the RB199 is at last beginning to be recognised as probably the best military engine ever, but this had to wait for a relaxation of security and the establishment of a massive in-service track record.

Traditional procedures for moving on to the next generation of engines have been to improve the fan/compressor blading, to get more work per stage, and thus higher pressure ratio with fewer stages; increase inlet diameter or in some other way increase the engine airflow; improve the combustion chamber to burn more fuel in a smaller space, without smoke; even out the temperature distribution at the HP turbine inlet so that the average gas temperature was almost the same as the maximum; improve the detail design, cooling and materials of the HP turbine to handle higher gas temperature; improve detail design of the blades, casings and seals to minimise air or gas leakage; introduce new materials, such as carbon-fibre composite for the cool fan duct; and generally make the engine more tolerant to distorted inlet airflow, incoming foreign objects such as birds, and even combat damage, whilst

Above: Supersonic gas blasts from a Volvo Flygmotor RM12 (GE F404 variant on test for Sweden's Gripen. It is difficult for hidebound engine designers to see that plain holes – no matter how their profile may vary – are no longer acceptable for any combat aircraft.

reducing IR signature and even noise (because stealth means quiet as well as invisible). All this adds up to a broad front on which to attack, and for good measure one can throw in the need to contain all the parts of an exploded engine, increase the operating life between major maintenance, raise reliability and handling response near to perfection and keep down all the costs, including fuel and spare parts.

It goes without saying that to a broad approximation the aircraft designer can be offered a choice between a tough, simple, reliable, cheap engine that weighs a ton more than it need and burns twice as much fuel or alternatively a fantastically com-

plicated, gold-plated, digitally controlled masterpiece built like a watch that has tremendous performance, handles beautifully, is light as a feather and burns very little fuel, but which has a thousand things to go wrong, is fragile, temperamental and costs an arm and a leg. That designers have achieved some success in merging all the requirements is demonstrated by the fact that – admittedly after years of problems – Pratt & Whitney is now delivering F100-PW-220 engines which not only put out 23,830lb (10,810kg) thrust, handle beautifully in "impossible" combat flight conditions and show exceptional cruising fuel economy, but also can fly 4,000 Tactical Air Command missions without even refurbishment of the hot section. This is just 3,920 missions more than the Tactical Air Command overhaul life of the same maker's J57 in the F-100 in January 1955.

In the past it has been usual for the engine designer to "play tunes" with the thermodynamic cycle in planning each new engine. Pressure ratio, bypass ratio and turbine entry gas temperature are still the foundations upon which the designer builds, but much of the effort is now devoted to other factors. The customer's demands are always rising. In the 1950s the average fighter pilot quite expected to get a fire or overheat warning, which might turn out to be false. Today even the false warnings are being all-but eliminated. In the 1950s bad handling and compressor stalls were par for the course, and got into the papers only in exceptional circumstances

PROPULSION

(for example, when the Hunter F.1 fired its guns the engine usually flamed out, which as a routine procedure was tiresome). Any off-design inlet condition was almost bound to cause trouble. Today no excuses are accepted; GE's new fighter engines, the F110 and F404, will keep running sweetly if you fly the fighter sideways or backwards.

Another contrast with the past is the revolution in maintenance procedures. Until well into the 1960s, and in some cases to the present day, it has been common to establish an "overhaul life" for each type of engine. After, say, 500 hours of operation the engine is removed from the aircraft, taken to a base depot or the manufacturer, torn apart and half the parts replaced. The whole procedure is labour-intensive and rapidly consumes expensive spare parts. Moreover, there was probably nothing wrong with the engine when it was removed for overhaul.

Today we have OCM (on-condition maintenance), modular construction, health monitors and a totally different approach. For a start, each engine is instrumented with devices such as chip detectors (which trigger warnings if any microscopic particles of metal start circulating with the lubricating oil). The most modern engines are tied in with the aircraft digital data bus system (as described later in this section) so that after each mission, or even once a month, maintenance engineers can play back the record and study when the engine flew, what the conditions were like throughout each mission and if, at any points it exceeded certain critical temperatures, rotational speeds or other major variables. In general, the engine is left severely alone (as we have seen, an F-15C can fly 4,000 missions without "pulling" either engine). The engine is made to tell us if it feels unwell.

Items such as hydraulic pumps, mounted on the engine or on a secondary power system gearbox, can in theory go on even longer than 4,000 mission cycles, because wear and tear can be reduced close to zero. Some crucial items change all the time, just like the ageing of our own bodies, and they have to be "lifed". An outstanding example is the turbine rotor blades, which when almost white hot are subjected to tremendous tensile and bending stresses by the centrifugal force or high-speed rotation plus the aerodrynamic driving force of the hot gas; a blade weighing 2oz (57g) typically experiences a tensile force of 2 tons (2,000kg) at full rpm. This results in very slow elongation, called creep, so the blade has to be one of the "lifed" parts. Others

Below: A Pratt & Whitney F100-PW-220, showing the completely new multi-flap nozzle used on this new version of the F-15 and F-16 engine. The Dash-220 is probably the most proven fighter engine there has ever been. One has run a test simulating nine years of combat.

AVIONICS

The oldest avionic (aviation electronic) system, is the communications radio. Even here things keep happening. Totally different wavebands are used to communicate with other aircraft, with surface airbases, with spacecraft, army units and warships; and to communicate with a submerged missile-firing submarine takes quite a package, pumping out VLF transmissions from a vertical wire 26,000ft (7,925m) long!

The obvious objective of any nation is that every individual in all its armed forces should be able to talk to anyone he or she needs to talk to, in clear voice contact, without delay – and without any enemy being able to eavesdrop. Bearing in mind the cleverness of modern Comint (communications intelligence) systems, this is no easy objective to realize. Indeed it was never even attempted until about 1970 when the vast architecture of the West's JTIDS (Joint tactical information distribution system) was first roughed out. Today many parts of JTIDS are coming into use, and thousands of terminals will be interlinked in the next few years.

It is one of a growing number of large systems that mean that no member of an Allied force, wherever he may be in the vicinity of Earth, need be either out of voice contact or lost.

It is a global network operating in the 960-1215 MHz band and using all available ECCM methods, such as frequency hopping and spread-spectrum waveforms to prevent anyone listening-in. TDMA (time-division multiple access) allows thousands of terminals, anywhere from deep beneath the sea to outer space, to talk to each other within one system. The signals take the form of streams of billions of pulses, but any series of 100 pulses might represent parts of 40 or 50 different messages. The receiver separates out his own pulses automatically, reconstituting them into digital data or the recognisable human voice of the original broadcaster. More, JTIDS serves a navigation function, in the case of aircraft usually by Tacan techniques.

Most of the JTIDS system is contracted to Singer-Kearfott, but the big Class 1 terminals and the successor HIT are Hughes Aircraft products, used for example in the E-3 Awacs. In Britain Marconi and Plessey share JTIDS terminals, used initially in the Nimrod AEW.3 and Tornado F.2 and eventually throughout NATO air defence forces. The Class 2 terminals carried in US fighters comprise two boxes with a combined mass of 95lb (43kg). We still do not know how many things this worldwide system will be able to do. Certainly it would be possible, for example, for an item of information in the form of data or a picture to be sent direct from an E-3 or Hawkeye to a particular fighter, or airbase, or warship; or for the five members of a low-level attack formation to transmit anything they wished, such as their HUD pictures or head-down radar displays, between each other.

Another widespread system is Rockwell Collins Navstar GPS (Global Positioning System). In 1985 GPS was already being used by many classes of customer, and the whole world-coverage system will be operational in early 1988. GPS will by that time use 18 satellites orbiting in three groups of six at a height of 6,772 miles (10,898km). Four spare satellites will be stored at fairly short readiness as insurance against loss or malfunction. All receiver stations are identical, no matter whether they are in a B-52, F-16, helicopter, aircraft carrier, submarine or tank. Each receiver station will at all times be able to read out his lat/long position, altitude (if airborne), local time (within 0.1s), position within 52ft (16m) and usually to considerably better accuracy, and velocity within 0.3ft (0.1m)/s. The first time GPS was used was to navigate a Sabreliner from Collins at include particular seals, flexible diaphragms and similar items.

An F100 fighter engine has 92 lifed items, so in mid-1985 the 3,300 engines of this type in the USAF contained 294,400 different lifed components. Each one is recorded in a computer memory, and each day that memory is updated with the flight time and LCF (low-cycle fatigue) count according to the actual missions flown by the F-15s and F-16s in which the engines are installed. At the correct moment the central computer gives notice that a particular engine has parts which have consumed their useful life. Modular construction makes life even easier in that it is

Engine	P&W F100	CE F100	ATF
First USAF service	1974	1986	1992?
Fan stages	3	3	1
HP comp. stages	10	9	5
HP stages	2	1	1
LP turb.	2	2	1

Below: By sheer technical capability General Electric has broken P&W's monopoly with the F110, a new fighter turbofan in the 29,000lb (13-tonne) class. Selected for the F-16C, D and N, it has a close relative in the F110-400 which will power the F-14D Tomcat.

possible, as a quick routine operation, to replace one major engine component, such as the fan, or LP turbine, without disturbing the rest.

At present the two US engine giants are locked in battle over the ATF engine. Either the GE37 or PW3000 will be chosen, and though it will have power at least as great as today's F100 and F110, it will have perhaps half as many parts. A rough idea is given by the accompanying table (which is hypothetical, details of the ATF candidate engines being classifed).

Fewer parts mean lower costs, and probably higher reliability. Other features of the ATF engine will be full-authority digital electronic control of the whole system — inlet, engine, afterburner and nozzle — forming part of the integrated aircraft digital control network, engine materials chosen for supercruise (sustained supersonic cruising flight), low-observable (stealth) blended inlet(s) and nozzles(s), and a vectoring nozzle for improved in-flight manoeuvrability. Obviously immense efforts are being devoted to reducing IR signature, but in general a powerful engine means a powerful signature.

What comes next, for the 21st century? USAF thinking - which is all the author can report on, because nobody else will admit to having any — expects the TAV propulsion system to put out double the thrust of the ATF engine, for the same weight and parts-count. It will possibly be a dual-cycle turboramjet. Mr Marquardt was 50 years too early.

Cedar Rapids, Iowa, to Paris in May 1983. The flight was deliberately made in five stages, yet terminal accuracy at Paris was 24.6ft (7.5m).

Important features of GPS are its global common nature, which for example will improve accuracy of cruise missiles and their carrier aircraft both using the same system, the fact that though the receiver antenna (aerial) is pointed at the local satellite(s) the signals are received during all combat manoeuvres, the fact that stealth aircraft or any other receiver station need not make any emission themselves, and the impossibility of hostile receivers tuning in to the same system.

Clearly there are exciting things happening in communications and navigation, the oldest forms of avionics. Most interest probably centres on EW (electronic warfare), and on advanced surveillance and attack radars. The latter are blossoming forth in many new forms, including DBS

Left: The Navstar GPS (Global Positioning System) promises to revolutionise a nation's force effectiveness. GPS is a 24-hour secure worldwide jam-resistant system which provides every customer – air, land, sea and undersea – with exact information on position, velocity and time. Here an aircraft box is seen front centre, with ship units at left rear and army at right.

(doppler beam sharpening) modes, the SAR (synthetic-aperture radar) and conformal radars. DBS is a mode in which by processing the received signals the clarity of the displayed picture is greatly enhanced (the effect is like bringing any optical system into sharp focus). The SAR has a similar effect, gained by emitting the signals in a phased sequence to achieve the simulated effect of a giant reflector; like DBS this can give at least an order of magnitude improvement in picture resolution. Conformal radars do not necessarily display a better picture but have the advantage that their aerial (antenna) is shaped to form part of the airframe, such as a forward fuselage and wing root, or the leading edge of a helicopter rotor blade. Best of all, from the stealth viewpoint, is not to send out any signals at all.

Over the whole field of avionics there are perhaps 1,000 areas in which progress is being made daily. FBW (fly by wire) control systems, in which the pilot's input demands are transmitted as electrical impulses along multiple-redundant wires, are beginning to look passé as the laboratories shift their efforts to FBL (fly by light) in which the transmission medium comprises bundles of optical fibres. Optics frequencies are so high that data-rates can be multiplied by several orders of magnitude, while other advantages include light weight, the ease with which the number of parallel data highways can be multiplied by 100 or 1,000 to take care of combat damage, and high resistance to nuclear blast and other effects.

Another big area of advance concerns the introduction of the VHSIC (very high-speed integrated circuit) or "superchip", which is crucial to a whole range of new

Above: An F-16 releases pyrotechnic flares. It looks impressive and is a simple but effective counter to many types of heat-seeking missile. However, many modern missiles sample the incoming infra-red energy at two wavelengths, and are less easily fooled.

developments including the next generation of aircraft. Yet another concerns standardization on Ada higher-order language for software, which one fervently hopes has already been chosen for the ATF and TAV. There is really no choice, previous languages such as Jovial being totally inadequate for these major long-term new "warplane" systems.

For several years the USAF has been trying to correlate all the new technologies into one integrated system, called Pave Pillar. Scheduled for introduction as a retrofit in the F-16C from 1990 (possibly 1989), this integrated system will have all the advances so far listed plus advanced colour graphics, voice control by the pilot's own voice, new software algorithms and total integration with the digital buses which will extend throughout the aircraft and also tie in the EW, sensors, flight controls and propulsion controls.

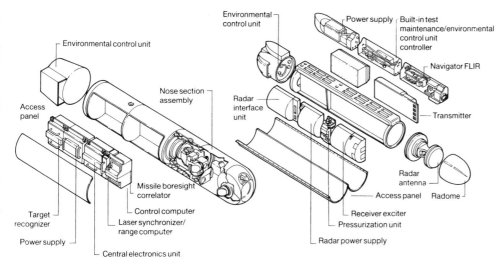

Environmental control unit

Access panel

Nose section assembly

Radar interface unit

Target recognizer

Power supply

Missile boresight correlator

Control computer

Laser synchronizer/ range computer

Central electronics unit

Environmental control unit

Power supply

Built-in test maintenance/environmental control unit controller

Navigator FLIR

Transmitter

Radar antenna

Access panel

Radome

Receiver exciter

Pressurization unit

Radar power supply

Above: The Lantirn targeting pod is one of two packages designed to be hung externally on USAF tactical aircraft in order to confer previously missing night (and limited all-weather) capability. This particular pod has given a great deal of trouble, but by 1985 apparently it was beginning to appear more reliable.

Above: In contrast, the Lantirn navigation pod gave reasonably good performance from the start, but even with both pods attached future USAF attack aircraft will not be able to equal the night and all-weather precision navigation and weapon-aiming ability designed into the Tornado in 1969. The ATF will have to do better.

One of the USAF's big handicaps has been the sunshine at most of its laboratories. As this is written the twin Lantirn pods (low-altitude navigation and targeting IR for night) are only just beginning to come out of the wood. When they work properly (and the main problem has been the targeting pod which contains a laser as well as a FLIR/forward-looking IR), the Lantirn pods will give aircraft such as the F-16 an all-weather and night attack capability somewhat less than that designed 15 years ago for the RAF Tornado, which has been in service four years. It is surely staggering that today the exciting new capability being spoken of in the corridors of USAF Systems Command is the ability to keep on fighting after sunset, and perhaps even if it rains!

The night and all-weather sensors of the Tornado are almost all internal, whereas its jammer pod and chaff/flare dispenser are pylon-mounted. The debate continues on whether it is better to hang mission electronics, such as EW subsystems, on a pylon or tuck them inside the aircraft. The RWR (radar warning receiver) is virtually always built-in; like a certain credit card, you don't leave home without it. Jammers are another matter, and many people, including front-line pilots, would rather have a smaller aircraft and hang the main ECM externally. The author does not subscribe to this view and welcomed the development of the

ASPJ (Advanced Self-Protection Jammer) which is designed where possible to be packaged internally.

Surprisingly, the rumours pouring into the US technical press about ATF design suggest that external EW systems are still very much in the running, not least because of severe pressure on internal space. This would be nonsense on an aircraft intended for some reason) to cruise at supersonic speed; in any case, a supercruise aircraft pumps out such intense IR that any kind of defensive electronics would appear superfluous.

In the past RWRs and ECM jammers have been almost unbelievably crude, and in some respects actually inferior to systems in RAF use in 1944. Today there is much greater sophistication, computer control of power and radiated direction, and coverage of an ever-widening spread of EM frequencies. With INEWS (integrated EW system), which should fly in 1991 and be ready in nice time for the ATF, the frequency coverage for the first time embraces the EO (electro-optical) region of the spectrum. INEWS has been described as having "revolutionary impact" and so is obviously one of the top-priority targets of Soviet intelligence.

It is difficult to see what completely new technique could be invented in traditional ECM, but as the frequencies increase a host of new possibilities emerge. IRCM using controlled pulsed emissions can go a long way to confusing heat-seeking missiles, though so far little has appeared even in the US trade press about how far such emitters can make a missile break lock from such a juicy source as an engine in full afterburner. (Incidentally one of dozens of USAF IR defensive systems under development, in this case to protect the E-3 Sentry, has the code name Have Charcoal; one wonders if this gives a clue to how it works, because the earliest IRCM products used white-hot bricks of ceramic !) To return to INEWS, this extends the art of countermeasures into broadly visual frequencies, and the obvious question is how far active emissions, or any other technique, can make something visually disappear. Perhaps we could learn from the showbiz magician who in 1984 made a hangared Learjet, surrounded by his audience, vanish?

Left: A Tornado of the German Marineflieger, with four Kormoran anti-ship missiles, Sidewinders, EL673 ECM jammer (left wing) and BOZ.100 chaff dispenser (right wing). Panavia's four original customers would not have bought an aircraft that was not truly night and all-weather capable.

Right: The electronics unit for the Marconi Avionics Lantirn HUD for the F-16C. As can be seen, all such "black boxes" are densely packed with the devices that are increasingly at the heart of on-board systems. The micro-electronic packages are soldered to easily replaced printed circuit boards.

COCKPITS

So rapid has been recent development in the cockpits of combat aircraft that anything offering an array of electromechanical dial or tape "instruments" looks positively prehistoric. This includes the F-15 and Tornado. There are some aircraft that dip one toe in the new-technology water; for example the Mirage 2000 has a primitive HDD (head-down display) which presents radar/TV data with three colours, while the two-seat 2000N has a form of moving-map display. Plenty of fighters have useful VSI and HSI (vertical/horizontal situation indicator) instruments, one example being the F-14A which is only now being drastically upgraded almost 20 years after it was designed. And of course the developing technology of the HUD has

swiftly made it the dominant item in every combat-aircraft cockpit, used by the pilot more than all other input devices combined.

One stepping stone to the future was the Comed (combined map and electronics display) developed by Ferranti. This combined in one HDD of standard format both a projected map and radar/TV pictures, with electronic annotations such as track, commanded track, present position, waypoints, targets, positions of known hostile defences and a wide range of alphanumerics such as time to the next waypoint. By the 1970s it was being realised that thanks to modern electronics such displays can serve as interfaces not only for navigation and weapon-delivery information but for

every kind of information the pilot needs, and more than he was previously given by serried ranks of "instruments". Today all combat aircraft are being designed with digital data bus systems into which are connected every functioning part of the aircraft, including every sensor. In theory it would be possible to confront the pilot with a single giant display filling his head-down range of vision. In practice it is better for suppliers to develop standard MFDs (multifunction displays) which are panel-mounted like old-fashioned instruments. Depending on the workload the cockpit may need from one MFD to four. Each MFD comprises a multicolour CRT display surrounded by buttons. These buttons enable the pilot to change the menu, the type of

Left: A 1979 picture of an F/A-18A Hornet cockpit, which ever since has been the yardstick against which other new tactical cockpits have been judged. It has a conventional stick and twin throttles (left), all with Hotas controls. Facing the pilot are three MFDs seen here with three different blue-green menus selected. At the centre, under the HUD, is the UFC. Altogether it just about enables one man to cope.

Right: Hughes AETMS (airborne electronic terrain map system) imagery showing the white cursor heading for Mt Rainier, Washington. Menu data show heading 028, range to point where cursor is centred 30,400ft, height AGL 1,650ft, and lat/long at upper right. Note accurate contour lines and different colours for vegetation, snow, rock and water. Stealth aircraft could use synthetic scenes to eliminate canopies.

Above: Simplified model of the Swedish Gripen cockpit, one of the few to be developed since the F/A-18. Ericsson's MFDs show flight data (left), navigation (centre) and radar/FLIR (right), while the Hughes HUD has a wide field of view achieved by using diffraction optics. On each side of the UFC are four traditional "instruments". By the time the Gripen reaches the squadrons these may have been considered superfluous.

Right: Collins (division of Rockwell) is one of the first to combine stroke-written and raster-written (made by TV-type lines) symbology in one display. The target reticle and green data are stroke-written, superimposed on the colour TV picture, while the colour blocks with messages are raster-generated. Obviously, even this display imposes a heavy workload on a single pilot making a low attack at high-subsonic speed.

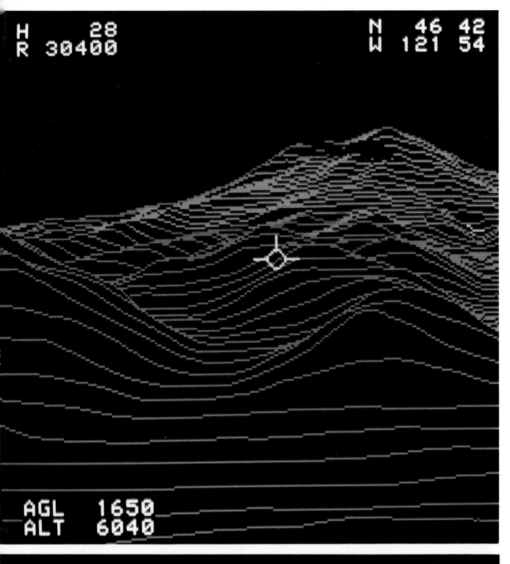

information presented, as well as call up alphanumeric data.

Now that everyone is doing it it seems obvious, but in fact it was as recently as 1976 that Kaiser Electronics was awarded the contract for the cockpit displays of the F/A-18A Hornet. These displays comprise three MFDs and an advanced HUD. Originally the three HDDs were to be identical, but production Hornets have two of the original kind and a slightly larger HI (horizontal indicator) which is basically a Comed. Each display is surrounded by 20 menu and input buttons with which the pilot can call up anything he could conceivably wish to look at or be told. In the twinkling of an eye he can switch a radar picture to a Flir picture, reverse the polarity so that blacks become whites and vice versa and then enlarge it to the magnification he wants. If he were to get any kind of malfunction warning he can call up thousands of BITE (built-in test equipment) readouts, trace the source of the fault and, if not rectifiable in the air, see if he can bypass it to restore the aircraft's full capabilities. Ordinary instruments are tucked away at the bottom of the panel in a standby role.

HOTAS CONTROLS

Though not peculiar to the Hornet, other new cockpit features of that aircraft include a combined UFC and Hotas. The UFC (up-front control) is a centralised panel right in front of the pilot, under the HUD, for all communications, navigation and IFF functions. This eliminates those vertigo-inducing explorations down into the depths looking for an elusive knob or switch. Hotas (hands on throttle and stick) simply puts every switch, button and other pilot control interface that might be needed during combat on either the control column handgrip or on the throttle(s). In combat the pilot has to keep his left hand on engine power and his right hand on the stick, and with Hotas he can do everything else as well, learning on part-task trainers and simulators until the correct finger or thumb reacts instantly, without conscious thought.

The Hornet has brought in a new cockpit generation, though it is far from being the final one. Still coming in are pilot helmet displays, with which weapons or sensors can be slaved to the pilot's eyes (among other things), and direct voice control. There is no problem in making the cockpit speak to the pilot; today's Hornet will tell him, in soothing female tones, such things as BINGO, ALTITUDE! and HOOK! What the backroom development teams have found more difficult is a cockpit that understands what the pilot says, no matter what his voice pitch, tonal quality, pronunciation insertion of "Er.." and "Um.." and voice variation under extreme stress. Displays are so good that ATF might have no transparent canopy; instead the pilot could be given total all-round view in a non-glinting bird-proof streamlined aircraft looking more like a missile.

PART THREE

WEAPONS OF THE FUTURE

In 1944 the Germans were using guided missiles and the Americans proximity fuzed ammunition for anti-aircraft guns. Today armament laboratories are wondering how long it will be before the aircraft gun, even in calibres as small as 25mm, will pump out shells which are both guided and proximity fuzed. Indeed, even the ''death ray'', beloved of fiction writers 50 years ago, now exists in huge and clumsy forms. Common sense tells us that directed-energy weapons will become smaller.

GUNS

The lesson has now been truly hammered home that the general belief in the period 1955-70 that aircraft guns are obsolete, at least for fighters, was a very mistaken one. Indeed it could be that the lesson has been learned just in time for it to be unlearned, but the value of guns is very far from being disproven. To take Britain's RAF as an example, the introduction of the Tornado F.2 interceptor not only marks the welcome arrival to combat duty of what can fairly be described as a "British fighter", for the first time in 26 years, but it also gives the RAF a modern fighter with an internal gun (the Jaguar, with two internal guns, is a close-support attack and recon aircraft). It is interesting to note that the Tornado F.2 has only one gun, whereas the IDS (interdiction/strike) version of the same aircraft has two. This was a considered choice by the Air Staff, based mainly on the supposition that the F.2 is designed to kill at long stand-off distances and (it is thought) is unlikely to engage in close dogfighting.

A comprehensive outline of air combat tactics and techniques appears in the companion volume Modern Air Combat. What did not appear there is how far it is sensible for NATO to try to build up fighter forces at the expense of other anti-aircraft systems. The universally accepted NATO scenario is not an invasion of the Warsaw Pact nations, but an invasion by the Soviet Union into Western Europe. This means that the entire battle would take place over NATO territory, and in the author's view the anti-air budget ought to be spent 99 per cent on the latest and most effective SAMs, with about 100 reloads per launcher (or roughly 98 more than we have at present). Trying to tangle with a vastly bigger force of hostile aircraft poses a very severe identification problem, cripples one's own SAM forces and at best may result in something like a 2:1 victory tally in NATO's favour (not the 900-odd to 1 ratios thrown up on

some simulations) which means that after a day or two there would be no NATO airpower left, even assuming the opposition remarkably neglected to destroy NATO's airbases first.

Aircraft guns, like ECM jammers, can be mounted internally, or conformally or in a pod. Internal guns designed in at the start can be very efficient, causing low drag and leaving all external hardpoints free for other stores. For a stealth aircraft they are infinitely preferable to any kind of external mounting, and the supercruise ATF is almost bound to have its gun(s) internally mounted. It so happens that the standard gun of nearly all US fighters is the General Electric M61, originally designed as Project Vulcan in 1949-52 and still with no visible replacement more than 30 years later. This gun is usually used in 20mm calibre with six barrels firing at up to 6,000spm (shots

per minute). Some versions have hydraulic or electric drive while others are self-powered, and most current installations have a linkless feed system.

This is an outstanding gun with almost every good feature including adequate projectile velocity and trajectory and truly remarkable reliability. Because it gets through ammunition so fast it tends to be given lots of ammunition. In Soviet fighters a 23mm gun tends to have 200 rounds and a 30mm weapon about 70, but the ammunition drum of the US Navy's F-14 contains 675 rounds, the F-15 has 940, the A-7 up to 1,032 and the F-111 (if a gun is fitted) has 2,084 rounds. Such ammunition is both bulky and very heavy, and the 2,084 rounds of the F-111 are just another of the early requirements numbers that looked good 25 years ago. In view of the rumoured intercontinental range being demanded of

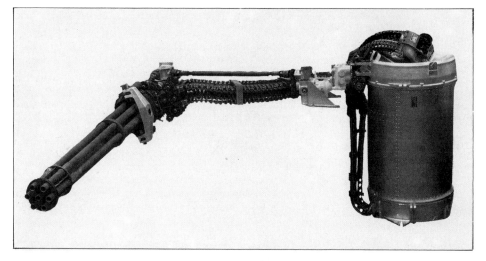

Above: The M61A-1 gun in the F-15 Eagle is mounted in the inboard edge of the right wing, well out from the centreline. When the gun is fired, rudder is automatically applied to hold the aim. The 940-round magazine is in the fuselage. Note the power drive shafting.

Below: In the F/A-18A the M61A-1 is on the centreline in a unique position, above the nose and almost touching the radar. As this photo shows, the muzzle flame is no problem in daylight (but could dazzle at night?). Each round leaves its own individual puff of smoke.

ATF, as well as supercruise capability, it could even be that an equally nonsensical ammunition capacity may be demanded, merely in order that, like the TFX in the early 1960s, the ATF shall be "the greatest". Incidentally, most of the US fighters have the M61 gun well away from the centreline, and in the F-15 firing the gun automatically applies just enough left rudder to hold the aircraft on target.

As the ATF is not due to become operational for another ten years it is bound to have a newer type of gun. Indeed, M61 replacements have been studied since 1957 if not earlier, and when the FX was about to become the F-15 in 1969 it was planned around a completely new and very impressive gun of 25mm calibre with many new features. It failed to work with adequate consistency, so the old M61 was put in as a temporary stop-gap. It is still there, and is

likely to be bolted into the last F-15 when that comes off the line around the middle of the 1990s.

There are many ways in which gun designers have tried to move ahead. Ideally one should leave the ammunition unchanged and produce a better gun, but to return to the RAF there seems to have been some lack of foresight because that very small air force has guns all similar in design and technology firing ammunition of 20mm, 25mm, 27mm and 30mm calibres! This is all the sadder when it is realised that to any gun designer the ammunition for all four guns is positively archaic; even the excellent 25mm Aden and 27mm Mauser, which are newer than the others, are still only improved in detail instead of by revolutionary new design. (Maybe the world really is upside-down; there is no doubt Plessey and Oto Melara are on to a

good thing with new turrets armed with the Browning "50 calibre" designed in 1916.)

How do you improve the ammunition? From a purely geometric viewpoint traditional ammo, being of circular cross-section, wastes space. Changing to a square section increases volumetric efficiency: space previously occupied by air is now occupied by propellant. We can thus either retain the original charge and make the ammunition shorter or keep the original length and put more energy into accelerating the projectile, which increases muzzle velocity (almost always a desirable objective). The fact the gun breech is now square in section, an undesirable form for a volume subjected to extremely high and rapidly pulsating pressures, is no unsuperable problem; we can make a gun with a square breech no heavier than one with a round breech.

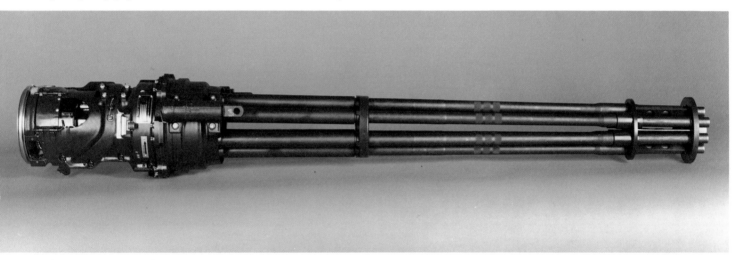

Above: General Electric's plant at Burlington, Vermont, developed the M61A-1 gun in 1949-53 as Project Vulcan. It has been virtually the standard US aircraft gun ever since. The 20mm model shown is externally powered and fires at up to 6,600 shots/ min. Basic weight is 265lb (120kg). Use of six barrels makes very rapid firing rates compatible with long barrel life and extremely high reliability. Most have linkless feed.

Below: Though 27 years later in development than the M61, the German Mauser 27mm gun used in the Tornado is a much more traditional gun, based on the firm's MK 213 of 1944. The IDS version of Tornado has two guns, both of which are seen firing in this photograph. Great care is taken to ensure that engine behaviour and performance cannot be affected by gun firing, even under the extreme manoeuvres of air combat.

Volumetric efficiency is improved further by telescoped ammunition. Instead of being long and tapering this is short and fat, and the projectile appears to have been pushed into the case. Following the process which has dramatically increased the flight performance of a submarine-launched ballistic missile, without increasing the size of the launch tube, modern ammunition can offer amazing improvements in efficiency on either a volume or mass basis, and can result in up to 50 per cent higher muzzle velocity.

Even more dramatic advances have been in the laboratory for 20 years, with hundreds of thousands of rounds fired. Consumable cases were to have been a feature of the gun that failed to mature in time for the F-15. Carrying back spent cases is not worth their scrap value, and ejecting them overboard causes all kinds of problems, both to one's own and to accompanying aircraft. A consumable case removes the problem entirely, and modern dumpy telescoped ammunition helps to overcome the problem that such ammunition has tended to be fragile. An alternative scheme is to use liquid propellant. In effect the gun barrel is converted into an internal-combustion cylinder (albeit of high fineness ratio), into which the liquid propellant is injected as soon as each fresh projectile is in place. One can use hypergolic (spon-

taneously reacting) liquids, but this is extremely hazardous and almost all liquid-propellant guns now on test require deliberate ignition of each charge. Released energy can be greater than for a solid charge, and there are ways of controlling the rate and location of combustion to achieve muzzle velocities much higher than the 3,300 (1,000m)/s common for modern aircraft guns.

Perhaps further down the road is the smart gun whose bullets do not miss. The

Above: Rearming an F-15 Eagle during an exercise requiring NBC masks. The 20mm ammunition is pulled off a special armament trolley and up the feed chute into the drum magazine. Note also the Sparrow AAM attachment.

author has no information on whether the gun firing guided projectiles would pose fresh problems in IFF; the subject has not been aired in public, and perhaps the answers are not known. Even today it is possible to fire one's gun at the wrong aircraft, but a man who does this might well

AIR-TO-AIR MISSILES

Air-to-air missiles are normally guided. Spin-stabilized or fin-stabilized rockets, much in vogue in the 1950s, are today seldom used in air-to-air operations, and the author knows of no modern fighter software programmed to assist firing "dumb" rockets in this role.

For over 30 years the two common methods of guiding AAMs have been SARH and IR. Semi-active radar homing relies upon "illumination" of the target aircraft by the radar of the fighter, usually with CW radiation. The missile has a passive receiver system not only operating on the same wavelength but probably keyed to the fighter's own individual emissions. The missile homes automatically on the radiation scattered or diffused back from the target. This is a very small fraction of that sent out, and the missile is also bothered by the fact that the centroid (apparent centre) of the returned radiation, on which it homes, continuously changes as a result of relative motion of the illuminating beam and target and the target's manoeuvres which keep changing its reflectivity.

A major advantage of SARH is that, provided the target is not too good at stealth technology and RAM (radar-absorbent material) coatings, it works well upon a non-co-operative target which has its own radars and engines shut down or at a low power. It also works better than IR over long ranges filled with rain or snow. The massive drawback is that all today's fighters have their target-illuminating radar pointing forwards, so they have to keep flying towards the enemy as long as their last missile is still in the air. Nothing more suicidal could be imagined, and this destroys the range advantage of SARH missiles in comparison with close-range IR dogfight missiles.

IR homing means that the missile has a very sensitive receiver in its nose, usually

Left: The fourth production Mirage 2000, showing the two standard AAMs carried, Matra Super 530 and the close-range Matra 550 Magic. The Super 530 is a vast improvement over the Matra R.530 carried by earlier Mirage fighters. Magic is similar to Sidewinder.

Right: Called AA-6 Acrid by NATO, the missiles carried by the MiG-25 "Foxbat" are the largest in the world. This Libyan MiG-25, seen in 1981, has one IR-homing missile (left wing) and one with semi-active radar guidance. The pilot can select either according to the weather, time of day or target.

be a bad shot anyway; if his rounds all home on the target the result would be serious. As for the technology, this has some features reminiscent of proximity (VT) fuzes, which arrived just in time to help shoot down flying bombs in July 1944. The basic problem, 40 years later, is that complex electronics must be made to work reliably after being fired from a gun, which today for specification purposes means launch acceleration of 30,000g.

Obviously, the smaller the calibre, the

Above: The General Electric GPU-5/A is one of the most powerful gun pods in the world, but it can be carried by the F-16 in the background. It contains the GAU-13/A four-barrel 30mm gun with a closed helical loop feeding the ammunition.

greater the difficulty of achieving a reliable guided projectile. The task is more difficult than the proximity fuze (which in fact is absent from the projectiles fired from today's aircraft guns) because as well as the guidance electronics there must be a method for changing the trajectory. The

high flight speed, typically between Mach 2 and Mach 3, means that the control system must be able to impart large forces if significant changes in direction are to be accomplished. Most current guided-projectile research does not use aerodynamic controls but reaction jets fed from solid charges (in effect, small rocket motors). It is wasteful to use side-thrusting rockets which fire throughout the flight, with deflectors to give trajectory control impulses during perhaps 1 per cent of the total time. Again, rapid-fire start/stop thrusters cannot yet operate sufficiently quickly. One programme uses a continuous firing motor with vectored nozzles which most of the time sustain projectile velocity but when needed rotate out to thrust sideways. Another uses 48 small motors fired in sequence as needed, rather like the US Army Dragon anti-tank missile. There has been some work on guided spinning projectiles fired from rifled barrels, but problems are much easier if the projectile is fin-stabilized and does not rotate. Of course, a little thought will show that the sharpest changes in trajectory are almost certain to be needed at the target end of the flight, when the projectile's speed is lowest. So far as is known 30mm is the smallest calibre yet guided in flight. In bigger calibres it is possible to combine guidance and a proximity fuze.

cryogenically cooled by liquid nitrogen or other cold medium to reduce background "noise", which detects the slightest spot of heat anywhere in its cone of vision. Some modern missiles have a staring focal-plane array, working very like a human eye, as explained in the Air Warfare chapter of the companion volume Advanced Technology Warfare. Most use a miniature telescope of the doubly reflecting Cassegrain or inverse-Cassegrain type, which focusses the feeble heat on to the detector by physically pointing towards it. The missile then steers itself to cancel out the difference between the pointing angle of the telescope and its own axis; in other words, it keeps flying towards the target. IR missiles see a funny target; most of it is invisible, but the engine nozzle(s) show up brilliantly, as do any other hot parts. The latest seekers even detect the enemy aircraft's cool areas against the slightly colder sky background, and so can be used from head-on or any other direction. IR homing works beautifully on a clear night, and even on a scorching day such systems no longer try to home on the Sun or its reflection in a friendly greenhouse; but the received signal is rapidly attenuated by snow, rain or even cloud. Thus the Soviet interceptors usually carry a mix of missiles including some of each type.

One of the major advantages of the IR missile is that it is autonomous, also called the "launch and leave" type. Thus, in exercises many Sparrow-armed F-15s have been lost to little IR Sidewinders fired at the last moment by F-5s and F-16s simply because the F-15 had to come into the latter's radar range in order to keep guiding its Sparrows. The Sparrow might knock out the little fighter, but by that time its Sidewinder would already be on its way, quite untroubled by the disappearance of the fighter that fired it. Thus SARH is a totally dead technology (the author suggested fitting Sparrow or Sky Flash carriers with target-illuminating radar facing aft, but somewhat facetiously).

In its place is eventually coming the Hughes AIM-120A Amraam (advanced medium-range AAM), which like Sidewinder is a launch-and-leave weapon. Fired in the general direction of its target – and several Amraams can be fired simultaneously against several different targets – this missile is an all-aspect, look-down, shoot-down weapon smaller and lighter than Sparrow but with tremendous advantages. The control system has been moved from the wings amidships to the tail controls. For much of its flight it streaks autonomously steered by its inertial platform, but in its nose it has its own active radar. This soon picks up its target, and from then on, even if the target detects the oncoming missile and tries to use countermeasures, there is almost bound to be a kill. Apart from the massive and extremely costly AIM-54 Phoenix fired by US Navy F-14s this missile is the first in history to offer BVR (beyond visual range) capability with autonomous (launch and leave) operation, so that the pilot who fires the missile can break away immediately and either get away or engage other targets. The main problems with Amraam are that it is running late and costing a lot more than expected, which is serious because it is

Below: If it can fully recover from technical delay and severe cost escalation the Hughes AIM-120A Amraam will soon be the West's most important AAM, with production by European companies as well as in the USA. The first firing was from this USAF F-16 in June 1981.

Above: This CSD solid-fuel integral rocket/ramjet model, on test at NASA Lewis laboratory, shows the type of propulsion needed for future missiles. Such air breathers will be able to fly much faster and much further than today's AAMs and ASMs. Plain rockets cannot compete.

Right: Every kind of weapon carriage offers advantages at the cost of various penalties. This Boeing study (with 2-D vectoring nozzles) carries four large missiles in deep recesses. This gives low drag but reduces the variety of weapons and demands high-power ejector rams.

Above: BAe Dynamics has an unrivalled range of air-launched missiles. This 1982 "ACA" mock-up is carrying Amraam, Asraam and Alarm (the first being a US AAM scheduled for European production). Asraam is Anglo-German.

very much needed by the USAF, USN and RAF (for Tornado F.2).

To the electronics and other workers in the laboratories Amraam is already crude and archaic. Today we have single-chip microprocessors so complex that the patterns etched into them have similar complexity to a street map (literally every street) of the USA. Such processors put colossal "thinking" capability into quite small missiles. It is no problem to make an Amraam-size AAM pick out a particular target, identify the exact type of aircraft, search its memory to check on the defensive capabilities of such aircraft (countermeasures, chaff and jammers), reprogram itself or change the radar wavelength, then

notice that the target has been destroyed by another friendly missile and immediately lock on to another hostile aircraft of the same type. A "brilliant" missile of this type could with perfect safety be fired towards a confused dogfight in the absolute certainty that it would pick out and destroy an enemy fighter; indeed it could be programmed to study all the hostile aircraft, perhaps taking a look at what they were carrying, and home on the one posing the greatest threat. Taking a quick look requires high-definition sensors, but that is no problem; the author is certain that we shall soon devise a sensor of this type.

The aforementioned book, Advanced Technology Warefare, does some thinking aloud on future AAMs and on the pros and cons of missiles possessing very long range and/or very high speed. Long range, and more especially sustained speed over a long range, can usually be shown to call for

air-breathing propulsion, the obvious choice being a ramjet. So far the only ramjet missiles have been SAMs and future anti-ship missiles, but there is every chance that AAMs of the 1990s will use such propulsion to cruise at about Mach 3.5 over ranges of at least 50 miles (80km). The drawback of high speed is that manoeuvrability falls very quickly indeed to unimpressive values; a Mach 3.5 manned aeroplane flies in essentially a straight line. AAMs with air-breathing propulsion can pull 20g or more without significant loss of speed, though it is no easy matter to pick the ideal speed for the vital last mile or so (say, 2km) to the target. With a microprocessor a missile can keep aiming at the target's future position instead of measuring the off-axis angle of the instantaneous LOS (line of sight) to the target's present position, and this usually makes it more difficult for the target to dodge.

AIR-TO-SURFACE WEAPONS

Apart from strategic weapons, discussed separately, this category includes anti-runway cratering devices, area-denial weapons, precision-target smart weapons, anti-armour missiles and anti-ship missiles. The last is perhaps the simplest species to design, because there could hardly be a nicer target than a ship. Modern ships, however, are now beginning to defend themselves with dedicated anti-missile weapons, and getting past these calls for a lot more thought in the design of the missile. The success of an AM.39 Exocet against HMS Sheffield in May 1982 is certain to go down in history as a unique event, never to be repeated with any other surface combatant. Exocet requires fairly sustained illumination of its target, first by the launch aircraft and then by the ADAC seeker radar of the missile, yet on that occasion the target either failed to detect such illumination with its own ESM systems or failed to respond; and in any case it had no defences. For such a combination of failures to occur again is inconceivable, and careful analysis of today's gun, rocket and missile defence systems against anti-ship missiles strongly indicates that the only way to hit warships in future will be by saturation or by stealth, or ineptness of the defender.

There is a slight chance that a combination of small radar cross-section and extremely high flight speed might get a missile to impact within the minimum reaction time of the defence system, but this is a challenge. Most of the latest ship anti-missile defence systems have unknown or classified reaction time, but 3 seconds is a typical design goal. At Mach 5 a missile would cover about 3 miles (5km) in this time, and as there are few limitations on the size and power of ship radars a missile would have to have exceptional stealth and low-flying capability to remain undetected at this range. An approach at the same speed at 100,000ft (30.5km) altitude, arching over into a dive (perhaps from just beyond the target) may have some merit, though radar cross-section would be enhanced in the plan aspect just before starting the dive 19 miles up. In any case the terminal homing must either be extremely clever or passive; this is clearly preferable to a brilliant missile which can "think" but which uses active homing broadcasting its attack.

In attacks on surface targets the same considerations apply. It is possible that future warplanes will be able to find minor wars in which it will be possible to overfly targets but, in general, hostile airspace in any war involving a major power is going to be deadly to manned aircraft. Why send a warhead fixed to a Ballute or tail retarder dropped from a vehicle offering a massive radar cross section, travelling at 500 knots in full afterburner and costing $30 million in preference to a stand-off missile with 5 per cent of the radar signature, 5 per cent of the IR signature, no human aboard, at least as high a speed, probably higher accuracy and better inflight agility, much less than 5 per cent of the cost and, if built that way,

able to deliver the same warheads and return for reuse?

Extraordinary attention has been paid to weapon systems intended to make craters in runways, and to methods of quickly restoring the runway to serviceability. Soviet Frontal Aviation, like the Swedish Flygvapen, recognises the obvious fact that airfields are the places not to be in any future war. Airfields are the ideal target to which any sensible enemy – ie, one who plays to win, not to lose – would deliver giant FAE (fuel/air explosive) warheads which would simply remove or flatten anything above ground level. Chemical weapons would almost be superfluous; there would be nobody left to incapacitate, and no point in spoiling the nice runways.

But the whole notion of sending manned aircraft to attack airfields is obvious lunacy; targets which do not move are for missiles. Even a moving armoured division is today capable of being engaged by what might be termed missiles, though some of them are fired by artillery. For at least 17 years American research programmes have addressed themselves to the problems of knocking out large numbers of moving armoured vehicles. The traditional methods of using a high-velocity gun firing special high-density ammunition able to penetrate by kinetic energy alone, and the low-velocity missile with a hollow-charge warhead are now being joined by systems

(often air-delivered) which dispense large numbers of smart (terminally guided) submunitions.

The biggest programme in the West has been the US Army's ERAM (extended-range anti-armour mine), which continues while many equally big schemes have been terminated. One of the ERAM payloads now declassified is Skeet, an Avco development, which is the first SFF (self-forging fragment) device to enter production. Skeet devices are dispensed in numbers from dozens to hundreds, either from an autonomous "bus vehicle" or from an aircraft overflying the target. Each Skeet comprises a cylindrical body which deploys four curved fins and an offset "wobble arm". The latter induces an oscillatory roll which makes the IR sensor in the nose "sweep over an area as big as a football field". A microprocessor converts image signals into steering commands which finally fire the warhead directly above the target vehicle. The transverse disc of explosive accelerates the slab of metal ahead of it to form a self-forging fragment, a dense streamlined globule of metal which at about 9,000ft (270m)/s punches straight through the thin top armour.

Skeet submunitions are the first of tomorrow's precision warheads. Only 15 years ago it was almost taken for granted that the user could buy a costly guided missile, which in fact was seldom brilliant and often failed to perform as advertised, or a shower of smaller warheads used scatter-gun fashion, making up in numbers for their random distribution. Today we can shower the land enemy with hundreds of

warheads, each of them likely to home on its target with much greater precision and reliability than the previous generation of expensive missiles. These modern submunitions can be strewn by an attacking aircraft, and if the target position is imprecisely known (the uncertainty exceeding submunition lateral travel) this may be the only method available. Alternatively they can be delivered roughly overhead by a rocket or artillery shell bus and dispensed high enough to see all the targets.

The key to weapons capability is microelectronics. With VHSICs, silicon-on-sapphire circuits and GaAs microwave devices the munition designer can add all

Above: Launch of a Super Etendard of the French Aéronavale. The Falklands war in 1982 showed the devastating effect its Exocet sea- skimming missile can have on ships which for whatever reason are not able to counter it. Exocet uses active radar in order to home on its target.

the brilliance he wants for the bulk and weight penalty of a pack of cards. One crucial item is likely to be the array processor, which looks at IR staring arrays (less often at TV) and processes the entire scene in microseconds. Even small submunitions can have not only precision guidance but also extra "intelligence", each able to select an individual target and be able to signal its intention to dozens of

other identical submunitions which can then concentrate on other targets. Clearly it would be frustrating if all 64 submunitions from one dispenser happened to pick the same tank. Invariably future warheads, whether dispensed in a cluster or individually propelled, will have at least one sensor if not two (such as homing on IR and millimetric wavelengths), feeding a whole family of tiny dedicated processors which, together with general mission processors to avoid duplicate attacks on the same target where possible, are all controlled by one or two microprocessors, which are slower but more versatile.

Thanks to integrated circuit progress we

Below: Actual photograph of a Skeet detecting and piercing a US Army tank target in a series of live firing demos. The explosive forging process is so rapid it is difficult to study, but sophisticated computer modelling has been confirmed in live tests. The original disc "lens" is of copper/steel/tantalum/uranium. Purity, contour, thickness, diameter, curvature, and the pressure wave, govern final shape.

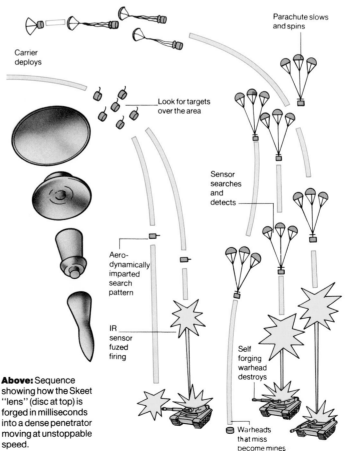

Carrier deploys

Look for targets over the area

Aerodynamically imparted search pattern

IR sensor fuzed firing

Above: Sequence showing how the Skeet "lens" (disc at top) is forged in milliseconds into a dense penetrator moving at unstoppable speed.

Parachute slows and spins

Sensor searches and detects

Self forging warhead destroys

Warheads that miss become mines

Left: Simplified sequence drawings for Avco's Skeet (left) and Aerojet's Sadarm (sense and destroy armour, right), showing alternative retarding techniques (Sadarm spins). Both can be delivered by tactical aircraft or any other "bus" including artillery. Both offer fire-and-forget all-weather day or night capability against the heaviest tanks. Skeet submunitions use IR seekers; Sadarm uses MMW radar (millimetre wave) to find its targets. Both can fire on the way down, but in alternative modes the warheads can behave as run-over mines to destroy from below. Skeet can even lie in wait and, when a tank comes within range, it can be fired to a height from which it can "see" the target and fire its EFP (explosively forged penetrator) through the top armour. Not least of the advantages of these versatile weapons is that the delivery system – such as an aircraft – only has to aim in the general direction of the target, and misses can hit later!

can have almost any amount of "thinking power" we want, and with extreme accuracy even in environments rich in radiation and electrical noise. We can slip these small processors into hundreds of dispensed warheads as easily as into a missile that will blow a ship in two. But it is still not easy to predict with any assurance how future weapons will be guided or even how they can best be delivered.

Artillery shells, even with base bleed or rocket boost, seldom go further than 30 miles (48km). Self-propelled missiles and warheads carried by aircraft can go any distance, and OTH (over the horizon) attacks can be handled by either. Increasingly it is going to be a suicidal waste of irreplaceable delivery systems to task manned aircraft directly against defended targets. The surface fleet or armoured division, in the Soviet forces at least, have probably reached the stage at which attack by manned aircraft would present no problem whatever. To try to overcome this situation there has been much recent effort to develop standoff stealth delivery systems which bring the warheads into the target area.

A current idea of the USAF is AWCIT (advanced weapon carriage integration technology), which is essentially a 2,000lb (907kg) brilliant stealth bus with a conformal shape to fit against a parent fighter. Four of these 13×3ft (4×1m) craft can fit conformally against the sides of an F-15. The fighter stands off outside the heavily

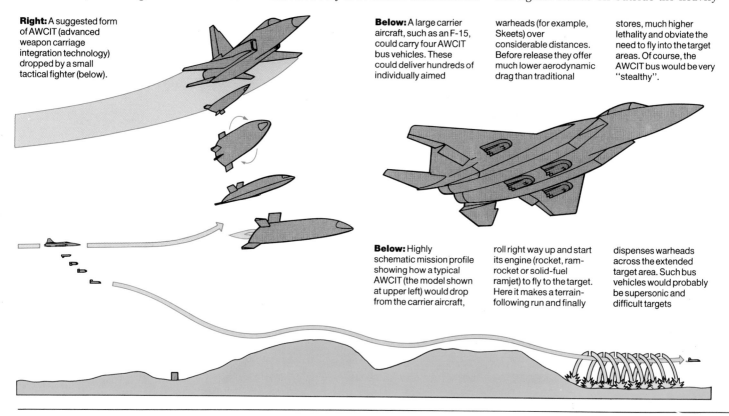

Right: A suggested form of AWCIT (advanced weapon carriage integration technology) dropped by a small tactical fighter (below).

Below: A large carrier aircraft, such as an F-15, could carry four AWCIT bus vehicles. These could deliver hundreds of individually aimed warheads (for example, Skeets) over considerable distances. Before release they offer much lower aerodynamic drag than traditional stores, much higher lethality and obviate the need to fly into the target areas. Of course, the AWCIT bus would be very "stealthy".

Below: Highly schematic mission profile showing how a typical AWCIT (the model shown at upper left) would drop from the carrier aircraft, roll right way up and start its engine (rocket, ram-rocket or solid-fuel ramjet) to fly to the target. Here it makes a terrain-following run and finally dispenses warheads across the extended target area. Such bus vehicles would probably be supersonic and difficult targets

COMPUTERS

Another way in which computer power is changing weapon development is in the basic design process. Until well into the 1960s the design of a major guided missile was a long and arduous process, typically taking 1,000 man-years. Once a missile had been fully developed it was used for as many applications as possible, changing the inside whilst leaving the shape and control system alone. The Terrier missile spawned Tartar, Standard and Standard ARM; Sparrow spawned Sea Sparrow, NATO Sparrow, Shrika and Sky Flash; Sidewinder became the Chapparal SAM (and was also copied in many other countries); and the Falcons led to the Phoenix and Maverick. Today CAD (computer-assisted design) has become such a powerful process that one engineer sitting at a graphic terminal can easily do the equivalent of 1,000 man-years of missile design before lunch. Different missile shapes and configurations are thus much less of a problem, and the difficulties lie mainly in bureaucracy and avoiding becoming submerged under mountains of paper.

defended area and launches its AWCITs, which fly in autonomously, dodging known defence positions, and finally put down warheads on tanks, runways or whatever the target might be. If AWCIT can avoid too big an IR signature it should have an excellent chance of reaching the target.

As for guidance methods, the point has been emphasized that it is desirable to avoid at all costs stridently advertising one's approach, even if clever radar is used with frequency hopping and very brief scans separated by long silences. It is obviously preferable to home on emissions from the target. But some of the best Western anti-ship missiles, including Harpoon, RBS 15F, Exocet and Sea Eagle, all broadcast their approach by radar. It is not necessary to do this, and Norway's Penguin family – now likely to be bought by the US Navy to give the SH-60B anti-ship capability – homes on IR from the ship. This immediately raises the interesting question of whether a ship can protect itself by appearing to be the same temperature as its background. Obviously it is possible to avoid or mask local hot spots, but bringing in stealth technology at IR wavelengths for a target as big as a surface combatant is a tall order. Such challenges will have to be faced by naval electronic warfare specialists, because with massive thinking power previously mentioned anti-ship missiles are going to ignore IR flares and similar decoys unless they are extremely clever simulations.

Below: One of the unusual features of the Norwegian Kongsberg Penguin family of anti-ship missiles is that they home on the IR (heat) emitted by the target. Here a Penguin Mk 3 is carried by Norwegian F-104G; similar missiles are now in service on F-16s and are likely to be carried by US Navy helicopters. IR homing makes it more difficult for the target to detect the missile, but the missile may be diverted by rocket-fired ECM flares offering a more attractive heat source. The black hemisphere on the missile nose covers the sensitive seeker.

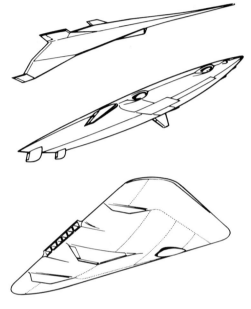

Above: Three shapes for an advanced stealth-type cruise missile with a design range of 6,000 miles (9,600km). Such vehicles have been studied by Boeing, General Dynamics and Lockheed. In 1983 GD Convair (composite airframe) and Willliams Research ("plastic" turbofan) were named winners.

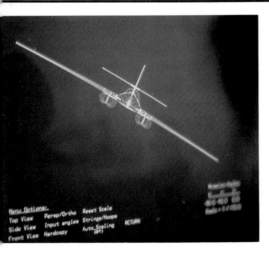

Left: Models of ASRAAM have been seen for years (this picture was taken in 1982) but because of the way NATO handles its programmes nothing looks like reaching the squadrons for another decade.

Above: This tail-on-view of a B-1 (or it could be Blackjack) can instantly be switched to any other view the operator wishes to study. Computers ought to have made missile design very much quicker than in the days of pencil drawings.

Modern computerized design processes ought to make the development of new weapon systems faster than ever before. In fact the reverse is true. Leaving aside the saga of the B-1, some of the physically smallest weapon systems are taking so long to develop that fathers are having to hand over to their sons. Consider the Anglo-German effort to find a new-technology successor to Sidewinder. Work began at BGT in Germany in 1966 on what became Viper, joined by Dornier in 1968. At Hatfield Hawker Siddeley Dynamics began work in 1967 on what in 1969 became Tail Dog. In 1972 Kongsberg joined Viper as propulsion subcontractor, while HSD changed the designation of their programme to SRAAM.100 with MoD funding in 1971. Shortsightedly both projects were cancelled in 1974; NATO was going to make Sidewinder AIM-9L, in other words to replace Sidewinder by Sidewinder.

The British and German governments did permit low-key development to continue, and in the second half of the 1970s HSD conducted many SRAAM test firings from ground launchers and from a Hunter. By 1980 the need to replace Sidewinder was beginning to sink in, and a year later ASRAAM was launched as a joint BGT/BAe programme, with US interest (the idea was, and still is, that Europe will adopt medium-range AMRAAM and the USA the short-range ASRAAM). In 1981 the "pre-feasibility" phase at last gave way to the "feasibility study", which was to last until 1983 but actually continued to April 1985. Project definition comes next, and instead of extending to 1984 is now unlikely to be complete before 1987. Then comes full-scale engineering development, originally scheduled for 1985-90 but now more likely to be 1988-99.

There seems little chance of getting ASRAAMs into the squadrons before about 2002. Now 1966 to 2002 is the same as 1916-52, so on that basis it would have taken until 1952 for the RAF to get its first Sopwith Camel. The adjective "glacial" was once used to describe the pace of a multinational fighter programme; the ASRAAM needs a new word.

INDEX

206